# Trade and development in sub-Saharan Africa

**Centre for Economic Policy Research**

The Centre for Economic Policy Research is a network of over 140 Research Fellows, based primarily in European universities. The Centre coordinates its Fellows' research activities, providing central administrative services and communicating research to the public and private sectors. CEPR is an entrepreneur, developing research initiatives with the producers, consumers and sponsors of research. Established in 1983, CEPR is already a European economics research organization with uniquely wide-ranging scope and activities.

CEPR is a registered educational charity. Grants from the Leverhulme Trust, the Esmée Fairbairn Charitable Trust, the Baring Foundation, the Bank of England and Citibank provide institutional finance. The ESRC supports the Centre's dissemination programme and, with the Nuffield Foundation, its programme of research workshops, while the Alfred P. Sloan and Ford Foundations support the Centre's programme of research in International Macroeconomics. None of these organizations gives prior review to the Centre's publications nor do they necessarily endorse the views expressed therein.

The Centre is pluralist and non-partisan, bringing economic research to bear on the analysis of medium- and long-run policy questions. The research that it disseminates may include views on policy, but the Board of Governors of the Centre does not give prior review to such publications and the Centre itself takes no institutional policy positions. The opinions expressed in this volume are those of the authors and not those of the Centre for Economic Policy Research.



15 June 1990

CEPR, 6 Duke of York Street, London SW1Y 6LA, 071-930 2963

# Trade and development in sub-Saharan Africa

*edited by*
Jonathan H. Frimpong-Ansah
S. M. Ravi Kanbur
*and*
Peter Svedberg

Manchester University Press
Manchester and New York
in association with the Centre for Economic Policy Research
Distributed exclusively in the United States and Canada by St. Martin's Press, New York

*Published by* Manchester University Press
Oxford Road, Manchester M13 9PL, UK
*and* Room 400, 175 Fifth Avenue,
New York, NY 10010, USA

*Distributed exclusively in the USA and Canada*
*by* St. Martin's Press, Inc.,
175 Fifth Avenue, New York, NY 10010, USA



*British Library cataloguing in publication data*
Trade and development in sub-Saharan Africa.
1. Africa south of the Sahara. Economic development
I. Frimpong-Ansah, J. H. II. Kanbur, S. M. Ravi
III. Svedberg, Peter IV. Centre for Economic Policy Research
330.967

*Library of Congress cataloging in publication data*
Trade and development in sub-Saharan Africa/edited by Jonathan H. Frimpong-Ansah, S. M. Ravi Kanbur, and Peter Svedberg. p. cm.
'Reports the results of a research project . . . organized by the Rockefeller Foundation, the Centre for Economic Policy Research, and the Commonwealth Secretariat' – Pref.
Includes index.
ISBN 0-7190-3478-7
1. Africa, Sub-Saharan – Commercial policy. 2. Africa, Sub-Saharan – Commerce. I. Frimpong-Ansah, J. H. II. Kanbur, S. M. Ravi. III. Svedberg, Peter. IV. Rockefeller Foundation. V. Centre for Economic Policy Research (Great Britain) VI. Commonwealth Secretariat.
HF1611.T73 1991
382'.0967 – dc20 90-13562

ISBN 0 7190 3478 7 *hardback*

Typeset in Hong Kong
by Graphicraft Typesetters Ltd., Hong Kong.

Printed in Great Britain
by Biddles Ltd., King's Lynn & Guildford

# Contents

# List of contributors

*T. J. Besley* Princeton University and Centre for Economic Policy Research
*Henry Bienen* Princeton University
*Vincent Cable* Commonwealth Secretariat
*Paul Collier* Institute of Economics and Statistics, Oxford
*Rob Davies* University of Zimbabwe
*Refik Erzan* World Bank
*Jonathan H. Frimpong-Ansah* International Foundation for African Capacity Building and University of Warwick
*S. M. Ravi Kanbur* University of Warwick, World Bank and Centre for Economic Policy Research
*Nguyuru H. I. Lipumba* University of Dar-es-Salaam
*Allechi M'Bet* National University of Côte d'Ivoire
*Benno J. Ndulu* University of Dar-es-Salaam
*Nehemiah K. N'geno* University of Nairobi
*Philip K. Quarcoo* United Nations African Institute for Economic Development and Planning, Dakar
*Peter Svedberg* Institute for International Economic Studies, Stockholm
*Joe U. Umo* University of Lagos

## List of abbreviations

| | |
|---|---|
| ACP | African, Caribbean and Pacific |
| CAP | Common Agricultural Policy |
| CCCN | Customs Cooperation Council Nomenclature |
| CPI | consumer price index |
| EC | European Community |
| GATT | General Agreement on Tariffs and Trade |
| GDP | gross domestic product |
| GNI | gross national income |
| GNP | gross national product |
| GSP | Generalized System of Preferences |
| GSTP | Global System of Trade Preferences |
| IBRD | International Bank for Reconstruction and Development |
| IMF | International Monetary Fund |
| ISI | import-substituting industrialization |
| LDC | less developed country |
| LLDC | least developed country |
| MFA | Multi-Fibre Arrangement |
| MFN | most favoured nation |
| MTN | multilateral trade negotiation |
| NGO | non-governmental organization |
| NIC | newly industrializing country |
| NTB | non-tariff barrier |
| OECD | Organisation for Economic Co-operation and Development |

| | |
|---|---|
| OPEC | Organization of the Petroleum Exporting Countries |
| PTA | Preferential Trading Area |
| S&D | Special and Differential treatment |
| SADCC | Southern African Development Co-ordinating Conference |
| SAL | Structural Adjustment Loan |
| SAU | South African Union |
| SDR | Special Drawing Right |
| SITC | Standard International Trade Classification |
| SSA | sub-Saharan Africa |
| UNCTAD | United Nations Conference on Trade and Development |
| VER | voluntary export restraint |

# List of tables

# List of figures

# Preface

This volume reports the results of a research project on 'Trade and Development in Sub-Saharan Africa', organized by the Rockefeller Foundation, the Centre for Economic Policy Research and the Commonwealth Secretariat. We are grateful to the Rockefeller Foundation for their financial support for the project, and to Catherine Gwin for her assistance from the New York office of the Rockefeller Foundation with organizing our meetings and for her many substantive comments during these sessions. We are likewise deeply grateful to David Court and Mrs de Sa, at the Nairobi office of the Rockefeller Foundation, who efficiently organized our three gatherings there and made them very pleasant as well.

Thanks are also due to the Commonwealth Secretariat, which by integrating our third meeting in their symposium on 'Trade Policy and Exchange Rate Management' made us confront many of the policy-makers in Eastern and Southern Africa. We wish to thank Carl K. Eicher, Jeffrey Fine and Bo Karlström, who very generously spent considerable time helping us to identify authors of country papers and discussants in the initial phase of the project. We are also indebted to Gerry K. Helleiner, Mohsin S. Khan and Tony Killick, who acted as outside discussants at one of our workshops. Their comments on many of the papers were most helpful.

Last but not least, we wish to thank Wendy Thompson for her

assistance with the administration of the project, and Paul Compton, David Guthrie and Sarah Wellburn, all at the CEPR, for coordinating the preparation and publication of the present volume.

JHF-A SMRK PS
May 1990

1

# Trade and development in sub-Saharan Africa: an overview

Jonathan H. Frimpong-Ansah, S. M. Ravi Kanbur and Peter Svedberg

The past twenty years have witnessed tremendous differences in the performance of countries conventionally lumped together under the label 'less developed' (LDCs). Some countries have seen their per capita real income quadruple and the production structure of their economies greatly diversify; a few are now industrialized or at least semi-industrialized. Some of these high-growth countries also have admirable records as regards income distribution, longevity, literacy, health, nutrition, etc. There are of course some countries where the pattern is mixed, but at the other end of the spectrum there are countries in which per capita real income has declined, economic structure remains undiversified, and poverty and nutritional standards have deteriorated severely.

With a few exceptions, countries in the latter group are to be found in sub-Saharan Africa – out of about forty-five[1] countries in this part of the world, twenty-five have experienced a decline in per capita real income since the end of the 1960s. There is, of course, no universally accepted theory to explain this record. One line of argument emphasizes ineffective indigenous economic policy. Manifestations of 'urban bias', such as an agricultural price structure skewed against farmers and in favour of urban consumers, have led to declining food production and also agricultural production for export. Inefficient parastatal operations in agriculture and in industry have compounded the problem and have blocked the emergence of a dynamic industrial sector. An overvalued exchange rate has penalized the traded goods sector and, together with large and uncontrolled government deficits, has led to severe balance of payments difficulties and the burden of a large external debt. On the other hand, there are those who emphasize external factors such as the secular deterioration of terms of trade, shortage of rainfall and other trends in climatic factors which have affected agricultural production, and the interests of foreign governments and multinationals. In between these two extremes are perhaps the majority of researchers, who would be inclined to think that there are varying elements of truth in both points of view.

Whatever their persuasions, however, few researchers would attempt to find the roots of the African problem in any simple theory of development which emphasizes either one or a small number of factors as being essential for success, be it savings, investment, foreign exchange, human capital, etc. While there are countries which have had both high investment and high growth, there are those which have had high investment but sluggish growth, and those which have had high growth despite low savings and investment. There are countries for which foreign exchange has been abundant for some periods, but where development has not been particularly impressive. Some countries well endowed with human capital have performed well; others less so. In the face of these realities, most researchers nowadays follow a more multifaceted approach which emphasizes different branches of conventional economics such as trade, macroeconomics, public finance, agricultural economics and labour economics, in their application to the special setting of a particular developing country. There are also those who urge that attention to be paid to the political economy of the development process.

However, the recognized interactions between different sectors of the economy do not contradict the approach of a focused analysis of particular sectors within the broader context. International trade is one such sector, whose importance in the development process has been recognized in the literature – if only through heated controversies on the terms of trade, export-led growth, import substitution, etc. Africa has not been immune from these controversies.

Most African countries' exports are still dominated by one or a few primary products. Except for a few countries that have struck oil or some other major mineral, the African countries' share of world (or third-world) total exports has fallen, in many cases quite drastically. Is this mainly the result of the fact that these countries have not maintained their *shares* of world exports of the *particular* goods they export, or is it that demand has grown especially slowly for these products? Have the barter terms of trade moved against the African countries during the last twenty years? Does the export sector act as an engine or 'handmaiden' of economic growth in the African context?

It is further notable that very few countries in the region have succeeded in advancing manufactured exports. Where countries have managed to get an industrialization process under way, it has catered for the domestic market and has often been heavily protected from outside competition. Various tariff and non-tariff trade barriers, or direct public subsidies (sometimes as support to state enterprises) have ensured the economic survival of many industrial projects. Is an outward-oriented industrialization strategy, with prime reliance on private market incentives, non-feasible in most of present-day Africa? Is it mainly overvalued exchange rates and other adverse government policies that have discouraged the export of manufactures in the past? Or is the explanation the lack of appropriate infrastructure, compounded by problems of market access and severe discrimination by protectionist developed countries?

The slow growth of export earnings and, possibly, capital 'flight', together with a strong import demand for oil derivatives, food, machinery and intermediate industrial products, have created large current account deficits which have been financed through extensive foreign (mainly public) borrowing over the past decade. Although small in absolute numbers, the accumulated foreign debts of many African nations are now significant in relative terms. What is the role of trade policies that boost new and traditional exports in facing these problems? Can imports be further curtailed without impairing overall economic activity through import compression?

These are some of the questions that motivated a project on 'Trade and Development in sub-Saharan Africa', organized by the Rockefeller Foundation, the Commonwealth Secretariat and the Centre for Economic Policy Research. It was decided at an early stage that the analysis would proceed through two types of paper. The first type would focus on issues that cut across countries. These 'issue papers' would be theoretical, empirical or institutional/policy oriented in nature. Their defining characteristic would be the treatment of phenomena at a general level and experience at a continent-wide level. The second type of paper would be a country-specific case study. The choice of countries was a compromise between selecting countries with interesting experiences, selecting them to give good coverage of East and West Africa, and selecting authors who would be willing to work on these countries. The country studies were all authored by economists from the countries themselves. While the authors of these case studies were given general guidelines, it was decided not to impose a strict template since this would inhibit intensive work on country-specific phenomena, should that prove of interest.

The countries that were eventually chosen were: Tanzania, Kenya and Zimbabwe in Eastern/Southern Africa and Ghana, Nigeria and Côte d'Ivoire in Western Africa. While balanced in terms of geographical coverage, this choice of countries also allowed us to cover many of the issues of interest. Country-specific concerns determined the eventual form of the case study. Thus in Zimbabwe it was immediately clear that very little basic analysis of trade data had been done since independence in 1980, and that the available time series would not permit serious econometric analysis. In Tanzania and Kenya, however, longer runs of data were available and earlier econometric studies of trade have been made. The East African studies are therefore more heavily econometric in emphasis. The Zimbabwean and Tanzanian case studies highlight a common theme, namely that of import compression, which has been a key problem in these two countries. In Côte d'Ivoire, import compression is not a problem given the Franc Zone arrangements of free capital movements and currency convertibility. The issue picked up in the Côte d'Ivoire study is that of non-traditional exports. Much has been written about Côte d'Ivoire's traditional primary exports of coffee and cocoa, but little is known about the trends and determinants of the exports of processed coffee and cocoa, and semi-manufactures. The Côte d'Ivoire study takes a first step in this direction, and highlights the problem of market access for these exports. Nigeria's dominant export is oil and is likely to remain so. For this reason the country study focuses rather on import demand and its price and income elasticities. The approach of the Ghana country study is based on the econometric modelling work of Project LINK of the UN system. Using this framework of system modelling, the paper attempts to answer the question of the links between exports and growth.

The issue papers attempt to cover the major themes in African trade and development. The paper by Peter Svedberg on the export performance of sub-Saharan Africa presents an aggregative, panoramic view of African performance in international markets, attempting to investigate whether it was terms of trade or export volumes that account for this performance. With this empirical background, Jonathan Frimpong-Ansah's paper sets the policy scene in the historical context, looking at the trade and exchange-rate policies followed by African governments in light of the forces and ideologies that propelled independence movements. He also considers changes of policy in the post-independence period, and introduces the international setting for African policy-making. Henry Bienen's paper on the politics of trade liberalization complements the Frimpong-Ansah paper in looking at one aspect of the political economy of trade policy in great detail – the domestic political constraints on, and the consequences of, a standard element in policy reform packages, namely trade liberalization. The next two papers take up the second theme of the Frimpong-Ansah paper – the international setting. The paper by Erzan and Svedberg documents the nature and pattern of protection against sub-Saharan Africa in the US, the EC and Japan, while the paper by Cable considers the issue in the context of the Uruguay Round of the General Agreement on Tariffs and Trade (GATT). What are Africa's interests in these negotiations, and how should these be pursued? The paper by Cable discusses these questions in the context of general issues as well as in the context of specific commodity groupings.

The final two issue papers are theoretical in nature, although directed towards key policy issues in the African context. The paper by Ravi Kanbur on the theory of structural adjustment and trade policy looks for the theoretical rationale behind the trade policy component of the sorts of structural adjustment packages that are now being adopted throughout Africa. The paper highlights three problems with the standard rationale: (i) it may not hold with a disaggregated model structure with many goods, policy towards some of which may remain unaltered; (ii) the distributional consequences of policy reform may cause a re-evaluation of certain policy instruments; (iii) with scale economies, the conventional wisdom needs to be re-examined. The paper by Tim Besley and Paul Collier on import compression and trade policy focuses on what might be optimal responses for an economy which is required to make a rapid and substantial reduction in import volumes. They distinguish between permanent and temporary import compressions. In the first case they argue that investment should increase to allow for sectoral adjustment if installed capital is immobile. In the second case, however, the conclusion is ambiguous because it may be optimal to weather temporary negative shocks by supporting consumption (and hence reducing investment).

Each of the papers in this volume has its own conclusions about the phenomena that it has chosen to analyse or highlight. It would be inappropriate simply to restate these conclusions here individually. But are there any general conclusions that emerge from these investigations – the 'issue papers' and the case studies? Recall that the object of the project was to analyse some of the determinants of trade performance, particularly of export performance, in Africa and to link this to policy. To begin with we can divide the relevant factors into two categories: (i) those that are 'internal' to a country and, in principle, under the control of a typical African government and (ii) those that are 'external' to a country and are not under government control. In the former category come the usual bunch of price and non-price instruments. Under price instruments we include the exchange rate, the producer price of major export crops, import subsidies, input subsidies for exports or import-competing commodities, etc. Under non-price instruments we include various export promotion and information dissemination schemes, efforts to strengthen infrastructure, etc.

Under the category of 'external' factors the most prominent are of course the external terms of trade and the international trading environment. If the long-run prices of primary exports are on an unfavourable downward trend, for a 'small' economy this is a given that has to be dealt with – and may itself explain poor export performance. Some of the behaviour of primary commodity prices may in turn be explained by developed country policy – such as agricultural subsidies and the dumping of the resulting high output on world markets. However, another aspect of developed country policy that has featured in recent policy discourse is that of protectionism. While most attention has been focused on protection from the newly industrializing countries (NICs), is their fate today the fate of Africa tomorrow? In any case, how much of Africa's trade performance is explained by developed country protection? The above discussion has been primarily economic in nature. Yet much policy is made in a political context. What are the prospects of liberalizing strategies, if these are appropriate from the economic standpoint, being acceptable politically?

These are the questions – what are the answers? While the experience reviewed in the papers in this volume is certainly mixed, some generalizations can nevertheless be attempted. Peter Svedberg's paper shows that the export performance of sub-Saharan Africa as a whole has been dismal. Its share in world exports and in LDC exports has fallen dramatically. Of thirty-three countries examined, fourteen experienced a fall in real export earnings over the period 1970–85. The performance over 1970–85 was in general worse than that over 1954–69. In general, very little change took place in the *structure* of exports. Both 'internal' and 'external' factors were responsible for the poor performance. For all countries of the region, with the exception of the oil exporters, there were stagnant or deteriorating barter terms of trade. However *export volume* growth also deteriorated in the period 1970–85 when compared with 1954–69. The case studies which focused on internal factors within each country shed further light on the export volume story. Nearly all of them that carried out the relevant statistical tests found that over the periods examined export supply of traditional exports was price-elastic (Tanzania, Kenya, Côte d'Ivoire, Ghana). This finding, together with a pervasive tendency to keep producer prices below world prices, explains some of the export performance. In Tanzania, for example, real producer prices of coffee, cotton, sisal, tea and tobacco all declined over the period 1978–84, with corresponding slowing down in growth rates of output (some of the growth rates even turning negative).

The political economy of these tendencies is examined by Jonathan Frimpong-Ansah in his paper. In the broad historical context, he locates the post-independence predilection for taxing primary exports in a reaction to the pre-independence, colonial, favouring of this sector in all respects. However, he describes how this initial reaction crystallized into a general strategy that favoured the urban groups at the expense of rural farmers. Henry Bienen dwells on the power of urban groups, for example in his discussion of Nigeria. Whether one is dealing with removal of import subsidies or the reduction of export taxes (which provide the revenue for urban expenditure), the politics of liberalization is important. The political economy of price reform is also taken up in Ravi Kanbur's paper, where it is argued that the political repercussions of a reform which adversely affects urban groups may lead to even greater distortions being created during the compensation process.

Thus, while confirming that prices can act as powerful incentives for increasing the supply of traditional exports, our studies warn of the need for political sensitivity in recommending such reform – if the price distortions reflect the balance of political power, what reason is there to believe that the distortions can be removed without first changing the balance of power? In fact, Jonathan Frimpong-Ansah speculates that the fundamental political stimulus required for reform 'must be rare and must be the result of extreme conditions'.

The studies highlight that price is not the *only* relevant factor in explaining traditional export supply. Export 'capacity' or 'capability' variables are found to be important in the studies on Kenya, Côte d'Ivoire and Ghana. The study on Tanzania also notes that infrastructure is important in supply. The Zimbabwe study identifies the impact of export promotion schemes. Thus prices matter, but so do other things. In fact, in the case of non-traditional exports, analysed in detail for Côte d'Ivoire, it is found that price incentives are not important in supply. In the case of Tanzania, the price effect was significant for manufactured exports, but as important was the supply of foreign exchange – which is used to purchase intermediate inputs for production. The Tanzania study also looked at services, in particular tourism. Here again, both price *and* supportive infrastructure proved to be important.

The foreign exchange constraints faced by Tanzania are similar to those faced by Zimbabwe, Ghana, Nigeria and Kenya. Côte d'Ivoire does not face foreign exchange rationing, and the analysis in the study reflects this. In Zimbabwe, however, import compression dominates the story. It is noted that this led to a 'stop–go' cycle as there was under-shooting and over-shooting by the authorities in their attempts to maintain short-term balance in trade using quantitative restrictions. In their theoretical paper Besley and Collier characterize *optimal* responses for an economy that has to undergo a sudden reduction in import volumes. They then go on to consider responses when governments are committed to maintaining the exchange rate, for example, at a fixed nominal level. In such a situation, the typical response (as in the case of Zimbabwe or Tanzania) is to tighten quotas and rations of foreign exchange. But this is invariably a second-best strategy which can also lead to fluctuations of the type described in the Zimbabwe case study. Thus maintenance of fixed exchange rates in the face of import compression is *not* supported by our studies. However, the use of the exchange rate as an import-reducing device is also not supported by our studies. Nigerian imports are argued to be highly price-inelastic. Tanzanian imports are determined almost entirely by 'import capacity' (foreign exchange availability for imports). Thus there appears to be an asymmetry between exports and imports, perhaps explained by the nature of the foreign exchange rationing regime. While for exports prices matter, alongside other factors, for imports there is an insignificant relative price effect.

Let us turn finally to the 'external' factors and export performance, emanating from the observation of a long-term decline in the relative price of the primary exports of sub-Saharan Africa. While in the short term this can be counteracted through increased export volume via domestic policies, it is clearly not a wise long-term strategy to divert more production resources into a declining unit value sector. Encouragement of non-traditional exports is clearly a possible strategy. Our studies are not clear on whether price instruments will or will not work here. However, whatever instruments are used, there is the question of market access. The case of Côte d'Ivoire is relevant. The country has had a liberal trade and financial regime, and has seen an increase in the production of processed primary exports such as coffee and cocoa. Yet in doing so it faces tariff and non-tariff barriers in developed countries. The extent of barriers against exports from sub-Saharan Africa is documented by Erzan and Svedberg. While in general they are low, and African countries benefit from preferential trade agreements, tariff barriers on processed raw materials are in general higher than those on the raw materials themselves. Then there is the matter of non-tariff barriers, which are difficult to quantify. Vince Cable notes that, even for tropical product exports, non-tariff barriers can be serious – in some cases they carry a tariff equivalent of over 100 per cent. Processed foods (e.g. fish products) face exacting health checks and other tests. Even where there is promise of unrestricted access, e.g. for textiles and clothing for Côte d'Ivoire under the Lomé Convention, restrictions are encountered. Thus, while our case studies have shown sufficient variation in trade structure and policy in the six countries to caution against the hope of a unified 'African' stance in multilateral trade negotiations, we must conclude that African nations must take an interest in the GATT, at least with the future in mind.

## Note

1 Different statistical publications provide data for different numbers of countries under the label 'sub-Saharan Africa'. In the following chapters there will therefore be some differences in the numbers of SSA countries covered. There are also different practices in different international organizations regarding which countries are considered to belong to sub-Saharan Africa. For instance, Sudan and Mauritania are sometimes treated as North African, sometimes as sub-Saharan African countries. Whenever data are available, all countries on the African continent, with the exceptions of Algeria, Egypt, Libya, Morocco and Tunisia in the north and the South African Union in the south, are counted as sub-Saharan Africa in this study. Also included are the island republics, Cape Verde, Malagasy, Mauritius, Réunion, Sao Tomé & Principe, and the Seychelles. All these countries, with the exception of Réunion, are members of the African Development Bank.

2

# The export performance of sub-Saharan Africa

Peter Svedberg

## 1 Introduction

Over the past decade and a half, the share of sub-Saharan Africa (SSA) in world trade has decreased dramatically. Export growth has dropped in absolute terms as well. In fact, real exports earnings have remained stagnant or declined significantly since the early 1970s in twenty-five out of the thirty-three countries in the region for which there are data. In 1988, the whole of SSA, with more than 400 million inhabitants, had export revenues below those of Singapore, a country of 2.5 million people.

The sluggish performance of the export sector in most of the SSA countries seems to have caused grave problems. Imports have been compressed and, given the composition of these (i.e. mainly industrial and investment goods, intermediate products and fuels), capacity utilization and growth have declined notably in most of the countries (Helleiner 1986).[1] This, in turn, has affected the export sector negatively; a vicious circle has been established. To finance imports, most SSA countries have become increasingly and heavily dependent on official foreign aid. In recent years, the tardy performance of the economy in the majority of the countries, and the ensuing large foreign debts,[2] have meant that their credit ratings abroad have generally become very poor. Since 1984 there has been a net outflow of private, non-concessional, financial funds from SSA, and private export credits have all but ceased (UNCTADa 1988, Tables 5.5 and 5.6).

There are two main, largely opposing, schools of thought when it comes to explaining the reason for the slow growth of exports in the 'typical' SSA country. One stresses factors that are 'external' to the individual country – slow volume growth of world primary commodity markets and deteriorating barter terms of trade being the main issues. The other line of thought emphasizes factors that are 'internal' to a particular country; that is, a variety of domestic policies that have affected export supply adversely. In brief, the arguments are that excessive import protection and overvalued exchange rates, and also high taxes on exports, have tilted domestic export producer prices downwards and, thus, reduced export supply.

This paper has two main objectives. The first is to assess the export performance of the SSA countries, jointly and by country. The main focus is on the period since 1970, although comparisons with earlier periods will be made when the availability of data permits. The second objective is to provide some broad explanations for the export performance observed. The main effort is directed towards estimating the relative role of changes in (i) the barter terms of trade, (ii) the export volume and (iii) the export composition.

The plan of the paper is as follows. In section 2, the *relative* export performance export performance of the SSA countries as a group is estimated by the *change* in their share of world exports. The *absolute* performance of *individual* countries over the 1970–85 period is analysed in terms of changes in the income terms of trade (i.e. real export earnings) in section 3, and also compared with own performance 1954–69. In section 4, a simple 'decomposition' model, in which the change in the *income terms of trade* is split up into changes in *export volume* and in *barter terms of trade*, respectively, is presented. The results of the statistical analysis are reported in section 5. In the next section, the focus is on the link between changes in *export structure* and export performance. In section 7, the relative importance of 'external' and 'internal' influences on export earnings growth is assessed. Section 8, lastly, sums up the findings and discusses a few qualifications to the results.

## 2 Sub-Saharan Africa's share of world exports

In the early 1950s, the share of SSA in *world* total exports was above 3 per cent (Table 2.1).[3] Since then there has been a gradual

Table 2.1 *Exports from world, less developed countries and sub-Saharan Africa, 1950–87*

| *Region* | *1950* | *1960* | *1970* | *1980* | *1987* |
|---|---|---|---|---|---|
| *Value (current US$bn):* | | | | | |
| World | 60.7 | 129.1 | 315.1 | 2,002.0 | 2,493.5 |
| LDCs | 18.9 | 28.3 | 57.9 | 573.5 | 507.2 |
| Sub-Saharan Africa | 2.0 | 3.8 | 8.0 | 49.4 | 29.0 |
| *% share of LDCs in:* | | | | | |
| World exports | 31.1 | 21.9 | 18.4 | 28.6 | 20.3 |
| *% share of SSA in:* | | | | | |
| World exports | 3.3 | 2.9 | 2.5 | 2.5 | 1.2 |
| LDC exports | 10.6 | 13.4 | 13.8 | 8.6 | 5.7 |

*Source:* UNCTADa (1988), Table 1.1, pp. 4–6.

decline, and by 1987 the share was down to 1.2 per cent. Over the period 1950–70, however, SSA increased its share of total exports from all *developing countries* (Table 2.1), but after that it declined dramatically: in 1987 it was 5.7 per cent. The sluggish export performance of the SSA countries as a whole since the early 1970s, and in the 1980s especially, can thus not be seen as a 'typical' developing country phenomenon. As a group, the developing countries have maintained their position in world exports over this period relatively well, although there have been large year-to-year swings (reflecting mainly changes in the relative price of oil).

*Crude oil* is the only major export product from SSA that has developed favourably since 1970. It then accounted for less than 10 per cent of total exports from the region; by 1985 it accounted for more than 50 per cent (Table 2.2). The growth of the world oil market, and the increased SSA share, contributed substantially to the region's total (nominal) export earnings growth. In fact, had the SSA share of oil exports remained at the 1970/71 level (*ceteris paribus*), the region's total export earnings would have been 13 per cent *lower* in 1984/85 than they in fact were.

In *non-oil products*, SSA held its position in the *world* market up to the mid-1970s. After that, the share fell sharply. In 1985, it was down to 0.9 per cent, about *one-third* of what it was only ten years earlier (Table 2.2). Over the same period, the SSA share of non-oil exports from *developing countries* declined from 16 to 5

Table 2.2 *Oil and non-oil exports from world, less developed countries and sub-Saharan Africa, 1970–85*

| *Region* | *Type of export* | *1970* | *1975* | *1980* | *1985* |
|---|---|---|---|---|---|
| *Value (current US$bn):* | | | | | |
| World | Total | 314.5 | 875.9 | 2,001.4 | 1,922.0 |
| | Oil | 15.6 | 113.3 | 332.2 | 205.3 |
| | Non-oil | 298.9 | 762.6 | 1,669.2 | 1,716.7 |
| LDCs | Total | 56.1 | 211.8 | 572.9 | 467.8 |
| | Oil | 13.9 | 104.3 | 296.4 | 146.7 |
| | Non-oil | 42.2 | 107.5 | 276.5 | 321.1 |
| Sub-Saharan | Total | 7.6 | 19.4 | 48.2 | 32.0 |
| Africa | Oil | 0.8 | 2.1 | 29.4 | 16.1 |
| | Non-oil | 6.8 | 17.3 | 18.8 | 15.9 |
| *% share of LDCs in:* | | | | | |
| World exports | Total | 17.8 | 24.2 | 28.6 | 24.3 |
| | Oil | 89.1 | 89.2 | 89.2 | 71.5 |
| | Non-oil | 14.1 | 14.1 | 16.6 | 18.7 |
| *% share of SSA in:* | | | | | |
| World exports | Total | 2.4 | 2.2 | 2.4 | 1.7 |
| | Oil | 5.1 | 1.9 | 8.9 | 7.8 |
| | Non-oil | 2.3 | 2.7 | 1.1 | 0.9 |
| LDC exports | Total | 13.5 | 9.2 | 8.4 | 5.2 |
| | Oil | 5.8 | 2.0 | 9.9 | 11.0 |
| | Non-oil | 16.1 | 16.1 | 6.8 | 5.0 |

*Sources:* Total exports – UNCTADa (1988), Table 1.1; Oil Exports – UNCTADa (1979), Table 4.3(D) and 4.4 (1970 and 1975); UNCTADa (1983), Table 4.3(D) and 4.4 (1980); UNCTADa (1988), Table 4.3(D) and 4.4 (1984/85).

per cent. This reflects to some extent (i) the sluggish growth of world non-oil primary commodity markets and (ii) a failure to boost alternative exports.

The share of non-oil *primary commodities* in world exports dropped from 26 per cent in 1970 to 17 per cent in 1985 (Svedberg 1988, Appendix Table 2). The relative decline in the share of 'tropical' primary products, or, in the terminology of the UN Conference on Trade and Development (UNCTAD), the eighteen Integrated

Table 2.3 *Share of sub-Saharan Africa and less developed countries in world exports of primary commodities (%)*

| | *All primary commodities* | | *18 IPC commodities* | |
|---|---|---|---|---|
| | *1970/71* | *1984/85* | *1970/71* | *1984/85* |
| *Share of LDCs in:* | | | | |
| World exports | 31.8 | 30.3 | 61.5 | 59.6 |
| *Share of SSA in:* | | | | |
| World exports | 7.0 | 4.1 | 16.1 | 10.2 |
| LDC exports | 21.0 | 13.5 | 26.1 | 17.1 |

*Sources:* UNCTADb (1984), Tables 1.4 and 1.10; and (1987), Tables 1.2 and 1.10.

Program Commodities (IPC), has been somewhat larger than for temperate zone ones – from more than 8 per cent in the early 1970s to 5 per cent in 1984/85 (Svedberg 1988, appendix table 2). The eighteen main tropical products make up more than 50 per cent of total export revenues in half the forty-four SSA countries. In an additional dozen countries, the share is above one-third (UNCTAD 1988a, Table 4.1). Had the share of non-oil primary products in world exports remained at the 1970/71 value (*ceteris paribus*), SSA export earnings would have been about $5 billion larger in 1984/85 than they actually were.

The share of *manufactured goods* in world trade increased marginally during the period 1970–86; this is by far the most dominant broad product category, accounting for 64 per cent of world exports in recent years. Over the same period, the equivalent share of exports from all developing countries increased from 16 to 42 per cent. Together, the LDCs have increased their share of world exports of manufactures from 5 to 13 per cent over this period. Manufactured goods remained a trivial 6 per cent of total SSA exports over the period (Erzan and Svedberg, Chapter 5 in this volume, Table 5.1). Only one SSA country, Mauritius, managed to take serious part in the expansion of world trade in manufactured goods.

The most noticeable phenomenon is, however, that the SSA countries on the whole failed to maintain their *shares* in the stagnating primary commodity world markets (Table 2.3). Between

1970 and 1985, the share fell from 7 to 4 per cent. Their share of the 18 IPC commodities declined from 16 to 10 per cent. Had the SSA countries maintained their shares of the world market for all non-oil primary commodities (*ceteris paribus*), export revenues in 1984/85 would have been about one-third, or $10 billion larger than they actually were.

Over the 1970–85 period, the combined share of the SSA countries remained intact or increased in eight of the thirty-one main primary commodity markets: fishery products, tea tobacco, sisal, bauxite, copper are, managanese ore and phosphate (Table 2.4). Only fishery products and tobacco are among the ten most important exports from SSA in general. The SSA countries lost their combined share in eight of the top ten primary commodity markets. In the six most important markets – coffee, cocoa beans, refined copper, cotton, timber and sugar – the decline was in the 22–38 per cent range. In the market for iron ore, the decline was almost 50 per cent; in the once large market for vegetable oil it was an astonishing 84 per cent.

Finally, it should be emphasized that the SSA countries generally have performed worse in the markets for semi-processed commodities than for unprocessed ones. While they have gained ground in bauxite and copper ore, they have lost shares in alumina and aluminium, as well as in blister and refined copper. Their share of the market for tin ore declined moderately; the share in tin metals declined drastically; the share in palm nuts decreased somewhat, while it fell significantly in palm oils.

## 3 Absolute export performance by country

In the preceding section, the focus was on the *relative* export performance of the SSA countries, as measured by changes in their *joint share* of world exports. In the following, the attention is shifted to the export performance of thirty-three *individual* countries in *absolute* terms. Export performance will be measured by exponential growth in the *income terms of trade*, which is another way of saying real export earnings or the import purchasing power of exports. Two periods, 1954–69 and 1970–85, each sixteen years long, will be examined separately. The main reason for this periodization is that we have data for thirty-two years and, since a reversal of the previous upward trend in real export growth took place

Table 2.4 *Share of sub-Saharan Africa in world and LDC exports of selected primary commodities (%)*

| *Commodity* | *Two main African exporters (1984/85)* | *Value of SSA exports (US$m.)* | | *Share of SSA in world exports (%)* | | *Share of SSA in LDC exports (%)* | |
|---|---|---|---|---|---|---|---|
| | | *1970/71* | *1984/85* | *1970/71* | *1984/85* | *1970/71* | *1984/85* |
| Fishery commod. | Mauritania, Senegal | 59 | 419 | 1.8 | 2.6 | 5.0 | 6.2 |
| Bovine meat | Botswana, Zimbabwe | 57 | 85 | 2.8 | 1.3 | 9.8 | 9.7 |
| Bananas | Côte d'I., Somalia | 35 | 41 | 6.7 | 2.7 | 7.2 | 2.9 |
| Sugar | Mauritius, Swaziland | 174 | 437 | 6.6 | 4.6 | 9.0 | 6.1 |
| Coffee | Côte d'I., Uganda | 805 | 2,451 | 27.7 | 21.8 | 28.5 | 23.8 |
| Cocoa beans | Côte d'I., Ghana | 650 | 1,785 | 80.6 | 62.0 | 81.3 | 66.8 |
| Cocoa products | Côte d'I., Nigeria | 102[a] | 271 | 28.5[a] | 11.0 | 56.2[a] | 29.0 |
| Tea | Kenya, Malawi | 89 | 412 | 12.8 | 15.7 | 15.5 | 20.8 |
| Vegetable oils | Côte d'I., Nigeria | 444 | 361 | 11.0 | 1.8 | 34.5 | 4.4 |
| Groundnuts | Sudan, Gambia | 123 | 41 | 57.3 | 7.2 | 77.0 | 24.0 |
| Groundnut oil | Senegal, Sudan | 75 | 92 | 51.7 | 30.6 | 68.4 | 53.6 |
| Palm nuts | Nigeria, Cameroon | 60 | 22 | 86.3 | 66.1 | 86.3 | 66.6 |
| Palm kernel oil | Nigeria, Zaire | 30 | 31 | 54.9 | 7.5 | 83.2 | 8.4 |
| Palm oil | Côte d'I., Liberia | 43 | 49 | 18.3 | 1.8 | 19.3 | 1.9 |
| Tobacco | Zimbabwe, Malawi | 110 | 392 | 8.5 | 9.6 | 24.5 | 21.9 |
| Hides, skins | Namibia, Ethiopia | 81 | 137 | 6.2 | 2.8 | 32.8 | 40.0 |
| Rubber | Liberia, Côte d'I. | 77 | 167 | 7.3 | 5.3 | 7.6 | 5.5 |
| Timber | Côte d'I., Gabon | 239 | 609 | 12.8 | 7.9 | 21.0 | 11.8 |

Table 2.4 *(cont.)*

| *Commodity* | *Two main African exporters (1984/85)* | *Value of SSA exports (US$m.)* | | *Share of SSA in world exports (%)* | | *Share of SSA in LDC exports (%)* | |
|---|---|---|---|---|---|---|---|
| | | *1970/71* | *1984/85* | *1970/71* | *1984/85* | *1970/71* | *1984/85* |
| Cotton | Sudan, Côte d'I. | 431 | 786 | 16.1 | 11.9 | 25.3 | 29.1 |
| Sisal | Tanzania, Kenya | 40 | 31 | 57.5 | 42.4 | 58.7 | 44.4 |
| Bauxite | Guinea | 9 | 411 | 3.2 | 42.1 | 4.1 | 50.4 |
| Alumina | Guinea | 46 | 130 | 7.8 | 4.8 | 17.5 | 17.1 |
| Aluminium | Cameroon, Ghana | 65 | 100 | 4.4 | 1.3 | 75.5 | 6.3 |
| Copper ore | Botswana, Zaire | 6 | 60 | 1.0 | 3.5 | 2.0 | 5.4 |
| Blister copper | Zaire, Namibia | 394 | 328 | 46.6 | 33.5 | 52.4 | 44.8 |
| Copper | Zaire, Zambia | 891 | 1,003 | 28.4 | 22.1 | 60.0 | 38.8 |
| Iron ore | Liberia, Mauritania | 311 | 431 | 11.8 | 6.2 | 29.8 | 15.0 |
| Tin ore | Zimbabwe, Namibia | 21 | 19 | 12.9 | 6.1 | 14.6 | 9.2 |
| Tin metal | Nigeria | 46 | 19 | 7.6 | 1.0 | 9.7 | 1.3 |
| Manganese ore | Gabon | 41 | 124 | 23.0 | 30.0 | 40.6 | 62.3 |
| Phosphate | Senegal, Togo | 28 | 154 | 6.6 | 9.4 | 12.2 | 15.5 |

*Note:*
[a] 1972/73

*Sources:* UNCTADb (1984 and 1987), various tables.

around 1970 in many of the countries, two equally long periods seem the most appropriate.

The estimates are presented in Table 2.5. The left-hand part of the table reveals that only eight countries had a *statistically significant* exponential annual growth of real export earnings over the 1970–85 period. This group is led by three oil exporters and Niger, for which uranium ore is the main export. For eleven countries, there was no statistically significant trend in real export earnings during this period. The remaining fourteen countries had an ascertained decline in real export earnings.[4]

The export performance in absolute terms of most SSA countries over the 1970–85 period also looks bleak when compared with their own performance during the earlier sixteen-year period. Over the years 1954–69, twenty-seven of the thirty-three countries saw statistically significant positive growth in real export earnings. For seventeen of these countries, the annual growth rate was above 5 per cent, something only four countries achieved over the later period. Seven countries had no trend in real export earnings, but not a single country saw them drop significantly.

## 4 Export earnings; price *v.* volume

Most of the SSA contries had a poor export performance over the years 1970–85 in the three dimensions examined, namely (i) relative to other countries, (ii) in absolute terms and (iii) compared with own performance in an earlier period. The question to be tackled in this section is to what extent the SSA countries' export performances are explained by different developments of the barter terms of trade and of export volume, respectively.

The real value of a country's exports for period $t$, or, in index form, the income terms of trade ($M_t$), is given by the following identity:

$$M_t \equiv B_t X_t, \qquad (2.1)$$

where $B_t$ is the barter terms of trade and $X_t$ is the export volume index. The barter terms of trade are defined as export prices over import prices. The constant exponential rates at which the barter terms of trade and the export volume are assumed to increase (or decline) are $\gamma$ and $\eta$, respectively:

$$B_t = B_0 e^{\gamma t}, \quad X_t = X_0 e^{\eta t}. \qquad (2.2\text{–}2.3)$$

Table 2.5 *Exponential growth of real export earnings of individual SSA countries, 1970–85 and 1954–69*

| *1970–85* | | *1954–69* | |
|---|---|---|---|
| *Country* | *Export growth rate (%)* | *Country* | *Export growth rate (%)* |
| Congo | 16.8 | Mauritania | 31.4 |
| Gabon | 11.3 | Rwanda | 14.9 |
| Niger | 7.8 | Congo | 12.7 |
| Nigeria | 7.4 | Gabon | 11.6 |
| | | Burkina Faso | 11.4 |
| Rwanda | 5.0 | Liberia | 10.0 |
| Mali | 4.4 | Côte d'Ivoire | 7.5 |
| CAR | 2.8 | Zambia | 7.3 |
| Malawi | 1.7 | Sierra Leone | 6.9 |
| | | Angola | 6.8 |
| Angola | . . | Mozambique | 6.5 |
| Burkina Faso | . . | Malawi | 6.4 |
| Cameroon | . . | Kenya | 5.8 |
| Chad | . . | Somalia | 5.8 |
| Côte d'Ivoire | . . | Togo | 5.7 |
| Gambia | . . | Niger | 5.7 |
| Mauritania | . . | Cameroon | 5.3 |
| Mauritius | . . | | |
| Senegal | . . | CAR | 4.9 |
| Somalia | . . | Nigeria | 4.9 |
| Togo | . . | Gambia | 4.5 |
| | | Tanzania | 4.3 |
| Réunion | –3.2 | Ethiopia | 3.9 |
| Ethiopia | –3.5 | Uganda | 3.3 |
| Kenya | –4.2 | Sudan | 3.0 |
| Sudan | –4.9 | Chad | 2.4 |
| Liberia | –5.8 | Senegal | 2.2 |
| Malagasy | –6.0 | Malagasy | 0.9 |
| Uganda | –6.2 | | |
| Ghana | –7.7 | Benin | . . |
| Tanzania | –8.0 | Ghana | . . |
| Sierra Leone | –8.3 | Mali | . . |
| Zaire | –8.6 | Mauritius | . . |
| Benin | –9.1 | Reunion | . . |
| Zambia | –10.9 | Zaire | . . |
| Mozambique | –13.8 | | |

*Note:*

. . No significant change in export earnings.

*Source:* Svedberg (1988), Appendix Table 5, based on UNCTADa, various issues.

We thus have that:

$$M_t = B_0 e^{\gamma t} X_0 e^{\eta t} = B_0 X_0 e^{\alpha t}, \qquad (2.4)$$

where

$$\gamma + \eta \equiv \alpha. \qquad (2.5)$$

Since (2.5) is an identity, the ratios $\gamma/\alpha$ and $\eta/\alpha$ will measure the *relative* shares (importance) of the exponential growth of the income terms of trade that are explained by changes in (i) the barter terms of trade and (ii) export volume, respectively.

In section 5, $\alpha$, $\gamma$ and $\eta$ will be estimated from *time-series* data for *M*, *B* and *X*, covering thirty-three SSA countries for the periods 1954–69 and 1970–85. The processed data that we will use are the UNCTAD estimates of export volume, income terms of trade and barter terms of trade. How these estimates are derived is not discussed in the UNCTAD publications. It is well known, however, that export volume and terms-of-trade indices are inherently tricky to estimate; the results usually depend on what weighting and other methods are used.[5]

## 5 Barter terms of trade *v.* volume; results

The following criteria will be used to classify the countries according to what has been the main determinant of their export performance. The barter terms of trade will be taken to have exerted the 'main' influence when they explain more than two-thirds of the growth of export earnings (whether positive or negative). Export volume will be asserted to have had the 'main' impact when it explains more than two-thirds. For countries where there is no significant trend in either entity, or for which both volume and barter terms of trade explain less than two-thirds of the growth of export earnings, the influence is taken to have been 'mixed'.

Out of the eight SSA countries that saw their real export earnings grow significantly over the 1970–85 period, the three oil exporters, Gabon, Nigeria and Congo, had improved barter terms of trade to thank for this (Table 2.6). Increased volume accounted for the entire growth of real export earnings for Niger and the four exporters of agricultural primary products in this group (Rwanda, Mali, the Central African Republic and Malawi). In the earlier period, 1954–69, export volume expansion was the main explanatory factor for all the twenty-seven countries that saw significant growth of real export earnings (Table 2.7). In fact, only two of the countries, Burkina Faso and Congo, saw the barter terms of trade improve significantly. More than two-thirds of these twenty-seven countries actually experienced a significant *deterioration* in the barter terms of trade.

In four of the eleven countries that had no growth of export earnings in 1970–85 (Mauritius, Burkina Faso, Mauritania and Somalia), this was due exclusively to deteriorating barter terms of trade. In fact, the first three countries expanded export volumes significantly. Five countries (Chad, Côte d'Ivoire, Gambia, Senegal and Togo) had no significant change in either entity. Angola and Cameroon experienced improvements in the barter terms of trade, but stagnant export volumes inhibited the income terms of trade from improving. During the 1954–69 period, only seven countries had no growth in real export earnings and only in the case of Zaire was failure of volume expansion the main explanation.

In four of the fourteen countries that had a statistically *significant decline* in the income terms of trade over the 1970–85 period (Reunion, Ethiopia, Liberia and Zambia), the problem was severely declining barter terms of trade. In Sierra Leone, Zaire and Benin, export volume decreased, and so did the barter terms of trade. In the remaining seven countries (Kenya, Sudan, Malagasy, Uganda, Ghana, Tanzania and Mozambique), volume accounted for 73–100 per cent of the deterioration in the income terms of trade over the 1970–85 period.

In summary, the different export performance between the two periods stems almost entirely from the *different export volume growth*. Over the earlier period, the export quantity grew rapidly in almost every African country. Over the later period, less than one-third of the countries managed to increase the volume. The most striking similarity between the two periods relates to unfavourable developments in the barter terms of trade. Nineteen countries saw their barter terms of trade deteriorate significantly between 1970 and 1985; also during the earlier period nineteen countries (although partly different ones) experienced declining real prices for their exports. Eight countries (Ethiopia, Ghana, Liberia, Malagasy, Malawi, Mauritania, Mozambique and Tanzania) had a significant decline in the barter terms of trade over both periods. Only five countries, all oil exporters, experienced an improvement in the barter terms of trade in 1970–85; in the earlier period, this applied to only two countries (Burkina Faso and Congo). Congo

Table 2.6 *Export performance by SSA countries, 1970–85*

| *Export performance* | *Main influence on export performance* | | | | | |
|---|---|---|---|---|---|---|
| | *Barter terms of trade*[a] | | *Mixed*[a] | | *Export volume*[b] | |
| Significant export earnings growth | Gabon | (100) | | | Niger | (>100) |
| | Nigeria | (100) | | | Rwanda | (100) |
| | Congo | (76) | | | Mali | (>100) |
| | | | | | CAR | (>100) |
| | | | | | Malawi | (>100) |
| No growth of export earnings | Mauritius | (>100) | Chad | (. .) | Angola | (>100) |
| | Burkina Faso | (>100) | Côte d'Ivoire | (. .) | Cameroon | (100) |
| | Mauritania | (>100) | Togo | (. .) | | |
| | Somalia | (100) | Senegal | (. .) | | |
| | | | Gambia | (. .) | | |
| Significant decline in export earnings | Réunion | (>100) | Sierra Leone | (63) | Kenya | (100) |
| | Ethiopia | (100) | Zaire | (60) | Sudan | (80) |
| | Liberia | (86) | Benin | (58) | Malagasy | (73) |
| | Zambia | (76) | | | Ghana | (76) |
| | | | | | Uganda | (100) |
| | | | | | Tanzania | (79) |
| | | | | | Mozambique | (86) |

*Notes:*

[a] The figure in brackets gives the estimate of the percentage share of the growth or decline in real export earnings that is explained by barter terms of trade improvement/deterioration (i.e. the ratio ($\gamma/\alpha$) from equation (2.5) above multiplied by 100); >100 means that there was a significant change in the opposite direction in export volume; 100 means that there was no significant change in export volume; (. .) means no significant change in either entity.

[b] The figure in brackets gives the percentage share of the increase in real export earnings or decline that is explained by volume (i.e. the ratio ($\eta/\alpha$) from equation (2.5) above muiliplied by 100).

*Source:* Svedberg (1988), Appendix Table 5.

Table 2.7 *Export performance by SSA countries, 1954–69*

| *Export performance* | *Main influence on export performance* | | | | | |
|---|---|---|---|---|---|---|
| | *Barter terms of trade*[a] | | *Mixed*[a] | | *Export volume*[b] | |
| Significant export earnings growth | | | | | Congo | (94) |
| | | | | | Burkina Faso | (83) |
| | | | | | Mauritania | (>100) |
| | | | | | Rwanda | (>100) |
| | | | | | Gabon | (>100) |
| | | | | | Liberia | (>100) |
| | | | | | Côte d'Ivoire | (>100) |
| | | | | | Zambia | (100) |
| | | | | | Sierra Leone | (100) |
| | | | | | Angola | (>100) |
| | | | | | Mozambique | (>100) |
| | | | | | Malawi | (>100) |
| | | | | | Kenya | (>100) |
| | | | | | Somalia | (100) |
| | | | | | Togo | (>100) |
| | | | | | Niger | (100) |
| | | | | | Cameroon | (>100) |
| | | | | | CAR | (>100) |
| | | | | | Nigeria | (>100) |
| | | | | | Gambia | (100) |
| | | | | | Tanzania | (>100) |
| | | | | | Ethiopia | (>100) |
| | | | | | Uganda | (>100) |
| | | | | | Sudan | (100) |
| | | | | | Chad | (>100) |
| | | | | | Senegal | (>100) |
| | | | | | Malagasy | (>100) |
| No growth of export earnings | Ghana | (>100) | Benin | (. .) | Zaire | (100) |
| | | | Mali | (. .) | | |
| | | | Mauritius | (. .) | | |
| | | | Reunion | (. .) | | |
| Significant decline in export earnings | | | | | | |

*Notes:*
See Notes to Table 2.6

*Source:* Svedberg (1988), Appendix Table 5.

alone saw the relative price of exports improve significantly over both periods.[6]

## 6 Export performance and export structure

The statistical analysis so far has focused on the separation of two components that determine a country's export earnings: volume and price. In this section we shall examine whether inter-country differences in growth of export earnings since the early 1970s can be related to *changes in the composition* of exports. We shall distinguish between 'deconcentration' and 'diversification'. By deconcentration we mean a lowering of the dominance of one or a few products (irrespective of which ones) in total exports, as conventionally measured by the Hirschman–Gini coefficient. Diversification means the introduction of 'new' export products on a notable scale. New export products will, somewhat arbitrarily, be identified according to the following criterion: a product that accounted for at least 15 per cent of total export earnings in 1985 and less than one-fifth of the 1985 share at the beginning of the period (1970).

The conventional view in the empirical literature is that *export concentration* is an impediment to growth of export earnings even though the exact reason is seldom made explicit (see the references in MacBean and Nguyen 1987). Standard trade theory does not predict a systematic relationship between export concentration and export growth. The principle of comparative advantage suggests that the composition of exports should be determined by relative factor supplies or technology differentials. This may mean highly concentrated exports for technologically unsophisticated countries where unskilled labour and one or a few natural resources are the main factor endowments. The little there is of dynamic theory does not postulate an unambiguous relationship between changes in export concentration and growth.

From a theoretical point of view, it is thus not very surprising this a cross-country examination of the thirty-three sub-Saharan countries shows that neither (i) and initially highly concentrated export structure, nor (ii) a deconcentration of exports over the 1970–85 period, are related to export performance.[7] Looking at individual countries, one finds that all the eight countries that saw significant growth of real export earnings in the period 1970–85 (Table 2.6) also had an *increase* in the concentration of exports.

The expansion of 'traditional' exports lies behind the achievement in most cases – oil in Gabon and Nigeria, coffee in Rwanda and the Central African Republic, cotton in Mali, and tobacco, tea and sugar in Malawi. When it comes to the twenty-five countries with stagnant or declining real export earnings between 1970 and 1985, there is no general pattern.

*Export diversification*, away from primary commodities with secularly deteriorating barter terms of trade, into 'new' products with a more favourable price development, one would expect (*ceteris paribus*) to enhance growth of export revenue. Over the 1970–85 period, one-third of the thirty-three SSA countries diversified into new (as defined above) export products. These eleven countries can be divided into three groups according to the type of new export commodity (Table 2.8). First, there is a group of six countries that became major exporters of oil or a mineral: Angola, Cameroon, Congo, Zaire, Niger and Sierra Leone. Second, there are three countries that started to export fishery products: Mauritania, Mozambique and Senegal. For these nine countries, the diversification thus reflects the tapping of a natural resource that was previously not exploited and that had favourable price developments. Finally, there is a third group comprising two countries – Mauritius and Chad – which diversified into the usual first-stage manufactured exports: textiles and clothing.

There is no (positive) correlation between diversification and overall export performance in 1970–85 across the thirty-three SSA countries. For nine of the eleven countries that 'diversified', real export earnings declined or remained stagnant. For only two of these countries (Mauritania and Mauritius) was the diversification accompanied by an expansion of the overall export *volume* (although export earnings failed to grow owing to deteriorating barter terms of trade in both cases). Among the eight countries that saw real export earnings grow significantly (Table 2.6), only Congo and Niger belong to the 'diversification' set.

## 7 External *v.* internal explanations of export performance

In the two preceding sections we have estimated the relative importance of changes in (i) barter terms of trade, (ii) export volume and (iii) export structure for the growth of real export earnings of the individual SSA countries. In this section we shall probe into the question of 'internal' *v.* 'external' influences on these three

Table 2.8 *SSA countries with a diversification of the export structure over the period 1970–85*

| *Country* | *SITC* | *New export product*[a] | *Export concentration index* | |
|---|---|---|---|---|
| | | | *1970* | *1985* |
| Angola | 331 | Petrol (76; 11) | 0.365 | 0.874 |
| Cameroon[b] | 331 | Petrol (43; 0) | 0.371 | 0.403 |
| Congo | 331 | Petrol (89; 1) | 0.486 | 0.894 |
| Zaire | 331 | Petrol (22; 0) | 0.656 | 0.417 |
| Niger | 286 | Ores (81; . .) | 0.569 | 0.738 |
| Sierra Leone | 283 | Non-ferrous metal (26; 4) | 0.543 | 0.391 |
| Mauritania | 031 | Fish (44; 7) | 0.864 | 0.622 |
| Mozambique | 031 | Fish (19; 1) | 0.234 | 0.274 |
| Senegal | 031+2 | Fish (25; 5) | 0.331 | 0.311 |
| Chad[b] | 652 | Cotton fabrics (24; 0) | 0.342 | 0.617 |
| Mauritius | 841 | Clothing (29; 0) | 0.930 | 0.656 |

*Notes:*

[a] The figures in brackets refer to the share of the commodity in the country's total exports in 1985 and 1970, respectively.

[b] Data for Cameroon and Chad are for 1983.

*Sources:* UNCTADa (1979), Tables 4.3(D) and 4.5; (1988), Tables 4.3(D) and 4.5.

variables. By internal and external are meant variables that can, and cannot, be influenced by the SSA countries themselves.

*Barter terms of trade*

When the individual country accounts for a few percent or less of the world markets of its exports (and imports), the demand (and supply) curves it faces are completely elastic. In such cases, (i) the *barter terms of trade* are unambiguously an *external* factor and (ii) the *volume* growth of the world market is of no concern. On the other hand, when the individual country accounts for a relatively large share of the world market for a particular product, the barter terms of trade are partly 'internally' determined and volume growth in the world market has to be considered. The demand curve facing the individual country will still be almost perfectly elastic, however, unless the country's share is relatively large (well above 10 per cent). Only in such cases is the price decline following an expansion of own exports not negligible.

In 1970/71, as well as in 1984/85, more than 90 per cent of all exports from SSA were in markets where the individual country had less than a 10 per cent share. On the whole, it thus seems appropriate to consider the barter terms of trade as an external factor and to disregard the volume growth of the world market. However, a little less than 10 per cent of total exports from SSA are from eight countries that (i) account for more than 10 per cent of the world market of one specific commodity that (ii) makes up an important share (above 20 per cent) of the country's total exports (Table 2.9). The six commodity markets of concern (bauxite, copper, manganese and uranium ore, cocoa beans and groundnut oil) remained stagnant over the 1970–85 period in volume terms (UNCTADb).

Four of the eight 'large' SSA countries increased their shares of the world market in the respective commodity over the 1970–85 period. It can thus justifiably be claimed that slow volume growth of the world market for these commodities is an *external* factor that has affected their export earnings adversely. Had the world market been growing more rapidly in terms of volume, these countries' supply expansion would have induced less downward pressure on world prices, and their own export earnings would have been larger.

When it comes to Zambia, Zaire and Ghana, it is a bit different. These countries saw their export volumes of copper and cocoa drop over the 1970–85 period and they lost shares in the world market. For these countries, the slow volume growth of the copper and cocoa markets must thus be considered a *favourable external factor*. Had the world market volumes grown more rapidly (*ceteris paribus*), the *upward* pressure on world prices induced by their declining absolute volumes, and thus their export earnings, would have been smaller.

*Export volume*

The delineation of internal and external influences on the SSA countries' export volume growth is rather complicated. The export supply functions found in the literature usually include production

Table 2.9 *SSA countries with more than 10 per cent of world exports of a primary commodity*

| *Country* | *Commodities* | *Value of export US$m.* | | *Percentage share of:* | | | |
|---|---|---|---|---|---|---|---|
| | | | | *World export* | | *Country's export* | |
| | | *1970/71* | *1984/85* | *1970/71* | *1984/85* | *1970/71* | *1984/85* |
| Zambia | Blister copper | 117.6 | — | 13.9 | — | 14.0 | — |
| | Refined copper | 675.7 | 750.6 | 21.7 | 16.5 | 80.4 | 87.7 |
| Zaire | Blister copper | 224.2 | 233.3 | 26.5 | 23.9 | 30.5 | 44.7 |
| Ghana | Cocoa beans | 242.0 | 338.5 | 30.0 | 11.8 | 59.9 | 66.1 |
| Côte d'Ivoire | Cocoa beans | 97.4 | 902.5 | 12.1 | 31.4 | 21.1 | 32.0 |
| Guinea | Bauxite | 4.2 | 387.5 | 1.5 | 39.7 | 8.7 | 80.1 |
| Gabon | Manganese ore | 31.1 | 114.5 | 17.4 | 28.7 | 20.8 | 5.7 |
| Senegal | Groundnut oil | 36.9 | 70.7 | 25.6 | 23.5 | 26.6 | 13.4 |
| Niger | Uranium ore | — | 211.8 | — | 29.3 | — | 80.8 |

*Sources:* UNCTADb (1984 and 1987) and UNCTADa (1988), Table 4.3(D).

capacity and export producer prices as the two independent variables. The producer prices, in turn, are determined by world market prices, the real exchange rate and net taxes levied on the export sector. World market prices are external in the small country case, while the real exchange rate and net taxes are internal variables. Without detailed estimation of export supply functions for individual SSA countries, which is beyond the scope of this paper, one can thus not answer the question of the more exact role of external and internal explanations of the export volume growth that has been observed.[8]

It is notable, however, that there is no correlation between developments in the barter terms of trade and export volume expansion during the 1970–85 period across the thirty-three SSA countries (Svedberg 1988, appendix table 1). Trade theory predicts not a positive relationship between price and quantity exported on a commodity-by-commodity basis, but a 'correspondence' across commodities; that is, in general, higher (lower) prices for a country's exports should lead to increased (decreased) export supply (Woodland 1982). The fact that this has not happened in SSA is an indication that internal variables, such as the real exchange rate and taxes, have distorted export incentives in many of the countries.

*Export structure*

Over the entire post-war period, the real world market prices for most primary products have declined and fluctuated wildly. There have thus been strong external incentives for moving into other products with more favourable price developments. Most commodity exporters in other parts of the world diversified into new products, mainly manufactures, during the 1970–85 period. Since there is no *discrimination* in the importing countries against exports from the SSA countries (Erzan and Svedberg, Chapter 5 in this volume), the fact that they have failed to renew their export structure, while others have succeeded, suggests internal reasons.

## 8 Concluding remarks

In this concluding section we shall discuss the extent to which our results permit generalizations about the countries in the region. A few qualifications to the results will close the paper.

There are at least three results which permit quite strong generalizations across the thirty-three countries that have been included in most of the study. First, it was found that the export performances of all the countries in the region, with the exception of the five oil exporters, were affected negatively by external forces in the form of stagnant or deteriorating barter terms of trade over the years 1970–85. The same happened also over the earlier period (1954–69), however, with the exception of even fewer countries (Congo and Burkina Faso). External factors were thus not any less unfavourable in this period, when real earnings grew rapidly in most cases.

The second generalization relates to the limited change in *export structure* that was revealed. Eleven of the countries have achieved some diversification (with the rather 'generous' criterion used). Most of this diversification was into new primary products, however, and only two of the SSA countries emerged as exporters of (light) manufactures on a notable scale (Mauritius and Chad). Thus, the SSA countries have yet to break with the export structure that was imposed upon them more than a century ago.

The third generalization pertains to the fact that the SSA countries did much better in terms of *export volume* growth in the 1954–69 period than more recently. Only four of the thirty-three countries had a higher growth rate during the later period (Mali, Mauritania, Niger and Reunion). About two-thirds of the countries had stagnant or declining export volumes over this period, while positive and significant growth over the earlier one. There were, however, large variations within this group (ranging from zero to a −13.8 per cent decline per annum) in the 1970–85 period. The large inter-country variations have not been explained here and should be subject to further investigation.

There are a few caveats to the above findings and conclusions that merit explicit comment. One is that the data underlying the analysis may not be very reliable. It is well known that there are large margins of error in SSA trade statistics and there may also be biases that have distorted the results. It should be noted, however, that the main general trends and findings that have been disclosed are so pronounced that potential data biases have to be large indeed to reverse them.

Moreover, the analysis has been mainly cross-sectional at a relatively high level of aggregation. This approach precludes indepth analyses of many country-specific issues that may be important. The analysis conducted here should thus be supplemented by detailed study of the individual countries, at best using a unified analytical approach. Above all, disaggregated estimates of export supply functions for individual countries and commodities are needed in order to untangle the relative role of external and internal influences on the export volume performance that we have observed. Such estimates are also required in order to identify the specific internal economic factors that have been at play in the individual countries, and also non-economic variables like weather and military strife.

Finally, it has to be noted that the focus in this paper has been on the first links in the long chain of analysis required fully to understand the role of trade in the overall economic decline of sub-Saharan Africa since the early 1970s. The relationship between export performance and overall growth has not been dealt with. Export earnings growth is not an ultimate objective, only what seems to be a necessary (although not sufficient) precondition for real-income growth. There is a relatively strong positive correlation between export and real-income growth across the SSA countries over both periods examined (Svedberg 1988, appendix table 1), but the question of causality has not been resolved. Much detailed study is required before the exact ways in which export earnings affect the rest of the economy (and vice versa) in the SSA context can be disclosed and understood.[9]

## Notes

The author is grateful for constructive comments from the participants at an Institute for International Economic Studies seminar and the Rockefeller Foundation and International Development Research Centre conferences on Trade in Sub-Saharan Africa held in December 1987 and March 1989 in Nairobi. Financial support from the Rockefeller Foundation and the Swedish Agency for Research Cooperation with Developing Countries is acknowledged.

1 The per capita GDP growth rate in SSA was about 2 per cent in the 1950s and the 1960s. In the 1970s, it declined to 0.6 per cent; during 1980–1987 it was –2.3 per cent (UNCTADa 1973 and 1989, Table 6.2).

2 The ratio of the *stock* of long-term foreign debt (outstanding and disbursed) to gross domestic product (GDP) at the end of 1989 was considerably higher in SSA than in Latin American and other 'developing

areas'. Moreover, the rate of *increase* in this ratio between 1985 and 1987 was drastically higher in SSA than in any other major bloc of countries. The *debt service ratio* in 1987 was about the same in SSA as in the other regions, but the projections by the International Bank for Reconstruction and Development (IBRD 1988) for 1988–92 suggest increases for SSA that outstrip those of all other regions by far.

3 In this section, all countries on the continent, with the exception of Morocco, Algeria, Tunisia, Libya, Egypt and the South African Union, are included. In subsequent sections, where the focus is on individual countries, data are often available only for the thirty-three countries listed in Table 2.5 (with 95 per cent of the total population of SSA).

4 More preliminary data show that the stagnation or decline in export earnings continued over the years 1986–88. Mauritius is the only SSA country among the thirty-three that had a significant increase in real exports earnings over the 1980s (mainly from light manufactures).

5 See Spraos (1980, 1985); Sapsford (1985); Scandizzo and Diakosawas (1987).

6 Real prices for almost all primary commodities have declined on a secular basis since the early years of this century (Scandizzo and Diakosawas 1987). By mid-1987, the real prices of thirteen out of the twenty commodities for which there are long price series were at an all-time low (Svedberg 1988). A recovery began in late 1987 and continued throughout early 1989 (IMF 1989).

7 The simple correlation coefficients are in fact positive, but not statistically significant (Sevedberg 1988, Appendix Table 1).

8 As far as is known, there has been no general discrimination against SSA exports. The data on tariff and non-tariff protection in the OECD countries in the mid-1970s suggest, on the contrary, that the SSA countries are favoured (Erzan and Svedberg, Chapter 5 in this volume).

9 See Helleiner (1986) and Ram (1987). For more detailed studies of two specific countries, see Ndulu and Lipumba (Chapter 9 in this volume) and N'geno (Chater 14 in this volume). Also see Gulhati *et al.* (1986).

## References

Gulhati, R. *et al.* (1986), 'Exchange rate policies in Africa: How valid is the scepticism?', *Development and Change* 17, pp. 399–423.

Helleiner, G. K. (1986), 'Outward orientation, import instability and African economic growth: An empirical investigation', in *Theory and Reality in Development; Essays in Honour of Paul Streeten*, S. Lall and F. Stewart (eds), Macmillan, London.

IBRD (1988), *World Debt Tables, 1988-89 Edition*, Washington DC.

IMF (1989), *Primary Commodities: Market Developments and Outlook*, Washington DC.

MacBean, A. I. and Nguyen, D. T. (1987), *Commodity Policies: Problems and Prospects*, Croom Helm, London.

Ram, R. (1987) 'Export and economic growth in developing countries: Evidence from time-series and cross-section data', *Economic Development and Cultural Change*, 36, pp. 51–72.

Sapsford, D. (1985), 'The statistical debate on the net barter terms of trade between primary commodities and manufactures: A comment and some additional evidence', *Economic Journal*, 95 pp. 781–8.

Scandizzo, P. L. and Diakosawas, D. (1987), *Instability in the Terms of Trade of Primary Commodities, 1900–1982*, FAO Economic and Social Development Paper 64, Rome.

Spraos, J. (1980), 'The statistical debate on the net barter terms of trade between primary commodities and manufactures', *Economic Journal*, 90, pp. 107–28.

Spraos, J. (1985), 'The statistical debate on the net barter terms of trade: a response', *Economic Journal*, 95, p. 789.

Svedberg, P. (1988), 'The export performance of sub-Saharan Africa 1970–1985', Institute for International Economic Studies, Seminar Paper No. 409, Stockholm.

UNCTADa, *Handbook of International Trade and Development Statistics*, Geneva, various issues.

UNCTADb, *Commodity Yearbook*, Geneva, various issues.

Woodland, A. D. (1982), *International Trade and Resource Allocation*, North Holland Publishing Company, Amsterdam.

3

# Sub-Saharan Africa and the international trade system: Perspectives of policy

Jonathan H. Frimpong-Ansah

## 1 Introduction: statement of the problem

Trade policy is usually defined as the methods by which a government manages its external sector through the use of price and non-price instruments, with a principal objective of maintaining correct relative prices between tradables. Often this is done by allocating resources (quotas) to, or levying taxation (tariffs) on, the economic sectors producing or marketing tradables. Exchange-rate policy aims at correcting the relative price of tradables to non-tradables. It can be non-interventionist, allowing market forces to regulate exchange rates, or interventionist, whereby a nominal exchange rate, which is different from the market rate, is complemented by various forms of rationing. Such rationing may also involve trade policies. Thus the nature and objective of trade policy are expected to be quite different in a regime in which the full instruments of exchange-rate policy are employed, as compared with that in which exchange-rate policies, particularly the nominal exchange rate, are passive. Where exchange-rate policies are passive or non-interventionist (e.g. in regimes of protracted fixed exchange rates against changing market rates), considerable dependence is expected on trade policies. Where exchange-rate policies are active, trade policies become positive and promotional, rather than restrictive. In this paper these definitions of trade policy and exchange-rate policy are implicit, but the analysis does not focus on the variety of management techniques employed in the two approaches to external sector management.

The literature on African trade and development is unanimous about the general decline in both exports and imports in the majority of African countries in the past decade and in some cases for a longer period. Poor export performance has been blamed as the primary reason, which in turn has necessitated import reductions in a dynamic process of trade compression and economic stagnation and decline.[1]

Exogenous factors listed in the literature include unfavourable barter terms of trade, overproduction of primary commodities, recent adverse climatic factors, and the breakup, in the post-independence period, of some regional economic integration arrangements that favoured liberalized regional trade, such as the East African Currency Board and the West African Currency Board.[2]

In the analysis of internal factors, the greater blame has been put on inappropriate public policies on trade and development. These include insufficient producer incentives, such as inappropriate prices, inadequate producer organization and services, fragmentation of peasant production and marketing, lack of modernization of production and therefore the perpetuation of low productivity particularly in agriculture, poor producer infrastructure, the protection of inefficient enterprises, especially those in the state sector, overvalued exchange rates, excessive producer taxation, excessive reliance on administrative controls in the allocation of scarce resources, and excessively expansive fiscal and monetary policies (World Bank 1987).

Areas that research has yet to concentrate on are the reasons why particular policies were adopted in the post-independence period, and why, in most cases, they failed and the policy issues of the reversal of the present trend.

This paper reviews the policies of African trade and development for some preliminary answers to these questions in a long-term perspective. It investigates whether pre-independence policies, post-independence strategies and current reforms are interlinked in a long-term causal relationship that better helps to explain the underlying reasons for trade and development policy formulation in sub-Saharan Africa.

The *prima facie* arguments are that: the course of immediate post-independence trade and development policies was largely the result of the perceptions by the immediate post-independence states in Africa of the effects of colonial policies on the indigenous economy. The methods of post-independence attempts aimed at reversing colonial policies were, in turn, the principal source of the adverse internal factors in trade and development. The current efforts at the reform of trade and development policies, and at trade negotiations, are largely targeted at what are believed to be the inappropriate policies in both the colonial and immediate post-independence periods.

Most studies that have attempted to analyse the current economic problems in Africa have taken a medium-term view and examined information relating to specific economic or political regimes.[3] Some, in effect, seem to have assumed that political independence was a landmark that distinguished clearly between significant macroeconomic regimes. By this approach most studies have not taken fully into account the dynamic causal factors influencing public policy in the succeeding historical period. In this paper, the view is taken that the problems of trade and development have existed for a very long period, even before colonization, and that the study of the perspectives of present policies stands to benefit from a long-run analysis which is able to examine the causal factors.[4]

## 2 The evolution of trade systems in Africa

It is not correct to speak of a common set of African trade policies. However, within the different patterns, there are similarities which derive largely from common economic history. The greatest factor has been the domination of European powers and trading interests in the past 200 years or so. Of particular influence were France and Great Britain. Our analysis therefore must concentrate on the evolution of British and French systems and their subsequent influence on trade and development in Africa.[5]

### *British-influenced systems*

The British influence on trade and development follows an easily discernible pattern. From early colonization to the end of the 1920s, the enthusiasm to develop the colonies as an integral part of the imperial trade network grew with the construction of transport systems and other infrastructural investments to promote the production of a wide variety of primary commodities and minerals. This phase saw the development of such commodities as coffee, tobacco, cocoa, tea, palm oil, groundnuts and cotton, and such minerals as gold, iron ore, copper and tin.[6] This was also the period of relative free trade in which most of these ventures were allowed to be developed by expatriate enterprises with the flow of private captial from Britain, where needed. Government assistance was offered through chartered companies that were specially created in the 1930s for the purpose.[7]

In the period that coincided with the great depression of the late 1920s to the late 1930s, a conscious attempt was made to reduce the pace of investment in the colonies. Official policy aimed also at lowering the prices paid for exports from the colonies, in order to 'limit the exaggerated ideas of value of their products and numerous expensive tastes'. The official view was that 'after the war (1914–1918) economic forces were broadly speaking left unchecked, and primary producers in the period immediately after the war had reaped rich harvests owing to the high prices which they received for their goods. . . . [with] consequences that were almost wholly evil'.[8] It was therefore in this period that most of the confrontation between primary producers and exporting companies took place.[9] Producers believed that the lower prices were due to the indifference of colonial governments, and demanded official intervention in pricing and storage.[10]

The period of the Second World War (1939–45) was, compared with the 1930s, one of renewed activity in African trade when the continent became fully drawn into British economic and war policies. The system of rationing foreign exchange for imports and invisible transactions was introduced, for the first time, on a comprehensive scale as part of the conservation of resources for the imperial war effort. The restrictive trade policies ran contrary to the trends in economic trade performance in the colonial countries (Ingham 1987). This experience in trade policy (*restriction culture*) was later to become extensively employed by post-independence African governments in situations when alternative macroeconomic policies might have been the more appropriate.[11] The loss of the Far Eastern colonial possessions to the Japanese and the hazards of the Mediterranean sea routes during the Second World War also led to a shift of trade to Africa. This occurred in two ways. There was the urgent need to revitalize export production of tropical raw materials to replace the loss from the Far East. There was also the urgent need to produce consumer goods, mainly food, for the British and American troops passing through West and East Africa on their way to the fronts in North Africa and the Far East.[12]

The period of the Second World War therefore produced a unique set of circumstances for African trade and development. In the immediate post-war trade liberalization, accompanied by the commodity boom of the Korean War of the 1950s, many African countries benefited from the higher levels of production created by the exigencies of the Second World War, and from the slow pace of reconstruction of the production facilities in the Far East. This advantage lasted throughout most of the period of decolonization in the late 1940s and 1950s. The perverse combination of import controls and export expansion led to several instances of external reserve accumulation with which aggressive development policies were attempted in the early post-independence period.[13] This and the euphoria of independence may have encouraged far more aggressive development programmes than the primary economic structures justified.[14]

After the acceleration of development and some successes in trade in the initial post-independence period, the pace of economic activities considerably slackened in most Anglophone countries. With very few exceptions, restrictions on trade and payments increased at approximately the same rate as economies stagnated or declined during most of the 1970s and 1980s (World Bank 1987). In the countries in which economic stagnation was prolonged or decline accelerated, the common factor was the poor performance of the export sectors in the first instance, followed by an accumulation of external debts and then import compression in the ratio of the loss of external resources.

*French-influenced systems*

There was essentially little difference in the objectives of colonization and the evolution of trade and development between Francophone and Anglophone Africa in the period before independence.[15] It is the greater post-colonial economic association between France and her former colonies that distinguishes the trade and development performance of Francophone Africa from Anglophone

Africa. This factor also determines the key domestic influence on trade policy and performance in Francophone Africa. Of greatest influence in this relationship was the creation at independence (in 1963) of two monetary unions in West Africa and in Central Africa, with two convertible common currencies – the CFA franc. Each union created a tightly integrated regional monetary and fiscal economy of the member countries, preserving free trade between them and relative free trade between the union and the rest of the international economy through full convertibility of the CFA franc through the French franc.[16]

The principal features of the two monetary unions that affect trade performance are the following. The African common currency systems by-pass the two hurdles of a customs union and a common market, directly to a theoretically possible and practically feasible optimum currency system.[17] The working conditions of the union are a rigid ceiling on fiscal deficits (usually fixed at 20 per cent of previous year's tax revenues), a common interest-rate policy (usually fixed in relation to the French interest-rate structure), a fixed exchange rate between the French franc and the CFA franc (currently fixed at 50 CFA francs to 1 French franc), a common external reserve pool managed by the common Central Bank, 65 per cent of which must be deposited with the French Treasury, and a ceiling on commercial bank credit in the member countries annually fixed by mutual agreement and implemented by National Committees in accordance with their respective domestic conditions.[18]

The regional and international convertibility that is safeguarded by these conditions facilitates free trade but does not guard against the polarization of investments or labour. The general result is that most of the capital and labour is concentrated in the coastal and forest belts in industry and agriculture. Notwithstanding this polarization, recent research indicates that the volumes of intraregional trade between the member countries of the West African Monetary Union have increased at a faster rate than those between the non-union West African countries. Trade between the two blocs has consistently declined over the years, despite the financing mechanism within the West African Clearing House.[19] The principal reason is the increasing indebtedness of the non-union members which have inconvertible currencies.

Another feature of the Francophone monetary system is the somewhat higher level of internal monetary and fiscal stability it generates and therefore the considerable moderation of the so-called adverse indirect factors on production of tradables attributable to domestic inflation and currency overvaluation.[20] Direct effects indicated by producer taxation, however, exist on the export crops in both Francophone and Anglophone systems.[21] The Francophone systems have not been able to eliminate all the adverse internal factors, even though the direct and indirect price distortions may not be as grave as those of some of their near neighbours.

The following conclusions emerge from the above analysis. The comparative experiences of the trade and exchange systems in Africa show that there has been greater trade expansion at both the regional and international levels in the regions and countries that continued with the more liberal systems than in those that abandoned such systems. The contrast comes out most clearly in the West African region.

It has also been illustrated in recent studies that efforts at economic integration, including the formation of clearing houses, as a method of liberalizing and expanding intraregional trade have been thwarted by the disharmony of the different exchange systems. In the West African region, for example, a significant factor in the failure of the clearing house has been the excessive accumulation of debts by the members with inconvertible currencies.

Those countries with liberal exchange rates have so far been better able to avoid producer price distortions and have better developed their productive facilities and organizations. If greater flexibility can be introduced into their exchange-rate system, they could still improve upon their export capacity. Those countries that have developed better organization for their productive sectors have also been able to withstand the predatory tendencies of the state, and have thereby ensured greater stability of production.

Against this background, it is easier to discuss the evolution of public policy on trade and development in the right perspective beginning from the pre-independence strategies and focusing on the dynamic causal linkages between the changing phases of public policy as the politics of decolonization gave way to accelerated development and then to stagnation and to decline in some instances.

## 3 Analysis of public policy on trade and development

*Causal factors from pre-independence public policies*

By excessively concentrating on primary production for international trade, the public policy of a typical government of the pre-independence African country did not promote broad-based economic development strategies that improved incomes and welfare of the indigenous sectors of the African economy. In some cases the colonial state directly discriminated against indigenous development.[22] The indigenous beneficiaries of wealth were those peasant sectors that were involved in export agriculture where this was permitted. In effect, the pre-independence governments in Africa preferred to distance themselves from the general public they governed. Rather greater reliance was placed on the administrative intermediation of traditional rulers who progressively failed the test of reforms indicated by the processes of economic, social and political change.[23]

There existed such a lopsided structure of economic development and trade and its financing as to encourage some strong views against colonial economic policy. One such celebrated authority wrote at the time:

> If they [colonial governments] re-orientate their outlook; if they think more in terms of local purchasing power; if they seek to increase the incomes of peasants and the wages of labourers; and *do not hesitate to tax the export industries* in order to keep purchasing power within the colony; all these things will attract capital. They may discourage mining capital and settler capital but they will attract industrial capital and so help to put an end to that lopsided concentration on exports which distinguishes colonial economic structures. (Lewis 1944, p. 30; emphasis added)[24]

It is necessary to elaborate on the characteristics of the lopsided structure of trade and development in order to establish the causal relationship that existed between post-independence and pre-independence policies on trade and development.

The wide disparity in wage and income structures between the bulk of populations, particularly between those in rural employment on the one hand, and those in urban and international trade related employment on the other, is that which drew the sharpest contrast. This was thought to express the inequities in pre-independence economic policies and gave credibility to the appeal for social justice in public policy. It became the mobilizing force against colonialism and the rhetorical cornerstone of the politics of decolonization It also provided some explanation for the tendency towards even more lopsided accelerated economic development in the early post-independence period aimed at curing underdevelopment.[25] While the colonial governments regarded international trade in selected items and the investments and associated infrastructure and transportation as the primary strategies for empire-wide economic development, the emerging African nationalists disagreed with the colonial intention and showed greater concern for the domestic economy, and for the need for rapid improvements in the welfare of the indigenous populations.[26] The effect was that some of the merits of the facilities created for export production, such as transport infrastructure and marketing, were not accorded the importance they deserved in the early post-independence phase. In designing programmes to correct the imbalance between the affluent export sectors and the deprived indigenous economy, there was no urgency to maintain established producer incentives in those productive sectors that served the previous colonial empire trade.

The second causal factor related to the policy on the taxation of the export sector. Following logically from the emphasis placed on international trade in pre-independence economic policy, taxation on international trade was the logical source of fiscal revenues. The bulk of the taxation was, however, on imports rather than on exports. There was considerable opposition against any form of export taxes that reduced the profits of mining companies or increased the cost of raw materials to manufacturing enterprises in the advanced countries. Such opposition extended even to taxation to finance road and rail infrastructure for the export sector itself (Guggisberg 1924).[27]

In so far as a policy of low export taxation led to higher producer incomes, it was advantageous to producer incentives and therefore to higher export production. However, in those countries in which there were single or few major products in the export sector, the relatively higher incomes had the tendency to reduce incentives in the other forms of production, including domestic foods (Cardinall 1931).[28] The other important argument against low export taxation in the pre-independence period was the adverse effect it had on domestic purchasing power and therefore on the growth of domestic demand as a stimulus for local manufacturing.[29]

Colonial economic thinking regarded importation of manufactured goods as a logical counterpart of exports of primary produce. Colonial governments were therefore prepared to countenance only discreet and gradual evolution of secondary industries 'with the object of providing the simpler needs of the population and so releasing overseas purchasing power for the acquisition of goods of greater social value' (Clauson 1941).[30]

The nationalist reaction to such policy in the politics of decolonization was to focus on a vigorous industrialization programme and to employ the instrument of taxation of the export sector for financing it.[31] Intellectual opinion at the time seemed also to support such a policy approach to trade and development. Falling into this category of economic thought were the several development theories launched in the 1950s and early 1960s (such as Prebisch 1959, 1963; Rostow 1960; Hirschman 1958; and Lewis 1954). However, the question of the degree to which the peasant export sectors could be squeezed to finance such modernization has yet to feature in the literature.

The third causal factor influencing the path of post-independence public policy on trade, and emanating from the underdevelopment of productive facilities and organization in the pre-independence period, was the view that the flow of productive external capital was a function of the facilities that the recipient country was able to offer. In the narrow sense this implied the granting of generous and often costly capital investment concessions. In the wider sense it implied the provision of an improved social and commercial environment for a modern sector. It called for such conditions as better transportation, better training in general education and professional and technical skills for indigenous workers. It was therefore justified, from the modernization point of view, in the immediate post-independence period, to squeeze resources from the savings and taxation of the established sectors and from external reserves and borrowing for such expanding social infrastructure – all tending to be urban oriented – in preparation for economic modernization.

This analysis shows how the state of the African economy in the pre-independence period and the policies of the colonial governments might have shaped immediate post-independence trade and development policies. The most significant difference between the pre-independence and post-independence governments was their relationships with the people they governed. Most post-independence governments saw themselves in the role of redeemers of the people from poverty, and therefore sought a sharp break in macroeconomic policies and strategies at independence in the hope that their objectives would be more quickly achieved.

The policy options between agricultural modernization and industrialization in the immediate post-independence period were an important determining factor in progress in trade and development. A major influence in the selection of the balance between the options was the perception, by incoming politicians, of the factors that had induced relative indigenous underdevelopment in the colonial era. Where the principal factors were thought to be excessive reliance on the international economy, policies focused on strategies for self-reliance in domestic supplies of essential consumer goods. Where excessive emphasis on agriculture for raw materials was thought to be a major disadvantage, policies focused on the need to shift the balance of investments in favour of local processing. Where the indifference and passivity of colonial governments in development were perceived to be the cause of underdevelopment, policies emphasized greater government involvement in mobilizing economic and commercial activities. Where a lack of indigenous private capital and entrepreneurship at the required scale was considered to be the greatest hindrance to modernization, state-centricity in industrial and business organization was considered desirable. Some of these considerations overlapped.

*Policies in the immediate post-independence period*

For the purpose of this analysis the immediate post-independence period is dated twenty-five years into the period of independence. For most countries this would span the 1960s to the mid-1980s. From the analysis of causal factors in trade and development policies in the transitional period of decolonization, it is possible to categorize the different approaches to policies on trade and development within a simple political economy framework constructed with the dimensions of economic ideology and nationalism. The spectrum of economic ideology would range from liberal, free market ideas in which private initiatives are protected on one pole to an opposite pole of state-centricity, economic controls and administrative pricing.[32] The spectrum of nationalism would range from a pole of active nationalism in which indigenous interests are

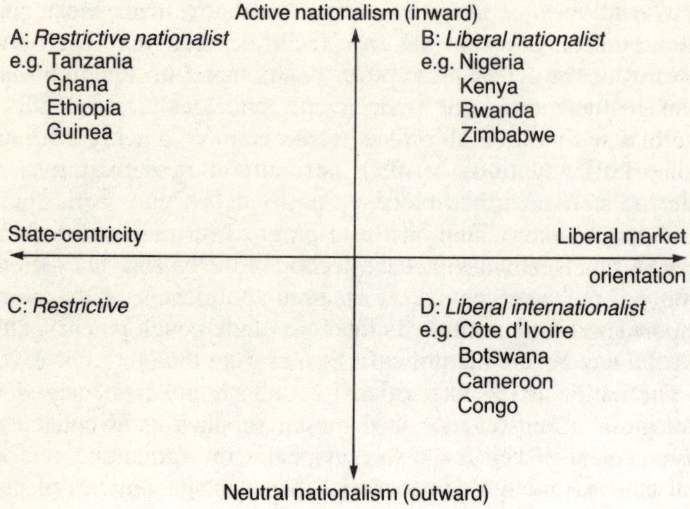


Figure 3.1 *Categorization of trade policy regimes*

favoured at the maximum levels possible, to the opposite pole of neutral nationalism where there is no significant discrimination between indigenous and external interests.[33] At the active nationalist pole one should expect preference for indigenous business initiatives and ownership of property. At the neutral nationalist pole, direct foreign investments and other forms of business involvement are expected to be liberally encouraged.

By superimposing the two spectral dimensions on each other, as in Figure 3.1 four general policy quadrants are formed. Most African trade and development policies in the immediate post-independence period can be generally categorized in these broad policy classifications. On either side of the vertical nationalist axis are restrictive and liberal systems respectively; and on either side of the horizontal ideological axis are policies favouring or giving preferential treatment to indigenous initiatives and those allowing free competition between indigenous and external interests, respectively. The four general policy classifications are: A – restrictive nationalist (inward) policies; B – liberal nationalist policies; C – monopolistic state/foreign bias; and D – liberal internationalist (outward) policies. It is in these general classifications that the immediate post-independence trade and development policies are discussed.

*A: Restrictive nationalist policies* Economic management policies in this classification are expected to be strongly restrictive and inward looking. This means that the countries in this group have managed their trade and exchange-rate policies by resorting to the use of a wide variety of trade and nominal exchange-rate policies. Countries in this category have generally allowed their exchange rates to be heavily overvalued and have therefore attempted to minimize market distortions by various forms of producer subsidies and incentives. Within the context of restrictive and nationalistic policies one should also expect a substantial bias towards import substitution strategies, and therefore a high level of effective protection for the domestic market.

The nationalist aspects of this classification of policies would indicate a strong bias for state initiatives, such as ownership and management of key establishments in the economic and commercial fields. Also to be expected is a bias for state control of international trade by way of marketing monopsonies and centralized state-managed import houses.

*B: Liberal nationalist policies* Trade and development policies in this classification are also inward looking but only moderately so. Public policies have tended moderately to favour import-substituting production for domestic consumption. Direct import quotas and licensing often exist but are not always rigidly enforced. In some cases their application is allowed to lapse in periods of relative prosperity. Policies in this category generally favour production for export through a high degree of producer incentives and lower taxes, but because countries in this classification often maintain overvalued exchange rates (despite their moderately liberal policies), some bias against the export sector exists. Attempts have usually been made to counter the effect of this bias through direct export incentives. A distinct characteristic of public policy in this general classification would seem to be the attempt to pursue, simultaneously, independent policies aimed at export promotion and import substitution. This approach to trade policy is the result of (a) the inability of public policy to decide on the appropriate policy alternative, (b) the existence in this regime of strong pressure groups in both export and import sectors, and (c) the failure to achieve more exchange-rate liberalization than is possible.

Though the countries in this classification have generally tended to favour a generally inward-oriented approach to economic modernization, the relatively more liberal attitudes to economic management in the immediate post-independence period would seem to have contributed to the moderate successes recorded in that period. Considerable distortions should be expected in such economies, though to a lesser degree than in the more restrictive economies. Of particular relevance have been the slow reactions in trade, in exchange-rate and other monetary policies and in fiscal policies to changes in the international economy.

*C: Restrictive internationalist policies* In this classification, one would expect trade and development policies to be outward looking, but, in a contradictory way, to be also restrictive and state-centric. This would present a disequilibrating set of policies, such as state monopolies in partnership with external interests and management, or an administratively restrictive economic and trade environment in which are located international free trading enclaves. Examples of these types of disequilibrium policies were rather rare in the immediate post-independence period for any countries to be so typified. The notable examples of the American-initiated Volta Aluminum venture in Ghana, and the bauxite operations in Guinea are not enough to enable any countries to be classified under this general policy label. It may be mentioned that this approach to policy on the exploitation of and trade in natural resources has always been a considered policy option in those countries in Africa with a deficit of capital and technology whose domestic public policies did not easily or naturally attract external capital. Indeed, this approach has been the key factor in the several liberal investment codes in many otherwise unattractive countries.

*D: Liberal internationalist policies* Not many countries in sub-Saharan Africa outside the Francophone regions are strongly outward oriented in their trade and development policies. Even in the Francophone regions, where there is little flexibility in the exchange-rate policy owing to the rather prolonged fixed ratio with the French franc, it cannot be said that the effective exchange rates for importables and exportables have generally remained equal.

Generally, therefore, the trade and development policies that are classified as liberal internationalist are those that are moderately outward oriented, in which public policies and incentives moderately tend towards import substitution for domestic markets. There therefore exists in most structures in this classification a wide range of moderate protection, with some tending to indicate some implicit bias against exports when comparisons are made of the effective rates of protection between export sales and domestic sales (World Bank 1987). Countries that can be placed in this classification include Côte d'Ivoire, Botswana, Congo, Gabon and Cameroon.

This analysis suggests the types of public policy environments that appear to have evolved in the immediate post-independence period in Africa. A combination of causal factors may have induced programmes of industrialization as the route to development in post-independence Africa, and led to policies that did not adequately recognize increasing productivity in agriculture as a basic condition for development. In most countries these policies did not yield the results that their designers had hoped for.

## 4 Failure of public policies

It is possible to argue, notwithstanding the above analysis, that in whatever model a country found itself, of greater importance to development and trade expansion is the quality of management and organization that it was able to pursue. An external sector management continuum of varying management styles, such as is formulated in Figure 3.2, illustrates the argument.[34]

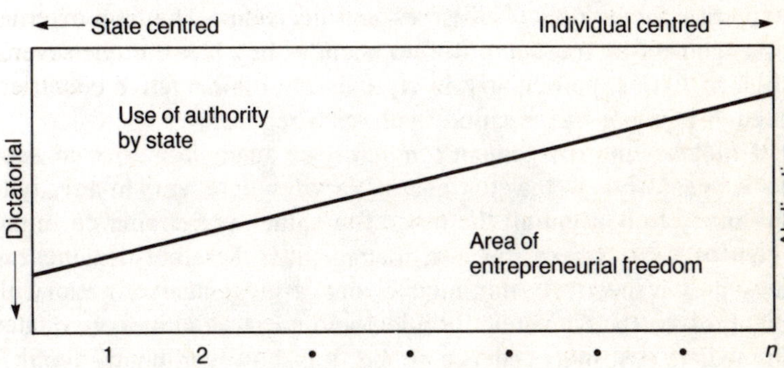


Figure 3.2 *A trade policy management continuum*

The most dictatorial management style is where the state, without consultation, decides the aims and objectives of policy in the light of its political objectives and the prevailing conditions in the domestic and international economies. The state selects its course of action, announces it, and expects compliance. The users of resources are not expected to have any direct involvement in the decision-making process. For greater efficiency in the allocation of resources, the officers or managers of the state must have a high degree of knowledge of both the domestic and external conditions. In the immediate post-independence period, such experience was not to be expected. The extreme dictatorial style has been common in countries with restrictive trade and exchange policies, where there is a strong direct role for the state in the management of resources.

The most liberal style is where the state sets the limits of resources available, through a market-related nominal exchange-rate policy. Trade policy is then used to promote domestic and international objectives that exchange-rate policies are unable to deal with. Until the current adjustment experience, this approach was rare in Africa, except in the member states of the Francophone monetary unions where their benefit is in situations where exchange rates are deemed to be market related.

Arguably an appropriate style in the period of post-independence, unavoidable statism would be somewhere in the middle of the continuum. Here the state is not made an excessive burden on productive resources; it is a manager and a promoter of development. The state depends on public experience, opinion and expertise for its policy measures and decisions. This approach to management of trade and development policy has not been common in Africa, particularly in regimes of administrative controls, though it is not incompatible with such regimes.

Efficiency in management can hardly be guaranteed, as a general rule, in any style in the continuum. Very few managers in any style are likely to be right all the time. The value to trade and development of the different styles of management therefore depends on how they respectively minimize errors of judgement and management, given the economic, political and social environment of the immediate post-independence period. It is, however, not difficult to link the management styles in the continuum to the different trade policy models discussed in section 3.

*Failure of exchange-rate policies*

In many African countries, the generally minimal use of the nominal exchange-rate tool for several years in the post-independence period has been due to certain incorrect intellectual perceptions. It was believed that exchange-rate devaluations are a primary cause of inflation, particularly where production responses to changes in monetary policy are weak. There has also been the political perception that they induce the overthrow of governments.[35] Also where a country does not have export manufacturing capability, the benefits of devaluation have been assumed to be minimal. However, where chronic exchange-rate overvaluation is allowed to erode both primary producer incomes and public sector revenues, the effect on the production of primary tradables has been known to be dramatic. The adverse indirect effects on economic and political stability have also been known to be devastating (Krueger *et al.* 1987).

A major effect of overvaluation of exchange rates in Africa has been to destroy export enterprises that had underpinned trade and development. In the primary agricultural sector, producer incentives were rapidly eroded because marketing boards, state treasuries or exporters could not pay adequate producer prices in local currency conversions.[36]

In the mining industry, the loss of profitability seriously eroded the capacity to undertake ore development. It also led to inefficient exploitation strategies that undermined the quality of proven ore reserves. Mining companies faced with unprofitable local currency earnings due to overvaluation have had to concentrate mining on richer ore deposits. The implied short-term operational viability has been achieved at the expense of longer-run efficiency.[37] Also relevant in this analysis is the excessive rigidity of the exchange-rate structure of the CFA franc. This has not allowed an effective nominal exchange-rate policy in the face of the recession in oil and commodity prices. The effect on Côte d'Ivoire and Cameroon has been devastating.[38]

*Failure of trade policies*

The effect of the failure of the primary export sectors has been complex. In most cases, the designers of trade polices thought their rationing policies and methods would conserve the dwindling foreign exchange. The evidence, however, shows that the trade policies themselves have become even stronger factors in the loss of production and foreign exchange. Most approaches were dictatorial in style and were not efficient. In the majority of countries, trade policies did not reduce the use of foreign exchange on imports or efficiently allocate what was spent.[39] Rather, large parallel markets grew up in such countries, which, coupled with smuggling activities, led to a steady dwindling of the relative size of the official markets for foreign exchange. The exchange-rate overvaluation worsened, tariffs and quantitative controls were made tighter and became even less efficient. The consequent reductions in the formal authority of governments led to increasing loss of confidence in the management of the formal external sector, and to the tendency to hold foreign exchange abroad or in the informal markets. Steadily the role of the state in managing the external sector became eroded.

Where the dictatorial use of state authority in trade policy management was the more predominant, the greater beneficiaries of scarce foreign exchange resources in the periods of quantitative restrictions were the state-owned enterprises. These were not necessarily the more efficient users of scarce resources.

A further factor in the failure of trade policy was its inefficient management. In most countries, evidence from numerous commissions of inquiry into corrupt practices in the allocation of import quotas illustrates the inefficient use of resources, and several cases of allocations in excess of resources that were available. In many instances, the power to allocate scarce foreign exchange, implied in trade policy, was transformed into political power to award largess to pressure groups and to promote certain political ideals.[40]

### *The failure of price controls*

Administrative pricing of consumables is to be distinguished from that of tradables. The former has usually been a complementary management strategy with quantitative restrictions. There is the need to limit the high rents that would accrue to sellers of scarce goods. There is also the need to limit the effect of inflation on sectors of the economy to which economic rents do not accrue. Policy-makers are also anxious to disown responsibility for the high levels of prices resulting from public policy. The higher price levels have been manifest in the parallel markets, and price control measures have focused particularly on the sensitive items in the cost of living. Price controls have therefore been pervasive in most countries and have covered thousands of items. In Ghana in the early to mid-1970s, the prices of nearly 6,000 items were controlled, and over 700 product groups were affected in both domestically produced and imported categories (World Bank 1987, p. 114).

Price controls on consumables have had significant adverse effects on production. Where producers remained law abiding, the lower prices led to lower revenues vis-à-vis costs and to lower profits. This discouraged production or encouraged poor-quality output.[41] Domestic products have progressively become uncompetitive, which has encouraged flourishing parallel markets in foreign goods.

The effect on the production of tradables of producer price controls and other direct and indirect distortions is even more devastating in a number of countries. Research in this area has been rather scanty and present efforts do not claim absolute success.[42] The results for the African countries show considerable distortions leading to significant loss of production. The loss of cotton production in Zambia from direct and indirect effects in 1980–84 was 61.7 per cent. In Côte d'Ivoire the loss of coffee production in the same period was 50.8 per cent and in Ghana the loss of cocoa production was 55 per cent (Krueger *et al.* 1987, p. 14).[43]

*Failure of state-centricity*

In the countries in which state initiatives and involvement in commercial activity were a factor in the deterioration of trade and development, there were three principal approaches. The mildest was the acquisition by the state of a majority interest in the principal commercial and industrial enterprises, often appointing the senior management but operating in partnership with the previous owners. This was the Nigeria model. In another approach the state did not acquire interest in existing enterprises but created larger ones and provided support for their expansion at the expense of non-state enterprises. This was the Ghana model. The third, and most comprehensive, was the nationalization (state ownership and management) of all major enterprises in banking, commerce and industry. This was the Tanzania model.

There were a number of effects: it led to less efficient production through the loss of profit motivation, the employment of less efficient persons, in some cases through political influence, several forms of politicization of business operations, loss of management incentives, reduced competition, and wastage of the larger scarce resources allocated to them.[44] It discouraged contact with technological improvements from the rest of the world, and led to the perpetuation of antiquated and uncompetitive techniques of production and management and the loss of export markets. These losses were additional to the drying up of markets and new investments from abroad.[45] The statist approach in its severe form discouraged the emergence of indigenous entrepreneurs by limiting their operations to small-scale enterprises and discriminating against them in the allocation of resources such as import quotas, domestic credits and external lines of credit.

## 5 Policy reforms in trade and development

Domestic and international aspects of the reform process are distinguished in this analysis. Domestic policies are defined as those of trade and exchange rates which governments may attempt to reform in order to return their economies to a stable growth path. International policies are those that deal with trade negotiations, such as those in the Lomé Convention, the GATT and UNCTAD.

### *Domestic policies*

What distinguishes current reforms from previous attempts is that the former were spasmodic and conceived largely within the existing models of economic and social policy. Almost all the attempts by the African countries that would be classified in our quadrants A and B in Figure 3.1 were unsuccessful. The common characteristic of the current reform attempts is the effort to change the primary models of public policy. The general evidence would seem to indicate that the failure of trade and development has been caused as much by the inappropriateness of the present models as by the inefficient operation within models. By our definition such reforms may therefore be properly described as processes of transition from the models of inward state-centric restrictive policy regimes to outward, liberal, private sector oriented regimes. In terms of management, the current efforts are an attempt to move along the management continuum (Figure 3.2) to find the style that is most suited to new policies in the particular conditions in different countries. This, arguably, is a hypothesis that many would wish to test more rigorously, but the general opinion, in many instances, is that a radical change of model is a crucial enabling factor in the long-term success of the current processes of reform. Given this condition, the problems of transition from one model to another, rather than those of reforms within existing models, should be regarded as the principal objective of policy formulation and implementation in trade and development in Africa in the current period. Experiences in the countries that have attempted radical economic reforms indicate that the process of ideological change is the most crucial, especially where a major deterioration of the productive facilities has taken place.

*The political dimension in the reform process.* The aspects of the political process that have been dealt with fairly exhaustively in the literature come under the subject of the political economy of economic stabilization, or of liberalization (e.g. Nelson 1984), and have dealt with the conflicts between interest groups in the processes of economic change. In a process of macroeconomic change that involves a radical transition from an inward restrictive model to an outward liberal model, the analysis of the political preconditions requires to be taken further. This may be subdivided into four conditions: the political conviction of change, the political authority to change, the political ability to enforce change, and the credibility of the process of change.

*The political conviction.* This is a combination of the political will for economic change on the part of a government and a decision to change the political and social ideology of domestic politics rather fundamentally. The combination of factors that can generate this kind of fundamental political stimulus must be rare and must be the result of extreme conditions. A change of political leadership or party may be an enabling factor but is not a necessary or sufficient condition, because, in the state of protracted economic stagnation or decline, successor governments are merely opposing factions in the same larger camp of interest groups that have benefited from economic deterioration at the expense of the productive sectors. Usually their first objective is to redistribute the shrinking cake in their favour. Thus the political stimulus that is required is one that is more patriotically inspired than those that have been known in post-independence Africa.

The experience so far in the few countries that have been able to attempt radical transformation of political conviction would indicate that a violent social and moral shock has been present resulting directly from a major economic decline. This is usually of such proportions that it leaves very little room for less radical alternatives. Usually this stimulus is endogenously inspired and therefore reforms are genuinely attempted. The radical turn-about of the present Ghana government in 1983, after one-and-a-half years of pursuing policies that worsened the already devastated economic conditions it had inherited, is a good example of the nature of the required shock and the degree of political stimulus and conviction that is required.

By this reasoning, many cases of radical political transformation should not be expected in those countries in Africa (quadrant A of Figure 3.1) where the economic shock has not quite happened, and where policy-makers still retain faith in their present models.

*The political authority to effect change.* Quite often what is assumed to be the preferences of the people for certain types of policies is rather what governments, intellectuals and ideologues have preached. In the case of economic restrictions, state-centricity and inward-looking policies in a declined environment, one often finds public policies that are quite at variance with the preferences of the bulk of the people. For example, governments may preach price controls and exchange controls while the bulk of the population are happy to buy and sell in the more realistic markets, generally now labelled the parallel markets. Those who are willing to enforce administrative prices are those in the bureaucracy itself whose wages are related to administrative prices.

Thus the political authority to effect a transition in policy is largely a function of the degree to which governments are able to re-educate themselves and to debunk inaccurate ideas about how an economy works. Political authority therefore depends very much on accuracy of thought and the public's perceptions of the correctness of public policies that affect their welfare. For example, given the choice between a currency dealer in the parallel market who posts his exchange rates and is able to defend them and a central bank governor who is unable to supply foreign exchange at the bank's published official rate, the public would give greater respect to the so-called currency trafficker and lesser authority to the central bank governor. An important condition in the process of radical change in economic policy is therefore the creation of greater authority and credibility through a comprehensive re-education on the content of the public policies to be pursued, so that they could be put across and defended convincingly.

*The political ability to enforce change.* The ability to enforce change is perhaps the most difficult aspect of the political process of transition, but, when this problem is carefully analysed, governments and policy-makers will find that they have precious little choice. A way of explaining this limitation is to conceive the problem in a model of the economic approach to the political process (Brennan and Buchanan 1980; Lal 1984, 1986; and Frimpong-Ansah 1989). In these models the government in a declined economy is conceived as a nucleus in a wider predatory state consisting of all beneficiaries of state largess, such as inefficient state enterprises, the bureaucracy and urban masses. The size of the predatory state has grown over time to be in excess of the surpluses that the productive sectors (the prey) can optimally generate for the services the state provides.

In most countries, domestic trade and development policies have failed because the prey has been taxed to the point of extinction. With the destruction of the prey or its withdrawal into occupations that are beyond the control of the state, as in cases of the failure of export crops or mineral companies or the minimal utilization of industrial capacity, the predatory state (better described now as the vampire state) must itself have no basis of survival. In most countries this is the stage at which an acute economic crisis occurs and the need for a radical review of policy becomes politically recognized as unavoidable. But at that stage most productive facilities are decayed, or are in such a state of disrepair that it would take a considerable time to rehabilitate them. The obvious priority in such a situation is to find urgent methods of transferring existing or new resources from the state to the productive sector if the state is to be transformed into a positive predator and if the productive sectors are to be nourished back to life.

The ability to enforce the desired change is therefore a condition for the survival, not only of the country as a stable and viable economy but of the state and its nucleus (the government). Since economic decline and political and social instability are best manifest in the struggle for survival within the vampire state, the greatest force that must be exerted to save the state must be within the state itself. Therefore, in an economy in decline, the restructuring of the state (i.e. the government and its integral institutions) must be the number one priority. But, while the productive sectors are often responsive to appropriate incentives, the state in decay can be reformed only by a nucleus (government) which recognizes the need to achieve such a change and is able to enforce its desire.

*The credibility of the process of change.* The credibility of the process of change is a final political condition. As economic reform, which involves a transition from one primary set of policies to another, often tackles the problem of long-term stagnation or decline, the process of recovery is always long, and several phases of fatigue and uncertainty are encountered. The political ability to persevere through these phases depends on a number of factors, chief among which are the rate at which the initial positive indications occur, the magnitude of external support, the flexibility of the multilateral institutions assisting in the reform process, and the credibility of the public education that the government is able to mount.

Most governments in the post-independence states in Africa have depended upon their various integral political wings for public mobilization. But, as has been explained in the preceding paragraphs, the excessive expansion of these groups has been a significant factor in the mutation of the vampire state, and therefore the political functionaries are usually the early victims of radical economic reform. A government that is committed to reform of a radical nature therefore cannot always depend fully on its traditional machinery of mobilization for the needed public education. The government will, in fact, face continued hostility from entrenched interests within the state such as trade unions and public servants (including the military and the police) in the difficult phases of transition.

This analysis points to some crucial aspects of the political dimension of the process of transition from one public policy model to another.

### *International policies*

The question that we now seek to answer is how, given the above background, sub-Saharan Africa can review its international trade relations in the current period in the context of the international trade system in support of its reform of internal policies. The attempt to answer this question is approached in three steps. First, we derive from our analysis what Africa's priorities should be in its international trade, given its present performance. Second, we look critically at the philosophy of the international trade system against the perspective of our determined priorities. Third, we examine the views gathered in Africa in the course of the research for the project on 'Trade and Development in Sub-Saharan Africa' and attempt to provide specific suggestions for policy-making towards the current trade negotiations.

*Sub-Saharan Africa's priorities in international trade.* The priorities that emerge from our analysis in section 2 of the paper may be set in the following order. For a majority of SSA countries, the first priority is to undertake those domestic policies that would bring their per capita production of tradables back to the levels that were achieved in the late 1960s. This is the focus of the economic reforms in which almost all SSA countries are currently engaged, either on their own initiative or with the help of multilateral institutions such as the International Monetary Fund (IMF) and the World Bank. The evidence that is emerging from these reforms indicates that for most countries the positive results should not be expected in the immediate term.

The second priority is the maintenance of stable and increasing prices for exports. The common long-term significant factor in export values in both the growth and decline phases of the whole of the post-war period has been the weak barter terms of trade. Many methods have been adopted in the international trade and monetary systems to cope with this problem, but the evidence of continued deterioration would indicate that effective methods are yet to be found. The present methods, including the commodity buffer stock agreements, export stabilization programmes within the Lomé Convention (Stabex), the compensatory finance fund in the IMF, etc., are obviously inadequate.

The third priority is the improvement of the structure of exports through diversification and deconcentration. The available evidence indicates clearly that there is need to make greater efforts to diversify into products that are more successful in the international markets, particularly light manufactures. It would seem that at Africa's present stage of development, the capacity to make this effort successfully is lacking. In the field of primary products the more general tendency has been towards unplanned deconcentration and diversification, implying that future strategies should become more orderly and more purposeful.

The fourth priority is to enlarge the volumes of intraregional trade. The present mechanisms for intraregional trade, which are based on the concept of limited currency convertibility, have been shown to be inefficient. The clearing systems in Western, Central, Eastern and Southern Africa have had problems coping with the less convertible currencies in the respective regions. It would seem from the evidence of the performance of the regional monetary unions that regional currency convertibility, where managed properly, is a better solution than the clearing mechanisms. The efforts in this direction relate to the economic reforms that have been mentioned in connection with the first priority.

This list is not exhaustive, nor are the priorities to be seen as common in the above order to all countries. For example, our field results indicate that public opinion in Kenya and Zimbabwe supports the export of manufactures as the number one priority. In Côte d'Ivoire, the public view is that greater emphasis should be placed on food production for the domestic market, while export concentration should be within the regional context followed by global export. Here the reduction of production costs in manufacturing would seem to be of high priority.

*The international trade system and Africa's priorities.* The problems of accommodating the African priorities in the philosophy of the international trade system are rather complex, largely because of the underlying mercantilist principles. Some fit well while others do not.

Africa's main priority of economic reconstruction can be interpreted as a desire for economic growth. In the present circumstances, there are two stages in this desire. The first is the journey back to the more satisfactory performance of the 1960s, and that is a repair job. The second involves real strategies for economic development within the context of a more viable development theory and political environment than were available in the 1960s and since then. In the context of both stages, and more so perhaps for the first, all types of preferential treatment (Special and Differential Treatment, the Generalized System of Preferences, the Lomé

Convention) are to be considered as aids to economic development in the international trade system. But these constitute only one aspect of the problem of reconstruction and development.

A second, and also important, aspect is trade liberalization. Though it would appear that the ultimate aim of the international trade system is free trade, it is arguable that its negotiation strategies can help developing countries, particularly those that are small in international trade terms (as most SSA countries are), in their programmes towards trade liberalization. Within the mercantilist-driven system, particularly of the GATT, argreements between small and large nations for trade liberalization lack credibility and are difficult to enforce in the eyes of interest groups. The developing countries' markets are too small for them to be able to negotiate reciprocal liberalization because the improved access is not likely to be significant enough to generate interest in the advanced countries.[46] On the other hand, unilateral liberalization by developing countries, using membership of the GATT as a pretext, has been found not to be of much value because membership of the GATT, by itself, has not been found to improve market access on the export side. Furthermore, this is a matter that would be of interest to countries that have attained export capability in manufactures. It would seem that there is little room in the international trade system for a specific agenda that would aid trade liberalization in Africa.

The fact that African countries were admitted into the GATT in the 1960s on geo-political arguments is still a hindrance. Though some of the arguments are outworn these countries still receive special treatment and little is expected of them, which does not enable the initiation of the kind of wider agenda that would aid the creation of the desired links between trade and economic development.

Africa's second priority, namely stable and increasing export prices, does not appear to be a matter of special and direct interest in the GATT. For this, African countries have had to depend on other forums, which accounts for their greater concentration on the Lomé Convention as a forum for international trade negotiations (apart from their traditional trade links with Europe). This problem also suggests the need to widen the GATT agenda by introducting items that are of special importance to the developing countries but that do not necessarily fall into the category of aid. The possibility of this happening through the initiative of the developing countries themselves has been discounted by observers who believe that earlier efforts in that direction failed. At the present negotiations, the idea of a wider agenda to include external debts, financial liberalization and trade links does not appear to be making any headway. We see again that one of Africa's major priorities has little room in the GATT process.

Africa's third priority, namely the improvement of its export structure, belongs more to the second stage of the economic development process than to the process of reconstruction, and also has more to do with domestic policy than with international factors, at least at the present time. The present facilities in GSP, S&D and also the Lomé Convention indicate that for the majority of countries there is room in the present framework for improvement. Again we come back to the question of how the international trade system can aid the improvement of the capacity of countries, such as those in Africa, to increase their performance. One cannot doubt that economic theory would support aid for such improvement; the problem is how such an item can be successfully introduced onto the mercantilist agenda of the GATT.

SSA's fourth priority, i.e. intraregional trade, would be in conflict with GATT rules if it became visibly protectionist in character. It has been shown that the present regional mechanisms, which have protectionist traits because they are based on currency inconvertibility, have been operationally unsuccessful. The new strategies for successful regional trade expansion are likely to be those that are based on liberal trade within the context of freer exchange systems. If this is so then there should be room for their encouragement within the GATT system.

As can be seen from our analysis, the major problems and priorities of sub-Saharan Africa are not of a nature that readily fits into the present GATT framework of an international trade system. Africa has two choices: it can maintain its present relative indifference, or it can explore opportunities in the present Uruguay Round in which its priorities may be assisted. The present economic reforms in Africa, which are aimed at reducing direct and indirect distortions, and at increasing trade liberalization, denote greater interest in new trade policies that are more compatible and more in harmony with the international trade system. It is therefore better for Africa to choose a strategy which, in addition to Lomé and UNCTAD, will make the continent become more interested in the

GATT as the embodiment of the international trade system, for better or for evil.

If we take the view that Africa should follow this course, the question is, what are the possible benefits and how should public policies be modified in order to achieve those benefits? The first part of the question can be answered by a review of some principal items on the GATT agenda that directly relate to the priorities of Africa's broader economic, financial and development policies. These are Tariffs, Agricultural and Tropical Products, Financial and Monetary Arrangements, Multifibre Arrangements, Trade in Services and 'New Issues', and Ideas on the Strengthening of the GATT System.

*Tariffs.* The discussion on Tariffs centres around the argument that probable reductions in most favoured nation status by major importing countries should be seen as conferring long-term benefits on African countries, if they can be made to eliminate tariffs on processed natural products. This would facilitate first-stage industrialization and therefore an increase in the value of tradables. It is also argued that certain products could be adversely affected by the future erosion of some of the facilities under the Lomé Convention and under present GSP preferences. Africa would do well, under these circumstances, to become involved in GATT negotiations that might have this effect. There is considerable evidence already that Africa has not been able to take full advantage of the facilities under Lomé or GSP because of supply, marketing, financing and other domestic constraints. There is a growing feeling that Africa's future in trade expansion depends more on efficiency in production and marketing than on preferential treatment.

*Agricultural and Tropical Products.* Considerable evidence has been produced in the studies of this project, and also in this paper, to show the failure of agricultural exports in a number of African countries. There is also considerable evidence on the efforts in many countries to reform their policies on production by the removal of some of the common distortions that adversely affect the farm sector. The question is what happens to Africa's export markets in the face of new competition from the Far East and the subsidies on agricultural products in the advanced countries. The removal of agricultural subsidies in the advanced countries and some negotiations with new producers in the Far East in the context of GATT should be seen as priorities of policy in Africa.[47]

*Financial and Monetary Problems.* Implicit in the GATT philosophy is a wide range of trade and exchange-rate liberalization. A considerable amount of financial support is needed to create this effective environment. African countries have already undertaken some very far-reaching monetary and financial reforms. It is logical that they should find an appropriate forum in which to press for agreement that gives credit for the painful measures that have been taken by them. Such measures should be matched by the removal of tariffs and non-tariff barriers to their exports. It is also logical for them to ask for more liberal rules of origin under present and future preferential arrangements that may be worked out under GATT.

*Multifibre Arrangement.* Like other developing countries, Africa's best interest, in the present and longer run, would be served by the termination of MFA. One of the areas in which Africa stands a chance of advancing exports is by shifting from low price elasticity to high price elasticity goods. It is in the textiles and apparel markets that such opportunities may exist for Africa. Those countries that are beginning to make some headway, such as Mauritius and Côte d'Ivoire, face problems of access and rules of origin, even in the context of Lomé.

*Services and 'New Issues'.* If negotiations on these issues are going to be important in the Uruguay Round, then Africa cannot remain aloof. It is in the services that African countries are significantly in deficit. These include banking, insurance and transportation, in which Africa will have comparative disadvantage for several years to come. In terms of future technological development, Africa must be interested in the negotiations on trade and production-related issues such as rules on investment and on intellectual property. These are directly related to the benefits that should be expected from the policy reforms that are being undertaken.

*Strengthening the GATT System.* A general focus in the Uruguay Round will be the strengthening of the GATT system itself. The question that Africa should ask is, in what direction is GATT likely to be strengthened and would it be to its advantage? There are a number of interests that Africa can pursue. Developing conceptual and practical links between the IMF–World Bank framework and that of the GATT is perhaps the most important. Another is the creation of new alliances within the GATT between Africa and the industrialized countries based on mutual interest. Also important is co-operation in the GATT environment between Africa and other third world countries on the basis of common interests.

*Africa's strength in the international trade system.* But is Africa strong and prepared enough to participate in the GATT along the lines discussed above? The following observations are based on the fieldwork conducted as part of the country studies. The attempt was made to ascertain Africa's present involvement and the strategies that can help in promoting Africa's interests.

A decade or two ago Africa's ideas about development and international economic relations were coloured by the euphoria of independence. Today the picture is quite different. Considerable knowledge has become available through the programmes of reform that most countries are pursuing. Not only the African politician but also the common man is today very conscious of the decline in production and trade that has taken place, and is prepared to support measures that a decade ago would have led to military revolutions. It is therefore easier to discuss very frankly what is required if Africa is to improve its participation in current and future negotiations.

What appears to be lacking is a clear identification of national and regional trade objectives in the different countries. Of particular importance is the distinction between short-term and long-term objectives. This problem is to be expected for two important reasons. First, most countries are today being virtually managed by the IMF or the World Bank or by donor countries. Policy-makers have little scope for reviewing the long-run perspectives of their economies in terms of policies they have not designed. Secondly, most policy-makers and politicians are not certain of the status of their public policies and cannot say whether the reforms are permanently radical or not. Until the present state of flux in policy has passed, it would be difficult for many countries to articulate long-term policies to deal with the international trade system.

Perhaps as a corollary of the above, we have observed a significant weakness in personnel and administrative support, and in general organization, for the formulation and management of trade policy. Also weak is negotiating capability. Individuals who have been involved in trade policy for several years in their countries or in their missions in Geneva are very knowledgeable in their subjects. However, their role in policy at the centre was not found to be significant. There appeared also to be little co-ordination between ministries or between departments.

We also observed that there was a complete absence of specialized centres, at the national or regional level, for research and analysis of matters relating to international trade. For the minimal information that this project needed, very primary research had to be undertaken. It would seem therefore that the basic knowledge upon which public policy on trade can be formulated at the quality required for constructive and beneficial negotiations may not exist in many countries. It is important that a cadre of trade policy specialists is developed quickly, and made to contribute to policy-making. For the time being, it is necessary that countries seek support from acceptable organizations, such as the African Development Bank, the Commonwealth Secretariat, non-governmental organizations (NGOs), etc., for the formulation of trade policies within the context of their economic recovery programmes.

We found no evidence of the formation of common regional interests, either in African political organizations or in regional organizations. Nor was there any evidence of initiatives to develop common positions for purposes of negotiations. In effect there seems to be little preparation at both the national and regional level for participation in the Uruguay Round. The evidence of involvement and preparation for the Lomé Convention contrasts very sharply with the passivity towards the GATT. The explanation we received was that Lomé was more specific in the provision of an agenda that was relevant to African interests. Lomé was also able to provide a desired link between trade and development.

## 6 Conclusions

Viewed in the context of the passivity of the colonial state, some of the aggressive approaches to development, which led to restrictive trade and exchange-rate practices, can be defended. In that sense, colonial policies contributed to some of the errors of immediate post-independence macroeconomic management. Likewise, some of the state-centric approaches to modernization can be justified.

Experience of economic problems in countries that went to the extreme in altering macroeconomic management policies, however, illustrates the futility of development strategies in which restrictive trade and exchange-rate policies dominate. The failure of development, particularly the failure of the production of tradables (both traditional and non-traditional), is largely accounted for by distortions that have resulted from inappropriate trade and exchange-rate policies. The political economy of failure poses even greater problems for economic recovery.

The cumulative effects of colonial passivity and post-independence aggression therefore pose major problems for economic recovery. Present adjustment policies, in which liberalization of exchange-rate and trade policies is at the centre, cannot by themselves eliminate the accumulation of policy failures. New philosophies on trade, development and the political economy have an important role to play in supporting current reforms. The new trade philosophy should aim at converting the elimination of distortions and the liberalization of trade into larger exports in the context of the mercantilist international trade system. The new political economy must lead the way towards a new philosophy of governance in which the producer's interests become at least as respected as those of the consumer. These must be recognized as tasks even more difficult than the current reforms themselves.

## Notes

1 See, for example, Khan (1974), London (1988), Krueger *et al.* (1987), Balassa (1977), and Frimpong-Ansah (1989).
2 Svedberg (1988) and World Bank (1987).
3 Examples are Killick (1978), Coulson (1982), World Bank (1987), Chazan (1983).
4 Such as introduced in Crowder (1968).
5 There have, of course, been other external influences in African international trade practices and policies apart from the ten or so countries that participated in the Berlin Conference at the end of the nineteenth century. There were Arab traders from North Africa and the Middle East before the Europeans, as the trading languages of Hausa and Swahili testify.
6 There is considerable literature on this subject. On West Africa the standard texts are McPhee (1926), and Crowder (1968). A more general standard work is Hancock (1942).
7 These include the Royal Niger Company in West Africa, the Imperial British East Africa Company, and the British South African Company. It was the Chartered Companies that acquired the large tin

concessions for expatriate mining in Nigeria, assisted in developing the copper belt of Zambia, opened up lands for settlement in South Africa and Rhodesia, and attracted settler farmers to Eastern Africa; Lewis (1944b)

8 G.M.L. Clauson, 1941, quoted from British Colonial Office File No. CO967/13. References beginning with the letters 'CO' are from files in the Public Records Office in London.

9 The farmers' riots are well described in Bates (1983), chapter 4. Ingham (1987) attributes the depressed state to unwarranted contractionary British Treasury policy for the colonies in the period.

10 Lord Bauer in several works (1971, 1981, 1984) has maintained opposition to state intervention through the creation of marketing boards.

11 In most cases, well-drafted exchange control laws were available in the archives of the Treasuries and only needed to be dusted up and made into law.

12 A detailed account of the change in policy is in Colonial Office Files Nos CO852/506/1 and 2. Also relevant was the creation of a West African War Council, headed by a British cabinet minister (Lord Swinton), to take charge of this operation. The detailed research on this subject must await the lifting of the present embargo on war files.

13 Uphoff (1970). Also Bauer (1981) and Frimpong-Ansah (1989).

14 This is detailed in Frimpong-Ansah (1989).

15 Cosnier (1921, p. xvi) states as follows: 'We have left almost nothing for the producer in return for the considerable riches our commerce has gained. Almost nowhere are there any riches.'

16 The present membership of the West African Monetary Union is Benin, Burkina Faso, Côte d'Ivoire, Mali, Niger, Senegal and Togo. That of the Central African Monetary Union is Chad, Central African Republic, Cameroon, Congo, Equatorial Guinea, and Gabon.

17 Grubel (1973, p. 101) provides the theoretical justification for such an approach.

18 The greatest criticism that has been levelled against the monetary unions in recent months is what appears to be a fixed exchange rate between the French franc and the CFA franc. The treaties of the two monetary unions, as well as the individual convertibility agreements between the French Treasury and the member states, do not make *immutability* of the exchange rate a condition. However, the fixed relationship has become a tradition which will require a major effort and much complicated negotiation between member states, between the two unions, and between them and France to resolve.

19 UNCTAD studies on the West African Clearing House are: Reference numbers ECDC/135, 1982, and ECDC/TA/20, 1987.

20 Krueger *et al.* (1987, p. 14) have estimated the indirect nominal protection rate for Ghana cocoa as –66.0 per cent in the period 1975–79 and –89.0 per cent in 1980–84. For the corresponding periods, the indirect nominal protection on Côte d'Ivoire coffee was estimated at –32.6 per cent and –25.6 per cent.

21 Direct nominal protection is defined as the difference between the relative producer price and the relative border price, or the relative adjusted border price measured at the equilibrium exchange rate and in the absence of all trade policies.

22 Bates (1983, chapter 3) cites several such instances in East Africa. Conspicuous areas of suppression of indigenous development were in discriminatory land and labour laws.

23 Crook (1985, p. 105): 'That it [the colonial state] failed was, it may be argued, very largely a product of the unchanged "externality" of the state from society.' In so far as the chiefs, as a medium of governance, were concerned, Crook argues that 'the only weapon they did have was the ability to call on a reservoir of traditional loyalties and sentiments . . .' (p. 104).

24 Lewis's argument was that an 'export industry wants low wages and low taxes – within limits, the lower the standard of living in the colony, the better it thrives. The domestic industry however depends on having a local market with a high standard of living, and purchasing power to spend.' Therefore the primary export industry perpetuates poverty.

25 In the words of Nkrumah, when he became Leader of Government Business in 1951, 'it was when they [colonial government] had gone that we were faced with the stark realities . . . there were slums and squalor in our towns . . . there was much ignorance and few skills . . . of industry we had none . . . we made not a pin, not a handkerchief, not a match' (1963, p. xiii).

26 Sir Gordon Guggisberg (1924, p. 41) states: 'No country can develop trade to its full paying capacity without incurring a debt for the construction of the necessary communication.' Compare with Nkrumah's view (1957, p. 38): 'To ensure increased efficiency in the handling of the colony's resources, the coloniser grants loans and invests capital in improving communications, social and welfare services, ostensibly to better the native.'

27 Guggisberg (1924, p. 26): 'we want all the money we can get to continue to build railways, harbours and roads . . . it is Government's opinion that the cost is a legitimate charge against the cocoa trade at the present moment.' Bates (1983, chapter 3) produces arguments to show that the peasant export sector was made to support unviable expatriate export sectors (often mining).

28 Cardinall (1931, p. 99) writes, for example, about cocoa: 'So easy is

cocoa to grow and so remunerative that a false idea of commercial values has been forced upon the native peasant. He has yet to think in pence instead of pounds . . . But the peasant-farmer if he is to survive must always remember that the crops which produce small but certain profits are those on which his existence depends. . . .'

29 See the Arthur Lewis quote in n24 above.

30 This quote is from British Colonial Office File No. CO967/13.

31 Writing on cocoa export revenues for development in Ghana, Nkrumah (1957, p. 157) wrote in defence of the government's strategy as follows: 'By using cocoa funds for development and for providing amenities, it would be possible to improve the general standard of living in the country as a whole at an early date.'

32 This would resemble the models in World Bank (1987).

33 This would be a continuum with characteristics similar in concept to Seers (1983, chapter 2). Seers, though, describes nationalist and anti-nationalist poles. However, 'neutral nationalism' used in this paper is not the same as Seers's 'anti-nationalism'. Neutral nationalism makes a high degree of protectiveness of national interest compatible with the acceptance of international co-operation.

34 The Tannenbaum and Schmidt Continuum Theory is well known in the business management literature. It postulates that the style of management depends on the situation, the personalities and the task, and that these provide enough variables to ensure that very few managers are going to be right every time. Tannenbaum and Schmidt (1960).

35 The overthrow of the government of Busia in January 1972 was classically attributed to the devaluation and other measures of late 1971. See Libby (1976). Otherwise, most examples are of Latin American origin.

36 For example, Ghana's cocoa production capacity in 1988 is estimated at the level of 1922 (Frimpong-Ansah 1989).

37 The Zambian copper industry and Ghana's gold-mining industry are typical examples.

38 It is estimated that half of Cameroon's public sector revenue has been wiped out. Both countries are experiencing problems paying producers of primary exports. For the first time in many years, cocoa smuggling from Côte d'Ivoire to Ghana has been observed.

39 ECOWAS (1987) showed that, among West African countries, restrictive trade policies were not a significant factor in determining the levels of imports in the periods when such policies were applied.

40 Several commissions of inquiry into trade malpractices in African countries have shown the prevalence of this practice. In Ghana, the Reports of Akainya, Abraham, and Ollenu contain such evidence; see Killick (1978).

41 The case of the textile industries is a typical example. The quality of yarn, weave count and dyestuff was lowered as uneconomic prices were enforced (author's interviews with manufacturers).

42 Reference here is to work pioneered by the World Bank under the supervision of Krueger, Schiff and Valdes. The studies have covered eighteen countries among which Côte d'Ivoire, Ghana and Zambia are the only sub-Saharan African countries. A. Atsain and A. M'Bet have been responsible for the Côte d'Ivoire study. The Ghana study has been conducted by D. Stryker. The Zambia study has been conducted by D. Jansen.

43 A more recent study for the period 1955–85 (Frimpong-Ansah 1989) gives the loss of production of cocoa in Ghana from direct and indirect effects at the peak of distortion in 1976–79 as 40.4 per cent (short-term effect), 51.5 per cent (long-term effect) and 62.9 per cent (very long-term effect).

44 Killick (1978) gives a number of examples in which productivity in state enterprises was only a fraction of that of the already low peasant systems. See also Dadson (1971).

45 A classic example is Tanganyika Packers in Tanzania. In its best years in the early 1960s, it produced corned beef under the Libby brand name and supplied 15 per cent of the UK market. After nationalization, it progressively declined, lost its hygiene licence, and therefore its export market. It now produces small quantities for the Tanzanian military, and has become a major loss-making enterprise.

46 There are other views on this subject; see Finger and Holmes (1987).

47 Cable's contribution in Chapter 6 of this volume goes into some detail on this issue.

## References

Balassa, B. (1977), *Policy Reform in Developing Countries*, Oxford University Press, London.

Bates, R. H. (1983), *Essays on the Political Economy of Rural Africa*, Cambridge University Press, Cambridge.

Bauer, Lord P. T. (1971), *Dissent on Development*, Harvard University Press, Cambridge MA.

Bauer, Lord P. T. (1981), *Equality, the Third World and Economic Delusion*, Methuen, London.

Bauer, Lord P. T. (1984), *Reality and Rhetoric*, Weidenfeld & Nicolson, London.

Brennan, G. and Buchanan, J. M. (1980), *The Power to Tax: Analytical Foundations of a Fiscal Constitution*, Cambridge University Press, Cambridge.

Cardinall, A. W. (1931), *The Gold Coast 1931*, Government Printer, Accra.

Chazan, N. (1983), *Anatomy of Ghanaian Politics*, Westview Press, Boulder, Colo.

Cosnier, H. (1921), *L'Ouest Africain française: ses resources agricoles – son organisation economique*, Paris.

Coulson, A. (1982), *Tanzania, A Political Economy*, Clarendon, Oxford.

Crook, R. (1985), 'Decolonization in the colonial state and chieftaincy in the Gold Coast', *African Affairs*, 85.

Crowder, M. (1968), *West Africa under Colonial Rule*, Hutchinson, London.

Dadson, J. A. (1971), 'Socialised Agriculture in Ghana, 1960–1965', unpublished PhD thesis, Harvard University.

ECOWAS (1987), *The Creation of a single ECOWAS Monetary Zone*, Economic Community of West African States, Lagos.

Finger, J. M. and Holmes, P. (1987),'Unilateral liberalization and the MTN', in *Uruguay Round: A Handbook on Multilateral Trade Negotiations*, World Bank, Washington DC.

Frimpong-Ansah, J. H. (1989), The State and the Economy in Ghana, PhD thesis, University of Salford.

Grubel, H. G. (1973), 'The theory of regional associations', in H.G. Johnson and A.K. Swoboda (eds), *The Economics of Common Currencies*, Harvard University Press, Cambridge, MA.

Guggisberg, Sir G. (1924), *The Post War Gold Coast*, Government Printer, Accra.

Hancock, W. K. (1942), *Survey of British Commonwealth Affairs, Vol. II: Problems of Economic policy, 1918–1939*, Oxford University Press, London.

Hirschman A. O. (1958), *The Strategy of Economic Development*, Yale University Press, New Haven, Conn.

Ingham, B. (1987), 'Colonialism and the economy of the Gold Coast', in B. Ingham and C. Simmons, *Development Studies and Colonial Policy*, Frank Cass, London.

Khan, M. (1974), 'Import and export demand in developing countries', *IMF Staff Papers*, 21, No. 4, November.

Killick, T. (1978), *Development Economics in Action*, St Martins Press, New York.

Krueger, A. O., Schiff, M. and Valdes, A. (1987), *Measuring the Impact of Sector-Specific and Economy-Wide Policies on Agricultural Incentives in LDCs*, American Economic Association Annual meetings, Chicago.

Lal, Deepak (1984), 'The political economy of the predatory state', World Bank, Development Research Department Discussion Paper, Washington DC.

Lal, Deepak (1986), 'The political economy of industrialization in primary exporting countries: some cautionary tales', World Bank, Development Research Department Discussion Paper, Washington DC.

Lewis, W. A. (1944), *Some Aspects of the Flow of Capital into the Colonies*, Colonial Office, London.

Lewis, W. A. (1953), *Report on Industrialization and the Gold Coast*, Government Printer, Accra.

Lewis, W. A. (1954), *Economic Development with Unlimited Supplies of Labour*, Manchester School of Economics and Social Studies, May.

Libby, R. (1976), 'External cooptation of a less developed country's policy-making: The case of Ghana', *World Politics*, XXIX.

London, A. (1988), 'Import compression and external adjustment policy: Some evidence for selected African countries', ADB Discussion Paper, Abidjan.

McPhee, A. (1926), *The Economic Revolution in British West Africa*, Routledge, London.

Nelson, J. (1984), 'The political economy of stabilization: Commitment, capacity and public response', *World Development*, 12.

Nkrumah, K. (1957), *Autobiography*, Panaf, London. Republished as *The Autobiography of Kwame Nkrumah*, Thomas Nelson, Edinburgh and New York.

Nkrumah, K. (1963), *Africa Must Unite*, International Publishers, New York.

Prebisch, R. (1959), 'Commercial policy in the underdeveloped countries', *American Economic Review*, May.

Prebisch, R. (1963), *Towards a Dynamic Development Policy for Latin America*, UN, New York.

Rostow, W. W. (1960), *The Stages of Economic Growth*, Cambridge University Press, Cambridge.

Seers, D. (1983), *The Political Economy of Nationalism*, Oxford University Press, Oxford.

Svedberg, P. (1988), 'The export performance of sub-Saharan Africa, 1970–1985', Seminar paper No. 409, Institute for International Economic Studies, University of Stockholm.

Tannenbaum, R. and Schmidt, W. (1960), 'Management of differences', *Harvard Business Review*, November/December.

Uphoff, N. T. (1970), 'Ghana's Experience in Using External Aid for Development, 1957–1966', PhD thesis, University of California, Berkeley.

World Bank (1987), *World Development Report*, World Bank, Oxford University Press, New York.

4

# The politics of trade liberalization

Henry Bienen

## 1 Introduction

The World Bank and many of the bilateral donors to African countries have urged a wide range of policy reforms on African countries including correcting overvalued exchange rates, reforming the public sector and trade liberalization. Here, I want to explore the prospects that external trade liberalization reforms will be undertaken and sustained in Africa. Many African countries have undertaken stabilization policies, including devaluation of their currencies. Some have embarked on fundamental public sector reform programmes; few have liberalized their trade extensively. This suggests that the political constraints may be greater for changing trade policies than for devaluing currencies or for restricting credit.

However, while analyses have been undertaken which examine the politics of stabilization and the components of adjustment programmes such as lowering consumer subsidies, and some work is in process on privatization and public sector reform, relatively little has been done on the politics of trade liberalization in Africa.[1]

By trade liberalization I mean: the relaxation or elimination of tariffs and removal of duties and/or quotas on exports; alteration in non-tariff barriers such as import quotas and quantitative restrictions; changes in licensing and direct allocation of foreign exchange, and in specific regulations for products; removal or relaxation of export subsidies.[2]

Many African countries have used tariff and non-tariff barriers to further import substitution strategies. Kenya, for example, in the 1970s placed increasing reliance on import controls and quantitative restrictions to save foreign exchange and to encourage domestic manufacturing production. In the 1980s, Ghana and Nigeria were at the high end of the scale of countries in terms of the numbers of goods covered by quantitative restrictions (Balassa 1986). The Sudan has made extensive use of quotas and tariffs. Taxes on external trade have been around 50 per cent of total government revenues in the Sudan.[3] Many examples could be given both of African trade restriction practices and of backing and forthing on trade policy reform. Kenya, to name only one country, has gone through periods where it reduced quantitative restrictions, lowered and rationalized tariffs and applied minimum tariff rates to goods previously exempted or which had very low tariffs. The idea was to reduce effective protection levels by reducing the spread between highest and lowest tariffs. The Kenya government's halting steps towards trade liberalization in the 1980s were typical. African governments have backed off trade reforms when their competitive trade positions did not improve, when they were losing foreign exchange, and when they had not devalued sufficiently. The Kenyan government moved from restrictive licensing by the Ministry of Commerce to restrictive foreign exchange allocations introduced by the central bank. Other countries auctioned or partially auctioned foreign exchange. This occurred in Uganda and Zambia among others.

I will argue below that halting steps towards trade liberalization and procrastination on tariff reform and export promotion, which characterized the Kenyan government's response in its second Structural Adjustment Loan (SAL II) programme, come less from large mass political protests against reform policies, protests which have frequently faced governments that tried to cut consumer subsidies, than they do from opposition within the government itself. While there have been import substitution strategies in Africa and the protection of infant industries, African countries have had fewer industries to protect than Latin American ones, weaker unions (public or private), and smaller concentrations of private capital.

It is the political issue of how countries get to a more liberal trade regime that I want to explore. This involves asking what will be the effects of trade liberalization on specific polities. It involves asking: What is the distribution of rewards in the old system? What will be the distribution of rewards in a new, trade liberalized regime? It involves asking: what kinds of political systems will be able more easily to put in place policies of trade liberalization? Is Bhagwati (1986, pp. 92–3, 101) correct in thinking that pluralistic democracies may find it harder to dismantle an import substitution strategy because they find it harder to dismantle the controls and protection that accompany this strategy and which are to be used for contesting elections than authoritarian political systems that have to worry less about political patronage?[4] In Africa, there are few pluralistic democracies. But what are the social, economic and political facts of African life which are most relevant to considering the politics of stability and implementation of trade liberalization?

There are many differences among African countries with respect to size, rates of growth, share of GDP in trade, structure of trade, nature of political competition with respect to institutional grids, ethnic heterogeneity, and colonial inheritance. None the less, painting with a broad brush, I want to draw out some salient features of Africa's political economy that are relevant for assessing the prospects for trade liberalization.

## 2 African political economy maps of the world

When we try to assess the prospects for implementing and sustaining trade liberalization policies, we require a political map of gainers and losers from various policies. We need to know whether or not new constituencies can be created to support reform policies or can be strengthened after such policies are put in place. This requires not only being able to delineate groups in Africa but being able to assess the impact of policies on individual and group welfare. It also requires being able to model out the interactions of economic and political factors. For, the success or failure of policies in raising incomes can provide resources for governments to compensate groups that might lose, in the first instance, from a policy shift. Before we can evaluate the prospects for successful policy alterations, we need to know whether governments can, during and after policy shifts, repress opposition or instability that might arise and what are the magnitudes of resources that may have to be devoted to repression.

I shall argue below that trade liberalization policies are often extremely hard to formulate and implement in Africa precisely because it is powerful officials (civilian and military) who benefit from the controls that have been established over imports and exports. It is government officials who ration and distribute scarce imports, including foreign exchange. They realize the rents which accrue from the systems they construct and control. Of course, officials have allies – import-substituting manufacturers and urban workers employed by state enterprises who are also interested in subsidized urban consumer goods.

Who are the proponents of trade liberalization in Africa? Rural producers who want to export freely have a stake in trade liberalization, but they are usually not well organized and have relatively little voice in government. Exporters of consumer goods and light industrial goods exist, but they too are not powerful actors.

There are elements in the bureaucracy who are usually committed to trade liberalization because they are trained to believe in less government regulation, to believe that corruption follows from illiberal trade regimes, or to believe that growth can take place only when trade is liberalized, or all of the above.

Moreover, bureaucrats have in the past often draped themselves in the garb of economic nationalism to justify protectionist policies. The justifications have been the need to protect infant industries, to defend national resource exploitation against foreigners, to increase the role of the state in trade in the name of national defence. Today, however, after precipitous declines in per capita income in many African countries, elements of the bureaucracy in many African countries are claiming that national survival requires a shift to more liberal trade policies in order to increase foreign exchange by raising exports and in order to rationalize domestic production.

Furthermore, as noted, Africa does not have large, well-organized private manufacturers to support import-substitution policies. And the trade unionized sector is also relatively weak, compared with Latin America. Thus, risks of generalized instability may not be too great if African leaders committed to trade policy reform can get past their own militaries and civilian bureaucrats.

Important issues in all structural adjustment and stabilization reforms are those of timing and sequencing. Should reforms be undertaken all at once or incrementally; should they be sweeping or modest? There are economic and political arguments on both sides of these questions and the answers depend in part on how well markets operate, how good is information, what resources can be gathered from external sources to smooth transitions to new policies, how unified are government elites in the formulation and implementation of the policies. Trade liberalization policies lend themselves to incremental change, in that tariffs or quotas can be removed product by product and also altered by degree. This does not mean that it necessarily will be a good idea to move incrementally but that the policy tools are there to do so. Whether coalitions can be built up to support liberalization measure by measure or can be brought about by more sweeping moves, and whether opponents of trade liberalization can be disarmed or will have time to organize if policies are gradual, are critical issues.

Before we can proceed with these issues and before we can discuss specific African cases, it is necessary to provide a fuller analytical statement for assessing opponents and proponents of trade policy reform in Africa.

Groups in Africa can be categorized in many ways, depending on the level of generality of the analysis and its purposes. We can think of rural and urban producers and consumers. For some purposes, this very rough division makes sense in Africa. For example, urban consumers rather than rural consumers usually benefit from subsidized foodstuffs. Most rural dwellers in Africa have access to the food production of relatives even when they do not work on a farm themselves. Some urban dwellers receive food packages from rural areas, but most now consume in urban markets.

Of course, not all Africans who live in rural areas produce food or other commodities that are traded. Many do, but we need to know the specifics in each country to learn how many people living in rural areas are producing goods for export, for trade on domestic markets, and for their own subsistence. Most imports to Africa are probably consumed in urban areas, but, once again, we would need to know how many people are using imported inputs for agricultural production, such as fertilizer, fuel and machinery. Also, rural dwellers do consume some imported clothing, food, and other consumption goods.

On balance, African exports originate in rural areas, not urban ones.[5] Manufacturing exports are a small share of total African exports. Aside from agricultural commodities, only the mining and minerals sectors account for significant exports. The only countries for which these sectors are significant are those producing oil and gas (Algeria, Gabon, Nigeria, Angola), copper (Zaire, Zambia), and manganese and other ores (Mauritania, Liberia, Zimbabwe, Senegal, Togo, Guinea, Ghana).

The minerals sector does have politically significant unionized labour in Zambia but even the minerals sector has not produced powerful trade unions in most African countries. And even where a country's share of exports is overwhelmingly in minerals exports, the number of workers in the industry may be very small. This is the case for the petroleum sector in Nigeria. Thus, the non-agricultural export sector has not given rise to powerful workers' groups in most African countries.

A sectoral breakdown that must be made if we are to assess the prospects for trade liberalization is within sectors that are roughly defined as rural or urban. The largest number of Africans who might benefit from policies that do not discriminate against exports are farmers who produce traditional exports and who usually are not well organized and are dispersed across wide areas (Bates 1976, 1981; Bates and Rogerson 1980).

It is striking that African agricultural exporters generally have not been well organized into powerful political groups. In general, African agricultural producers have not been well organized politically. In part, this is because most agricultural producers are not highly specialized by crop and thus both are difficult to organize and do not form coalitions with other non-specialized producers.[6] Modern specialization of agricultural production would be likely to make political organization easier – better means of communication between producers, surplus resources to finance specialists in lobbying and information, etc. Having large numbers of undifferentiated producers makes free-rider problems intense; size increases the cost of co-ordination and the individual producers see higher costs and fewer benefits from organizing (Bates and Rogerson 1980). This argument does not apply, however, to many exporters of cocoa or palm products, who are relatively specialized. Why have these producers been so hard to organize politically in Africa?

The political weakness of agricultural exporters has been striking from the colonial period onwards, compared with the political strength in Africa of traders, administrators, politicians, military personnel and urban workers. Small producers have been forced to export through state-organized commodity boards, which have skimmed profits by paying lower than world market prices or have short-changed farmers through many other practices. The response to the state's pricing and other monopoly practices has been in the first instance to smuggle where possible. Smuggling has been significant in Uganda, Ghana and many other countries.

On occasion, would-be exporters have resorted to force. This was the case during 1968–69 in Western Nigeria when farmers in the Agbekoya movement (literally, farmers who reject suffering) attacked government offices and policy as they protested against low prices, taxes and poor service delivery. But, while order broke down in a number of Yoruba-speaking and cocoa-producing areas of Western Nigeria, farmers were not well organized and their leaders were soon co-opted by the Western State of Nigeria government.[7] A more common farmer response has been to move out of export production and sometimes to withdraw from markets and even physically to move away from export-producing areas if government taxes become too onerous or if public order breaks down and personal safety becomes questionable (see Hyden 1980).

One reason why African exporters have typically been hard to organize politically is that coffee, tea, cocoa and cotton producers have been small farmers. Although a World Bank Report once referred to Nigerian cocoa producers as 'cocoa barons', they too have been smallholders.[8] While some large cocoa and coffee plantations have been in African hands in the Côte d'Ivoire, most large exporters in Africa have been European farmers living in Africa, sometimes as citizens in Kenya or Zimbabwe. Where large farmers have been prevalent, especially before independence in Kenya and Zimbabwe, they have formed effective lobby groups. Indeed, Kenya, Zimbabwe and Côte d'Ivoire have maintained a responsiveness to farming interests in part because their ruling political organizations retain rural ties and roots. But most African countries do not have well-organized rural exporters, nor do they have well-maintained political structures in rural areas.

Another reason for the difficulty of organizing exporters is that associational ties (communal, religious, language) have all cut across rural–urban and class affiliations in Africa.

While some commentators such as Frantz Fanon have argued that the real class division in Africa is between rural and urban areas and others have argued that class differentiation is proceeding within rural areas, what has been striking to perhaps most observers of rural Africa is not collective action of countryside against town or class division in the countryside, but complicated internal divisions in rural areas that cannot be subsumed by class analysis.

In many countries, communal solidarities have not been breached and rural communities have not broken down on class lines. Political cleavages in rural Africa still do not seem to be drawn between those with a few acres more or less or those with a hundred dollars income more or less or even between 'medium' and 'small' farmers. The major basis of differentiation in the rural areas may be not between progressive farmers and less-well-off farmers but between those who have wage employment from government in the rural sector, or who otherwise have strong urban links, and those who do not.[9] It is interesting that, in both Kenya and Senegal, rural elites increasingly tie themselves to urban businesses and trade. Still, rural–urban ties are also mediated by ethnic affiliations. For example, Mouride Brotherhood urban businessmen in Senegal are tied to their ethnic affines who control groundnut production in rural areas.

It is true that in specific cases an export crop may be grown largely by a particular ethnic language group. Thus cocoa producers in Ghana are frequently Ashantis; coffee producers in Kenya often are Kikuyu; cocoa producers in Nigeria are Yoruba. Where an ethnic community and a particular cash crop for export overlap, organization of producers is easier. But if the government is controlled by a different ethnic community, and government then taxes the cash crop, as occurred in Ghana under Nkrumah, ethnic conflict is intensified.

As African governments ponder whether they can alter their policies and perhaps move towards a more liberalized trade policy, they must consider a number of things in addition to the political stength of various producers and consumers. They have to consider how mobile are factors of production. They must also assess their own strengths and weaknesses and the likelihood of political instability arising not only from economic policies but from ethnic tensions and institutional factors in their countries.

African political leaders, whether civilian or military, worry first about political instability in urban areas. Leaders themselves reside in urban areas, so they feel pressures from urban groups more than rural ones. Moreover, their immediate constituencies are often inside the very bureaucracies of the state over which they preside.

Trade liberalization policies in Africa frequently confront governments with hard decisions because opposition to them resides within the government's civil and military bureaucracies more than within embedded and powerful constituencies 'out there' in society. Africa's domestic private manufacturers are fewer and less powerful than Latin America's. The most politically powerful pressures for import-substitution policies and or overvalued exchange rates have come from civil servants, politicians and military men. Their demands are often couched in the name of nationalism and the need to be modern and industrial. These may be sincerely held beliefs or they may be cloaks for the interests of government officials who benefit from corrupt practices or from policies that provide them with cheap imports.

Since African countries have less well developed private manufacturing sectors than most Latin American or Asian countries, private sector non-agricultural workers make up a smaller percentage of the labour force in Africa than in Latin America or Asia. Public sector workers in the early 1980s were 54 per cent of all non-agricultural employees in Africa compared with 36 per cent in Asia and 27 per cent in Latin America (Heller and Tait 1983). Of course, this aggregate figure for Africa disguises important differences between countries such as Kenya, Nigeria and the Côte d'Ivoire, which have private manufacturers who can benefit from a protected domestic market, and countries such as Angola, Mozambique and Tanzania, where a private domestic manufacturing sector exists hardly at all.

In the main, however, a policy that moves away from tariff protection of domestic industries will not face strong *private* sector capitalists or workers in Africa. Similarly, a policy of moving away from administrative rationing of foreign exchange, which has the same effects as a tariff that expands domestic production of the imported good (usually capital intensive) and decreases production of the exported good (correspondingly labour intensive), will not face strong *private* sector opposition. Such policy shifts face strong *public* opposition in Africa.

## 3 The impact of trade liberalization policies

Trade liberalization policies have the effect of changing relative prices of final goods, intermediate inputs and factors of production. Thus these policies alter the relative welfare of different social groups. These social groups can be defined in terms of clusters of owners of different factors of production, for example, land, labour and capital. They can be defined in terms of different sectors, say agriculture versus industry or import versus export.

Trade liberalization policies may also alter the power, status and income of institutionally based groups as well as occupational ones. Militaries tend to be importers of equipment and luxury goods. Militaries in Africa also frequently are recruited disproportionately from particular ethnic communities. Thus a trade liberalization policy may be, in the short run, costly to an armed force which has benefited from a cheap import policy, and this means costs will be incurred by a particular ethnic community. The same argument can be made for the civil service when and if it is disproportionately recruited from a region or an ethnic community and it loses control over licences and quantitative controls in a trade liberalization policy.

A large body of economic theory permits systematic analysis of the effects of trade liberalization policies on the incomes of different sectors and owners of factors of production. These factors of production in Africa can, in turn, be correlated with institutional, ethnic, regional and rural–urban factors. One crucial concept in understanding the relationship between the impact of trade liberalization programmes (or, more generally, International Monetary Fund stabilization programmes or World Bank structural adjustment programmes) on economic sectors and their impact on individuals who own different factors of production employed in those sectors is intersectoral factor mobility. It denotes the ability of different factors of production to switch among sectors of the economy, for instance between export and import sectors. Only if one knows whether factors of production can move easily between sectors can one tell if it is analytically preferable to group individuals by the sectors in which they produce or by the factors of production they own. For example, is it better to think about capitalists regardless of where their capital is employed, or about individuals whose incomes depend on the export sector regardless of whether they are workers or capitalists?

Factors of production are said to be completely mobile if they always earn the same return regardless of the sector in which they are employed. Some factors may be almost perfectly mobile in this sense, others may not be. Over time, factors can be reallocated among sectors at costs lower than when shifts are rapid.[10] Using the concepts of relative price changes, intersectoral factor mobility and ownership of factors of production, we can divide a society into gainers and losers from various policies.[11] But, as I have noted, gainers and losers must be understood in institutional and ethnic terms as well as in economic ones.

Further complications arise when we not only try to assess the impact of economic reform policies on various groups but also try to understand the political consequences of these policies. All economic policies are undertaken in an environment of uncertainty. This is especially true in Africa, where weather is so important to production for export and for domestic consumption. Unforeseeable variations in the international terms of trade can be critical. Important uncertainties in Africa arise from lack of knowledge about the functioning of economies because data are poor. Furthermore, the very success or failure of economic policies affects political stability down the line. Uncertainties concerning success, together with other uncertainties, lead politicians usually to want to proceed slowly in implementing new policies, although this tactic may entail economic costs and also may allow groups to adjust so as to circumvent the new policies.

In addition to uncertainties of information, neither social scientists nor political leaders have strong theories which allow them to predict with confidence how economic decisions affect political alignments. We know that, once political stances are taken in favour of or against economic policies, these stances become new facts that affect economic outcomes. For example, massive opposition to cuts in consumer subsidies may lead to strikes, violence in the cities, increasing costs of repression and alternative use of government resources, which lowers production. But which policies will trigger the most opposition in specific African countries? Can we generalize about the conditions for support for or opposition to policies, the magnitude of opposition, the forms it takes? For not only are we interested in the impact of trade liberalization policies on groups, but we also want to assess the impact of policy reform on the stability of individual countries, regimes and governments.

It is tempting to predict that stabilization policies that impose austerity on a wide range of actors (such as devaluation, credit contraction and cutting government budgets) will have more profound impacts on stability in the short run than more targeted and specific policies associated with trade liberalization. This is because stabilization policies are thought to affect the widest group of actors. Indeed, politicians often are leery of large devaluations because they believe that costs are generalized and benefits may come only at a later time. But devaluations can make exporters better off immediately. Similarly, cuts in consumer subsidies, *if* translated into high producer prices, can also improve the lot of producers right away. Cutting government budgets, through abolishing unproductive enterprises or unproductive civil service units, may take time to be translated into more efficient use of funds. It might be thought that trade liberalization policies can rather quickly bring about more efficient use of resources and thus will find supporters among those who benefit from the more liberalized regime. The problem is that opponents of liberalization may be especially well placed to resist liberalizing measures and to force backsliding from them because they are in strategic places inside African governments.

Governments cannot estimate precisely the political impact of economic policies. Elites frequently hedge their bets since they know that the consequences of their actions may be great but cannot estimate the effects of particular policies. We have seen this as governments cut subsidies, face opposition, cancel the subsidy cuts, and then reimpose the subsidy cuts later. This has occurred in many countries (including Sudan, Egypt, Liberia, Morocco) at various times. Or governments cut subsidies but announce wage increases. In the trade area, they may move from direct controls to a phased controlling of foreign exchange, as Kenya did.

Politicians who depend on electoral support try to hold on to as many constituencies as possible; they aim for tactical implementations. Holding fair elections can be an important contribution to legitimacy. Moreover, elections can help diminish urban bias since most voters live in rural areas in Africa. Zimbabwe has used elections to mobilize rural constituencies in favour of reform policies. In some African countries, even though elections have not determined the formation of governments in open competitive settings, an elite may have close ties to rural constituencies which allow it to seek support for policies that benefit agriculture or even to be pressured by these constituencies. This has occurred in Kenya and in the Côte d'Ivoire.

The prospects for implementing trade liberalization policies and the attendant stability impacts of these policies will depend on the kinds of coalitions that form in different countries within the state and between state and non-state actors. Again, we return to the concept of factor mobility to help form a typology of gainers and losers.

Ending the rationing of foreign exchange by a devaluation will raise the price of agricultural exports relative to industrial products. This will benefit the producers of such exports. In Ghana and Nigeria these will be small and medium-sized farmers who produce cocoa for traditional exports. In Kenya this would be coffee and tea producers who are both smallholders and sometimes larger African and non-African farmers. In Uganda it would be coffee and cotton producers, again mostly middle-sized farmers (by African standards) and smallholders. In Malawi, it would mean favouring agricultural estates, but this is rather rare in Africa since most traditional exports are not produced by estates but by peasant households. In the Côte d'Ivoire, large planters are important producers.

Economists would expect labour to be helped by a devaluation that replaces administrative controls, raises the relative price of labour-intensive light manufacturers and expands this sector at the expense of capital-intensive heavy industry, which is import-competing in countries such as Brazil or Korea. In Africa, however, few countries have significant heavy industry. Still, labour should benefit compared with capital, and the labour-intensive export sector could increase the demand for labour. But light industries might suffer overall if protection is withdrawn in Africa. In any case, African private sector trade unions are relatively weak, and African leaders have to worry less about erosion of support from private sector workers than do leaders in Latin America. But trade unions, when acting together with urban elites, are not negligible. In Senegal, this alliance delayed for more than a year an increase in the price of imported rice and domestic food grains.

One question is how high or low is intersectoral factor mobility in Africa? Land is used mostly in agriculture and capital in large industry. But workers may be able to switch between industry and agriculture, especially where skills in industry are modest. Nigerian rural to urban migration was very high during the oil boom years and has slowed appreciably. Some workers have returned to the land.

What about producers of domestic foodstuffs in Africa? It is often hard to net out the effects of the different policy instruments that have been used in Africa and which affect food producers. Prices for inputs, prices for final products, controls on imports and overvalued exchange rates have tended to have contradictory effects (see Bienen 1986). Often data are so poor that it is hard to calculate the terms of trade between rural and urban sectors. Many African countries did develop a cheap food policy, and subsidized urban food consumption through low prices to domestic producers, often supplemented by significant imports of grains through aid programmes. Domestic farmers were hurt by this policy and urban consumers were helped.

One of the most complex and striking cases is that of Nigeria. Nigeria increased its food imports significantly during the oil boom years. This helped to keep farmgate prices of rice and other foods down, but the Nigerians, who at least in the buoyant oil price years (1973–81) perhaps could have afforded it, did not develop a 'cheap food' policy. While imports did compensate, to some extent, for falling per capita food production, the system of import licences that controlled food imports gave high profits to distributors and kept food imports lower than unregulated markets would have produced. Probably, relative prices for agriculture did not change much between 1973 and 1979. But in some years rice prices fluctuated violently, creating uncertainty for both producers and consumers.

In this situation, trade margins are very important. Individuals with access to licences for food imports and individuals who have information about policies that impose or remove direct controls stand to make large windfall gains. This happened frequently with respect to rice imports. Indeed, accusations of corruption associated with the rice trade in Nigeria, Liberia and other African countries turned out to be a destabilizing issue for rulers in those countries. Before the Nigerian 1979 elections, imports were increased and this may have provided short-run political gains, but by using import policy in this manner the legitimacy of government was called into question.

The post-1983 Nigerian military governments were less beholden to licensed buying agents and to the political networks in which party politics were enmeshed. But, in the past, military and civil servants have created their own political networks and have enjoyed the benefits that go with control of economic resources. After all, it was not the Shagari civilian regime but preceding military governments which instituted a system for licensing rice imports and which promulgated unpredictable and rapidly shifting policies with respect to the amounts of food, especially rice and wheat, that could enter duty free under government account.

Much effort has gone into trying to explain Nigeria's policy on food imports. Some would argue that Nigeria simply imported when it had foreign exchange available, since it desired to keep urban consumers happy. It especially was concerned to bring in cheap rice when elections were about to take place in 1983 or earlier when the Shagari government assumed control, or even earlier still when General Obsanjo replaced the assassinated General Murtala Mohammed. Others have a less benign view and argue that government officials systematically lowered and raised import quotas in order to make windfall profits. However, while there was undoubtedly large-scale corruption in the selling of licences, it is doubtful that government officials could systematically manipulate the import system well enough to make profits through price changes, although they could make profits by selling licences and rewarding followers. It is more reasonable to suggest that clever people could manipulate a system and take rents once that system was put in place.

We can generalize from the Nigerian case and argue that the whole panoply of import controls has increased corruption in Africa. Those who have benefited most have been public sector officials with the power to control licences, quotas and access to foreign exchange and who have knowledge about future policy. Also benefiting have been business associates of public officials who have been awarded scarce goods. The scarce imported goods have not reached sectors that could use them most efficiently. Controls on external trade have, of course, been supplemented by internal trade networks controlled by marketing boards and state corporations. Again, those who received wages from the state and parastatal corporations and who received compensatory payments from their operations benefited enormously from the system.

Kenya is another country that has used import licensing, which was already important by the early 1970s. In Kenya, where industry was more advanced than in most African countries, producers did lobby for protection. Since Kenya's membership in the East African Community ruled out unilateral changes in tariffs, the government used import bans, quotas and 'no objection' certificates (Bevan *et al.* 1987, pp. 6–7). It has been pointed out that rules governing Kenya's quantitative restrictions were vague: 'the detailed allocation of imports was left to the discretion of officials and corruption was inevitable' (p. 7).

Import bans were supposedly abolished by the Financial Act of 1980, but they continued to be used. The Ministry of Commerce in Kenya was the target of lobbying and wanted to retain item-specific quotas. Some shift from quantitative restrictions to tariffs went on, but uniform and lower tariffs were politically hard to implement (Bevan *et al.* 1987, p. 37).

Removal of trade restrictions and import controls helps to end artificial scarcities and decreases the benefits that accrue to the middlemen involved in smuggling and other illegal actions by which profits are made. But export subsidies can lead to serious administrative problems too. In Senegal they have led, reportedly, to substantial amounts of fish caught by foreign-flag fishermen being brought to port and re-exported in order to receive a subsidy. Export subsidies can also lead to over-invoicing.[12]

## 4 Conclusions

I raised the question as to whether Bhagwati was correct in thinking that pluralist democracies find it harder to dismantle the system of controls that have been developed because they need patronage networks to contest elections. Most African regimes are not pluralist democracies. But they have found it hard to dismantle systems of control precisely because the authoritarian military and civil service coalitions that have ruled African countries are dependent on the compliance of their own institutional bases. It is opposition within the armed forces, civil services and state and parastatal enterprises involved in trade and marketing that has made ending regulated trade so difficult. It is also the same public sector officials who are urban based and work for a wage who want to maintain the system of cheap foodstuffs and consumer goods and who favour building up large-scale industry through import substitution in the name of modernization and national security.

African leaders believe that policies which increase food costs to growing urban populations are politically dangerous. Leaders do not believe that they can base their power on peasants, who are hard to mobilize. Kenya and Zimbabwe have been exceptions where political networks have mobilized small farmers in support of policies which do not discriminate against agriculture.

The fears of African leaders, while not baseless, are overblown. Urban food prices in African countries have in fact risen in recent years without endemic instability occurring (see Bienen and Gersovitz 1986). Prices are being raised in order to increase agricultural production. While increased prices may be a shock in the short run, political stability over the medium and long run should improve as food supplies increase. African leaders hope to bridge the short run with food aid and the gradual implementation of IMF programmes that end subsidies and increase food prices. Together with devaluation, such programmes will allow them to shift priorities toward rural areas without provoking large-scale instability in urban areas.

Nigeria provides an interesting case. An elected government in Nigeria between 1979 and 1983 did not dismantle the system of trade controls that it inherited from military regimes. The second post-1984 military government of Major-General Ibrahim Babangida has implemented an 'austerity policy without the IMF'. The policy package of the Babangida government includes some measures which are trade liberalizing in their thrust but others which are not. Prices of imported goods rose precipitously when Nigeria imposed a major devaluation in the autumn of 1986. The government created a second-tier foreign exchange market. The new foreign exchange system hit middle-class people, including army officers and civil servants. Some of them were hit again by the abolition of the import-licensing system which allowed for corrupt fortunes to be made by government officials and importers. The government also closed various commodity boards. While officials who manned these systems were recruited from all parts of Nigeria, probably those hurt worst in regional-ethnic terms were Moslem northerners who had benefited the most through government control of trade because they had greatest political access to the system. While northerners still dominate the armed forces, the Babangida regime is less northern and Moslem than its predecessor, the Buhari military regime.

Nigeria still does not have a free trade regime. Licences are now issued to successful bidders at weekly foreign exchange auctions. The system is certainly more open. However, a number of goods are banned completely. These include wheat (which accounts for less than 10 per cent of Nigeria's food requirements), live poultry, eggs, rice, vegetables, vegetable oils, furniture. Banning these goods, of course, helps domestic producers of them and their substitutes. Since it has been impossible to seal Nigeria's ports and borders from smuggling in the past, presumably imports will still get in and fetch premiums. Smugglers will benefit; manufacturers and their workers who rely on industrial imports will be hurt.

General Babangida has been able to harness feelings of Nigerian nationalism for his programme. The fact that he received a loan from the World Bank for the country's efforts to liberalize trade but decided not to draw on any IMF credits helped him mobilize support for an austerity programme. Of course, there are financial costs to forgoing IMF loans.

The Nigerians have been implementing a policy reform package incrementally, whereas the economics of the situation may have called for rapid adjustments. But Babangida has been able to develop support through debate, commissions and differentiated policies. African leaders who have tried to impose policies without debate and explanation have got into trouble.[13] It is also important that the policy-making and policy-implementing elites be cohesive as they embark on trade reform (or other adjustment measures). Within Tanzania and Zambia, policy elites were split in the 1970s and 1980s; this hindered implementation of reforms.

As African economic problems have deepened, there may be greater consensus over what needs to be done than in the early 1980s or the 1970s. Indeed, as Lal and others have suggested, increasing government intervention in economies may be perceived finally as diminishing areas of government control (Lal 1987, p. 281). This point has special force in Africa where governments have a weak administrative and political base and where the tools to control economies have also been weak. None the less, leaders have extended governments' scope widely, if ineffectively. They have acted in an unrestrained way, but this has not meant that they have controlled political and economic life.

A motive for liberalization may be to try to assure long-run stability by improving resource bases and also by restricting the sphere of government activity, in order to assert more meaningful control over a narrower band of activities (Lal 1987, p. 281). If the formal economies collapse, as occurred in Ghana and Uganda in the 1970s, urban workers and civil servants sometimes return to rural areas since they cannot sustain themselves in the cities. Rationing of foreign exchange and maintaining trade controls require a large bureaucracy and thus promote government employment. But trade repression may help bring on economic collapse. Furthermore, systems that increase corruption at some point – albeit at a point hard to specify – increase the risk of instability.[14] Political unrest and instability under these conditions are likely to be at least as great or greater than instability arising from implementation of adjustment policies in general and trade liberalization policies in particular.

There is a broad consensus by now that policies implemented by African governments accounted for a major share of the fall in imports that could be purchased out of export earnings. Weather and terms of trade effects were significant, but the failure to generate sufficient export revenues through increased volumes was crucial.[15] This argues for trade liberalization policies being stability enhancing in the medium to long run. In the short run, the policy risks are no worse than those associated with business as usual and probably they are better.

Of course, the timing, sequence and speed of implementation of new policies are relevant to the ways that gainers and losers organize to support or oppose policies.[16] It has been argued that undertaking structural adjustment programmes is easier during periods of favourable external shocks when rising public expenditure can be used to compensate politically powerful groups (Bevan *et al.* 1987, p. 43). The experiences of African countries, however, suggest that during a rise in world prices or when weather conditions are favourable is not when adjustment programmes are undertaken. On the contrary, new commitments are made when revenues increase. It is under the conditions of adversity, not of windfall gains, and under the pressures of external actors, that adjustment programmes are likely to be implemented. Implementations, including trade liberalization ones, are likely to be piecemeal and not fully realized as governments backslide under various pressures. But these piecemeal implementations often fail economically (Bevan *et al.* 1987, p. 53). Thus it may be that things have to get very bad indeed before politics induces sustained trade liberalization.

## Notes

I am most appreciative of comments from Ravi Kanbur, Warwick University; and to my Princeton colleagues Mark Gersovitz, Gene Grossman, Atul Kohli, John P. Lewis, Robert Tignor, John Waterbury, and Michael Doyle.

1 The impacts of IMF conditionality policies have been assessed by Bienen and Gersovitz (1985). Also see Nelson (1984a, b); Cline and Weintraub (1981); Williamson (1983). Among the general discussions of structural adjustment in Africa see: Zulu and Nsouli (1985); World Bank (1986); Hardy (1986). With Mark Gersovitz, I have

analysed the impacts of consumer subsidy cuts in Africa and elsewhere in Bienen and Gersovitz (1986). Also see Herbst (1988).

2 I am aware that some would argue that devaluation should at least sometimes be considered part of a liberalization programme independent of the decision on stabilization. See Branson (1984), p. 38.

3 Grossman (1986), citing IMF paper, 'Sudan: Recent Economic Developments', unpublished, 1983.

4 Also see Bhagwati and Krueger (1973).

5 Among other sources, see Svedberg in Chapter 2 of this volume.

6 Bates and Rogerson (1980) provide a formal analysis.

7 The most extensive analysis of the Agbekoya riots and earlier peasant revolts in Yoruba areas can be found in Beer (1976). An account can also be found in Williams and Beer (1976). Bates (1976, pp. 256–60) argues that in Zambia, too, villagers have advanced their interest through political turmoil, using tactics that impose costs on government.

8 This phrase is cited by Rimmer (1981, p. 39).

9 For Kenya, see Bienen (1974, pp. 181–2). As non-farm employees buy land, these divisions do get transformed into rural class ones. For a discussion of class and communal relations in Nigeria, see Bienen (1981).

10 Among the idealized situations with respect to factor mobility that economists often consider are: (1) an economy with the same two factors of production, both of which are perfectly mobile between both sectors; (2) an economy with final goods, each produced using two factors of production, one of which is specific to a particular sector and one of which is common to both sectors and perfectly mobile between them; (3) an economy with two final goods, each of which is produced using two factors of production, all four factors being specific to their particular sectors and hence immobile. See also, Lal (1986).

11 Bienen and Gersovitz (1985, p. 738). Deepak Lal models out gainers and losers in economic liberalization policies – not just trade liberalization ones – in Lal (1987).

12 Bevan, *et al.* (1987, pp. 19–20) make an interesting argument about the damaging effects of over-invoicing, which have consequences similar to a deterioration in the barter terms of trade. They distinguish between the effects of over-invoicing by public and private enterprises in a system of rationed foreign exchange. 'Both types of enterprise are encouraged to inflate costs, but there is a special incentive to inflate the import component in the private case, and the domestic component in the public case' (p. 20).

13 This can be seen clearly as policies are implemented to cut subsidies. When Zimbabwe cut subsidies in 1983 its leaders went to great lengths

to explain policies. General Nimeiri in the Sudan cut subsidies in 1985 and two days later left for a trip abroad, without preparing the ground for new policy measures.

14 High-level corruption poses risks for individual leaders. Witness the first Rawlings coup and subsequent executions of military officers in Ghana, the first Nigerian coup and assassinations in 1966, and subsequent coups in Nigeria, the Doe coup and executions in Liberia. Wholesale purges of civil servants by General Murtala Mohammed occurred in Nigeria in 1975.

15 A partial dissent is Wheeler (1984). Wheeler's econometric analysis puts more weight on environmental factors than on policy ones.

16 Lal (1987, p. 288), citing Latin American experiences, has a preferred sequencing of: first, reduction of the fiscal deficit, accompanied by a removal of domestic capital market distortions; second, limitation of exchange controls and free floating of the exchange rate, accompanied by an announcement of a phased programme for removing commodity market distortions; and third, implementation of this preannounced phased programme.

## References

Balassa, Bela (1986), 'The importance of trade for developing countries', mimeo, for the Conference on the Role and Interests of the Developing Countries in the Multilateral Trade Negotiations, Thai Development Research Institution and IBRD.

Bates, Robert (1976), *Rural Responses to Industrialization: A Study of Village Zambia*, Yale University Press, New Haven, Conn.

Bates, Robert (1981), *Markets and States in Tropical Africa: The Political Basis of Agricultural Choice*, University of California Press, Berkeley, Calif.

Bates, Robert and Rogerson, William (1980), 'Agriculture in development: A coalitional analysis', *Public Choice*, 35, pp. 513–26.

Beer, Christopher (1976), *The Politics of Peasant Groups in Western Algeria*, University of Ibadan Press, Ibadan.

Bevan, David, Bigsten, Arne, Collier, Paul and Gunning, Jan Willem (1987), *East African Lessons on Economic Liberalization*, Gower, London.

Bhagwati, Jagdish N. (1986), 'Rethinking trade strategy', in John P. Lewis and Valeriana Kalla (eds), *Development Strategies Reconsidered*, Transaction Books, New Brunswick.

Bhagwati, Jagdish N. and Krueger, Anne (1973), 'Exchange controls, liberalization and economic development', *American Economic Review*, 63, pp. 419–27.

Bienen, Henry (1974), *Kenya: The Politics of Participation and Control*, Princeton University Press, Princeton, NJ.

Bienen, Henry (1981), 'The politics of distribution: Institutions, class and ethnicity', in Henry Bienen and Vremudia Diejomaoh, *The Political Economy of Income Distribution in Nigeria*, Holmes & Meier, New York.

Bienen, Henry (1986), *Politics and Agricultural Policy in Nigeria*, World Bank Paper.

Bienen, Henry and Gersovitz, Mark (1985), 'Economic stabilization, conditionality and political stability', *International Organization*, 39, pp. 739–54.

Bienen, Henry and Gersovitz, Mark (1986), 'Consumer subsidy cuts, violence and political stability', *Comparative Politics*, 19, pp. 25–44.

Branson, William (1984), 'Stabilization programs, stagflation and investment: The case of Kenya', National Bureau of Economic Research/The World Bank, Conference on Structural Adjustment and the Real Exchange Rate, Washington DC, 29 November–1 December.

Cline, William R. and Weintraub, Sidney (eds) (1981), *Economic Stabilization in Developing Countries*, The Brookings Institution, Washington DC.

Grossman, Gene (1986), 'An evaluation of trade policy in the Sudan', paper prepared for USAID/Princeton University project in the Sudan, Princeton, January.

Hardy, Chandra A. (1986), 'Africa's debt: Structural adjustment with stability', in Robert Berg and Jennifer Seymour Whitaker (eds), *Strategies for African Development*, University of California Press, Berkeley, Calif.

Heller, Peter and Tait, Alan (1983), 'Government employment and pay: Some international comparisons', *Finance and Development*, 20, pp. 44–7.

Herbst, Jeffrey (1988), 'Societal demands and government choices: Agricultural producer price policy in Zimbabwe', *Comparative Politics*, April, pp. 265–8.

Hyden, Goran (1980), *Beyond Ujamma in Tanzania: Underdevelopment and an Uncaptured Peasantry*, University of California Press, Berkeley, Calif.

Lal, Deepak (1986), 'A single framework for analyzing various real aspects of stabilization and structural adjustment policies', World Bank Economics and Research Staff Research Center Paper.

Lal, Deepak (1987), 'The political economy of economic liberalization', *The World Bank Review*, 1, pp. 273–99.

Nelson, Joan (1984a), 'The political economy of stabilization: Commitment, capacity and public response', *World Development*, 12, pp. 983–1006.

Nelson, Joan (1984b), 'The politics of stabilization', in Richard E. Feinberg and Valeriana Kallab (eds), *Adjustment Crisis in the Third World*, Transaction Books, New Brunswick, pp. 99–118.

Rimmer, Douglas (1981), 'Development in Nigeria: An overview', in

Henry Bienen and V. P. Diejomaoh, *The Political Economy of Income Distribution in Nigeria*, Holmes & Meier, New York.

Wheeler, David (1984), 'Sources of stagnation in sub-Saharan Africa', *World Development*, 12, pp. 1–24.

Williams, Gavin and Beer, Christopher (1976), 'The politics of the Ibadan peasantry', in Gavin Williams (ed.), *Nigeria: Economy and Society*, Rex Collings, London, pp. 135–58.

Williamson, John (ed.) (1983), *IMF Conditionality*, Institute for International Economics, Washington DC.

World Bank (1986), *Financing Adjustment with Growth in Sub-Saharan Africa, 1986–90*, Washington DC.

Zulu, Justin B. and Nsouli, Saheh M. (1985), *Adjustment Programs in Africa*, Occasional Paper No. 34, International Monetary Fund, Washington DC, April.

5

# Protection facing exports from sub-Saharan Africa in the EC, Japan and the US

Refik Erzan and Peter Svedberg

## 1 Introduction

The real export earnings of a great majority of sub-Saharan African (SSA)[1] countries declined over the 1970–85 period. Moreover, the African countries lost shares in most of the world primary commodity markets on a substantial scale. It has been shown that, although supply shortcomings were the predominant cause of the poor export performance of most SSA countries, the demand side – specifically the deterioration in the barter terms of trade – also played a role (Svedberg 1988).

The objective of this paper is to investigate yet another constraint on the demand side, namely, the extent to which protection in the major industrial market economies facing SSA products might have hampered their export growth. The incidence of protection encountered by SSA is analysed and compared with that faced by all developing countries taken together.

Industrial market economies are represented by the EC (10), Japan and the US, which together absorb more than three-quarters of total African exports. This share has remained largely unaltered during the past two decades, particularly in the 1980s. Both tariffs and non-tariff barriers (NTBs) which were effective in the 1980s are analysed. However, since tariffs in industrial market economies, especially those on primary products (the bulk of SSA exports), are relatively low, the critical area is the incidence of NTBs, although tariff escalation is a potential problem.

The plan of the paper is as follows. The export performance of the SSA countries over the 1970–85 period is briefly summarized in section 2. In section 3, a short description of the export structure of these countries is provided as additional background. In Section 4, the general developments in tariff and NTB protection of the industrial market economies and escalation of trade barriers are discussed. In section 5, the average tariffs on African exports and the incidence of NTBs are compared with those faced by all developing countries taken together. Also the main NTBs affecting sub-Saharan Africa are singled out. In section 6, the SSA countries are considered individually. Tariff averages, preference margins and the incidence of NTBs are investigated. Furthermore, products affected by specific NTBs are examined. In the case of the EC, NTBs on major product groups are scrutinized to distinguish the purely restrictive ones from those that actually allow preferential treatment of sub-Saharan Africa. A concluding section summarizes the main findings of the study.

## 2 The export performance of sub-Saharan Africa

Over the past two decades, the purchasing power of the combined export earnings of the SSA countries remained stagnant (see Svedberg, this volume). An overwhelming majority of SSA countries for which data were available saw their real export earnings dwindle or stagnate. Only three oil-exporting SSA countries had increasing export earnings on a par with the rest of the world; another four countries (Central African Republic, Malawi, Mali and Rwanda) had more modest increases in real export earnings. Compared with the export achievements of the African countries over the period 1954–69, their performance during the years 1970–85 was strikingly bleak. During the earlier period, their real export earnings grew by 6 per cent annually; in fact, no single SSA country experienced declining real export earnings in that period.

The meager performance of the SSA countries since the early 1970s has meant drastically declining shares in world markets. Between 1970 and 1986, their share of total world exports fell from 2.4 to 1.3 per cent. In non-oil exports the decline was even more drastic. In all primary commodities excluding oil, their world share fell from 7 per cent to below 4 per cent.

The predominant causes of the poor export performance for most African countries are found on the supply side. On the demand side, the most notable event over the 1970–85 period was the deteriorating barter terms of trade that all the SSA countries, except the oil exporters, experienced. The price decline of primary products accounted for about one-third of the total world market share loss of the SSA. The remaining two-thirds was due to failures to expand export volumes. The volume decline has so far been ascribed to problems on the supply side. In the following, we shall investigate to what extent protection in the main importing countries could have been part of the explanation.

## 3 Commodity composition and destination of sub-Saharan Africa's exports

The structure and intensity of protection that exporters encounter differ considerably across products and markets. Commodity composition and destination of exports were thus important determinants of the overall protection faced by SSA.

Since the time when the African countries were drawn into world trade by the colonial powers, primary commodities have dominated their exports. Manufactures defined narrowly (as SITC 5 to 8 less 68) accounted for only 6 per cent of SSA's total exports in both 1970 and 1985 (see Table 5.1).[2] Two major changes occurred in the composition of SSA's exports during this period. First, the total value of crude oil exports expanded roughly twenty times and its share jumped from 13 to 60 per cent. Second, there was a drastic decline in the share of the exports of ores and metals, from 32 to 9 per cent. Exports of foodstuffs and agricultural raw materials roughly doubled, yet their share in total exports dropped by half.

The predominance of primary products in SSA's exports is a mixed blessing from the point of view of protection in the industrial market economies. Mineral fuels, ores and metals face negligible duties and often only nominal NTBs. Also most tropical products which do not compete with production in the developed countries are relatively less protected goods. However, since agriculture is the most heavily protected and subsidized sector in the industrial market economies, their markets are nearly closed to temperate zone products (see OECD 1987). Furthermore, there is considerable

Table 5.1 *Commodity composition of sub-Saharan Africa's exports,*[a] *1970 and 1985 (%)*

| *Sector* | *(SITC)* | *1970* | *1985* |
|---|---|---|---|
| Non-manufactures | (0 to 4 + 68) | 94[b] | 94[b] |
| Food | (0 + 1 + 22 + 4) | 37 | 20 |
| Agricultural raw materials | (2 less (22 + 27 + 28)) | 13 | 6 |
| Ores and metals | (27 + 28 + 68) | 32 | 9 |
| Fuels | (3) | 13 | 60 |
| Manufactures | (5 to 8 less 68) | 6 | 6 |
| Total | (0 to 9) | 100 | 100 |
| (US$m.) | | (7,887) | (37,294) |

*Notes:*
[a] Based on partner country import statistics.
[b] Owing to rounding up, the components add up to 95 per cent.

*Source:* COMTRADE Data Base, United Nations Statistical Office.

escalation in trade barriers at higher levels of processing for most goods; agricultural and mining (Yeats 1988), as well as in tropical products (Cable 1988, and UNCTAD 1988).

Only a very small number of SSA countries have managed to diversify their export base during the 1970–85 period. The most notable example was Mauritius where textiles and clothing became the predominant exports (see Appendix Table A5.1).[3] Some other countries added 'non-traditional' primary products to their exports. These included horticultural and fishery products, which also comprised some processed items.[4]

Concerning destination, Europe and, in particular, the EC, is the dominant market for SSA's exports. Ten SSA countries had more than two-thirds of their exports to the EC in 1985 (see Appendix Table A5.2). Only around one-third of the SSA countries had less than half of their exports going to this market. Botswana, the Seychelles and Somalia had less than 20 per cent of their exports to the EC. For these countries, and also for Burkina Faso, Cape Verde, Kenya, Mozambique and Sudan, other developing countries (or the South African Union in the case of Botswana) have become important markets, absorbing roughly half of their exports.

The concentration of SSA's exports to Europe, and in particular to the EC, largely reflects the colonial heritage. The special ties of the industrial countries with their ex-colonies still have a considerable influence on trade patterns (see Svedberg 1981 and Kleiman 1977). Nevertheless, during the 1970–85 period, in addition to the increasing importance of other developing countries, there was also some reshuffling between the EC and the US markets for SSA's exports. Angola, Congo, Gabon and Nigeria – which are the main oil producers – shifted the bulk of their exports from the EC to the US. For the coffee exporters, Ethiopia, Burundi and Rwanda, the opposite happened (see Appendix Table A5.2).

The market concentration on Europe had important implications for Africa's export growth. Of the three main markets considered here, the US is by far the largest in terms of non-oil imports from developing countries. In fact, in 1985, US imports from developing countries were roughly the same as those of the EC and Japan taken together (see Table 5.2). In the early 1970s the situation was quite different; the EC was then the largest market for non-oil exports from developing countries. Over a decade, the growth in the US market for developing country exports was about twice the rate of that in the EC. The share of SSA's exports going to the US did increase significantly during this period, from 9 to 21 per cent. However, petroleum accounted for most of this increase. A noteworthy development was that the share of SSA's exports to Japan dropped dramatically, from 8 to 2 per cent, while this market absorbed an increasing share of developing countries' exports in general. It should be emphasized, however, that while fuels (mainly crude oil) constituted approximately half of SSA's total exports to the EC, and over three-quarters of its exports to the US, they were negligible in SSA's exports to Japan.

It seemed that sub-Saharan Africa did not have the 'right' products to exploit the potential in the fast-growing US market for labour-intensive manufactures. Despite an increase in 'new' forms of protection, the US largely remained an open market, and the developing countries on the whole managed to penetrate it with great success (see Yeats 1989b). Nevertheless, lost opportunity aside, it will be argued in sections 5 and 6 that the fact that SSA's exports were concentrated to the EC – rather than to the US – did not necessarily imply relatively less favourable conditions in terms of trade barriers faced. This was due to the preferential treatment the SSA enjoyed in the EC.

Table 5.2 *Destination of developing countries' exports,*[a] *1970 and 1985 (%)*

| *Exports from* | *Year* | *Developed market economies* | | | | *Developing countries*[b] | *All other countries* |
|---|---|---|---|---|---|---|---|
| | | *Total* | *EC* | *Japan* | *US* | | |
| All developing countries | 1970 | 80 | 40 | 12 | 18 | 18 | 2 |
| | 1985 | 77 | 25 | 16 | 27 | 22 | 1 |
| Non-OPEC developing | 1970 | 79 | 35 | 12 | 22 | 20 | 1 |
| | 1985 | 77 | 21 | 15 | 34 | 22 | 1 |
| Sub-Saharan Africa | 1970 | 87 | 58 | 8 | 9 | 11 | 2 |
| | 1985 | 85 | 50 | 2 | 21 | 15 | 0 |
| Memo item: World | 1970 | 80 | 41 | 7 | 14 | 18 | 2 |
| | 1985 | 81 | 37 | 8 | 21 | 18 | 1 |

*Notes:*

[a] Based on partner country import statistics. Owing to non-reporting centrally planned economies and poorly reporting developing countries, the figures overstate the actual shares for developed market economies.

[b] Developing countries are defined in accordance with the UN.

*Source:* COMTRADE Data Base, United Nations Statistical Office.

## 4 Tariff and non-tariff protection in industrial market economies

The major accomplishment of the post-war multilateral trade negotiations (MTNs) was the drastic reduction of industrial country tariffs. Through seven rounds of negotiations – Geneva (1947 and 1956), Annecy (1949), Torquay (1951), Dillon (1962), Kennedy (1968) and Tokyo (1979) – the average for the developed country most favoured nation tariffs was slashed from 40 per cent to about 5 per cent (see GATT 1980, UNCTAD 1968 and 1982).[5]

*'New' protectionism*

As tariffs have been progressively reduced, the importance of non-tariff barriers (NTBs), or non-tariff measures (NTMs) as they are sometimes called, have increased significantly (see Laird and Yeats 1988).[6] While governments were under legal obligation with respect to tariffs, they responded to domestic protectionist pressures by resorting to NTBs, which were only loosely monitored by the General Agreement on Tariffs and Trade (GATT). Moreover, the most favoured nation (MFN) principle, the cornerstone of the GATT, has been eroded as NTBs were increasingly directed against specific countries and country groups.

The spread of these measures and their domination of major sectors, such as agriculture, textiles and steel, is widely considered a threat to the functioning of the GATT and, more generally, the international trading system. The system is challenged in at least three important respects. First, there has been an increase in the use of formally permissible instruments of non-tariff protection. Agriculture is the case in point where the EC, for example, has become one of the world's largest exporters of sugar and beef through price support policies. Secondly, agreements such as the Multifibre Arrangement (MFA), which are in essence discriminatory against products of importance to developing countries, have been 'legitimized'. Thirdly, the use of 'grey area measures', such as 'orderly marketing arrangements' and 'voluntary export restraints', has increased. These measures lack transparency and involve *de facto* discrimination among trading partners.

Among the objectives of the current round of MTN, the Uruguay Round, which was launched in 1986, are the reversal of the trend concerning NTBs and the full integration of agriculture and other exceptions, such as textiles, back into the GATT discipline. This makes it the most ambitious MTN round so far.

*Non-tariff barriers*

There is no commonly agreed term to describe non-tariff instruments, let alone a consensus on their coverage. While NTB is the term preferred by economists, who consider the distortions they create the common denominator, policy-makers often wish to classify them among other policy measures and hence prefer the term non-tariff 'measures'. The UNCTAD Date Base on Trade Control Measures, which we use in our analysis, defines non-tariff measures as all government regulations and practices that may distort international trade by introducing differential treatment for imported and domestically produced goods. In doing so, no prior judgement is made as to the restrictiveness of specific NTBs, or whether they conform to national or international trade rules.

The information thus includes a wide range of non-tariff measures, some of which might have been implemented for legitimate non-protection reasons, such as concern for public health and safety. Since the discriminatory effect of some measures, such as health and safety regulations, technical standards and excise taxes, against imports vis-à-vis domestic products is arguable, they have been generally excluded from the analysis of official trade interventions. The 'broad' group of NTBs used in such analysis includes para-tariff measures (such as tariff quotas, seasonal tariffs, supplementary tariffs, etc.), variable levies, countervailing and anti-dumping actions, quantitative restrictions, the surveillance of quantities and/or prices of imports, and various types of licensing. What is commonly referred to as the 'narrow' group of NTBs excludes para-tariff measures, 'automatic' licensing and authorizations and import surveillance measures. Finally, measures which with some certainty constitute effective trade barriers, such as tariff quotas, variable levies, quantitative restrictions and non-automatic import authorizations and licences, are often called 'hard core' NTBs.

Most assessments of the general extent of the application of NTBs use two indicators: trade coverage and frequency ratios (see Laird and Yeats 1989). The trade coverage ratio measures the value of imports affected by selected NTBs as a share of imports from a particular source. The frequency ratio gives the number of trade flows covered by NTBs as a share of the total number of trade flows (where trade flows are defined as the number of national tariff lines times the number of trading partners in which imports originate in each tariff line in the base year). The profile of NTBs has been analysed by computing these indicators for selected NTBs and for specific groups of products. The trends in trade intervention have been analysed by calculating these indicators for a number of years, using the trade flows of a fixed base year as weights. A major shortcoming of this method, however, is that the underlining trade flows are already affected by NTBs. In the extreme case, when an import barrier is prohibitive, it would appear that trade is not affected at all. It is therefore important to remember that trade coverage and frequency ratios do not necessarily measure the restrictiveness of the NTBs considered.

*Escalation of trade barriers*

Most 'tropical' primary (unprocessed) commodities in industrial market economies are either free of import duties or face the lowest tariff rates – with the duties escalating as the goods undergo increased fabrication. The same pattern holds, although to a lesser extent, for non-tariff protection. Such escalation of trade barriers provides a disincentive for increased processing of primary commodities in the developing countries. This general phenomenon holds true in the case of tropical products as well. Furthermore, following the Tokyo Round tariff reductions, tariff escalation in highly processed tropical products has also increased (Cable 1988).

A recent study by Yeats (1988) considering sixteen material groups – meat, fish, vegetables, fruit, vegetable oils, tobacco, sugar, cocoa, rubber, leather, wood, cotton, iron, other metal ores, phosphates and petroleum – revealed that, in all but fish, average tariffs (incorporating preferential rates) increased on the average by five to ten percentage points as one moved higher in the processing chain. Furthermore, in eleven of these cases, the incidence of NTBs also escalated considerably. Studies by Cable (1988) and UNCTAD (1988) corroborated these findings in tropical products. Ironically, developing countries export a much smaller proportion of processed tropical products than do industrial countries. Escalation of trade barriers certainly does not help to improve this imbalance.

It should also be underlined, however, that escalation of trade barriers is not a developed country phenomenon only. The pattern is the same in the case of developing countries (Yeats 1988), where the level of protection is several times higher than in the industrial economies (Erzan *et al.* 1989).

*Preferences*
In previous MTN rounds, most developing countries preferred to stand by and enjoy the benefits of MFN concessions which resulted from negotiations among the major industrial market economies rather than participate actively on a reciprocal basis.[7] They also argued strongly for unilateral preferential treatment by the developed countries. Following discussion under the auspices of the GATT and UNCTAD in the late 1960s and early 1970s, the unilateral preferential schemes of industrial countries concerning tariffs were somewhat harmonized and put under a framework known as the Generalized System of Preferences (GSP). GSP covers only tariffs, not NTBs.

As the GSP schemes are unilaterally granted by the industrial countries, the list of beneficiary developing countries, the product coverage and the depth of the preference margins vary considerably across the donors. In the US, GSP beneficiaries are further subject to a 'competetive need limit' for each product under the scheme. An eligible country exceeding this limit is temporarily disqualified from GSP treatment of the product in question. Otherwise, imports under the GSP are duty free. More advanced developing countries, however, have 'graduated' from the GSP beneficiary status altogether. In most other developed countries, the preference margin for beneficiaries is a certain percentage of the MFN rate (see UNCTAD 1989). The least developed countries (LLDCs) usually enjoy deeper preference margins and their product coverage is somewhat broader.

A survey of the GSP schemes of the major industrial countries revealed that, on the whole, the product coverage of GSP schemes in high tariff items was significantly narrower compared with lower tariff items (Erzan and Karsenty 1989). The Japanese, US and EC GSP schemes covered, respectively, 69, 51 and 68 per cent of all tariff positions. In the EC, GSP coverage in high tariff products was 69 per cent compared with 78 per cent in lower tariff items and in the US 27 and 57 per cent, respectively.

Almost all sub-Saharan countries are GSP beneficiaries in all developed country markets. Under this scheme, many of them also qualifying as LLDCs[8] enjoy wider product coverage and deeper preference margins compared with other developing countries. In the US, LLDCs are not subject to the 'competetive need' criterion. Furthermore, all SSA countries belong to the ACP (Africa, Caribbean and Pacific) Group (except Namibia and Réunion). *In principle*, as beneficiaries of the Lomé Convention, their exports enter the EC without being subject to any barriers – tariff or non-tariff.

## 5 Tariff and non-tariff protection facing sub-Saharan Africa's exports[9]

This section investigates the overall incidence of tariffs and non-tariff barriers on exports from SSA in the major industrial market economies and compares this with the exports of all developing countries in the same markets.

*Tariff protection*

The major exports of sub-Saharan Africa, being primary products, are subject to relatively low tariff rates in developed market economies. Besides enjoying most favoured nation (MFN) status, they are eligible for preferential treatment under the GSP schemes and the Lomé Convention.

Table 5.3 gives trade weighted average tariffs for all products excluding fuels faced by sub-Saharan Africa and by all developing countries in the EC, Japan and the US. The averages are based on the tariffs which were actually applied to the individual countries' exports, taking into account preference margins. It was found that, in the EC, where SSA was virtually exempt from tariff duties,[10] the weighted average tariff rate for all developing countries was 1.76 per cent for all products. In Japan, the corresponding figures were 4.03 per cent for all developing countries and 1.64 per cent for SSA; in the US these were 6.67 per cent and 0.48 per cent respectively. Hence, the average preference margin, in percentage points, appeared to be the highest in the US, followed by Japan.

Part of these apparent preference margins was due to differences in the product mix of SSA compared with the rest of the developing countries. To remove the effect of this difference, yet another comparison, limited to the same products as SSA countries exported, was conducted. In weighting tariffs for the constrained list of products, actual trade weights were retained to reflect the relative importance of particular products for each country. When the tariff

Table 5.3 *Trade weighted average tariffs faced by sub-Saharan Africa and all developing countries in the EC, Japan and the USA (all products, excluding fuels), 1983 (%)*[a]

| *Exporter* | *Market* | | |
|---|---|---|---|
| | *EC* | *Japan* | *USA* |
| Sub-Saharan Africa | 0.01 | 1.64 | 0.48 |
| All developing countries | 1.76 | 4.03 | 6.67 |
| (for same products as SSA)[b] | (1.75) | (1.71) | (6.63) |

*Notes:*

[a] The averages are based on actual tariffs faced by individual countries including preference margins in 1983. Weights also pertain to actual 1983 trade.

Tariff lines for which data were not available were excluded. This was particularly important in the case of the EC where over 400 items, predominantly in the food sector, mostly pertaining to variable levies with no fixed component, had to be excluded.

[b] Average for all developing countries, yet restricted to the list of products exported by sub-Saharan countries to the relevant markets – using aggregate trade weights of all developing countries.

*Source:* GATT Tariff Study computer files; Svedberg (1988), p. 54.

averages in the EC and the US were calculated accordingly, the results did not change. It can thus be concluded that the difference between the average rates faced by SSA and the rest of developing countries was the reflection of actual preference margins. In Japan, however, the average tariff facing all developing countries, when restricted to the same list of products, was not much different from that facing sub-Saharan Africa. The apparent margin in the first calculation was thus mainly due to differences in the composition of imports from the SSA and other developing countries.

It is noteworthy that duty-free treatment in the EC under the Lomé scheme provided only a negligible margin to SSA's exports. On the other hand, the relatively higher tariff average in the US facing other developing countries yielded a substantial margin to Africa.[11]

*Non-tariff protection*

Using the two measures for the incidence of NTBs – their frequency and trade coverage ratios (described on page 104) – Table 5.4 presents the overall situation faced by SSA's exports in comparison with that for all developing countries taken together. For all products in the three markets combined, the frequency of NTBs on SSA's exports was 14 per cent, as opposed to 24 per cent for all the developing countries. On the other hand, NTBs covered around 16–18 per cent of the exports of both groups. When fuels were excluded, however, the trade coverage of NTBs was considerably lower for SSA compared with the aggregate group of developing countries: 14 per cent versus 24 per cent.[12]

The picture in the EC market, which dominated the aggregate figures, closely resembled the overall situation described above. In the US, the frequency of NTBs and their trade coverage of SSA's exports did not exceed a few percentage points, except in manufactures. In Japan, NTB incidence on SSA appeared to be greater than that encountered by other developing countries. An intersectoral comparison revealed that, among SSA's exports, the products most affected by NTBs were foodstuff and manufactures in all three markets, and mineral fuels in the EC.

In making these comparisons, it should be observed that the purpose of using the NTB frequency and trade coverage ratios is to give a snapshot by summarizing the information involving large and diversified trade flows encountering a variety of NTBs. However, for SSA's limited exports, the NTB incidence indices are somewhat irrelevant, as we can look into the products and barriers in a detailed fashion – a task which would have been insurmountable in the case of major exporters.

We start this detailed investigation with the NTBs faced by SSA. Table 5.5 lists the individual NTBs and gives the value of imports which were affected by the respective barrier in the EC, Japan and the US. Individual NTBs are not mutually exclusive in their coverage of imports. The information provided in Table 5.5 considerably modifies the impression of the relatively high NTB protection conveyed by Table 5.4. The predominant tool used by Japan against SSA happens to be import authorization (covering US$133 million worth of imports) – which usually is not a restrictive barrier. In the US, the largest item was flexible import fees used in combination

Table 5.4 *NTB frequency and trade coverage ratios facing sub-Saharan Africa and all developing countries in the EC, Japan and the US*[a]

| *Sector*[b] | *Exporter* | *Market* | | | | | | | |
|---|---|---|---|---|---|---|---|---|---|
| | | *EC* | | *Japan* | | *US* | | *Total* | |
| | | *Frequency ratio*[c] *%* | *Coverage ratio*[d] *%* | *Frequency ratio %* | *Coverage ratio %* | *Frequency ratio %* | *Coverage ratio %* | *Frequency ratio %* | *Coverage ratio %* |
| Food | SSA | 31 | 15 | 47 | 42 | 5 | 8 | 29 | 15 |
| | All Dev.[e] | 41 | 26 | 48 | 56 | 9 | 15 | 35 | 28 |
| Agricultural raw materials | SSA | 8 | 2 | 13 | 1 | 3 | 1 | 8 | 1 |
| | All Dev. | 11 | 5 | 17 | 6 | 3 | 12 | 11 | 6 |
| Ores and metals | SSA | 5 | 5 | 12 | 4 | 0 | 0 | 5 | 4 |
| | All Dev. | 3 | 5 | 6 | 5 | 1 | 3 | 3 | 5 |
| Mineral fuels | SSA | 28 | 31 | 0 | 0 | 0 | 0 | 22 | 18 |
| | All Dev. | 25 | 27 | 12 | 2 | 0 | 0 | 18 | 11 |
| Chemicals | SSA | 6 | 1 | 0 | 0 | 0 | 0 | 5 | 1 |
| | All Dev. | 3 | 1 | 12 | 19 | 1 | 15 | 3 | 11 |
| Manufactures (excl. chem.) | SSA | 12 | 56 | 9 | 8 | 2 | 18 | 11 | 48 |
| | All Dev. | 26 | 42 | 8 | 8 | 18 | 24 | 24 | 29 |

| | | | | | | | | | |
|---|---|---|---|---|---|---|---|---|---|
| All sectors | SSA | 15 | 23 | 21 | 17 | 2 | 2 | 14 | 16 |
| | All Dev. | 25 | 28 | 15 | 8 | 15 | 14 | 24 | 18 |
| Excluding fuels | SSA | 15 | 14 | 21 | 17 | 3 | 3 | 14 | 14 |
| | All Dev. | 25 | 28 | 15 | 21 | 15 | 23 | 24 | 24 |

*Notes:*

[a] The broad group of NTBs used in the analysis includes para-tariff measures such as tariffs with quotas, seasonal tariffs, supplementary tariffs, etc., variable levies, countervailing and anti-dumping actions, quantitative restrictions, the surveillance of quantities and/or prices of imports, and various types of licensing. Health and safety regulations, technical standards and excise taxes are excluded. While data on NTBs pertain to 1986, trade data employed to calculate frequency and coverage ratios are of 1984.

[b] Sectors are defined in SITC as the following: Food – SITC 0 + 1 + 22 + 4; Agricultural raw materials – SITC 2 less (22 + 27 + 28); Ores and metals – SITC 27 + 28 + 68; Mineral fuels – SITC 3; Chemicals – SITC 5; Manufactures – SITC 6 to 8 less 68; All sectors – SITC 0 to 9.

[c] Frequency Ratio gives the number of trade flows covered by NTBs as a share of the total number of trade flows where the number of trade flows is the number of national tariff lines times the number of trading partners in which imports originate in each tariff line in the base year.

[d] Trade Coverage ratio measures the value of imports affected by selected NTBs as a share of all imports.

[e] All Dev. = all developing countries

*Source:* UNCTAD Data Base on Trade Control Measures.

Table 5.5 *List of NTBs facing sub-Saharan Africa's exports in the EC, Japan and the US and value of trade affected (US$m.)*

| | *Imports[b] from SSA affected in* | | |
|---|---|---|---|
| *NTB[a]* | *EC* | *Japan* | *US* |
| Tariff quotas | 44.0 | 9.3 | — |
| Seasonal tariffs | 41.3 | — | — |
| Anti-dumping duties | — | — | 0.1 |
| Countervailing duties | — | — | 0.4 |
| Variable levies | 372.4 | — | — |
| Variable component | 4.9 | — | — |
| Flexible import fees | — | — | 82.0 |
| Licences | 395.6 | 0.1 | — |
| Import authorization | — | 133.1 | — |
| Global quotas, unallocated | — | 33.8 | — |
| Global quotas, allocated | — | — | 0.2 |
| Bilateral (country) quotas | 1.2 | — | 82.2 |
| MFA quotas | — | — | 59.9[e] |
| Seasonal quotas | 15.2 | — | — |
| Quotas not elsewhere specified | 2,984.7[c] | — | — |
| Surveillance licence | 711.4[d] | — | — |
| Retrospective surveillance | 1.3 | — | — |
| Community surveillance | 12.1 | — | — |
| Reference prices | 118.8 | — | — |
| Price surveillance | 1.5 | — | — |
| Anti-dumping investigations | — | — | 0.2 |
| Countervailing duty investigations | — | — | 0.6 |
| Sole importing agency | — | 12.5 | — |
| Memo item: Total imports | 18,266.4 | 1,005.0 | 7,943.5 |
| (excl. fuels) | (9,063.3) | (1,005.0) | (1,722.2) |

*Notes:*

[a] All NTBs in place during 1986, except health and safety regulations, prohibition for conservation, etc., technical standards and excise taxes.

[b] 1984 imports. The reported import coverages of the individual NTBs are not mutually exclusive and hence there can be overlapping up to 100 per cent.

[c] The bulk of this amount, US$2.7 billion, was mineral fuels subject to quota systems in some EC member states.

[d] US$49 million of this amount was mineral fuels.

[e] 1986 MFA import value.

*Source:* UNCTAD Data Base on Trade Control Measures.

with bilateral quotas (US$82 million) followed by MFA quotas (against imports from Mauritius worth US$60 million in 1986).

In the case of the EC, the relatively large array of NTBs and the volume of trade they cover give a partially misleading impression. Most of these NTBs relate to agricultural products, especially foodstuffs, which are regulated by the Common Agricultural Policy (CAP). However, while CAP is an extremely protectionist mechanism, for the beneficiaries of the Lomé Convention it implies certain rewards. For instance, while other exporters are subject to extremely high variable levies,[13] for the ACP countries – including the SSA – these levies are often reduced or eliminated. In turn, SSA countries have quota allocations under which they can sell their produce at artificially high EC domestic prices – several times the price prevailing in international markets. These special provisions obviously cannot be taken into account in Tables 5.4 and 5.5, and consequently they are not distinguished from the purely restrictive barriers. To clarify this matter, important items are scrutinized in the sub-section on the EC market below (pages 118–20).

In the EC, national quota systems constitute the biggest item in terms of import coverage (nearly US$3 billion). The bulk of the imports subject to this tool is petroleum – whose flow is monitored in compliance with national energy conservation policies, particularly by France.

To conclude this section: the incidence of NTBs facing sub-Saharan Africa was somewhat lower compared with that for all developing countries taken together. However, there was a more significant difference if one took into account that (i) over 20 per cent of all developing countries' non-fuel exports encountered 'hard core' NTBs in the OECD markets (Laird and Yeats 1989), (ii) while the NTBs most frequently faced by SSA were relatively 'soft'. The following section further narrows down the focus of the investigation by considering the SSA countries and their products individually.

## 6 Tariff and non-tariff protection by exporter and product

This section addresses the following questions: (i) which SSA countries were most affected by tariff and non-tariff protection, (ii) what was the depth of preference margins in tariffs for individual countries, (iii) in which products did exporters encounter tariff 'peaks', (iv) on which products were specific NTBs concentrated, (v) in the EC, did NTBs allow preferential treatment of SSA, and (vi) did the incidence of NTBs on SSA countries exports intensify during the 1980s? Table 5.6 summarizes the country-specific information for SSA on trade, tariffs and NTBs in the EC, Japanese and US markets. Exporter- and product-specific data on NTBs in the respective markets are provided in Appendix Tables A5.4–A5.6.

*Tariffs and preference margins*

Weighted average tariffs (including preferences) encountered by individual SSA countries and the averages in the corresponding products for the 'control group' covering all developing countries were computed in the same fashion as the overall averages reported in section 5. Furthermore, as a second check of the underlying tariff rates, the corresponding unweighted tariff averages were also calculated (reported in Appendix Table A5.3).

The results revealed that, in the EC, where SSA enjoyed virtually duty-free treatment,[14] weighted preference margins were around two percentage points. The smallness of these margins was due to (i) the relatively low level of EC's MFN and GSP tariffs (given that most highly protected foodstuffs were covered by variable levies with no fixed component),[15] (ii) the fact that SSA had little to export in processed goods with higher tariffs, and (iii) the preferences which the Mediterranean associates of the EC enjoyed.

In Japan and the US, the SSA countries were beneficiaries of the GSP, which implied duty-free status in the US for eligible products.[16] Weighted average tariffs encountered by SSA countries in the Japanese market ranged from zero to 4 per cent. Weighted preference margins were generally negligible. In ten cases, SSA countries faced slightly higher weighted average tariffs compared with the control group of all developing countries. This was not, however, due to less favourable treatment of SSA, as revealed by arithmetic averages of the underlying tariffs in Appendix Table A5.3.[17]

While the weighted average tariffs facing most SSA countries in the US were zero or under 1 per cent, for five countries – Chad, Equatorial Guinea, Lesotho, Malawi and Mauritius – this rate was between 10 and 30 per cent. Also Malawi and Mauritius encountered considerably higher averages compared with the aggregate control group of all developing countries. Behind all these cases were the extremely high tariffs on textile yarn and clothing items which were excluded from the GSP.[18] The relative weight of the few high tariff products in SSA's exports accounted for this outcome. Otherwise, almost all other SSA countries had a weighted average preference margin often above 4 per cent in the US market.

*Non-tariff protection*

While most SSA countries apparently encountered some NTBs in the EC, this was not the case in Japan, and especially not in the US (see Table 5. 6).[19] The main reason for the difference in the distribution of the NTB burden across the SSA countries in the EC versus Japan and the US was the volume and diversity of exports to the EC market. A great majority of the SSA countries had exports to the EC amounting to several hundred million US dollars – covering a relatively wide range of products – as opposed to exports worth a few hundred thousand or a few million US dollars to the other two main markets. The second major reason for the difference in the apparent NTB incidence relates to the penetration of some SSA exports into otherwise extremely restricted EC markets for temperate zone agricultural products.

Excluding the major petroleum exporters, which encountered quota systems on fuels in some member states of the Community,[20] nine countries – Botswana, Gambia, Guinea-Bissau, Mauritius, Mozambique, Senegal, Seychelles, Swaziland and Zimbabwe – had over 20 per cent of their export products affected by NTBs in the EC market. Among them, Guinea-Bissau was the only one with exports less than US$10 million to the EC. All these countries, except Swaziland and Zimbabwe, also had very high NTB incidences in Japan, exceeding 90 per cent in most cases. However, with the exception of Mozambique and Senegal, all had exports to Japan below US$10 million. There were seven other SSA countries in this market which had high NTB coverage. These were Djibouti, Madagascar, Malawi, Mauritania, Nigeria, Sierra Leone and Somalia. Three of them – Djibouti, Sierra Leone and Somalia – exported less than US$100,000 to Japan.

Finally, in the US, only Mauritius, Mozambique and Swaziland had NTB coverage ratios over 20 per cent. Madagascar and Zimbabwe were the only others facing NTBs to a significant extent.

Table 5.6 *Weighted tariff averages and NTB coverage on SSA countries' exports in the EC, Japan and the US*

| *Exporter*[d] | *EC* | | | | *JAPAN* | | | | *US* | | | |
|---|---|---|---|---|---|---|---|---|---|---|---|---|
| | *Imports*[a] *(US$m.)* | *Weighted average tariffs*[b] *(%)* | | *NTB*[c] *coverage ratio (%)* | *Imports*[a] *(US$m.)* | *Weighted average tariffs*[b] *(%)* | | *NTB*[c] *coverage ratio (%)* | *Imports*[a] *(US$m.)* | *Weighted average tariffs*[b] *(%)* | | *NTB*[c] *coverage ratio (%)* |
| | | *Facing the exporter* | *(Facing all DCs)* | | | *Facing the exporter* | *(Facing all DCs)* | | | *Facing the exporter* | *(Facing all DCs)* | |
| Angola | 600.2 | 0.0 | (0.7) | 0.1 | 0.6 | 0.0 | (0.0) | 0.0 | 599.7 | 0.7 | (0.8) | 0.0 |
| Benin* | 109.8 | 0.0 | (0.5) | 1.6 | 1.2 | 4.1 | (0.5) | 0.0 | 0.1 | 0.7 | (4.0) | 0.0 |
| Botswana | 60.2 | 0.0 | (1.7) | 71.2 | 0.2 | 0.8 | (0.1) | 23.8 | 2.3 | 1.8 | (15.3) | 0.0 |
| Burkina Faso* | 41.9 | 0.0 | (1.3) | 13.4 | 2.6 | 0.6 | (1.3) | 0.0 | 0.9 | 8.6 | (11.1) | 0.0 |
| Burundi* | 104.5 | 0.0 | (1.9) | 0.1 | 1.8 | 0.0 | (0.0) | 0.0 | 10.0 | 0.2 | (1.7) | 0.0 |
| Cameroon | 1,255.2 | 0.0 | (0.9) | 0.6 | 42.2 | 1.1 | (3.2) | 0.1 | 230.7 | 0.8 | (3.5) | 0.1 |
| Cape Verde | 2.1 | 0.0 | (2.1) | 1.4 | . . | . . | . . | . . | 1.0 | 0.0 | (0.0) | 0.0 |
| CAR* | 109.0 | 0.0 | (1.6) | 0.5 | 5.6 | 0.0 | (0.0) | 0.1 | 3.0 | 0.4 | (5.0) | 0.0 |
| Chad* | 43.6 | 0.0 | (1.6) | 0.0 | 1.5 | 0.0 | (0.0) | 0.0 | 0.1 | 29.9 | (32.0) | 0.0 |
| Comoros* | 12.6 | 0.0 | (2.2) | 0.4 | 0.2 | 0.2 | (0.1) | 6.1 | 3.5 | 0.7 | (7.5) | 0.0 |
| Congo | 419.8 | 0.0 | (0.6) | 0.7 | 5.6 | 0.0 | (0.0) | 0.0 | 161.1 | 0.6 | (0.7) | 2.7 |
| Djibouti* | 3.4 | 0.0 | (1.9) | 14.5 | 0.1 | 1.9 | (5.0) | 38.5 | 0.2 | 2.2 | (6.0) | 0.0 |
| Ethiopia* | 236.8 | 0.0 | (1.7) | 4.0 | 43.5 | 0.2 | (0.1) | 0.6 | 73.0 | 0.3 | (3.5) | 0.0 |
| Eq. Guinea* | 36.3 | 0.0 | (1.5) | 0.1 | . . | . . | . . | . . | 0.2 | 17.0 | (27.7) | 0.0 |
| Gabon | 750.5 | 0.0 | (0.9) | 2.2 | 15.7 | 0.0 | (0.0) | 0.0 | 195.1 | 0.7 | (3.5) | 0.3 |
| Gambia* | 14.2 | 0.0 | (1.9) | 27.8 | 8.3 | 0.5 | (4.0) | 100.0 | 0.5 | 0.0 | (1.2) | 0.0 |
| Ghana | 344.0 | 0.0 | (1.4) | 0.3 | 74.1 | 0.4 | (1.2) | 8.7 | 190.8 | 0.0 | (1.8) | 0.1 |
| Guinea* | 250.5 | 0.0 | (1.6) | 0.2 | 1.1 | 0.8 | (4.3) | 17.1 | 89.1 | 0.0 | (4.0) | 0.0 |
| Guinea-Bissau* | 4.3 | 0.0 | (1.1) | 30.0 | 0.3 | 0.5 | (4.0) | 100.0 | 0.8 | 0.7 | (4.3) | 0.0 |
| Ivory Coast | 2,102.9 | 0.0 | (1.2) | 2.1 | 43.8 | 0.2 | (0.1) | 0.1 | 423.9 | 0.1 | (4.1) | 2.2 |
| Kenya | 586.8 | 0.0 | (1.7) | 11.7 | 12.3 | 3.1 | (1.7) | 10.1 | 140.6 | 0.6 | (7.1) | 0.1 |
| Lesotho* | 2.8 | 0.0 | (1.8) | 5.2 | 0.1 | 0.0 | (5.6) | 0.0 | 3.3 | 13.6 | (18.6) | 0.3 |
| Liberia | 526.1 | 0.0 | (1.2) | 0.6 | 91.7 | 0.0 | (0.0) | 0.1 | 80.8 | 0.0 | (6.1) | 0.0 |
| Madagascar | 193.9 | 0.0 | (1.4) | 6.5 | 44.3 | 1.6 | (1.9) | 72.7 | 62.4 | 0.0 | (2.4) | 7.0 |
| Malawi* | 172.9 | 0.0 | (1.7) | 6.9 | 14.1 | 0.0 | (0.0) | 99.9 | 17.3 | 11.1 | (3.7) | 0.1 |

| | | | | | | | | | | | | |
|---|---|---|---|---|---|---|---|---|---|---|---|---|
| Mali* | 57.8 | 0.0 | (1.3) | 2.0 | 2.9 | 4.3 | (3.4) | 0.0 | 7.8 | 1.9 | (7.9) | 0.7 |
| Mauritania* | 206.0 | 0.0 | (1.3) | 15.8 | 135.4 | 0.7 | (4.1) | 100.0 | 2.0 | 4.3 | (11.5) | 1.2 |
| Mauritius | 459.9 | 0.0 | (2.1) | 47.5 | 1.3 | 2.6 | (5.1) | 46.9 | 115.7 | 14.4 | (8.7) | 61.2 |
| Mozambique* | 22.0 | 0.0 | (1.0) | 64.2 | 17.4 | 2.9 | (2.6) | 95.9 | 18.4 | 0.2 | (2.5) | 47.5 |
| Namibia | . . | . . | . . | . . | . . | . . | . . | . . | 18.4 | 0.4 | (1.4) | 0.0 |
| Niger* | 176.5 | 0.0 | (0.6) | 0.3 | 0.1 | 0.0 | (0.0) | 0.0 | 8.6 | 0.9 | (4.4) | 0.2 |
| Nigeria | 4,409.1 | 0.0 | (0.8) | 0.1 | 5.1 | 2.6 | (3.1) | 85.6 | 2,519.6 | 0.7 | (2.0) | 0.1 |
| Réunion | . . | . . | . . | . . | . . | . . | . . | . . | . . | . . | . . | . . |
| Rwanda* | 146.6 | 0.0 | (1.8) | 0.2 | 1.7 | 0.0 | (0.0) | 13.5 | 10.8 | 0.3 | (5.9) | 0.0 |
| Sao Tomé* | 6.3 | 0.0 | (2.3) | 0.7 | . . | . . | . . | . . | 1.0 | 1.9 | (3.5) | 0.0 |
| Senegal | 299.1 | 0.0 | (1.4) | 24.6 | 26.8 | 3.4 | (2.3) | 71.4 | 5.4 | 2.6 | (9.2) | 0.1 |
| Seychelles | 22.0 | 0.0 | (2.1) | 91.1 | 0.2 | 3.5 | (4.6) | 95.9 | 6.6 | 3.3 | (6.7) | 0.0 |
| Sierra Leone* | 138.1 | 0.0 | (1.2) | 7.3 | 0.1 | 3.0 | (3.0) | 100.0 | 10.4 | 0.7 | (5.8) | 0.0 |
| Somalia* | 22.9 | 0.0 | (2.2) | 3.6 | 0.1 | 0.0 | (0.0) | 93.5 | 0.4 | 6.1 | (8.7) | 0.0 |
| Sudan* | 118.2 | 0.0 | (1.2) | 13.3 | 43.5 | 0.0 | (0.1) | 4.3 | 12.2 | 1.1 | (18.5) | 0.2 |
| Swaziland | 119.9 | 0.0 | (2.4) | 77.8 | 9.0 | 0.0 | (0.0) | 0.0 | 18.6 | 2.2 | (7.9) | 56.4 |
| Tanzania | 260.7 | 0.0 | (1.6) | 7.0 | 22.2 | 0.2 | (1.3) | 12.1 | 11.9 | 0.4 | (1.0) | 0.0 |
| Togo* | 158.2 | 0.0 | (1.3) | 2.9 | 5.2 | 0.0 | (0.0) | 0.2 | 24.1 | 0.0 | (3.8) | 0.0 |
| Uganda* | 295.0 | 0.0 | (1.6) | 0.1 | 18.2 | 0.0 | (0.0) | 0.0 | 133.0 | 0.0 | (1.6) | 0.0 |
| Zaire | 1,200.2 | 0.0 | (0.8) | 0.2 | 54.1 | 0.0 | (0.1) | 3.3 | 221.0 | 0.5 | (1.0) | 0.0 |
| Zambia | 264.9 | 0.0 | (2.1) | 0.3 | 202.8 | 0.0 | (0.1) | 0.1 | 63.1 | 0.7 | (2.0) | 0.0 |
| Zimbabwe | 453.3 | 0.0 | (2.0) | 22.6 | 61.3 | 1.2 | (0.1) | 1.6 | 69.1 | 3.2 | (8.1) | 10.4 |

*Notes:*

[a] 1986 imports. Apparently irrelevant items such as return goods, postal packages, stamps, etc., are excluded from the trade values reported.

[b] Trade weighted actual average tariffs in 1986, including preferences. The average for the individual SSA country is based on its own trade weights in the market concerned. The corresponding average for 'all developing' is restricted to the same products – however uses aggregate trade weights of all developing countries.

[c] All NTBs in place during 1986, except health and safety regulations, prohibition for conservation, etc., technical standards and excise taxes. This broad definition of NTBs includes para-tariffs, i.e. tariffs with quota, seasonal tariffs, supplementary tariffs, etc. In the case of the EC, the NTBs are confined to those applied uniformly by the Community, leaving out those NTBs used only by some member state(s).

[d] * = Least developed countries (LLDCs) according to the UN. Mozambique was added to the list in 1988.

*Sources:* GATT Tariff Study computer files and UNCTAD Data Base on Trade Control Measures.

*NTBs by exporter and Product*
Documenting the limited number of specific NTBs affecting the export products of the individual SSA countries in the Japanese and the US markets is fairly straightforward. In the EC, however, the number of products involved is far greater and some of the apparent NTBs actually allow preferential treatment of SSA. We should also remember the differences in the magnitude of the three markets' imports from SSA and the share of petroleum in this: (i) the EC, total over US$18 billion, approximately half of it non-fuel, (ii) Japan, around US$1 billion, no petroleum, and (iii) the US, roughly US$8 billion yet less than one-quarter of it non-fuel.

*The EC market* In ninety-five product categories,[21] SSA countries' exports to the EEC were affected by NTBs (see Appendix Table A5.4). When fuels – which were subject to quotas under energy policies of some EC states – were excluded, imports from SSA subject to NTBs were US$1.3 billion, or roughly 14 per cent of non-fuel imports. These products can be studied under four large clusters: (i) agricultural products, mostly foodstuffs, subject to the CAP, (ii) textiles and clothing, exempt from the MFA in the case of SSA, nevertheless somewhat affected by it, (iii) precious and semi-precious stones and ores and minerals, and (iv) other manufactured goods.

In addition to reduced levels of barriers in most agricultural goods, in five products – sugar, beef, rice, bananas and rum – imports from ACP countries are regulated by special 'regimes' or 'protocols'. Other than rice and rum, which had little relevance for Africa, these provided guaranteed export revenues for the SSA countries. The arrangement in sugar is an outright income transfer mechanism, not different from the deal the European farmers in the EC get. For the stipulated annual ceilings, SSA countries receive the artificially high EC prices and pay no duties or variable levies. To provide the EC with the agreed quantities of sugar is not only a right but also a duty for the SSA suppliers. In beef, the SSA countries enjoy exemption from duties of around 20 per cent – and Botswana and Kenya have major reductions in the variable levies too – subject to annual ceilings, which are often highly utilized. Under the banana protocol, the EC pledges to provide and maintain the advantages of the ACP countries in market access. Particularly in the British,

French and Italian markets, ACP countries enjoy guaranteed market shares provided by quotas. However, ACP countries, including those in SSA, often failed to exploit this advantage fully.

An inspection of Appendix Table A5.4 reveals that imports of meat (including beef) from Botswana, Djibouti, Ivory Coast, Madagascar, Swaziland and Uganda totalled US$43 million (in 1984). The NTBs facing products falling in this category were variable levies, licences and tariff quotas.[22] The information conveyed here is that, when annual ceilings are surpassed, exemption from or reduction in tariffs and variable levies may no longer hold. Sugar imports from Congo, Ivory Coast, Kenya, Madagascar, Malawi, Mauritius, Swaziland, Tanzania and Zimbabwe totaled US$271 million. Licences and variable levies are listed as the effective NTBs for the same reason explained above. Bananas from Benin, Cameroon, Guinea, Ivory Coast, Madagascar and Togo, worth US$86 million, came under quotas devised for promotion of these imports.

A large number of SSA countries supplied the EC market with fish and shellfish totalling US$72 million. Some of these products were subject to reference prices and surveillance licences. In most of these goods, the EC's Common Customs Tariff was around 20 per cent and ACP countries were exempt from it. However, if the landed import price was below a certain reference price, they were subject to a compensatory charge. Similarly, imports of prepared or preserved fish from Cape Verde, Ivory Coast and Senegal, worth US$73 million, were subject to these provisions. Fruits and vegetables were also important export items for a large number of SSA countries. Most of these were exempt from tariffs, yet some were subject to tariff quotas according to which tariffs were restored above certain annual ceilings. For some, reference prices applied. Especially in fruits, there were seasonal tariffs, often with a reduced rate for the ACP countries.

In textiles and clothing, despite free access provisions of the Lomé Convention, voluntary export restraints (VERs) have been imposed on Mauritius in France and the UK. Furthermore, ACP countries' exports of MFA products were put under import surveillance. Imports into France from the Ivory Coast and Senegal faced some limitations.

Precious and semi-precious stones, and minerals and metals (mostly copper), constituting a very large category of imports (worth nearly half a billion US$), were subject to surveillance licences – which, however, amounted to a monitoring measure rather than a restrictive barrier.

The last cluster of goods, diverse manufactured products – many of them originating in duty-free zones of SSA countries – were subject to surveillance licences. Some of these products, such as radios, also came under quotas in some member states of the EC, notably in France, Greece and Italy. We have no information on the restrictive effect of these measures. Nevertheless, the trade values involved were extremely small and the statistics include some irrelevant items such as used ships, etc.

Finally, we found no evidence of a significant deterioration in the preferential treatment enjoyed by SSA in higher levels of processing. For instance, meat, fish, fruits and vegetables appeared to penetrate the market with not much greater formality or difficulty when they were in prepared or preserved forms. In preparations which used inputs subject to variable levies – such as macaroni made of hard wheat – the 'variable component' charged at the border for the final product was often reduced or eliminated for the SSA countries.

*The Japanese market* Fresh, chilled or frozen fish (excluding fillets) and other produce from the sea (such as shrimps, prawns, lobsters, squids and octopus), adding up to approximately US$130 million, constituted the bulk of SSA's exports to Japan which encountered NTBs (see Appendix Table A5.5). These products were all subject to import authorization and some of them, worth around US$20 million, were under global quotas as well.

Import authorization in Japan is a general measure, used mainly to monitor imports of goods considered 'sensitive', particularly vis-à-vis domestic production. In cases where informal VERs exist, the monitoring may have important implications. In the absence of other arrangements, however, as is often the case for SSA countries, their restrictive impact is usually negligible. A number of exporters, such as Djibouti and Sierra Leone, which had extremely small export volumes covered by import authorization, fall into this category. On the other hand, for example in the case of Mauritania, the largest supplier of octopus in the Japanese market, the authorizations might be more than a mere formality.

Global quotas – with no country allocations – are potentially more potent barriers. As they are administered on a first-come-first-served basis, at times they may hinder even the small quantities which the SSA countries supply. In addition to some sea products, global quotas affected a variety of goods, most importantly chromium, niobium and tantalum ores from Madagascar, Nigeria, Rwanda and Zaire. Another major mineral export of SSA, manganese from Congo, Gabon and Ghana, was subject to tariff quotas.[23] Details of these barriers are not readily available. However, it can be expected that, in a country like Japan, which is poor in natural resources, their main purpose would not be to curtail imports. Tariff quotas also covered leather from Tanzania and maize supplied by Zimbabwe. Textile fabrics, fibres, cordage and ropes from Burkina Faso, Kenya and Tanzania were subject to import authorization only. Imports of tobacco in Japan are virtually under the monopoly of the state. Hence tobacco supplied by Malawi and Zimbabwe fell under this constraint.

*The US market* Sugars, syrups and molasses worth over US$80 million were the main items encountering NTBs in the US (see Appendix Table A5.6). These products, originating from Congo, Madagascar, Malawi, Mauritius, Mozambique, Swaziland and Zimbabwe, were subject to country quotas as well as flexible import fees – the counterpart of the variable levies of the EC. Owing to the artificially high US domestic prices, exports were profitable for the SSA countries despite the import fees. Consequently, the country quotas were generally filled or highly utilized, implying that the quantitative restrictions were effective barriers in most cases.

The second major NTB in the US facing SSA was the MFA quotas on textile and clothing exports of Mauritius totalling US$60 million (in 1986). These quotas were also fully or highly utilized. However, while this was an effective constraint, some of the production in Mauritius might not have been there in the first place had there been no MFA restrictions on exports of major developing country suppliers of textiles and clothing.

Sudan's cotton exports, worth around US$200,000, were also subject to bilateral quotas. Furthermore, miscellaneous edible preparations with roughly the same value from Burkina Faso, Ivory Coast, Kenya, Mali and Swaziland were subject to global quotas with allocations. Kenya's exports of carnations and other cut flowers, totalling US$300,000, were subject to anti-dumping investigations and some of them came under anti-dumping duties. Finally, less than US$500,000 worth of wire rods of iron and steel from Zimbabwe triggered countervailing duties in the US.

*Change in the incidence of NTBs*

The incidence of NTBs on a country's exports might change over time as a result of (i) changes in the destination of exports – assuming differences in NTB usage across markets, (ii) changes in the commodity composition of exports, and (iii) changes in the trade practices within each market.

As observed in section 3, there were no significant changes in the commodity composition and destination of most SSA countries' exports over the period under consideration. However, the considerable intensification in the usage of NTBs by developed market economies in the 1970s and the 1980s (see Laird and Yeats 1988, and UNCTAD 1988) could have affected sub-Saharan Africa as well. The earliest NTB data comparable with the 1986 information reported in this paper pertain to 1981. Using these, NTB coverage ratios were computed for individual SSA countries in the EC, Japanese and US markets. For the great majority of the SSA countries, however, there was little or no change in the share of their exports covered by NTBs. The main exceptions were the oil-exporting SSA countries. Owing to the abolition of import surveillance on oil in the US, the shares of total exports from these six countries (Angola, Cameroon, Congo, Gabon, Nigeria and Zaire) that were subject to NTBs fell drastically.

The finding here, that SSA countries were not adversely affected in any significant way by the general intensification of NTB protection during the 1980s, is mainly due to the commodity composition of their exports. Labour-intensive manufactures from developing countries – which triggered most of the NTB action in developed market economies, and nevertheless achieved a dramatic expansion – constitute only a minute portion of SSA's exports.

The longer-term evolution of the incidence of the NTBs encountered by sub-Saharan Africa could not be studied owing to the fact that comparable information was not readily available on earlier periods. However, it can be safely stated that the increase in the relative share of agricultural products in SSA countries' exports coupled with a decline in non-fuel minerals and ores has made SSA more vulnerable to protection.

## 7 Summary and conclusions

Two main questions were addressed in this paper: (i) how did the incidence of protection encountered by SSA's exports in the major industrial market economies compare with that faced by all developing countries, and (ii) to what extent might protection in these markets have constrained SSA's export growth?

The findings on the first issue were conclusive. On the whole, SSA had a better deal in terms of both tariff and non-tariff protection in all three markets. This was in part due to special preferential treatment, especially in the EC, and in part a consequence of the commodity composition of its exports, heavy in primary goods.

As to the second question, there was no compelling evidence suggesting that protection in the major industrial markets has been a significant constraint on SSA's export growth. In fact, we found evidence to the contrary. Some SSA countries have benefited from protection restricting (MFA) – and in some cases virtually barring (CAP) – other developing countries' exports.

In case where SSA's exports were subject to 'hard core' barriers, they nevertheless had most often an advantage over other developing countries in market access. This finding rules out protection in the major markets as a cause of the poor *relative* export performance of SSA countries with respect to other developing countries. We do not, however, in any definite manner rule out the negative impact of protection on SSA's exports – most importantly, because we lack information on the actual application of the various licence and authorization requirements which affect the bulk of SSA's exports. This, and a more thorough investigation of the true value of the preferential treatment SSA countries receive for their major export products, especially in the EC, are among the issues for further research.

We have identified two other developments pertaining to the demand side which might have had some bearing on SSA's poor export growth. One was the increase in the share of agricultural products in SSA countries' exports coupled with the decline in non-fuel minerals and ores. This has made SSA potentially more vulnerable to protection. The second development was the slow growth in the EC, the traditional market for Africa. The growth in the US market for developing countries' exports was over twice that rate in Europe.

Finally, we would like to remind the reader that evaluations of the type undertaken in this paper necessarily have an *ex post* and myopic nature, which becomes evident in forward-looking endeavours such as the current Uruguay Round of multilateral trade negotiations under the auspices of the GATT. Apparently, SSA has very little to gain from multilateral trade liberalization in the short term; in fact it has much to lose on several accounts. For instance, if there were to be a substantial tariff reduction in tropical products (accompanied by an adjustment in GSP rates), ACP preferences in the EC would be severely eroded. Similarly, SSA would suffer in the short run if agricultural protection and subsidies in this market were to be reduced. The abolition of MFA might cut down some of the textile and clothing production in SSA. The simple fact remains, however, that protection in the major industrial market economies did not harass SSA countries in general, mainly because SSA did not have much to export in the first place. The longer-run interest of the SSA countries, like any other country for that matter, lies in a liberal, non-discriminatory and stable trade environment. In this context, as the industrially more advanced developing countries constitute an increasing share of this environment, improvements in the conditions of market access in these countries will also be of prominent importance for sub-Saharan Africa.

## Appendix

Table A5.1 *Export structure of SSA countries by main product category (%)*[a]

| *Country* | *Year*[b] | *Primary commodities* | | | | | *Manufactures* | *Others* |
|---|---|---|---|---|---|---|---|---|
| | | *Total* | *Food* | *Agric.* | *Fuels* | *Ores* | | |
| Angola | 1970 | 79 | 45 | 8 | 13 | 12 | 21 | — |
| | 1981 | 88 | 5 | — | 82 | — | 12 | — |
| Benin | 1970 | 89 | 71 | 18 | — | — | 11 | — |
| | 1982 | 53 | 36 | 12 | 4 | 1 | 46 | 1 |
| Burkina Faso | 1970 | 97 | 68 | 28 | — | 1 | 3 | — |
| | 1983 | 90 | 34 | 56 | — | — | 10 | — |
| Burundi | 1970 | 99 | 85 | 10 | — | 4 | 1 | — |
| | 1985 | 91 | 90 | 1 | — | — | 5 | 4 |
| Cameroon | 1970 | 92 | 63 | 19 | — | 10 | 8 | — |
| | 1987 | 73 | 40 | 16 | 18 | 9 | 18 | — |
| Cape Verde | 1970 | 94 | 81 | 2 | — | 11 | 6 | — |
| | 1984 | 97 | 84 | 1 | 3 | 9 | 3 | — |
| CAR | 1970 | 56 | 26 | 29 | — | — | 44 | — |
| | 1980 | 74 | 31 | 43 | — | — | 26 | — |
| Chad | 1970 | 95 | 24 | 71 | — | — | 2 | 3 |
| | 1975 | 92 | 16 | 67 | 8 | 1 | 8 | — |
| Congo | 1970 | 71 | 18 | 52 | 1 | — | 29 | — |
| | 1985 | 96 | 1 | 2 | 93 | — | 3 | — |

Table A5.1 *(cont.)*

| *Country* | *Year*[b] | *Primary commodities* | | | | | *Manufactures* | *Others* |
|---|---|---|---|---|---|---|---|---|
| | | *Total* | *Food* | *Agric.* | *Fuels* | *Ores* | | |
| Ethiopia | 1970 | 98 | 86 | 11 | 1 | 1 | 2 | — |
| | 1985 | 99 | 71 | 18 | 10 | — | 1 | — |
| Gabon | 1970 | 91 | 2 | 33 | 43 | 14 | 9 | — |
| | 1983 | 94 | — | 7 | 80 | 7 | 6 | — |
| Gambia | 1970 | 100 | 100 | — | — | — | — | — |
| | 1977 | 99 | 99 | — | — | — | — | 1 |
| Ghana | 1970 | 100 | 78 | 9 | — | 13 | — | — |
| | 1981 | 99 | 51 | 6 | 12 | 30 | 1 | — |
| Guinea-Bissau | 1970 | 98 | 94 | 4 | — | — | 2 | — |
| | 1980 | 87 | 85 | 2 | — | — | 8 | 4 |
| Ivory Coast | 1970 | 94 | 68 | 25 | 1 | 1 | 6 | — |
| | 1985 | 90 | 68 | 12 | 10 | — | 9 | 1 |
| Kenya | 1970 | 88 | 63 | 12 | 12 | 1 | 12 | — |
| | 1983 | 89 | 59 | 6 | 21 | 3 | 11 | — |
| Liberia | 1970 | 97 | 4 | 20 | — | 74 | 2 | 1 |
| | 1984 | 99 | 9 | 26 | — | 65 | — | 1 |
| Madagascar | 1970 | 93 | 79 | 5 | 4 | 5 | 7 | — |
| | 1986 | 91 | 81 | 3 | 2 | 5 | 8 | — |
| Malawi | 1970 | 96 | 88 | 8 | — | — | 3 | 1 |
| | 1983 | 96 | 96 | — | — | — | 4 | — |

| | | | | | | | | |
|---|---|---|---|---|---|---|---|---|
| Mali | 1970 | 90 | 65 | 24 | — | 1 | 10 | 1 |
| | 1982 | 97 | 40 | 57 | — | — | 2 | 1 |
| Mauritania | 1970 | 99 | 8 | 3 | — | 88 | 1 | — |
| | 1984 | 99 | 50 | — | — | 49 | — | 1 |
| Mauritius | 1970 | 98 | 98 | — | — | — | 2 | — |
| | 1983 | 70 | 69 | — | — | — | 30 | — |
| Mozambique | 1970 | 91 | 57 | 23 | 8 | 2 | 9 | — |
| | 1984 | 87 | 69 | 11 | 6 | 1 | 1 | 12 |
| Niger | 1970 | 96 | 91 | 5 | — | — | 3 | 1 |
| | 1981 | 98 | 16 | 1 | 1 | 80 | 2 | — |
| Nigeria | 1970 | 99 | 31 | 5 | 58 | 4 | 1 | — |
| | 1981 | 99 | 2 | — | 97 | — | — | 1 |
| Réunion | 1970 | 95 | 94 | — | — | 1 | 5 | — |
| | 1987 | 89 | 88 | — | — | 1 | 10 | — |
| Rwanda | 1970 | 99 | 61 | 3 | — | 35 | — | 1 |
| | 1980 | 100 | 80 | 10 | — | 10 | — | — |
| Senegal | 1970 | 81 | 65 | 4 | 3 | 9 | 19 | — |
| | 1981 | 80 | 27 | 2 | 37 | 14 | 20 | — |
| Seychelles | 1971 | 96 | 90 | 1 | — | 5 | 4 | 1 |
| | 1985 | 93 | 11 | — | 82 | — | 7 | — |
| Sierra Leone | 1970 | 40 | 16 | 1 | 3 | 20 | 60 | 1 |
| | 1983 | 71 | 33 | 1 | 4 | 34 | 29 | — |
| Somalia | 1970 | 94 | 86 | 8 | — | — | 5 | 1 |
| | 1981 | 100 | 98 | 2 | — | — | — | — |
| Sudan | 1970 | 100 | 24 | 74 | 1 | 1 | — | — |
| | 1981 | 99 | 59 | 36 | 4 | 1 | 1 | — |

Table A5.1 *(cont.)*

| *Country* | *Year*[b] | *Primary commodities* | | | | | *Manufactures* | *Others* |
|---|---|---|---|---|---|---|---|---|
| | | *Total* | *Food* | *Agric.* | *Fuels* | *Ores* | | |
| Tanzania | 1970 | 87 | 50 | 30 | 7 | 1 | 13 | — |
| | 1981 | 89 | 63 | 21 | — | 5 | 11 | — |
| Togo | 1970 | 94 | 67 | 2 | — | 25 | 6 | — |
| | 1981 | 85 | 26 | 6 | 1 | 52 | 15 | — |
| Uganda | 1970 | 100 | 68 | 22 | — | 9 | — | — |
| | 1976 | 100 | 90 | 7 | 1 | 2 | — | — |
| Zaire | 1970 | 93 | 12 | 3 | — | 78 | 7 | — |
| | 1978 | 93 | 29 | 8 | 1 | 55 | 5 | 2 |
| Zambia | 1970 | 100 | 1 | — | — | 99 | — | — |
| | 1982 | 93 | — | — | — | 93 | 3 | 4 |
| Zimbabwe | 1976 | 86 | 36 | 9 | 1 | 40 | 13 | — |
| | 1984 | 80 | 36 | 12 | 1 | 31 | 16 | 4 |

*Notes:*
[a] Due to rounding, the percentages do not always add up to 100.
[b] 1970 or the nearest year and the latest year available for each country.

*Source:* UNCTAD, Handbook of International Trade and Development Statistics, 1988, Table 4.1.

Table A5.2 *Export structure of SSA countries by main destination (%)*[a]

| *Country* | *Year*[b] | *Industrial market economies* | | | | *Developing countries* | | *Socialist countries* |
|---|---|---|---|---|---|---|---|---|
| | | *Total* | *EC* | *US*[c] | *Japan* | *Total* | *Africa* | *Total* |
| Angola | 1970 | 92 | 66 | 18 | 7 | 6 | 5 | — |
| | 1981 | 68 | 27 | 37 | 1 | 28 | 2 | 2 |
| Benin | 1970 | 81 | 66 | 5 | 10 | 19 | 18 | — |
| | 1981 | 69 | 56 | 1 | 9 | 24 | 20 | — |
| Burkina Faso | 1970 | 47 | 31 | — | 15 | 51 | 49 | 2 |
| | 1983 | 35 | 29 | 1 | 4 | 54 | 26 | 11 |
| Burundi | 1970 | 96 | 32 | 59 | 5 | 4 | 3 | — |
| | 1986 | 90 | 62 | 5 | 2 | 7 | 6 | — |
| Cameroon | 1970 | 86 | 73 | 10 | 3 | 10 | 8 | 4 |
| | 1987 | 78 | 68 | 7 | 1 | 20 | 18 | 2 |
| Cape Verde | 1975 | 96 | 79 | — | — | 4 | 4 | — |
| | 1984 | 50 | 46 | — | — | 50 | 50 | — |
| CAR | 1970 | 92 | 71 | — | 4 | 8 | 7 | — |
| | 1985 | 96 | 91 | — | — | 4 | 4 | — |
| Chad | 1970 | 71 | 71 | — | — | 29 | 29 | — |
| | 1982 | 65 | 63 | — | 2 | 28 | 28 | — |
| Congo | 1970 | 81 | 65 | 2 | — | 16 | 13 | 4 |
| | 1985 | 95 | 35 | 60 | — | 5 | 3 | — |
| Ethiopia | 1970 | 81 | 20 | 50 | 6 | 17 | 6 | 1 |
| | 1985 | 71 | 49 | 11 | 10 | 20 | 6 | 9 |

Table A5.2 *(cont.)*

| *Country* | *Year*[b] | *Industrial market economies* | | | | *Developing countries* | | *Socialist countries* |
|---|---|---|---|---|---|---|---|---|
| | | *Total* | *EC* | *US*[c] | *Japan* | *Total* | *Africa* | *Total* |
| Gabon | 1970 | 72 | 63 | 4 | 1 | 28 | 9 | 1 |
| | 1979 | 66 | 40 | 19 | 1 | 31 | — | 3 |
| Gambia | 1970 | 99 | 87 | — | — | 1 | 1 | — |
| | 1980 | 68 | 68 | — | — | 30 | 30 | — |
| Ghana | 1970 | 81 | 47 | 20 | 7 | 8 | 1 | 11 |
| | 1983 | 68 | 32 | 6 | 5 | 20 | 16 | 12 |
| Guinea | 1980 | 91 | 56 | 35 | — | 9 | 6 | — |
| | 1983 | 89 | 52 | 37 | — | 10 | 5 | — |
| Guinea-Bissau | 1970 | 94 | 94 | — | — | 7 | 3 | — |
| | 1981 | 83 | 62 | — | — | 8 | 8 | 10 |
| Ivory Coast | 1970 | 90 | 69 | 19 | 2 | 8 | 8 | 1 |
| | 1985 | 72 | 58 | 13 | 1 | 18 | 16 | 6 |
| Kenya | 1970 | 64 | 41 | 12 | 2 | 22 | 12 | 3 |
| | 1984 | 56 | 45 | 6 | 1 | 35 | 24 | 1 |
| Liberia | 1970 | 98 | 67 | 23 | 8 | 2 | 1 | — |
| | 1984 | 92 | 71 | 20 | 1 | 6 | 3 | 2 |
| Madagascar | 1970 | 70 | 43 | 23 | 3 | 27 | 20 | 1 |
| | 1986 | 85 | 58 | 15 | 11 | 9 | 4 | 5 |
| Malawi | 1970 | 77 | 65 | 4 | — | 21 | 19 | — |
| | 1986 | 88 | 58 | 10 | 7 | 12 | 11 | — |

| | | | | | | | | |
|---|---|---|---|---|---|---|---|---|
| Mali | 1970 | 29 | 25 | — | 4 | 63 | 62 | 2 |
| | 1979 | 76 | 71 | — | 3 | 24 | 24 | — |
| Mauritania | 1970 | 94 | 86 | 1 | 6 | 6 | 6 | — |
| | 1986 | 81 | 54 | — | 27 | 15 | 13 | 4 |
| Mauritius | 1970 | 98 | 69 | 26 | — | 2 | 1 | — |
| | 1986 | 94 | 75 | 18 | — | 5 | 4 | — |
| Mozambique | 1970 | 77 | 54 | 10 | 1 | 20 | 10 | — |
| | 1983 | 51 | 31 | 13 | 7 | 49 | 12 | . . |
| Niger | 1970 | 65 | 65 | — | — | 35 | 35 | — |
| | 1982 | 85 | 70 | — | 15 | 14 | 14 | — |
| Nigeria | 1970 | 89 | 71 | 14 | 1 | 8 | 1 | 3 |
| | 1981 | 90 | 34 | 51 | 2 | 11 | 3 | — |
| Réunion | 1970 | 97 | 96 | 1 | — | 3 | 1 | — |
| | 1987 | 93 | 89 | — | 3 | 7 | 7 | — |
| Rwanda | 1970 | 82 | 29 | 52 | — | 18 | 18 | — |
| | 1986 | 95 | 90 | 3 | 1 | 5 | 3 | — |
| Senegal | 1970 | 75 | 71 | — | 1 | 22 | 22 | — |
| | 1984 | 50 | 48 | — | 2 | 28 | 22 | — |
| Seychelles | 1975 | 29 | 14 | 14 | — | 76 | 14 | — |
| | 1984 | 16 | 5 | 7 | 3 | 85 | 11 | — |
| Sierra Leone | 1970 | 95 | 64 | 14 | 17 | 3 | 2 | 3 |
| | 1984 | 65 | 56 | 9 | — | 6 | 2 | — |
| Somalia | 1970 | 30 | 29 | 1 | — | 67 | 3 | 3 |
| | 1985 | 11 | 10 | — | — | 89 | 4 | — |
| Sudan | 1970 | 49 | 34 | 4 | 9 | 22 | 6 | 29 |
| | 1983 | 34 | 25 | 2 | 5 | 47 | 5 | 18 |

Table A5.2 *(cont.)*

| *Country* | *Year*[b] | *Industrial market economies* | | | | *Developing countries* | | *Socialist countries* |
|---|---|---|---|---|---|---|---|---|
| | | *Total* | *EC* | *US*[c] | *Japan* | *Total* | *Africa* | *Total* |
| Tanzania | 1970 | 60 | 39 | 11 | 6 | 34 | 10 | 5 |
| | 1985 | 71 | 58 | 3 | 4 | 24 | 5 | 2 |
| Togo | 1970 | 91 | 88 | — | 3 | 3 | 3 | 6 |
| | 1984 | 66 | 63 | 1 | 1 | 22 | 13 | 12 |
| Uganda | 1970 | 77 | 35 | 24 | 11 | 15 | 4 | 8 |
| | 1983 | 89 | 53 | 31 | 5 | 8 | 3 | — |
| Zaire | 1970 | 76 | 74 | 2 | — | 24 | 24 | — |
| | 1982 | 98 | 83 | 3 | 1 | 3 | 2 | — |
| Zambia | 1970 | 87 | 58 | — | 23 | 7 | 1 | 6 |
| | 1984 | 68 | 32 | 10 | 24 | 22 | 5 | 10 |

*Notes:*

[a] Due to rounding and data inconsistencies, the percentages do not always add up to 100.

[b] 1970 or the nearest year and the latest year available for each country.

[c] US and Canada

*Source:* UNCTAD, *Handbook of International Trade and Development Statistics*, 1987 and 1988, Table 3.4.

Table A5.3 *Arithmetic average of actual tariffs*[a] *on SSA countries' exports and that for all developing countries in corresponding products in the EC, Japan and the US (%)*

| *Exporter*[b] | *EC* | | *JAPAN* | | *US* | | *Exporter* | *EC* | | *JAPAN* | | *US* | |
|---|---|---|---|---|---|---|---|---|---|---|---|---|---|
| | *For the exporter* | *For all DCs* | *For the exporter* | *For all DCs* | *For the exporter* | *For all DCs* | | *For the exporter* | *For all DCs* | *For the exporter* | *For all DCs* | *For the exporter* | *For all DCs* |
| Angola | 0.0 | 1.4 | 0.0 | 0.0 | 0.3 | 1.1 | Mali* | 0.0 | 1.8 | 1.1 | 2.5 | 3.3 | 5.2 |
| Benin* | 0.0 | 1.5 | 2.3 | 2.3 | 1.6 | 3.2 | Mauritania* | 0.0 | 3.2 | 4.6 | 5.0 | 8.4 | 9.8 |
| Botswana | 0.0 | 1.9 | 0.8 | 0.8 | 5.7 | 6.8 | Mauritius | 0.1 | 1.9 | 4.6 | 4.6 | 5.9 | 7.8 |
| Burkina Faso* | 0.2 | 1.6 | 0.8 | 2.4 | 8.3 | 9.1 | Mozambique* | 0.2 | 1.6 | 0.8 | 0.8 | 1.3 | 3.7 |
| Burundi* | 0.0 | 1.6 | 0.0 | 0.0 | 3.5 | 3.7 | Namibia | . . | . . | . . | . . | 2.9 | 2.5 |
| Cameroon | 0.0 | 1.5 | 0.4 | 0.4 | 4.7 | 6.0 | Niger* | 0.0 | 1.4 | 0.0 | 0.0 | 3.0 | 4.6 |
| Cape Verde | 0.0 | 2.1 | . . | . . | 0.0 | 0.0 | Nigeria | 0.0 | 1.3 | 1.4 | 1.5 | 5.3 | 4.5 |
| CAR* | 0.0 | 1.9 | 0.0 | 0.0 | 2.4 | 4.2 | Réunion | . . | . . | . . | . . | . . | . . |
| Chad* | 0.0 | 1.2 | 0.0 | 0.0 | 31.3 | 31.3 | Rwanda* | 0.1 | 1.4 | 0.0 | 0.0 | 4.0 | 5.2 |
| Comoros* | 0.0 | 0.6 | 0.8 | 0.8 | 2.7 | 6.7 | Sao Tomé* | 0.0 | 1.5 | . . | . . | 6.3 | 7.5 |
| Congo | 0.0 | 1.3 | 0.0 | 0.0 | 0.1 | 2.4 | Senegal | 0.1 | 2.3 | 2.5 | 2.6 | 4.1 | 5.7 |
| Djibouti* | 0.0 | 1.3 | 2.5 | 5.0 | 3.0 | 4.9 | Seychelles | 0.0 | 2.0 | 2.5 | 3.3 | 6.7 | 8.5 |
| Ethiopia* | 0.2 | 1.4 | 1.7 | 1.7 | 5.4 | 4.2 | Sierra Leone* | 0.0 | 2.9 | 3.0 | 3.0 | 4.9 | 5.7 |

Table A5.3 *(cont.)*

| *Exporter*[b] | *EC* | | *Japan* | | *US* | | *Exporter* | *EC* | | *Japan* | | *US* | |
|---|---|---|---|---|---|---|---|---|---|---|---|---|---|
| | *For the exporter* | *For all DCs* | *For the exporter* | *For all DCs* | *For the exporter* | *For all DCs* | | *For the exporter* | *For all DCs* | *For the exporter* | *For all DCs* | *For the exporter* | *For all DCs* |
| Eq. Guinea* | 0.0 | 1.1 | . . | . . | 19.8 | 19.8 | Somalia* | 0.0 | 2.2 | 0.0 | 0.0 | 7.4 | 8.4 |
| Gabon | 0.0 | 1.4 | 0.0 | 0.0 | 4.3 | 3.6 | Sudan* | 0.2 | 1.4 | 0.4 | 0.5 | 7.8 | 8.4 |
| Gambia* | 0.0 | 2.9 | 3.0 | 3.8 | 0.0 | 1.8 | Swaziland | 0.2 | 2.9 | 0.0 | 0.0 | 5.4 | 7.0 |
| Ghana | 0.0 | 1.9 | 0.6 | 0.6 | 2.3 | 3.9 | Tanzania | 0.1 | 1.3 | 0.8 | 0.9 | 1.2 | 1.9 |
| Guinea* | 0.0 | 1.7 | 5.0 | 6.3 | 2.1 | 3.3 | Togo* | 0.0 | 1.6 | 0.0 | 0.0 | 2.3 | 4.1 |
| Guinea-Bissau* | 0.0 | 2.9 | 2.5 | 4.1 | 0.3 | 3.8 | Uganda* | 0.3 | 1.5 | 0.0 | 0.0 | 5.4 | 5.8 |
| Ivory Coast | 0.1 | 2.3 | 1.1 | 1.1 | 4.2 | 6.4 | Zaire | 0.0 | 1.5 | 0.0 | 0.2 | 1.1 | 2.3 |
| Kenya | 0.0 | 2.2 | 1.3 | 1.4 | 3.8 | 6.3 | Zambia | 0.1 | 1.7 | 0.0 | 0.0 | 0.1 | 2.0 |
| Lesotho* | 0.1 | 2.1 | 0.0 | 5.6 | 11.6 | 12.2 | Zimbabwe | 0.1 | 1.7 | 1.1 | 1.2 | 7.0 | 7.8 |
| Liberia | 0.0 | 1.5 | 1.3 | 1.3 | 3.6 | 4.6 | | | | | | | |
| Madagascar | 0.0 | 1.4 | 0.9 | 0.9 | 2.2 | 2.6 | | | | | | | |
| Malawi* | 0.0 | 1.4 | 0.0 | 0.0 | 4.5 | 5.0 | | | | | | | |

*Notes:*

[a] Actual tariffs taking into account preferential rates.

[b] * = Least developed countries (LLDCs) according to the UN.

*Source:* GATT Tariff Study computer files.

Table A5.4 *SSA's products affected by NTBs in the EC by product and exporter*

| *Product*[a] | *Exporter*[b] | *Value*[c] *(US$m)* | *NTB*[d] |
|---|---|---|---|
| Meat, fresh, chilled or frozen | Botswana, Djibouti, Ivory Coast, Madagascar Swaziland, Uganda | 43.1 | Variable levy, licence, tariff quota, surveillance licence |
| Fish, fresh, chilled or frozen | Cape Verde, Gabon, Ghana, Ivory Coast, Madagascar, Mauritania, Mauritius, Senegal, Seychelles | 13.0 | Reference prices |
| Shellfish, fresh, frozen salted, etc. | Benin, Cameroon, Eq. Guinea, Gabon, Gambia, Ghana, Guinea-Bissau, Ivory Coast, Kenya, Liberia, Madagascar, Mauritania, Mozambique, Senegal, Seychelles, Sierra Leone, Somalia, Tanzania, Togo | 59.5 | Reference prices, surveillance licence |
| Cut flowers | Ethiopia, Ivory Coast, Kenya, Mauritius, Zimbabwe | 15.3 | Seasonal tariffs, community surveillance |
| Vegetables, fresh or chilled | Burkina Faso, Cameroon Ethiopia, Ivory Coast, Kenya, Mali, Mauritius, Niger, Nigeria, Senegal, Sudan, Togo, Zaire | 31.3 | Quotas n.e.s.,[e] reference prices, seasonal tariffs, seasonal quota, surveillance licence |

Table A5.4 *(cont).*

| *Product*[a] | *Exporter*[b] | *Value*[c] *(US$m)* | *NTB*[d] |
|---|---|---|---|
| Vegetables, provisionally preserved | Kenya, Madagascar, Swaziland | 0.1 | Licence, quotas, surveillance licence |
| Dried, dehydrated, etc. Vegetables | Swaziland | 0.2 | Surveillance licence |
| Dried leguminious vegetables | Kenya, Tanzania, Zimbabwe | 4.2 | Licence, surveillance licence |
| Roots | Cameroon, Ivory Coast, Nigeria, Tanzania | 1.0 | Tariff quota, variable levy, licence quota by country |
| Dates, bananas, coconuts, etc., fresh or dried | Benin, Cameroon, Guinea, Ivory Coast, Madagascar, Togo | 86.3 | Quotas n.e.s. |
| Citrus fruits, fresh or dried | Burkina Faso, Burundi, Cameroon, Ivory Coast, Kenya, Mozambique, Sierra Leone, Swaziland, Zaire, Zimbabwe | 9.2 | Seasonal tariffs, reference prices |
| Grapes, fresh or dried | Ivory Coast | 0.1 | Seasonal tariffs, reference prices |
| Other nuts, fresh or dried | Malawi | 0.1 | Reference prices |
| Berries, fresh | Ethiopia, Ivory Coast, Kenya, Zimbabwe | 1.1 | Seasonal tariffs, reference prices |

| | | | |
|---|---|---|---|
| Other fruit, fresh | Ethiopia, Ivory Coast, Kenya, Madagascar, Mauritius, Senegal Zimbabwe | 3.3 | Reference prices, seasonal quota |
| Maize | Zambia | 0.7 | Variable levy, licence |
| Rice | Togo | 0.1 | Variable levy, licence |
| Buckwheat, millet, other cereals | Kenya, Malawi, Sudan | 0.4 | Variable levy, licence |
| Cereal groats and cereal meal | Sudan | 0.1 | Variable levy, licence |
| Seeds | Kenya, Madagascar, Tanzania, Zimbabwe | 0.6 | Licence, surveillance licence |
| Other prepared, preserved meat | Botswana, Ethiopia, Kenya, Zimbabwe | 21.6 | Variable levy, licence |
| Prepared, preserved fish | Cape Verde, Ivory Coast, Senegal | 73.0 | Quotas n.e.s, surveillance licence, reference prices |
| Shellfish, prepared, preserved | Gambia, Ivory Coast, Senegal, Togo | 0.4 | Surveillance licence, reference prices |
| Beet and cane sugar | Congo, Ivory Coast, Kenya, Madagascar, Malawi, Mauritius, Swaziland, Tanzania, Zimbabwe | 271.0 | Licence, variable levy |
| Molasses | Ethiopia, Ivory Coast, Kenya, Madagascar, Mauritius, Mozambique, Senegal, Somalia, Sudan, Tanzania | 35.5 | Variable levy, licence |
| Sugar confectionery | Mauritius | 0.1 | Quotas n.e.s., variable component |
| Chocolate and other preparations containing cocoa | Ivory Coast | 4.6 | Variable component |

Table A5.4 *(cont)*.

| *Product*[a] | *Exporter*[b] | *Value*[c] *(US$m)* | *NTB*[d] |
|---|---|---|---|
| Macaroni, spaghetti, etc. | Ivory Coast | 0.1 | Variable component, surveillance licence |
| Tapioca and sago | Madagascar | 0.3 | Variable component |
| Vegetables, prepared, preserved | Cameroon, Ethiopia, Ivory Coast Kenya, Madagascar | 2.0 | Quota by country, surveillance licence, licence |
| Jams, marmalades, etc. | Kenya, Malawi, Zimbabwe | 0.5 | Variable levy, licence |
| Fruit otherwise prepared or preserved | Ivory Coast, Kenya, Lesotho, Swaziland, Uganda, Zimbabwe | 28.5 | Variable levy, licence, surveillance licence |
| Fruit juices | Ivory Coast, Kenya | 1.4 | Surveillance licence, variable levy |
| Extracts, etc. of coffee, tea, mate | Ivory Coast, Tanzania | 0.8 | Surveillance licence |
| Food preparations, not elsewhere specified | Ivory Coast, Nigeria, Senegal | 0.3 | Variable component, surveillance licence |
| Wine | Comoros, Nigeria | 0.1 | Licence, reference prices |
| Spirits | Madagascar | 0.1 | Quotas n.e.s. |
| Residuals derived from cereals or leguminous vegetables | Benin, Cameroon, Gabon, Ivory Coast, Liberia, Nigeria, Togo, Uganda, Zaire | 8.0 | Variable levy, licence |
| Residuals from sugar, starch, etc. manufacture | Liberia | 0.1 | Licence |
| Other vegetable products | Ghana, Guinea, Ivory Coast | 0.9 | Licence |

| | | | |
|---|---|---|---|
| Matallic ores | Mozambique, Zaire | 0.1 | Surveillance licence |
| Petroleum oils and oils obtained from bituminous minerals, crude | Cameroon, Congo, Gabon, Nigeria | 2,745.3 | Quotas n.e.s. |
| Petroleum oils and oils obtained from bituminous minerals, other than crude | Angola, Cameroon, Gabon, Kenya, Nigeria, Sierra Leone, Tanzania | 62.0 | Quotas n.e.s., surveillance licence |
| Petroleum gases | Angola, Nigeria | 3.6 | Quotas n.e.s. |
| Vaccines, toxins, etc. | Senegal | 0.2 | Surveillance licence |
| Medicaments | Djibouti, Kenya, Nigeria | 0.1 | Surveillance licence |
| Woven fabrics of man-made fibres | Togo | 0.1 | Quotas n.e.s. |
| Wool | Kenya | 0.1 | Surveillance licence |
| Cotton, not carded or combed | Mali, Sudan, Tanzania | 3.1 | Surveillance licence |
| Cotton yarn | Cameroon, Ivory Coast, Senegal, Sudan, Tanzania, Zimbabwe | 7.3 | Surveillance licence |
| Terry towelling of cotton | Cameroon | 1.4 | Surveillance licence |
| Other woven fabrics of cotton | Benin, Cameroon, CAR, Chad, Eq. Guinea, Ivory Coast, Liberia, Madagascar, Malawi, Rwanda, Senegal, Zambia, Zimbabwe | 36.7 | Quotas n.e.s., surveillance licence |
| Yarn of man-made fibres | Mauritius | 0.1 | Surveillance licence |
| Woven fabrics of man-made fibres | Ivory Coast, Mauritius, Togo, Zimbabwe | 0.8 | Surveillance licence, quotas n.e.s. |
| Other vegetable textile fibres | Kenya, Tanzania | 0.3 | Surveillance licence |
| Woven fabrics of jute | Kenya | 0.1 | Surveillance licence, quotas n.e.s. |

Table A5.4 *(cont).*

| *Product*[a] | *Exporter*[b] | *Value*[c] *(US$m)* | *NTB*[d] |
|---|---|---|---|
| Twine, cordage, ropes, etc. | Kenya, Madagascar, Tanzania | 0.5 | Surveillance licence |
| Gloves, mittens, etc. | Mauritius | 1.4 | Surveillance licence, quotas n.e.s. |
| Under garments, knitted or crocheted | Djibouti, Ivory Coast, Mauritius Senegal, Tanzania, Zimbabwe | 3.3 | Surveillance licence, quotas n.e.s. |
| Outer garments, knitted or crocheted | Gambia, Ivory Coast, Lesotho, Malawi, Mauritius, Zimbabwe | 24.9 | Surveillance licence, quotas n.e.s. |
| Men's and boys' outer garments | Burkina Faso, Chad, Ivory Coast, Kenya, Lesotho, Mauritania, Mauritius, Niger, Zambia, Zimbabwe | 7.4 | Surveillance licence, quotas n.e.s. |
| Women's, girls' and infants' outer garments | Cameroon, Congo, Ivory Coast, Kenya, Liberia, Malawi, Mali, Mauritius, Sudan, Zimbabwe | 2.8 | Surveillance licence, quotas n.e.s. |
| Men's and boys' under garments | Liberia, Mauritania, Mauritius, Tanzania | 6.5 | Surveillance licence, quotas n.e.s. |
| Women's, girls' and infants' under garments | Zimbabwe | 0.2 | Surveillance licence, quotas n.e.s. |
| Bed linen, table linen, curtains, etc. | Cameroon | 0.8 | Surveillance licence, quotas n.e.s. |
| Sacks and bags | Ethiopia, Ivory Coast, Mauritius | 0.6 | Surveillance licence, quotas n.e.s. |

| | | | |
|---|---|---|---|
| Footwear with rubber, etc. soles | Senegal | 0.1 | Community surveillance, surveillance licence |
| Footwear with leather soles | Burkina Faso, Congo, Ethiopia, Kenya, Liberia, Rwanda, Senegal, Zimbabwe | 0.4 | Community surveillance, surveillance licence |
| Footwear with wood or cork soles | Djibouti | 0.1 | Community surveillance |
| Footwear with soles of other materials | Mauritius | 0.1 | Community surveillance |
| Parts of footwear | Burkina Faso | 0.1 | Community surveillance |
| Precious and semi-precious stones | Botswana, Burundi, CAR, Congo, Gambia, Ghana, Guinea, Ivory Coast, Lesotho, Liberia, Madagascar, Mali, Mauritius, Nigeria, Sierra Leone, Tanzania, Togo, Zaire, Zambia | 362.0 | Surveillance licence |
| Ferro-alloys | Zimbabwe | 24.5 | Surveillance licence |
| Iron or steel coils | Zaire | 0.1 | Community surveillance, price surveillance |
| Bars and rods of iron or steel | Togo | 0.1 | Retrospective surveillance |
| Angels, shapes, etc. of iron or steel | Zimbabwe | 1.2 | Retrospective surveillance, community surveillance, price surveillance |
| Tubes and pipes of iron and steel | Congo, Ivory Coast | 0.3 | Surveillance licence |
| Stranded wire, cables, etc. of iron or steel | Congo, Ivory Coast, Uganda | 0.1 | Surveillance licence |
| Copper | Benin, Cameroon, Congo, Gabon, Ivory Coast, Kenya, Senegal, Zaire, Zambia, Zimbabwe | 84.2 | Surveillance licence |

Table A5.4 *(cont)*.

| *Product*[a] | *Exporter*[b] | *Value*[c] *(US$m)* | *NTB*[d] |
|---|---|---|---|
| Nickel | Tanzania, Zaire, Zambia, Zimbabwe | 4.2 | Surveillance licence |
| Electrical goods | Chad, Liberia | 0.1 | Surveillance licence |
| Sound equipment | Gabon | 0.1 | Surveillance licence |
| Transmission and reception equipment | Cameroon, Congo, Gabon, Guinea, Ivory Coast, Madagascar, Mali, Niger, Senegal | 0.4 | Quotas n.e.s. |
| Electrical apparatus | Benin | 0.1 | Surveillance licence |
| Insulated electric wire, cable, etc. | Cameroon | 0.1 | Surveillance licence |
| Motor vehicles | Cameroon, CAR, Congo, Niger, Nigeria, Togo | 1.5 | Surveillance licence |
| Parts and accessories of motor vehicles | Angola, Cameroon, Congo, Djibouti, Gabon, Ivory Coast, Madagascar, Mail Nigeria, Senegal, Zimbabwe | 0.5 | Surveillance licence |

| | | | |
|---|---|---|---|
| Trucks and tractors | Ivory Coast | 0.1 | Surveillance licence |
| Flying machines | Burkina Faso, Gabon, Ivory Coast, Mali, Senegal | 1.2 | Surveillance licence |
| Ships and boats | Benin, Ivory Coast, Liberia | 13.4 | Quotas n.e.s. |
| Photographic equipment | Zambia | 0.1 | Surveillance licence |
| Medical instruments | Cameroon, Congo, Djibouti, Gabon, Ivory Coast | 0.1 | Surveillance licence |
| Watches | Benin, Mauritius | 0.5 | Quotas n.e.s. |
| Watch movements | Mauritius | 2.5 | Quotas n.e.s. |
| Other clock and watch parts | Mauritius | 0.1 | Quotas n.e.s. |

*Notes:*

[a] EC import classification at the 4-digit aggregation level.

[b] Exporters with US$10,000 or more in a single product within the aggregate product group.

[c] Import values for 1984 in the aggregate product group from all SSA exporters.

[d] NTBs covering one or more products/exporters concerning the aggregate product group.

*Source:* UNCTAD Data Base on Trade Control Measures.

Table A5.5 *SSA's products affected by NTBs in Japan by product and exporter*

| *Product*[a] | *Exporter* | *Value*[b] *(US$m)* | *NTB*[c] |
|---|---|---|---|
| Live animals, n.e.s. | Botswana, Ethiopia, Ghana, Kenya, Liberia, Senegal, Seychelles, Zimbabwe, Togo, Tanzania | 0.5 | Global quota (unallocated), import authorization |
| Aquarium fish | CAR, Kenya | 0.1 | Import authorization |
| Aji, frozen (excluding fillets) | Mauritania, Senegal | 0.1 | Global quota (unallocated), import authorization |
| Other fresh, chilled or frozen fish (excluding fillets) | Djibouti, Ghana, Gambia, Mauritania, Mauritius, Namibia, Senegal, Seychelles, Sierra Leone | 22.0 | Import authorization |
| Fish, salted or dried, n.e.s. | Reunion, Senegal, Seychelles | 0.1 | Global quota (unallocated), import authorization |
| Shrimps, prawns and lobster, fresh, chilled or frozen | Guinea, Madagascar, Mozambique, Nigeria, Senegal, Tanzania | 44.5 | Import authorization |

| | | | |
|---|---|---|---|
| Cuttle fish and squid, fresh, chilled or frozen | Ghana, Mauritania, Nigeria, Senegal | 21.2 | Global quota (unallocated), import authorization |
| Octopus, fresh, chilled or frozen | Guinea Bissau, Mauritania | 41.8 | Import authorization |
| Bekko | Kenya, Seychelles, Somalia, Tanzania | 0.2 | Global quota (unallocated), import authorization |
| Shells | Comoros, Kenya, Tanzania | 0.1 | Import authorization |
| Other live plants | Ivory Coast, Liberia, Madagascar | 0.1 | Licence |
| Dried vegetables, n.e.s. | Zimbabwe | 0.1 | Global quota (unallocated) |
| Maize | Zimbabwe | 0.4 | Tariff quota |
| Seaweeds | Madagascar | 0.1 | Import authorization |
| Fish liver oil | Ivory Coast, Senegal | 0.2 | Import authorization |
| Bacon | Ethiopia | 0.1 | Import authorization |
| Flours and meal, not for human consumption | Ethiopia | 0.3 | Import authorization |
| Tobacco | Malawi, Zimbabwe | 12.5 | Sole importing agency |
| Manganese | Congo, Gabon, Ghana | 8.8 | Tariff quota |
| Chromium, niobium and tantalum | Madagascar, Nigeria, Rwanda, Zaire | 5.5 | Global quota (unallocated) |
| Leather, tanned | Tanzania | 0.1 | Tariff quota, global quota (unallocated) |

Table A5.5 *(cont.)*

| *Product*[a] | *Exporter* | *Value*[b] *(US$m)* | *NTB*[c] |
|---|---|---|---|
| Textile fabrics, fibers, cordage and ropes | Burkina Faso, Kenya, Tanzania | 2.0 | Import authorization |
| Worked ivory, etc. | Congo, Kenya, Sudan | 0.1 | Global quota (unallocated) |
| Collections, zoological, botanical, anatomical, etc.[d] | Kenya | 5.9 | Global quota (unallocated) |

*Notes:*

[a] According to Japan's tariff classification. Some related items are aggregated for the presentation.

[b] Total import values for 1984.

[c] NTBs in 1986.

[d] In more recent years extremely low trade owing to prohibition.

[e] n.e.s. = not elsewhere specified.

*Source:* UNCTAD Data Base on Trade Control Measures.

Table A5.6 *SSA's products affected by NTBs in the US by product and exporter*

| *Product*[a] | *Exporter* | *Value*[b] *(US$m)* | *NTB*[c] |
|---|---|---|---|
| Sugars, syrups and molasses | Congo, Madagascar, Malawi, Mauritius, Mozambique, Swaziland, Zimbabwe | 82.0 | Bilateral quotas, flexible import fees |
| Edible preparations, n.e.s. | Burkina Faso, Ivory Coast, Kenya, Mali, Swaziland | 0.2 | Global quota (ailocated) |
| Fresh cut carnations | Kenya | 0.2 | Anti-dumping investigations |
| Fresh cut flowers, n.e.s. | Kenya | 0.1 | Anti-dumping investigations and anti-dumping duties |
| Raw cotton (short and long staple) | Sudan | 0.2 | Bilateral quotas |
| Textiles and clothing[d] | Mauritius | 59.9[e] | MFA quotas |
| Wire rods of iron and steel | Zimbabwe | 0.4 | Countervailing duty investigations and countervailing duties |

*Notes:*

[a] According to the US tariff classification. Some related items are aggregated for the presentation.

[b] Total import values for 1984.

[c] NTBs in 1986.

[d] All textile and clothing items subject to MFA.

[e] 1986 MFA import value.

*Source:* UNCTAD Data Base on Trade Control Measures.

## Notes

The authors gratefully acknowledge valuable comments by Bela Balassa, Paula Holmes, Sam Laird, Paul Meo and Alexander Yeats on an earlier draft.

The views expressed in this paper are those of the authors and do not necessarily reflect the views of the institutions to which they are affiliated.

1 SSA is broadly defined as all countries in the continent excluding the North African countries and South Africa. The 47 SSA countries under study are listed in Table 5.6.

2 Tables 5.1 and 5.2 are based on partner country import statistics. This gives a more accurate profile since import data of the OECD countries – which constitute the major market – are considerably more reliable and up to date. Yeats (1989a) found that, especially in crude oil, cocoa and coffee – which are under cartels – many SSA countries under-report their exports by a large margin. Furthermore, in many cases the most recent data pertain to 1983 (see Appendix Tables A5.1 and A5.2). There are two major shortcomings, however, in using partner country import statistics. One is that the data are in c.i.f., rather than f.o.b., prices – including freight and insurance. Secondly, owing to non-reporting centrally planned economies and poorly reporting developing countries, the actual share of industrial market economies is overstated.

3 Appendix Tables A5.1 and A5.2, which give information for individual SSA countries, are based on these countries' own export data – in contrast to Tables 5.1 and 5.2 in the main text which use partner country import statistics. This is due to the fact that, at an individual level, for some SSA countries, non-reporting centrally planned economies and some poorly reporting developing countries are relatively important markets. It these cases, a tabulation based on partner countries would yield an even more inaccurate picture.

4 Certain processed goods do not fall into the conventional definition of manufactures. Conversely, items such as precious and semi-precious stones are captured as manufactures (see, e.g., Sierra Leone in Appendix Table A5.1).

5 Nevertheless, there are tariff 'peaks', especially on products of special export interest for developing countries, such as textiles and clothing (see Erzan and Karsenty 1989).

6 See, also, Finger and Laird (1987), Nogues *et al.* (1986) and Olechowski (1988).

7 This was probably a major reason why tariff cuts in products of particular interest for developing countries did not achieve the same depth.

8 Of the 42 LLDCs according to the UN, 25 are in SSA (denoted by

* in Table 5.6). Mozambique received this status in 1988. In addition to this list, both the EC and the US treat Botswana, Cape Verde and Tanzania (also the Seychelles in the EC) as LLDCs. However, Mauritania in the EC scheme and Ethiopia, Mauritania, Mozambique and Sao Tomé in the US scheme do not have LLDC status.

9 The NTB data used in this section pertain to 1986 and 1981 (for comparison). The base year for the data on trade and tariffs, on the other hand, is not always the same. The apparent inconsistency stems from the use of various specially designed computer programs which cannot easily accommodate year-to-year changes in the product classifications of the markets studied.

10 According to GATT sources, in 1986, 58 per cent of ACP imports in the EC had duty-free treatment under MFN and another 41 per cent were admitted duty free under the Lomé Convention. At the same time, 9 per cent of these imports were eligible for GSP treatment, implying full exemption or reduced tariffs.

11 In the US, a number of developing countries have 'graduated' from GSP beneficiary status. Furthermore, exceeding 'competitive need limits', some beneficiaries are temporarily disqualified concerning certain products.

12 Computations by Laird and Yeats (1989) corroborate our figures on the aggregate control group of all developing countries. Confining their analysis to 'hard core' NTBs in 1986 facing non-fuel exports of developing countries in the OECD markets, they arrived at 18 per cent for the frequency ratio and 21 per cent for trade coverage.

13 Variable levies are used to maintain an artifically high guaranteed domestic price in the face of fluctuating international market prices.

14 Arithmetic tariff averages in the EC for fourteen SSA countries were non-zero, yet a fraction of 1 per cent (see Appendix Table A5.3). This was due to a handful of items and seasonal tariffs on some fruits. In most of these cases, SSA enjoyed some preference margin over other developing countries.

15 These items, which constitute roughly 10 per cent of tariff lines in the EC (see Erzan and Karsenty 1989), are excluded from the tariff averages.

16 Apart from the two OPEC members (Gabon and Nigeria) and Ethiopia and Namibia, all SSA countries were beneficiaries of the US GSP scheme.

17 Although the tariff averages were limited to the same products for comparison, differences in the trade weights used (the country's export basket versus overall trade weights of developing countries in that market) generated this result concerning weighted averages.

18 Even the most generous US scheme for developing countries, the

Caribbean Basin Initiative (CBI), excludes textiles and clothing. The only exception is for imports under the off-shore assembly provision 807, some of which enter the US duty free (see World Bank 1988).

19 NTB coverage ratios reported in Table 5.6 for individual SSA countries are not fully comparable with the aggregates given in Tables 5.4 and 5.5 owing to the fact that the underlying import values pertain to different years (1986 versus 1984). Another difference concerning the EC is that Table 5.6 pertains to NTBs applied uniformly by the Community, leaving out those NTBs used only by some member state(s).

20 Not accounted for in Table 5.6, which pertains to NTBs applied uniformly by the Community.

21 Defined at the 4-digit aggregation level of EC's import classification – which is at this level identical with the CCCN.

22 The list of NTBs given in Table A5.4 relates to one or more – not necessarily all – products in the product group. Similarly, not necessarily all exporters listed are affected.

23 This reflected the general transition in the Japanese foreign trade regime from global quotas to tariff quotas since the mid-1980s.

## References

Cable, V. (1988), 'Tropical products', in M. Finger and A. Olechowski (eds), *The Uruguay Round: A Handbook on the Multilateral Trade Negotiations*, The World Bank, Washington DC, pp. 171–9.

Erzan, R. and Karsenty, G. (1989), 'Products facing high tariffs in major developed market economy countries: An area of priority for developing countries in the Uruguay Round?' *UNCTAD Review*, 1, pp. 51–73.

Erzan, R., Kuwahara, H., Marchese, S. and Vossenaar, R. (1989), 'The profile of protection in developing countries', *UNCTAD Review*, 1, pp. 29–49.

Finger, M. and Laird, S. (1987), 'Protection in developed and developing countries: An overview', *Journal of World Trade Law*, 21, pp. 9–23.

GATT (1980), *The Tokyo Round of Multilateral Trade Negotiations: II Supplementary Report*, Geneva.

Kleiman, E. (1977), 'Heirs to colonial trade', *Journal of Development Economics*, 4, pp. 93–103.

Laird, S. and Yeats, A. (1988), 'Trends in non-tariff barriers of developed countries: 1966 to 1986', *PPR Working Papers*, No. 137, The World Bank, Washington DC.

Laird, S. and Yeats, A. (1989), 'Quantitative methods for trade barrier analysis', Macmillan, London; Prentice Hall, New York: (forthcoming).

Nogues, J., Olechowski, A. and Winters, A. (1986), 'The extent of non-tariff barriers to imports of industrial countries', *The World Bank Economic Review*, 1, Washington, DC.

OECD (1987), *National Policies and Agricultural Trade*, Organisation for Economic Cooperation and Development, Paris.

Olechowski, A. (1988), 'Non-tariff barriers to trade', in M. Finger and A. Olechowski (eds), *The Uruguay Round: A Handbook on the Multilateral Trade Negotiations*, The World Bank, Washington, DC, pp. 121–6.

Svedberg, P. (1988), 'The export performance of sub-Saharan Africa: 1970–1985', Institute for International Economic Studies, Seminar Paper No. 409, Stockholm.

Svedberg, P. (1981), 'Colonial enforcement of foreign direct investment', The *Manchester School*, 49, pp. 21–38.

UNCTAD (1968), *The Kennedy Round Estimated Effects on Tariff Barriers* (TD/6/Rev.1), New York.

UNCTAD (1982), *Assessment of the Results of the Multilateral Trade Negotiations* (TD/B/778/Rev.1), New York.

UNCTAD (1988), 'Problems of Protectionism and Structural Adjustment' (TD/B/1081) and (TD/B/1160), Geneva.

UNCTAD (1989), 'Operation and effects of the generalized system of preferences' (TD/B/C.5/109), New York.

World Bank (1988), *The Caribbean: Export Preferences and Performance*, Washington DC.

Yeats, A. (1988), 'The escalation of trade barriers', in M. Finger and A. Olechowski (eds), *The Uruguay Round: A Handbook on the Multilateral Trade Negotiations*, The World Bank, Washington DC, pp. 110–20.

Yeats, A. (1989a), 'On the accuracy of economic observations: Implications of the quality of sub-Saharan African trade statistics', *PPR Working Paper* 307, The World Bank, Washington, DC.

Yeats, A. (1989b), 'Developing countries' exports of manufactures: Past and future implications of shifting patterns of comparative advantage', *The Developing Economies*, 27, pp. 109–45.

6

# African trade policy and multilateral negotiations

Vincent Cable

The principal question that this paper addresses is how sub-Saharan Africa can review its trade policies in the context of the international trade system so that it can help retrieve the losses of the past two decades and achieve acceptable rates of growth. The attempt to answer this question is approached in three steps. First, from the general picture of Africa's post-independence trade performance, we derive what Africa's priorities should be in its international trade. Second, we look at Africa's involvement in, and perception of, the multilateral trade negotiations. Third, we look at the main issues in the current round of multilateral trade negotiations (MTNs) and Africa's interests in relation to them.

## 1 Sub-Saharan Africa's priorities in international trade negotiations

For a majority of sub-Saharan African countries, the main priority is to undertake domestic policies that will bring their per capita production of tradables at least back to the levels that were achieved in the late 1960s. This is the focus of the economic reforms in which almost all SSA countries are currently engaged, either on their own initiative or as part of programmes agreed with multilateral institutions such as the International Monetary Fund (IMF) and the World Bank. The evidence that is emerging from these reforms indicates that, for most countries, the positive results will be long term. The issue here is whether the objectives and possible results of multilateral trade negotiations – in particular, improved market access for African exports – can serve as an incentive to persist with economic reforms.

In the short run, Africa's main external trade priorities lie in better and more stable returns from traditional export earnings. The issues of terms of trade and earnings stabilization are addressed not in the General Agreement on Tariffs and Trade (GATT); but rather through methods such as commodity buffer stock and export quota agreements, as well as earnings stabilization programmes within the Lomé convention (Stabex), or the compensatory and Contingency Financing Facility in the IMF.

If reforms are successful, however, and increased tradable output is produced, this will in the short run involve more exports of traditional commodities: in 1987, no less than 90 per cent of Africa's exports were primary commodities, a proportion that has grown from 80 per cent in 1970. For those products where African producers – taken as a whole – are the major suppliers, the effect of improving supply performance could be to aggravate the problem of declining terms of trade. Where price elasticity of demand is low, incremental supplies from major suppliers could lead to low, or even negative, earnings growth. One estimate, based on available elasticity and market share estimates, suggests that 50–60 per cent of sub-Saharan Africa's earnings from agricultural exports – coffee, cocoa, groundnut oil, sisal, tea and sugar – could suffer from this 'fallacy of composition', such that export volume increases would definitely result in earnings decline (Godfrey 1985). There are ways in which multilateral trade negotiations could help alleviate this problem directly if, for example, total import demand in consuming countries could be raised by the removal of trade barriers (sugar, vegetable oils, beef) or if heavy excise taxes were to be reduced (coffee, tea, cocoa, spices, tobacco).

In the long term, the most important contribution trade negotiations can make is to provide an incentive to diversify African exports from low to high price elasticity goods (non-traditional agricultural items, manufactures including raw material processing, and some services). At present, however, the share of manufactures in sub-Saharan Africa's exports is small – 6 per cent – almost all of that occurring in intraregional trade or specialized products such as partially processed bauxite and uranium ore. Few countries have so far succeeded in diversifying exports away from the traditional commodity-based pattern, the most conspicuously successful exception being Mauritius. If this picture is to change as a result of the structural reforms now being undertaken, secure and enlarged access to overseas markets is an important prerequisite.

To summarize, the major problems and priorities of sub-Saharan Africa do not readily fit into the present GATT framework of an international trade system. But, as African exports expand and become more diversified, this will change.

## 2 Africa's role in multilateral trade negotiations

The overwhelming majority of African countries are members of the GATT or applicants.[1] Yet the experience of past trade rounds has not encouraged active membership. The documentation and subject matter are generally regarded as too technical to be easily understood. Only very few personnel deal with them and attend the meetings. The information on GATT is not widely circulated and is largely ignored. One cannot therefore say that there are powerful interest groups in Africa directly following the GATT. Also the GATT agenda is rarely of direct interest to Africa, making GATT a rather distant institution. In practice, more resources have been put into negotiating in forums such as OPEC (for the oil exporters), the Lomé Convention, the UN Conference on Trade and Development (UNCTAD) and the regional integration movement, such as the Economic Community of West African States (ECOWAS) and the Preferential Trading Area (PTA), than in the GATT.

This overall detachment appears to have influenced the approach to the Uruguay Round. Generally, the negotiating resources devoted to the GATT have been low and both politicians and private institutions have shown little interest in the proceedings.[2] Nor is there any evidence of the formation of common regional interests either in African political organizations or in regional organizations. These conclusions have been borne out by other, country, studies. A paper on Kenya states, 'there is no evidence of serious formal preparations by the Kenyan trade officials for the current GATT negotiations. Little effort has been made to investigate possibilities of common negotiation strategies' (G. K. Ikiara in Whalley 1989). Nigeria is described as having played a 'rather passive role' in earlier rounds of trade negotiations and, despite being more actively involved in the run-up to the Uruguay Round (as a member of the Group of Ten), the 'current preoccupation' of policy-makers is with 'domestic policy reforms and special preference arrangements' (T. A. Oyejde in Whalley 1989). Tanzania, also a member of the Group of Ten, is described as having taken stands which are 'not derived from a well articulated consideration of Tanzania's economic interest . . . but rather are a political act of solidarity with other radical Third World countries' (N. Lipumba in Whalley 1989).

The relative passivity of African involvement in multilateral trade negotiations stems, in part, from the belief that domestic policy reform to improve supply response is so much more important; partly also from the complex and manpower-intensive nature of GATT processes. But it also stems from a judgement that little could be achieved from more active participation. There are several, distinct, strands to this belief:

(i) the conviction that, as small actors in the world trading system, African countries have little capacity for negotiating significant concessions over and above those enjoyed as 'free riders' from application of the most favoured nation (MFN) principle. To some extent, of course, this limitation of scale can be countered by individual countries adopting a common position with like-minded countries in the region or elsewhere;
(ii) resistance, along with other developing countries, to reciprocity in negotiations, as part of a broader belief in 'special and differential treatment' (S & D);
(iii) a belief in the value of special preferential arrangements outside the MTNs, notably those enjoyed under the Lomé convention, and anxiety about the erosion of preferences through multilaterally agreed liberalization.

*S&D and reciprocity*

'Special and differential treatment' and 'non-reciprocity' are principles for which developing countries have fought hard in earlier rounds of negotiations (and in the preparatory work for the Uruguay Round). They rest on the underlying belief that, in trade, equal treatment of unequals is unjust. More particularly, they derive from the 'infant industry' argument for protection applied both to new export industries (hence the case for tariff preferences) and to import-competing activities (hence, non-reciprocity in respect of liberalization of tariff and non-tariff barriers).

This overall approach by developing countries to negotiations has been questioned both on economic grounds (that protection may be damaging to the developing countries themselves) and on tactical grounds (that it achieves less in improved market access to developed country markets than a willingness to offer reciprocal concessions). But this questioning has not been directed at Africa. Here, the 'infant industry' argument has been held to apply *a fortiori*. Even strong critics of generalized preferences for developing countries have argued not for wholesale abolition but for the surrender of preferences by more 'advanced' developing countries, concentrating them, without any of the present restrictions, on low-income countries (Wolf 1984, p. 84). Nor do African countries have a great deal to offer through negotiations in terms of market access (the largest countries, notably Nigeria, obviously do; and negotiation could be about broader objectives than reciprocal market access). The only important recorded case of an African country having made concessions in MTNs is Côte d'Ivoire in the Tokyo Round (along with Indonesia, Morocco, Colombia and Thailand).

While special and differential treatment and non-reciprocity remain important principles for African trade negotiators, various factors have raised questions about whether they need some adaptation. Several African countries have unilaterally embarked on far-reaching trade liberalization. Nigeria, Kenya and Ghana, for example, have unilaterally made sharp tariff reductions on a wide range of products and have eliminated large numbers of quantitative restrictions on imports and exports as part of structural adjustment programmes negotiated with the IMF or the World Bank. There should be some means of obtaining credit for these measures in GATT negotiations, perhaps if consolidated through bindings.

Further, the new Round involves serious discussion on some issues which are central to African economic interests (agriculture) as well as some new issues, like services, trade-related aspects of intellectual property rights (TRIPs) and trade-related investment measures (TRIMs), which could be central. The new Round does moreover – at least in the language of the Ministerial Declaration – promise to address issues of concern to Africa in a way that earlier MTNs have not, by looking at the response of the GATT system to 'serious difficulties in commodity markets and the importance of an improved trading environment providing, inter alia, for the ability of indebted countries to meet their financial obligations', and also 'contribute towards continued, effective and determined factors to improve the functioning of the international monetary system and the flow of financial and real investment resources to developing countries'. All of this suggests the need for more active participation in the rule-making and negotiating process.

Lastly, there may be an interest in encouraging the 'graduation' of newly industrialized countries from preferential and non-reciprocal participation and requiring them to offer preferences in turn. So far, such a position has not been openly stated, but recognition that African countries' negotiating interests diverge from those of other developing countries is directly reflected in the importance attached to the ACP (Africa, Caribbean and Pacific) Group and to the undertaking in the Ministerial Declaration of special measures for 'least developed' countries.

*The Lomé Convention and special ACP preferences*

The Lomé Convention – over and above its aid and compensatory financing provisions – provides, in principle, free access for tropical products, manufactured and semi-manufactured exports to the EC market as well as special arrangements under the Common Agricultural Policy and quota-based preferences for sugar, rum, bananas and beef. Any advance obtained by African countries in the MTNs in terms of improved access to industrial countries' markets has to be set against the dilution of preferences in the EC market. The real, or imagined, benefits of these arrangements have hitherto acted as a major constraint on African, and other ACP, exporters seeking improved MFN access.

The actual value of the Lomé preferences has been the subject of much debate. At first sight, their importance to Africa is very large, simply because the EC is such an important market. As can be seen from Table 6.1, African exports to the EC far exceed in value those to the the rest of the OECD: $17.5 billion in 1986 as against $8.7 billion, of which $6.2 billion, was to the US; if oil is excluded, the EC accounts for $11.4 billion against $3.7 billion to the rest of the OECD, of which $1.8 billion was to the US. How much could preferential access explain this imbalance? Overall, as Table 5.3 showed, African countries face virtually no tariff barriers in the EC

Table 6.1 *Imports of OECD countries from sub-Saharan Africa,*[a] *1986. (US$m.)*

| *Group category* | *(SITC)* | *OECD total* | *US* | *Japan* | *EC* | *Other* |
|---|---|---|---|---|---|---|
| Total | | 26,178 | 6,245 | 988 | 17,465 | 1,480 |
| Live animals and food | (0) | 7,645 | 1,040 | 434 | 5,785 | 386 |
| Vegetables and fruit | (05) | 440 | 14 | 2 | 398 | 26 |
| Sugar and honey | (06) | 531 | 50 | 0 | 452 | 29 |
| Coffee, tea, cocoa | (07) | 5,890 | 940 | 208 | 4,419 | 323 |
| Beverages and tobacco | (1) | 333 | 36 | 16 | 244 | 37 |
| Tobacco | (12) | 323 | 34 | 16 | 237 | 36 |
| Crude materials | (2) | 3,166 | 297 | 129 | 2,559 | 181 |
| Hides and skins | (21) | 111 | 5 | 8 | 94 | 4 |
| Oils and seeds | (22) | 57 | 0 | 7 | 41 | 9 |
| Rubber, crude | (23) | 189 | 67 | 0 | 120 | 2 |
| Cork and wood | (24) | 862 | 4 | 21 | 817 | 20 |
| Textile fibres | (26) | 372 | 0 | 23 | 331 | 18 |
| Mineral fuels | (3) | 11,066 | 4,446 | 13 | 6,019 | 588 |
| Animal and vegetable fats | (4) | 134 | 0 | 7 | 126 | 1 |
| Processed fats | (43) | 4 | 0 | 1 | 3 | 0 |
| Chemicals | (5) | 336 | 10 | 0 | 322 | 4 |
| Manufactured goods | (6) | 2,573 | 318 | 295 | 1,867 | 93 |
| Machinery | (7) | 291 | 26 | 82 | 169 | 14 |
| Miscellaneous | (8) | 444 | 141 | 1 | 286 | 16 |

*Note:*
[a] Excludes South Africa

*Source:* OECD, *Foreign Trade by Commodities, 1986 Imports.*

in trade weighted terms. But that is, in large part, because tariffs are generally low; other developing countries with the same export composition would pay an average of under a 2 per cent tariff (it is, in fact, in the US that African countries enjoy their greatest preference margin against other developing countries, because of the way the GSP system operates there). Overall, around 60 per cent of ACP (and African) exports to the EC are non-dutiable commodities – the percentage varies over time, depending on commodity price movements, particularly oil. Another 4 per cent or so consists of items that still face significant barriers in the EC – mainly agricultural products – though, in most cases, ACP exporters still have preferential terms of access. Of the remaining third or so of ACP exports to the EC that do enjoy unrestricted preferential access, there is in some cases 'redundancy': either the exports are competitive anyway, or else they are so uncompetitive that a small margin of preference would make little difference. One German study argues that 'redundancy' of one kind or another is quite substantial (Agarwal *et al.* 1983).

In terms of any demonstrated impact of preferences there is little satisfactory, let alone conclusive, evidence. ACP exporters have seen their share of EC imports decline – overall and among developing countries – though this must be explained by the relatively poor overall supply performance; were this improved, preferences might still be a helpful incentive. There is evidence of very rapid growth of ACP exports to the EC of some industrial, non-commodity, items which preferences have been particularly designed to encourage: a survey in the 1975–80 period showed seventy-five items and another, extending the data up to 1984, showed 128. Low-income African countries were among the main exporters of these items, but the leading countries – in terms of numbers of items – were Mauritius and Côte d'Ivoire with Kenya, Senegal and Cameroon some way behind. Taken as a whole, however, these 'new' items accounted for only 2 per cent of ACP exports to the EC and of this 40 per cent was accounted for by one item – canned tuna – and one-third by textiles and clothing (McQueen and Read 1987).

While the experience of these growth items suggests a long-term potential for stimulating new exports with the help of (almost) guaranteed liberal access on a preferential basis, the main concern of ACP exporters has been to protect preferences in respect of some traditional items against erosion from GSP and, to a lesser extent, from MTNs. However, as Table 6.2 tries to show, overwhelmingly the most important items in terms of actual exports are tropical beverages where there is a small tariff preference for ACP exporters. Arguably a much more serious issue for them is the access barrier presented by the high level of consumption taxes in some European countries. Reduction of these taxes cannot occur on

Table 6.2 *Tropical products and preference margins in the EC*

| *SSA tropical products exports to EC Group* | *ECU m.* | *% of total exports to EC (% of non-oil in brackets)* | *Tariff preferences (%)* | | | *NTBs*[b] | *Main beneficiaries* |
|---|---|---|---|---|---|---|---|
| | | | *MFN* | *GSP* | *ACP*[a] | | |
| *Beverages* | *4,707* | 17.8 (31.1) | | | | | |
| Coffee, raw | 2,798 | | 5 | 4.5 | 0 | I | Madagascar, Rwanda, |
| Roasted, extracts, etc. coffee | 41 | | 15–18 | 9–12 | 0 | | Tanzania, Uganda, Angola, Burundi, Cameroon, CAR, Côte d'Ivoire, Ethiopia, Kenya |
| Cocoa, beans and shells | 1,386 | | 3 | 3 | 0 | I | Côte d'Ivoire, Ghana |
| Cocoa butter and paste | 139 | | 12 | 8 | 0 | I | Sierra Leone, Togo, Equatorial Guinea |
| Tea | 247 | | 5 | 0 | 0 | I | Kenya, Malawi, Rwanda |
| *Spices and flowers* | 108 | 0.5 (0.8) | | | | | |
| Cut flowers | 29 | | 17–24 | 17–24 | 0 | S | Kenya, Comoros, Madagascar, Tanzania |
| Vanilla | 24 | | 11.5 | 11.5 | 0 | | |
| Cloves | 7 | | 15 | 10 | 0 | | |
| Cinnamon, nutmeg, | | | 10 | 0 | 0 | | |
| mace, cardamons | 6 | | 10 | 3 | 0 | | |
| Pepper | 7 | | 10 | 3 | 0 | | |
| *Oil seeds and fats* | 269 | 2.1 (3.7) | | | | | |
| Groundnut oil | 53 | | 10 | 10 | 0 | | Côte d'Ivoire, Gambia |
| Palm oil | 81 | | 10 | 7 | 0 | | |

| | | | | | | | |
|---|---|---|---|---|---|---|---|
| Coconut oil | 26 | | 10 | 7 | 0 | | |
| Other dutiable oils | 81 | | 6 | 4 | 0 | | |
| *Tobacco and rice* | 326 | 1.5 (2.7) | | | | IQ | Zimbabwe, Malawi |
| Virginia flue-cured tobacco | 236 | | 23[c] | 23[c] | 0 | | |
| Other type | 34 | | 14[c] | 14[c] | 0 | | |
| Manioc/arrowroot | 20 | | 16 | 16 | 0 | | |
| Rice | 6 | | 6 | 0 | 0 | | |
| *Tropical fruits* | 606 | 2.6 (5.3) | | | | SQ | Somalia, Cameroon, Côte d'Ivoire, Kenya |
| Bananas | 301 | | 20 | 20 | 0 | | |
| Pineapples | 110 | | 9 | 9 | 0 | | |
| Pineapples juice | 12 | | 19 plus additives | 17 | 0 | | |
| *Wood and rubber products* | 1,070[d] | 4.1 (7.4) | | | | | Côte d'Ivoire, Gabon, Liberia |
| Tropical hardwood | 55 | | 4–6 | 4–6 | 0 | | |
| Plywood | 25 | | 10 | 10 | 0 | | |
| *Jute, sisal and hard fibres* | *19* | 0.1 (0.2) | 0 | 0 | 0 | Q | Tanzania |
| Total tropical products | 7,105 | 28.8 (51.3) | | | | | |

*Notes:*
[a] Also non-ACP least developed
[b] I: internal taxes; Q: Quotas; S: Sanitary regulations
[c] With price floor
[d] The total is so much larger than the components since very few sub-items are dutiable.

*Sources:* EC Eurostat and ACP sources (1986).

any other than a non-discriminatory basis. Those product areas where ACP producers do enjoy significant NTB preference are sugar and bananas but, here, the main beneficiaries are Caribbean rather than African producers (other than Mauritius for sugar). Some of the most substantial preferences, in fact, are in some small, high-tariff, items such as spices – where trade is not large in aggregate but is crucial to one or two small African states which face competition from Asia.

While the benefits of preferences are still perceived to be real and important, the ACP countries themselves acknowledge (ACP 1988) that it is not feasible to use them to block progress in the MTNs: 'it is to be noted that it is not possible for the ACP Group to fully safeguard its position in the EC market during these negotiations. However, the ACP group should ensure that any losses in the EC market are more than compensated by gains in the markets of other developed countries.' Given this acknowledgement it becomes all the more important for African countries, and the ACP countries as a whole, to be able, through active participation in the Round, to secure access advantages elsewhere to compensate for those advantages that will be lost through eroded Lomé preferences.

## 3 Issues in the Round

*Tropical products*

It is in the field of tropical products that the main negotiating interests of African countries are centred, since it is here that are the bulk of products still facing tariff and non-tariff barriers in major markets and also where Lomé preferences are most important. Tropical products, in a broad sense (SITC 0 to 4 less metals and oil), account for two-thirds of African exports to OECD markets. However, in an MTN context, only a select group of tropical products – those categories dominated by developing countries – are subject to negotiations (tropical beverages; spices and cut flowers; some oilseeds and vegetable oils; tobacco, rice, manioc and tropical roots; tropical fruits and some nuts; tropical fruit and products; tropical timber, natural rubber and some rubber products; jute and hard fibre). There are significant exclusions even from these categories – for example, soya and olive oil. And in one case – tropical timber and rubber – there are very few tariffs or NTBs in any event. Some 'tropical' products are dealt with elsewhere (e.g. sugar in agricultural negotiations, fish products among natural resource products). Even with these exclusions, however, tropical products as defined in a GATT sense still account for 30 per cent of all African exports to the EC, and over half of non-oil exports (see Table 6.2).

In past rounds, negotiations have centred on nominal tariffs. A situation has been arrived at where, for most items within the tropical products groups of concern to Africa, MFN duties are low or nil albeit with some exceptions. The EC maintains MFN (and GSP) tariffs of 10 per cent or more for such important categories as tobacco, manioc, some spices and vegetable oils; in each case there may be some protective intent, but there is no tariff on ACP exports from Africa. The EC also maintains small tariffs on some important items – cocoa, coffee – where there is no domestic competition, purely for preferential purposes. If an essentially static view of EC preferences is taken and their value measured by the multiple of the current value of trade and the preference margin, the sum considerably exceeds what could be obtained on an MFN basis in other OECD countries by cutting high tariff barriers – albeit reduced by GSP: e.g. in the US, tobacco (20–23 per cent for the main categories), manioc and tropical fruits and juices; in Japan on fresh fruit particularly; and in some smaller countries (Australia and New Zealand for example have generally high tariffs). In particular, African exporters have EC tariff preferences to protect in the case of coffee or cocoa (mainly against Brazil), palm oil (against Malaysia), Virginia flue-cured (VFC) tobacco (where Zimbabwe and Malawi compete with Brazil, Korea and India), bananas (against Latin America) and spices (against South Asia).

Nominal tariffs are only part of the story, however. A major issue for many tropical products (as with raw materials more generally) is the extent to which the tariff structure acts as a disincentive to export processing. This occurs because of tariff escalation (tariffs increase in nominal terms at higher stages) and because tariffs are charged on the final sales value, not on the processing value added. In some cases the effective protection rate can be much higher than the nominal rate. There have been many attempts to quantify this effect and they suggest that tariff escalation is generally high on processed tropical products, especially in those areas where the processing is labour intensive (Yeats 1984; Balassa

1964). In the Tokyo Round, developing countries tried to have a tariff-cutting formula adopted under which tariffs for processed items were cut more than for raw materials. This did not happen; in fact, more items experienced an increase than a decrease in tariff escalation, and tariff reductions were proportionately greater on raw materials than on processed goods (UNCTAD 1980). African countries share with other developing countries a general interest in reducing tariff escalation where it exists. But here, also, the issue of ACP preferences intrudes. Under the Lomé Convention (as in the GSP schemes), duty-free access for processed goods ensures that there is little or no tariff escalation problem in the EC market. African exporters sell cocoa butter, vegetable oil, pineapple juice and plywood, among other processed items, to the EC and in each case they have preferential access to protect. In the case of West African plywood and veneer manufacturers competing against those from Taiwan and Korea and pineapple juice producers competing against exporters from the Philippines, the preference margin may be of significant value.

Non-tariff barriers are often more serious obstacles to tropical product exports than tariffs. In some cases – rice, for example, in Japan and the EC – NTBs have a tariff equivalent of over 100 per cent. *Variable levies* are widely used to protect agriculture: in the EC (mainly on temperate products, but including rice and the sugar content of tinned fruit, though African producers often have preferential access conditions); and in some smaller OECD countries (Sweden on vegetable seeds and oils and cut flowers; Switzerland on vegetable oils and some fresh flowers; Austria on a wide variety of items). *Quantitative restrictions* are used by Japan (on fruit processing, groundnuts and rice – through the operation of state trading agencies), the US (groundnuts) and Scandinavia (manioc). But, again, African ACP producers have an ambigous position – for example, favouring EC banana quotas against non-ACP competition from Latin America.

There are some ways in which preferential treatment cannot operate in respect of non-tariff barriers and, here, all developing countries have a common interest in reducing them. The main case is special *internal taxes*, which are widespread on major tropical products: roasted and instant coffee (EC and Japan); tea (the EC); cocoa (all forms in the EC; as products in Japan; as butter and powder in Norway); bananas (the EC); spices and tobacco (in many industrial countries). Mainly revenue considerations are involved, though health factors may explain high tobacco excises. The price elasticity of demand for these products appears low, but as long as it is above zero there should be a stimulus to demand from reducing taxes, which are very high in some cases (over 50 per cent on coffee and tea in Germany). Of lesser, but some, importance are *health and sanitary barriers*, which may go beyond reasonable levels to the extent of constituting a trade barrier (for flowers and fresh fruit in Japan; spices and tropical fruit in the US). *Export subsidies* may have had a damaging effect on some African tropical product exports, for example EC and US subsidies for oil seeds and vegetable oils.

Given the preferential treatment available in the EC market and the removal of most tariff and quota barriers to their exports, the interests of African countries are, in significant part, defensive – to prevent an erosion of EC preferences. But there are two fields in which African negotiating energies can be channelled into coalitions with other developing countries:

(i) big cuts in the internal excise taxes (imposed over and above standard rates of consumption tax or VAT) charged in some developed countries, especially the EC, on beverages and spices (tobacco presents special – health – problems). No producer interests are threatened in industrial countries and the revenue costs would not be large overall;

(ii) improved access to non-EC markets. The US has some highly protected areas – fruit and fruit processing, tobacco and groundnuts – but access is otherwise quite liberal. The main target could be Japan, which has high tariffs in some cases (fruit processing) and a substantial number of NTBs. Some African countries with dynamic non-traditional exports – like Kenya's horticultural exports – have significant interests in this type of market diversification.

The tropical products offers so far made in the Round go a small way to meeting the above objectives. The EC has committed itself to a progressive reduction in taxes on tropical beverages as well as the progressive elimination of other NTBs. The offer to eliminate tariffs on unprocessed items and cut tariffs by 50 per cent on unprocessed items will, however, undoubtedly reduce preference margins. Where products have been excluded from the offer – mainly tobacco, vegetable oils, rice, fruits – this clearly reflects EC domestic interests rather than ACP interests (except in the case of bananas). The EC has also emphasized 'reciprocity' and 'burden sharing'; and this appears to be directed to Asian and Latin American rather than ACP producers. Japan has made an offer similar to that of the EC, albeit with less emphasis on reciprocity but with important exclusions (on, *inter alia*, tobacco, rice, most fruits and vegetables, ginger, tea and groundnuts) reflecting the concerns of domestic interest groups. The US has made an offer including tariff cuts on cocoa paste and powder, copra, palm kernel and nuts and oilcake, but actual concessions will depend on progress on agriculture. The ACP countries have in fact expressed strong reservations to the Tropical Products package in the Round because they consider the reduction in preference on items accounting for 12 per cent of ACP exports to the EC is not justified in terms of the advantages elsewhere. In fact these concerns may be exaggerated a little since almost all the preference loss is accounted for by a cut from 5 to 4 per cent on unroasted coffee tariffs. For African countries, there is scope for considerable further improvement in tropical products treatment along the lines sketched above.

*Agriculture*

Agreement on a liberalization of world agricultural trade (that is, temperate agriculture and sugar) is close to the top of the priorities of the major participants in the Uruguay Round. This may be the first Round to make significant progress in that area. Agreement is still a long way off, but the overall effects of such an agreement are clear: an increase in world prices (a consequence of the reduction in export subsidies and of the reduction in supply following reduced protection), which should in turn stimulate world agricultural trade.

Most of the academic studies which have tried to simulate the effects of such a change for the main product areas – grain, dairy products, livestock, non-tropical vegetable oils and sugar – have argued that there would be large net economic welfare gains globally. But, for developing countries, the net effects may be negative because of the 'terms of trade' effect of higher prices, unless developing countries themselves liberalize (for example, Tyers and Anderson 1987; also Don *et al.* 1989). Moreover, among developing countries there are significant losers, mainly net food importers, as well as gainers. These studies suggest that sub-Saharan Africa, as a food-importing region, would lose from liberalization whether it occurred in industrialized countries alone or globally. There have been numerous variants of these studies using different commodity weights, different assumptions about the price effect and different time periods. A radically different set of conclusions, however, has come from 'general equilibrium' studies, which take into account not just the effects on the agricultural sector but wider economic effects – such as the expansion of the farm sector relative to the industrial sector as a result of higher global prices. The efficiency gains from such a shift – which are shown to swamp the terms of trade effects – have been used to argue that developing countries as a whole, including low-income African countries, would benefit from global liberalization (Loo and Tower 1988).[3]

African countries with agricultural exports should welcome moves that reduce agricultural support measures that give rise to surpluses and depressed prices in international markets, and also those which act as trade barriers. Potential beneficiaries should include sugar exporters such as Mauritius and Swaziland and, on a smaller scale, Malawi and Zimbabwe; beef exporters, notably Botswana; and exporters of oil seeds and vegetable oils like Côte d'Ivoire, Gambia and Senegal, which would gain indirectly from liberalization of temperate oil seeds and oils. There are, however, few African exporters of products that would be covered by agricultural liberalization (other than tropical products) and the interests of these in liberalization are ambiguous. Sugar and beef exporters enjoy preferential access, through agreed quotas at guaranteed prices, to the EC market. They could gain to the extent that prices are increased and market access improved for sales in non-EC markets; they could lose to the extent that the EC becomes less willing to provide preferential access – albeit restricted – at guaranteed prices. Calculations of the loss of 'economic rent' by the ACP Group suggest a range of overall losses from sugar liberalization of $175–260 million a year to the ACP countries as a whole calculated on 1978–80 values – though almost all the losses would accrue to a small number of countries mainly Mauritius, whereas Kenya would gain (summarized in Mathews 1985, and Valdes 1986). There are much larger gains to developing countries as a whole from EC and global sugar liberalization. One factor these model simulations cannot capture, however, is the long-term effects of creating more stable international markets as a result of restricting the use of instruments like variable levies that accentuate price instability. Another is the gains that might accrue to developing countries in general if greater multilateral discipline over agriculture were to reduce the use of subsidized corn by US firms to produce sugar substitutes – which are emerging as a major threat to developing country sugar exporters even outside the US.

African countries that are net food importers lose from higher world prices as a result of terms of trade effects. It can be seen from Table 6.3 that several African countries are net importers of foodstuffs covered by agricultural negotiations on a substantial scale: Nigeria, Côte d'Ivoire, Ghana, Zaire, Senegal, Zambia, Somalia, Cameroon, Ethiopia, Madagascar, Gabon. Only Zimbabwe, Malawi and Mauritius are major net exporters. It could be, however, that current policies designed to provide greater incentives to the farm sector will reduce import dependence and create net exports in some cases. But, in the short term, there would still be costs to be borne. In some cases, import substitution is not feasible in any event. Two of the foodstuffs whose imports have grown rapidly into Africa are wheat and dairy products, neither well suited to production in many parts of Africa – local dairy production would probably be slow to develop and quite import intensive. The terms of trade costs would be reduced if food aid is available. But to the extent that liberalization reduces agricultural surpluses in major food-producing economies, the willingness to provide such surpluses in the form of food aid may be reduced (indeed, one of the flashpoints of recent trade conflict between the US and the EC has been the terms of concessionary sales of grain to developing countries such as Egypt). There is, of course, a widely held view that food aid has had a negative effect on African development by depressing domestic prices and encouraging food dependence. But a broad consensus of recent writings suggests that food aid has a role, provided it is applied carefully as a substitute for commercial imports and as a source of revenue for local food security programmes (Common Agricultural Policy Briefing 1987). It seems unlikely that a withering of food aid and higher world prices as a result of global agricultural reform would be the best way of assisting domestic reform.

In the longer term, if the current bias against agriculture is corrected, the issue may arise as to whether multilateral disciplines against agricultural protection would apply to Africa. African and other (notably Indian) negotiators in the Uruguay Round have argued forcefully that the overwhelming predominance in African culture of small-scale peasant farmers, many producing for subsistence only, will require (probably for generations) a developmental perspective which may be at odds with policies appropriate to commercial agriculture in developed countries. In such an environment there is a long-term case for government intervention for research, extension services and price support, which developing countries are concerned may be undermined by the commitments required in the GATT.

In the GATT agricultural negotiations, African interests are complex. They are not necessarily congruent with those of middle-income agricultural exporters whose views have been expressed through the Cairns Group (except in as much as individual countries like Kenya, Zimbabwe or Botswana might over the long term become net exporters to non-EC markets of sugar, beef, grain and dairy produce on a scale sufficient to generate net gains from a more liberal environment). African interests in general would seem closer to those of other low-income countries such as India and China or Egypt whose agriculture is dominated by small-scale peasant farming and which are not net exporters on any scale (or are net importers). For these countries, the main requirement would seem to be a clause in the agreement which recognizes, not merely as a transitional feature, the case for agricultural incentives and price support on development grounds. Additionally, those countries which are expected to remain net importers will require assurances on food security (by considerably enlarging multilateral disaster food reserves and agreeing stock levels to meet emergencies) and expanded assistance to cushion the balance of payments effects of higher prices.

### *Other sectoral issues*

No other sectors are as important as tropical products and agriculture but two will necessitate attention by African negotiators. The first relates to the negotiating group on *natural resource products*. These negotiations are still at a most rudimentary stage, but three areas have been considered appropriate for the negotiations: non-ferrous metals; forestry products (other than those covered under tropical products); fish and fisheries. The US and Australia (strongly opposed by the EC) have sought to enlarge the agenda to include

Table 6.3 *SSA trade in agricultural group items (US$m, latest year)*

| *Country* | | *Dairy Products* | *Meat* | *Foodgrains* | *Vegetable oils* | *Sugar* |
|---|---|---|---|---|---|---|
| Cameroon | X | — | — | — | — | 3 |
| (1983) | I | 9 | 8 | 24 (of which 13 rice) | 2 | — |
| Benin | X | — | — | — | 5 | 1 |
| (1983) | I | 2 | 3 | 24 (10 rice) | — | — |
| Ethiopia | X | — | 2 | — | 1 | 5 |
| (1981) | I | 7 | — | 44 (4 rice) | 4 | — |
| Gabon | X | — | — | — | — | — |
| (1983) | I | 9 | 31 | 22 (4 rice) | 5 | — |
| Ghana | X | — | — | — | — | — |
| (1981) | I | 3 | 9 | 52 (18 rice) | 7 | 3 |
| Côte d'Ivoire | X | — | — | — | 47 (plus 4 seed) | 17 |
| (1983) | I | 51 | 17 | 144 (94 rice) | — | — |
| Madagascar | X | — | 4 | 1 | — | 2 |
| (1982) | I | 5 | — | 55 (43 rice) | 10 | — |
| Malawi | X | — | — | 3 (3 rice) | 1 (13 seed) | 68 |
| (1981) | I | 5 | — | 19 | 1 | — |
| Mali | X | — | — | — | 1 (7 seed) | — |
| (1980) | I | 4 | — | — | 1 | — |

| | | | | | | |
|---|---|---|---|---|---|---|
| Mauritius | X | — | — | — | — | 234 |
| (1983) | I | 17 | 10 | 41 (18 rice) | 9 | — |
| Kenya | X | — | 6 | 20 | — | 4 |
| (1983) | I | 5 | — | 38 (15 rice) | 66 (3 seed) | — |
| Nigeria | X | — | — | — | — | — |
| (1984) | I | 329 | 30 | 920 (405 rice) | 187 | 804 |
| Senegal | X | — | — | — | 23 | 3 |
| (1981) | I | 23 | — | 116 (82 rice) | 38 (3 seed) | 27 |
| Somalia | X | — | — | — | — | — |
| (1980) | I | 6 | — | 68 (9 rice) | 8 | 13 |
| Sudan | X | — | — | 116 | 8 | — |
| (1982) | I | 26 | — | 70 (11 rice) | 4 (3 seed) | 70 |
| Zaire | X | — | — | — | 9 | — |
| (1978) | I | 21 | 28 | 58 (5 rice) | — | 4 |
| Zambia | X | — | — | — | — | — |
| (1982) | I | 9 | — | 32 | 11 | — |
| Zimbabwe | X | — | 30 | 1 | — | 32 |
| (1984) | I | 4 | — | 4 (4 rice) | — | — |

*Source:* UN, *Trade Statistics Year Book*, 1986.

energy (oil, coal, gas and uranium) and ferrous metals. In general, there is an African interest in reducing access barriers (exacting health checks, for example, on fish products) and in reducing tariff escalation where this acts as a disincentive to processing (for fish preparations and metal processing). Leaving aside energy (crucial to oil-exporting Nigeria, Gabon and Congo and uranium-exporting Nigeria) and ferrous metals (iron ore exported by Liberia and Mauritania and ferro alloys by Zimbabwe), there are African interests in negotiations that affect access for fish and fish products (Angola, Guinea-Bissau, Mauritania, Mozambique, Senegal, Seychelles) and non-ferrous metals (Ghana, Rwanda, Sierra Leone, Mauritania, Zaire, Zambia and Zimbabwe).

There are, however, some respects in which African countries have interests that do not coincide with those of countries simply trying to liberalize trade. There are Lomé preferences on fish products – though their value is eroded by some onerous rules of origin requirements. Preferences have less value in the case of metals, where raw materials are usually non-dutiable and finished goods attract GSP concessions too. There is also the call by the EC for reciprocal 'access to supplies' by beneficiaries of improved market access to the Community; 'guaranteed' access to countries' exclusive economic zones has been cited as an example of what may be required. In response to this, some developing countries have called for negotiations to be extended to cover control by multinational corporations over the international marketing of such commodities as bauxite and aluminium, phosphate, tin, petroleum, copper and iron ore. At present, however, these exchanges seem to have the character of debating points rather than serious negotiating moves.

In the case of *textiles and clothing*, Africa has little by way of exports to OECD markets, notably Mauritius and Côte d'Ivoire so far. These two countries have, in fact, encountered restrictions in the EC despite the promise of unrestricted access under the Lomé Convention. Rules of origin are also a problem in a Lomé context. In the long term, economic reform, and in particular real exchange rate depreciation, may make more countries generally competitive in this sector – both in garments assembly and, possibly, in cotton textiles utilizing local raw materials (though it is by no means certain that new African producers would be able to compete against low-cost Asian or NIC exporters in a deregulated environment). To safeguard this possibility, African countries have generally adopted a strong position in favour of liberalization in the sector and for the return of textiles and clothing to GATT rules.

*General and systemic issues*

Other than in specific negotiating forums, African countries have a strong interest in the design of a basic framework for the international trading system which will protect their interests for decades to come – a period in which they may, as a result of current adjustment policies, have a much larger and more diversified export capability. As small players in the world trading system – excepting Nigeria – sub-Saharan African countries have an interest in arrangements which provide for a generally open liberal trading system, strengthen multilateral rules and disciplines and prevent strong trading partners exercising coercion and discrimination against weaker partners. To this extent, African countries endorse the general principles of the negotiations but give particular emphasis to those which highlight the particular needs of developing countries (as embodied in Part IV of the General Agreement) and the particular needs of the least developed countries, the majority of which are in Africa (as provided for in the GATT Ministerial Declaration).

Given this background, African countries have an interest, with other developing countries, in pressing for strong *standstill and rollback* provisions (though the particular features of the Lomé Convention that give ACP countries preferential access through the EC's trade barriers create some conflicts of interest); stronger and streamlined *dispute settlements* provisions that protect weak trade partners (where progress has already been made in the Round); through the *FOGS* (functioning of the GATT system) negotiations, for a stronger GATT and a stronger link between the GATT and organizations dealing with monetary, financial (for example debt) and commodity matters; and for a *safeguards* clause under Article XIX that reinforces GATT rules, puts the onus of proof of injury and the obligation to adjust on the country imposing restrictions, and avoids selective voluntary export restraints (there is a safeguards clause with the Lomé Convention that permits unilateral action and has occasionally been imposed, creating considerable doubts about the EC's long-term commitment to unrestricted market access for ACP exports).

In the *tariff negotiations*, there is, as in the tropical products, agriculture and natural resource groups, an interest in cutting high tariffs and tariff escalation (and binding tariffs at a lower level). Areas of actual or potential interest include hides, leather and leather products. But, here again, there are ACP preferences to defend: Benin footwear exporters, for example, have been able to take advantage of preferential access to the EC to build up a useful business. A further general interest is in ensuring that African countries are not precluded by the GATT from offering tariff preferences to each other (through PTAs or customs unions). In *NTB* negotiations, the objective is essentially one of achieving maximum access to major markets. However, in the NTB field the adoption of a code approach (in the Tokyo Round) has created some difficulties for developing countries that wish to benefit from easier market access while avoiding reciprocity. Where codes are adopted, these apply only to signatories that adhere to their principles. An issue has already surfaced that exemplifies the dilemma of African countries – in the relatively uncontroversial area of customs documentation and procedures. If streamlined procedures were to be adopted, this would create difficulties for African countries that have contracted external agencies to check invoices so as to reduce dishonest or damaging pricing practices. Another potential area of difficulty is the *balance of payments safeguards clause* (Article XVIII) which permits the use of trade restrictions under certain circumstances: to ensure adequate reserves for developmental needs. Hitherto, special and differential treatment has been applied to this article. This reflects a belief that the balance of payments restrictions in many developing countries originate in structural problems, with only a sluggish response likely from conventional adjustment policies. According to this view, where there is insufficient external finance to cover the adjustment period it is difficult to avoid recourse to physical controls. The approach of many African countries to this question has, however, changed somewhat and some countries have removed extensive controls imposed for balance of payments reasons. There is, however, some reluctance to accept GATT disciplines in this area as against liberalization undertaken as part of World Bank/IMF programmes with supporting external finance.

*New issues*

The Uruguay Round has a more complex and ambitious programme than earlier rounds. For countries that have had difficulty participating effectively in earlier rounds, the prospect is intimidating, particularly in getting to grips with the 'new issues'. Several have major, and potentially disturbing, implications for Africa.

The negotiations on trade-related aspects of intellectual property rights (*TRIPs*) have so far attracted little public discussion or debate. Yet there has been a significant change in the thrust of the negotiations and it is rapidly emerging as a major stumbling block in the talks. At the outset, in the Ministerial Declaration, this was seen as a relatively uncontroversial area dealing mainly with the clarification of GATT provisions to reduce trade distortions arising from intellectual property rights and to develop rules and disciplines to deal with counterfeiture (which hardly impinged on Africa). But it has been extended to a much broader review of the intellectual property rights involving patents and copyright. The US proposals, in particular, incorporate blanket protection for intellectual property holders. As regards patents, these proposals give developing countries serious cause for concern, especially where, as in Africa, new technology is mainly imported and development depends on having as much access as possible to new ideas. The US proposals (which have been diluted a little in EC counter-proposals to allow shorter protection and exceptions to safeguard developing country acquisitions of new agricultural technology and biotechnology) reverse much of what developing countries have tried to achieve in relation to the Paris Convention on patents: they acknowledge no link between access to technology and development; and they make no concession to the wider public interest beyond the right of intellectual property holders. Some of these concerns have begun to be aired on behalf of developing countries (UNCTAD 1989), but the African dimension – particularly of small, less developed, technology importers – has not yet received adequate attention in the GATT.

The *TRIMs* (*trade-related investment measures*) negotiations raise issues that are no less important. What was initially envisaged as a set of negotiations to look at those aspects of countries' investment policies which impinged directly on trade flows has been broadened greatly in scope. US and Japanese proposals would entail a comprehensive review of foreign investment measures, not just those (like export performance and local content requirements) that directly influence trade. This approach should be worrying to African negotiators. First, it attempts to use GATT rules to influence foreign investment policy in a way never envisaged under the GATT rules. As it happens, many African countries are voluntarily adopting more liberal foreign investment regimes, but this is quite different from having such regimes imposed. Moreover, issues of concern to developing countries such as restrictive practices by multinational companies (relevant, for example, for potential African exporters of sisal and cigarettes) are not being considered. Second, even in the more specific area of genuine TRIMs, which is where the EC is trying to limit negotiations, many African countries are seeking to attract foreign investors specifically into export activities rather than into protected domestic markets where the benefits of foreign investment are more questionable. No doubt, in time, as economies liberalize generally, the case for export-processing zones and minimum local content requirements will disappear; and there may be benefits in limiting competition for export-oriented investment. But, as now conceived, the industrial country proposals seem to represent a threat to efforts to acquire specifically export-oriented investment.

The *services* issue is a wide and complex one and, while there has been considerable discussion of developing country interests in this area, it has mainly reflected the interests of major countries such as India and Brazil and, to a lesser extent, services exporters such as Singapore and Korea. The smaller, less developed, developing countries have distinctive interests (see Cobban 1988). The distinctive position of these countries is that they do not have a major commitment to 'infant' service industries; most import technological knowledge in fields such as technology services, data processing and consultancy; and they allow foreign companies to operate in such specialized financial services as insurance and banking. Thus, in general, they have an interest in liberalization to cheapen the cost of imported services. The 'right of estabilishment' of foreign companies is of less concern than how they operate.

But this generalization has to be qualified. Some, especially among the large African countries, are trying to establish domestic banking and insurance industries under domestic ownership; and there are genuine anxieties about national sovereignty and cultural penetration in relation to the services industries. One domestic service industry that would benefit from liberalization is airlines, but that is a matter for the International Air Transport Association and not GATT. In the long term, Africa may acquire service export industries, but the only one of short-term significance is tourism, about which little thought seems to have been given in GATT negotiations; indeed, it is not at all clear what 'liberalization' of tourism means.

At present, Kenya is Africa's only net services exporter in the main identifiable categories and most African countries, including the largest (Nigeria), are heavy net importers of shipping, other transportation, travel and miscellaneous services (see Table 6.4). Africa has an interest, too, in trying to seek equal status for 'labour only' services (as carried out by overseas migrant labour) and not only in those non-factor services where developed countries have a comparative advantage. The tightening immigration rules facing African workers in Europe and elsewhere underline the fundamental asymmetry in the approach of developed countries in the GATT, in relation to both services and TRIMs.

*Coalitions and negotiating strategies*

An attempt is made in Table 6.5 to summarize the main negotiating forums in which African countries have interests within GATT. In many respects, African negotiating interests and positions coincide with those of other developing countries. But there may be some divergences. These are most explicit in relation to tropical products and some agricultural items (sugar) where ACP preferences are enjoyed. But it is possible to envisage a common approach to tropical products based on giving priority to NTBs – particularly excise taxes – and access to non-EC markets with severe barriers, notably Japan. Agriculture is another potentially divisive issue, since African food-importing countries could lose, at least in the short term, as a result of policies being promoted by the export-oriented Cairns Group. Positions could, however, be reconciled if a strong 'developmental clause' were built into any agreement on agriculture. For manufactured exports, Africa has, like other developing countries, an interest in the long term in ensuring – in relation to textiles and safeguards – that opportunities are not blocked by protectionist barriers. African, like other developing, countries also have good reason to be concerned at some of the concepts which may be introduced into the GATT through the 'new issues' negotiations. While African countries appear to have less to lose than some other developing countries from a more liberal global services regime, the proposal for all-embracing protection of intellectual property rights under TRIPs is particularly threatening to small technology importers, and there are legitimate concerns about the course taken by TRIMs negotiations. Overall, a good many African interests can be safeguarded in the GATT by major developing countries and by

Table 6.4 *SSA trade in services, 1985 (SDRm.)*

| *Country* | *Shipping/freight* | | *Travel* | | *Transportation incl. airlines* | | *Professional services,*[a] *technology, etc.* | |
|---|---|---|---|---|---|---|---|---|
| | *Earnings* | *Balance* | *Earnings* | *Balance* | *Earnings* | *Balance* | *Earnings* | *Balance* |
| Burkina Faso[c] | — | –60 | 4 | –21 | 7 | –32 | 3 | –20 |
| CAR | 3 | –29 | 2 | –21 | 3 | –4 | 1 | –12 |
| Cameroon[b] | 129 | –72 | 63 | –46 | 50 | –10 | 142 | –214 |
| Chad[b] | — | –43 | 10 | –9 | 8 | +3 | 0 | –17 |
| Congo[b] | — | –138 | 5 | –49 | 46 | +31 | 13 | –156 |
| Côte d'Ivoire[b] | 88 | –190 | 44 | –50 | 149 | +31 | 79 | –316 |
| Gabon | 4 | –147 | 2 | –79 | 42 | –6 | 72 | –636 |
| Ghana | 13 | –46 | 1 | –9 | 15 | –24 | 6 | –41 |
| Kenya | 25 | –155 | 251 | +236 | 159 | +114 | 20 | –26 |
| Madagascar[b] | 7 | –39 | 1 | –19 | 32 | –9 | 6 | –5 |
| Malawi | 2 | –76 | 9 | +3 | 9 | –1 | 36 | +16 |
| Mauritania[b] | — | –35 | 7 | –11 | 8 | –55 | 2 | –42 |
| Mauritius | 2 | –63 | 54 | +35 | 61 | +30 | 22 | +2 |

| | | | | | | | | |
|---|---|---|---|---|---|---|---|---|
| Niger[c] | — | −44 | 5 | −9 | 13 | −6 | 8 | −21 |
| Nigeria | 170 | −441 | 33 | −139 | 78 | −65 | 29 | −597 |
| Rwanda[b] | — | −50 | 6 | −5 | 7 | −5 | 2 | −6 |
| Senegal[c] | 7 | −95 | 76 | +30 | 80 | −36 | 23 | −20 |
| Sierra Leone[b] | — | −21 | 7 | +2 | 11 | +10 | 11 | −6 |
| Tanzania[c] | 19 | −126 | 16 | +1 | 33 | +14 | 44 | −2 |
| Togo | — | −153 | 31 | +9 | 18 | +2 | 8 | −17 |
| Uganda[c] | — | +42 | 3 | −11 | 0 | −17 | 0 | −7 |
| Zaire[b] | 3 | −162 | 7 | −35 | 20 | −3 | 97 | −163 |
| Zambia | 16 | −75 | 8 | −8 | 21 | −28 | 1 | −39 |
| Zimbabwe[b] | 17 | −123 | 24 | −41 | 55 | +7 | 16 | −65 |

*Notes:*

[a] Advertising, brokerage, management fees, leasing, merchanting, professional and technical services, non-merchandise insurance, communications.

[b] 1984

[c] 1980

*Source:* GATT, *International Trade 1986/87*.

Table 6.5 *Major SSA export interests by negotiating group (% of total exports)*

| *Country* | *Tropical products* | *Agriculture* | *Natural resources* | *Textiles and clothing* | *Other Manufactures* | *Others* |
|---|---|---|---|---|---|---|
| Angola (1979) | Coffee 15 | | | | | Oil 73<br>Diamonds 1 |
| Benin (1982) | Coffee 7<br>Vegetable oil 6<br>Nuts 6<br>Residues 5 | | | | Leather shoes 39 | Cotton 1 |
| Botswana (1983) | | Beef 11 | | Textiles 4 | | Diamonds 6 |
| Burkina Faso (1982) | (Karike) nuts 15 | | | | | Cotton 7 |
| Burundi (1985) | Coffee 89<br>Tea 5 | | | | | |
| CAR (1980) | Coffee 27<br>Timber 23 | | | | | Diamonds 2<br>Cotton 7 |
| Cameroon (1983) | Coffee 33<br>Cocoa 12<br>Cocoa, paste and butter 2 | | Aluminium 7 | | | Oil 3 |
| Chad (1983) | Oilcake 8 | Meat 23 | | | | Live cattle 15<br>Hides and skins 17 |

| | | | | |
|---|---|---|---|---|
| Cape Verde (1979) | | | Crustaceans 32 | |
| Comoros (1980) | Spices 56 | | | |
| Congo (1980) | Timber 2 | | | Oil 89 |
| Ethiopia (1982) | Coffee 62<br>Vegetables and fruit 5<br>Pulses 6 | | | Hides and skins 10 |
| Equatorial Guinea (1981) | Cocoa 71 | | | |
| Gabon (1983) | Timber 8 | | | Oil 77 |
| Gambia (1979) | Groundnut oil 23<br>Groundnuts 55<br>Oilcake 8 | | Fish 10 | |
| Ghana (1981) | Cocoa 46<br>Cocoa butter and paste 2<br>Timber 6 | | Aluminium 27 | |
| Guinea (1980) | Pulses and seeds 3 | | Bauxite 97 | |
| Guinea-Bissau (1980) | Oilseeds 42<br>Timber products 7 | Crustaceans 30<br>Other fish 5 | | |

Table 6.5 *(cont.)*

| *Country* | *Tropical products* | *Agriculture* | *Natural resources* | *Textiles and clothing* | *Other Manufactures* | *Others* |
|---|---|---|---|---|---|---|
| Côte d'Ivoire (1983) | Coffee 22<br>Cocoa paste and butter 5<br>Timber 13<br>Timber products 1<br>Fruit products 3<br>Vegetable oils 2 | | Fish 3 | Textiles and clothing 3 | | |
| Kenya (1983) | Coffee 24<br>Tea 19<br>Vegetables and fruit 4<br>Processed fruit 4<br>Flowers 1 | | | | | |
| Liberia (1984) | Rubber 20<br>Timber 5<br>Coffee 6<br>Cocoa 41 | | | | | Iron ore 62 |
| Lesotho (1979) | | | | | | Diamonds 5<br>Wool and mohair 20 |
| Madagascar (1982) | Spices 37<br>Coffee 28 | | Crustaceans 7 | Textiles 4 | | |

| | | | | | | |
|---|---|---|---|---|---|---|
| Malawi (1982) | Tobacco 41<br>Tea 12<br>Oilseed 5<br>Vegetable oil 3 | Sugar 25 | | Textiles 4 | | |
| Mali (1980) | | | | | | Cotton 67 |
| Mauritania (1984) | | | Fish 46 | | | Iron ore 49 |
| Mauritius (1983) | Tea 2 | Sugar 64 | | Clothing 22 | Watches and other manuf. 5 | |
| Mozambique (1983) | Cashewnuts 14<br>Tea 11<br>Tobacco 3 | | Crustaceans 30 | | | |
| Niger (1981) | | | | | | Uranium 97 |
| Nigeria (1981) | Cocoa 2 | | | | | Oil 97 |
| Rwanda (1980) | Coffee 55<br>Tea 18 | | Tin and tungsten 10 | | | |
| Senegal (1980) | Vegetable oil 12<br>Oilcake 4 | | Crustaceans 6<br>Other fish 14 | Textiles 5 | Fertilizers 4 | Phosphates 16 |
| Seychelles (1983) | Copra 45<br>Spices 12 | | Fish 36 | | | |
| Sierra Leone (1984) | Cocoa 16<br>Coffee 9 | | Bauxite 29 | | | Diamonds 36 |
| Somalia (1981) | Bananas 6 | | | | | Live animals 68 |
| Sudan (1982) | Oilseed 18<br>(Natural gums 8)<br>Vegetable oil 3 | [Cereals 23] | | | | Cotton 25 |

Table 6.5 *(cont.)*

| *Country* | *Tropical products* | *Agriculture* | *Natural resources* | *Textiles and clothing* | *Other Manufactures* | *Others* |
|---|---|---|---|---|---|---|
| Swaziland (1981) | Canned fruit 4 | Sugar 39 | Wood pulp 15 | | | |
| Togo (1984) | Cocoa 25<br>Coffee 4 | | | | | Phosphate 4<br>Cotton 9 |
| Tanzania (1981) | Coffee 27<br>Tea 4<br>Fruit and vegetables 13<br>Spices 9<br>Sisal 6 | | | | | Cotton 14<br>Diamonds 6 |
| Uganda (1979) | Coffee 96 | | | | | |
| Zambia (1982) | | | Copper 90<br>Other non-ferrous 5 | | | |
| Zaire (1978) | Coffee 20<br>Rubber 5 | | Copper 51 | | | |
| Zimbabwe (1984) | Tobacco 22 | Sugar 3<br>Meat 3 | Non-ferrous 7 | | Ferrous alloys 12<br>Iron and steel 3 | |

*Sources:* UN, *International Trade Yearbook*, 1988; *Africa South of the Sahara*, Europa Publications, London, 1986.

those African countries sufficiently well prepared to participate. But the distinctive voice of the smaller and weaker developing countries – what has been called the Group of 100 – is not being effectively heard. At present, the ACP group, representing sixty-six countries – forty-five in Africa – is the nearest approximation to an organized force on their behalf.

A further issue is how far African countries should go in seeking support from particular industrial countries. The EC is committed to protect ACP interests in respect of items covered by the Lomé Convention – tropical products and agriculture (though, in the latter case, ACP interests are very much subordinate to those of EC farmers). The EC has also taken up positions in relation to new issues, particularly TRIPs and TRIMs, which are likely to be more acceptable than those of the US and Japan. While the EC's support is obviously to be welcomed, there are dangers in too close an association. Africa has much to gain also from better access to the US, Japanese and other OECD markets and, in the long term, it has a strong interest in an open, non-discriminatory, system to which the EC may not be as wholeheartedly committed.

Perhaps most important of all, it is important not to lose sight of the variety of African national interests which have to be negotiated individually. For Zimbabwe a delicate balance of advantage has to be struck, trading off preferential access for tobacco (and some beef and sugar) in the EC market against potential gains elsewhere. Mauritius, with its large sugar exports and successful garment and other manufacturing export sector, has interests quite distinct from almost all other African countries. The interests of the large agricultural importers, like Nigeria, Côte d'Ivoire and Zaire, are distinct from those of actual or emerging net food exporters like Kenya or Malawi. For the Comoros, the EC's preferential tariff regime for cloves and vanilla is the major national interest of substance in the Round, an issue where it has common interests with Madagascar and Tanzania but few other countries. Kenya is breaking new ground in exporting cut flowers and exotic fruits and vegetables to a wide variety of markets. Some countries have developed successful export industries in new areas not covered by the main tropical products and agriculture negotiations (Mozambique and Guinea-Bissau with crustaceans; Zimbabwe in ferro alloys; Benin with footwear) but where there are important trade barriers and preference issues to be fought. All of this suggests the need for strong and effective national representation as well as broader coalition-building in the negotiations.

## Notes

1 The following sub-Saharan African countries are members of the GATT: Benin, Burkina Faso, Burundi, Cameroon, Central African Republic, Chad, Congo, Côte d'Ivoire, Gabon, The Gambia, Ghana, Kenya, Lesotho, Madagascar, Malawi, Mauritania, Mauritius, Niger, Nigeria, Rwanda, Senegal, Sierra Leone, Tanzania, Tongo, Uganda, Zaire, Zambia and Zimbabwe. The following countries applied GATT provisions: Angola, Botswana, Cape Verde, Equatorial Guinea, Guinea-Bissau, Mali, Mozambique, Sao Tomé and Principe, Seychelles, Swaziland.

2 In a number of countries, it was the national 'dialogues', organized by this project's country authors, that gave the first major press coverage of the present round.

3 A similar conclusion emerges from the work of Burniaux and Waelbroeck.

## References

African, Caribbean and Pacific Group (1988), 'Memorandum on Trade Issues to be Covered by the Uruguay Round of Multilateral Trade Negotiations', January.

Agarwal, J., Dippl, Martin and Langhammer, R. (1983), *EC Trade Policies towards Associated Developing Countries: Barriers to Success*, Kieler Studies 193.

Balassa, B. (1964), *The Structure of Protection in the Industrial Countries and its Effects on the Exports of Processed Goods from Developing Countries*, World Bank Economic Department Report EC152.

Cobban, M. (1988), 'Small states and the Uruguay Round negotiations on services', mimeo, Commonwealth Secretariat, London.

Common Agricultural Policy (1987), *EEC Food Aid*, Briefing, Catholic Institute for International Relations, London.

Don, H., Gunasekera, B. H., Parsons, D. and Kirby, M. (1989), 'Liberalizing agricultural trade: Some perspectives for developing countries', in J. Whalley (ed.), *Rules, Power and Credibility*, Center for the Study of International Economic Relations Research Monograph, Ontario.

Godfrey, Martin (1985), 'Trade and exchange rate policy', in Torre Rose (ed.), *Crises and Recovery – Sub-Saharan Africa*, OECD Development Seminar.

Loo, T. and Tower, E. (1988), *Agricultural Protectionism and the Less Developed Countries*, Centre for International Economics, Canberra.

McQueen, M. and Read, R. (1987), 'Prospects for ACP exports to the enlarged Community', in C. Stevens (ed.), *The EC and the Third World*, Overseas Development Institute, London.

Mathews, A. (1985), *The Common Agricultural Policy of the Less Developed Countries*, Gill & McMillian, Dublin.

Tyers, R. and Anderson, K. (1987), 'Global interactions and trade liberalisation in agriculture', in A. Ray and D. Gale Johnson (eds), *Economic Policies and World Agriculture*, World Bank, Canberra.

UNCTAD (1980), *The Influence of Protectionism on Trade in Primary and Processed Commodities: The Results of the Multilateral Trade Negotiations*, Geneva, August.

UNCTAD (1989), *Trade Related Aspects of Intellectual Property Rights*, UNCTAD/MTN/INT/CB/S, Geneva.

Valdes, A. (1986), 'Agriculture in the Uruguay Round', International Food Policy Research Institute paper for World Bank conference in Thailand, October.

Whalley, J. (ed.) (1989), *Developing Countries and the Global Trading System*, vol. II, Macmillan, London.

Wolf, Martin (1984), *Some Are More Equal*, Trade Policy Research Centre, London, October.

Yeats, A. (1984), 'On the analysis of tariff escalation', *Journal of Development Economics*, 15.

7

# The theory of structural adjustment and trade policy

S. M. Ravi Kanbur

## 1 Introduction

During the 1980s, country after country in Africa entered into a World Bank/Fund supported programme of 'structural adjustment'. Well over twenty countries either have current programmes or are negotiating to put programmes in place. For some countries, structural adjustment programmes are into their third or fourth year. These adjustment programmes are in response to unsustainable external deficits, which arose because of internal or external shocks. The precise circumstances vary from country to country, but by and large most programmes include measures to (i) attain stabilization through demand-side measures, (ii) increase production of tradables, (iii) liberalize the domestic and international sectors, (iv) reduce the scope of the public sector – cut-backs in expenditure and investment, with encouragement to privatization. Most, but by no means all, of these measures interact with trade policy in a significant way.

The object of this paper is to discuss a theoretical framework for evaluating the process of structural adjustment, paying particular attention to the realm of trade policy. To set the stage for the theoretical discussion, we begin in section 2 with a brief account of the process in one particular African country – Côte d'Ivoire. In this case the process has been going on since 1981 and it provides an indication of how programmes in other countries might develop.

After this background, section 3 proceeds to a theoretical framework in which a programme such as that of Côte d'Ivoire could be analysed. Section 4 takes up a factor often neglected in the design of programmes – their distributional consequences. Section 5 moves on to a discussion of the extent to which the 'new' trade theory can help us in the analysis. Section 6 concludes the paper.

## 2 The Structural adjustment process in Côte d'Ivoire

The broad contours of Côte d'Ivoire's economic development are too well known to need detailed rehearsal. After a strong growth performance in the 1960s and 1970s, in the context of external equilibrium and domestic financial prudence, the 'Ivorian miracle' began to falter in the late 1970s. The sharp increases in coffee and cocoa prices in 1975, 1976 and 1977 led to large increases in government revenue. A huge public investment programme followed, of which a substantial portion was financed through external borrowing. With this over-expansion the stage was set for a crisis, which came with the dramatic falls in coffee and cocoa prices between 1977 and 1980. Immediate steps were taken towards financial stabilization, and alongside this the government also put into place a Structural Adjustment Programme.

The Côte d'Ivoire Structural Adjustment Programme has been supported by three World Bank Structural Adjustment Loans (SALs) in 1981, 1983 and 1986. The content of the agreements is specified in the Economic Policy Statement (EPS) of 1981, the Letter of Development Policy (LDP) of 1983 and the Statement of Development Policy (SDP) of 1986. In what follows we will review these agreements briefy, focusing in particular on their trade policy content. As argued in Kanbur (1987c), these SAL agreements have become progressively more specific and detailed in terms of their policy content. The EPS (1981) discussion is largely institutional, and announces the launching of a set of studies. On pricing, the policies were geared largely to financial stabilization – the producer prices of the export crops coffee and cocoa were left unchanged, although increases in the future were indicated. Palm-bunch prices were increased by 50 per cent, as were copra prices. By the time of SAL II the commitment to increasing producer prices of export crops was much stronger. The LDP (1983) announced definite increases in coffee and cocoa prices for the 1983–84 season. This emphasis on increasing real prices of export crops continued under SAL III.

On industry, the three SAL agreements again reveal a progressive tightening of the focus. The culmination is in SAL III. The SDP (1986) notes that the overall objective is to 'achieve an effective protection of 40 per cent across-the-board for the entire manufacturing sector'. The details of this vary from industry to industry, but involve reforms of export incentives and of tariff and non-tariff import protection.

Overall, then, the Côte d'Ivoire SALs focus on encouraging the production of tradables and liberalization of the domestic protected sectors. While the agreements do mention the need to encourage food production, for those staples which are non-traded (such as root crops) this goes against the overall thrust of increasing the profitability of cash crop production for export. However, given these emphases in the Côte d'Ivoire SALs, we might ask what theoretical framework and rationale underlies them. We turn to this in the next section.

## 3 The theory of structural adjustment and trade policy

Côte d'Ivoire presents us with a classic case of structural adjustment necessitated by an unsustainable external deficit. The policy imperatives were to control this deficit. In this section we will develop a theoretical framework for analysing the role of trade policy in this adjustment, basing our discussion on the work of Knight (1976), Addison and Demery (1985, 1987) and Kanbur (1987a, b).

We begin in the usual Salter–Swan framework, diving the economy into tradables (T) and non-tradables (NT). We take the economy to be one of the 'small-open' variety, so that the world price of tradables is a given. The relative price of tradables to non-tradables is a crucial element in the structural adjustment process, whether or not the initial disturbance from equilibrium is of the price or the expenditure variety. Starting from equilibrium, consider an expansion of expenditure. At the same relative prices, there is excess demand in both the tradable and non-tradable sectors. The latter is of course translated into a trade deficit. However, since the price of non-tradables is domestically determined, we would expect it to increase in response to the excess demand, eventually leading to a situation where there is no excess demand in the market for tradables but an even larger trade deficit.

This situation is the one which comes closest to the situation facing the Côte d'Ivoire and other countries at the outset of the adjustment process, with excess demand being reflected in inflationary pressure *and* external deficits. The immediate reaction to this situation, caused by the initial expansion and absorption, might be to recommend a reduction in expenditure. However, it should be clear from the above that both expenditure reduction *and* a change in relative price are required to get back to the initial equilibrium. If this expenditure switching policy is *not* enacted, then a far greater deflation is required in order to attain external equilibrium. To the extent that there are downward rigidities in the price of non-tradables, the deflation will exact a toll in terms of lost output and income.

What is the role of trade policy instruments in the above process? If there are rigidities in the labour market which prevent the relative price of non-tradables from falling, then the standard prescription is nominal exchange-rate devaluation. This will increase the nominal price of tradables and hence their relative price via-à-vis non-tradables. However, in Côte d'Ivoire, as in all the countries of the West African Monetary Union, the nominal exchange rate is *not* a policy instrument. All exchange rates in the union are pegged to the French franc. If devaluation is ruled out, then tariff and subsidy instruments become relevant instruments for affecting the relative price of tradables and non-tradables. In fact, it is well known that an export subsidy and import tariff scheme can always be enacted to simulate the effects of a currency devaluation.

In Côte d'Ivoire, as in other African countries, the marketing of key export cash crops is controlled. The government sets the producer prices, and the difference between these and world prices acts essentially as an export tax. A major plank in the platform of adjustment policies is that of increasing producer prices for export crops. To the extent that the supply of export crops is elastic, the effects of this on government revenue will be mitigated. However, in terms of the tradables/non-tradables analysis, such an increase in producer prices will allow a less deflationary demand-side policy than would otherwise be necessary for external deficit correction.

We have seen that making certain assumptions allows us to

conduct a coherent discussion of one of the major components of a structural adjustment programme – the relative price of tradables to non-tradables. However, it should be recognized that the theory advanced is in many ways oversimplified. The existence of trade policy in itself raises questions about the basic framework. The rationale for being able to aggregate exportables and importables into a single composite called 'tradables' is that the relative prices of exportables and importables are given by world prices. In this situation we can form a Hicksian composite commodity. If export taxes and import tariffs are of the constant proportionate variety, then the simple Salter–Swan analysis goes through. But if, as is sometimes the case, these taxes and tariffs are fixed in nominal terms, then the assumptions underlying the Hicksian composite are violated. Moreover, an important type of trade policy is that of a quota. In this case the shadow price of the quantity ration will depend on the general equilibrium and cannot be taken as given. In addition to the above problems on the tradable side, the assumption of a simple non-tradable aggregate is also questionable. In an African context, at least two types of non-tradables come to mind – food crops and the urban formal sector. The former do indeed have a flexible price; the latter tend not to.

In order to incorporate these criticisms, we need a more detailed model and the simplicity of the diagrammatic formulation is lost. However, having such a disaggregated framework may be important for discussing trade policy in the context of structural adjustment. In what follows we develop a model introduced in Braverman and Kanbur (1987) and put it to work on the structural adjustment question. The model consists of markets for four goods – an exportable cash crop ($g$), a domestically non-produced importable food crop ($r$), a non-traded food crop ($m$) and non-traded urban sector output ($s$). While the model itself is general, the dichotomy is quite relevant for some African countries ($g$ = groundnut, $r$ = rice, $m$ = millet, $s$ = services and construction).

It is assumed that $g$ and $m$ are substitutes in production, while $r$ and $m$ are substitutes in consumption. The good $s$ is special in that the sole demand for it is from the government, which taxes the export of $g$ and the import of $r$ in order to finance purchases of $s$. The demand for $m$ and $r$ comes from two sources – rural farmers and urban workers. The demands of the former are modelled in terms of the behaviour of a farm household, and depend on prices $p_g$, $p_r$ and $p_m$ of the goods. The demand for $r$ is

$$Q_r(p_r, p_m, p_g) + D_r(p_r, p_m, W_s), \tag{7.1}$$

where $Q_r$ is rural demand, $D_r$ is the urban demand and $W_s$ is the urban wage bill. If the urban demand for $m$ is $D_m(p_r, p_m, W_s)$ while the rural net supply of $m$ is $q_m(p_r, p_m, p_g)$, then $m$ market equilibrium is given by

$$D_m(p_r, p_m, W_s) = q_m(p_r, p_m, p_g). \tag{7.2}$$

If the world prices of $g$ and $r$ are $P^*_g$ and $P^*_r$, and the nominal exchange rate is $e$, then world prices in domestic currency are $P_g = eP^*_g$ and $P_r = eP^*_r$. The government sets domestic prices $p_g$ and $p_r$ and hence, implicitly, the taxes (or subsidies)

$$t_g = P_g - p_g$$
$$t_r = P_r - p_r. \tag{7.3}$$

Given this, government revenue is

$$R = t_g q_g(p_g, p_m) + t_r[Q_r(p_r, p_m, p_g) + D_r(p_r, p_m, W_s)], \tag{7.4}$$

where $q_g$ is output of $g$. If government expenditure is $G$, the government deficit is

$$G^D = G - R. \tag{7.5}$$

Since we assume that there is no other demand for urban services except from the government, we can clearly choose units so that

$$G = W_s = P_s. \tag{7.6}$$

Given $G$, $t_g$ and $t_r$, the equilibrium is determined. From (7.6), $G$ determines $W_s$. Given this, from (7.2), $p_m$ is determined. Given $p_m$, government revenue follows from (7.4) and this leads to the government deficit $G^D$ in (7.5). One feature of this model is that the external deficit, in domestic currency terms, is exactly equal to $G^D$. This is not surprising. Since all markets clear and all agents except the government meet their budget constraint, the government's deficit must equal the economy's deficit. Finally, notice that the system is homogeneous of degree zero in domestic prices and the exchange rate if the deficit is fixed in foreign currency terms.

With this model, let us investigate the role of trade policy in structural adjustment. Let us start with an initial situation with

$$G = R, \text{ i.e. } G^D = 0, \tag{7.7}$$

and consider an increase in $G$. From (7.6) this will increase $W_s$ and $P_s$. From (7.2), the effect on $p_m$ is given by

$$p_{mG} = \frac{\mathrm{d}p_m}{\mathrm{d}G} = \frac{D_{mW}}{q_{mm} - D_{mm}}, \tag{7.8}$$

where $D_{mW}$ and $D_{mm}$ are income and price derivatives of demand for $m$ and $q_{mm}$ is the price derivative of the net supply of millet. Assuming the usual shapes, $p_m$ will indeed increase. Thus the relative price of non-tradables as a whole will increase relative to that of tradables. The effect on the government deficit is got from (7.5) and (7.4), together with (7.8):

$$\frac{\mathrm{d}G^{\mathrm{D}}}{\mathrm{d}G} = 1 - \{t_g q_{gm} p_{mG} + t_r [Q_{rm} p_{mG} + D_{rm} p_{mG} + D_{rW}]\} \tag{7.9}$$

where the second subscript indicates the derivative with respect to the relevant argument. The expression (7.9) shows the different influences at play. An increase in $G$ will have a direct effect on $D_r$ through $D_{rW}$, and hence on $G^{\mathrm{D}}$ since $r$ is taxed at rate $t_r$. The second-round effects of an increase in $G$ come through the increase in $p_m$. This leads to a reduction in $q_g$ and an increase in $Q_r$ and $D_r$. If $t_r$ is negative, i.e. a subsidy, then the term in curly brackets on the right-hand side of (7.9) would be expected to be positive, thereby magnifying the first-round effect of an increase in $G$ and hence increasing further the deficit problem.

Now consider adjustment to this deficit, assuming it to be unsustainable. Fairly clearly, a reduction of $G$ back to its original value will restore equilibrium if the prices of the non-traded goods are flexible downwards. However, if they are not, the story is different. The crucial price here is $p_m$ since $p_s$ is delinked from the rest of the model and determined directly by $G$ (if $W_s$ is rigid, then unemployment will follow a reduction in $G$). If $p_m$ is indeed fixed, then

$$\frac{\mathrm{d}G^{\mathrm{D}}}{\mathrm{d}G} = 1 - t_r D_{rW}. \tag{7.10}$$

Comparing (7.9) and (7.10), it is seen that, if $p_m$ is flexible upwards but rigid downwards, a far greater reduction in $G$ is needed to restore equilibrium, when compared with the initial increment in $G$ which led to the disequilibrium. This is again in keeping with the simple analysis discussed earlier.

Let us consider now a standard policy in structural adjustment programmes – an increment in producer prices of export cash crops. What is the effect of this on other prices and on the government deficit? From (7.2), the effect of a change in $p_g$ is given by

$$\frac{dp_m}{dp_g} = \frac{q_{mg}}{D_{mm} - q_{mm}}. \qquad (7.11)$$

If we suppose that $q_{mg} < 0$, $D_{mm} < 0$, $q_{mm} > 0$, then (7.11) is positive, i.e. the price of *m* increases. This is because with the increase in $p_g$ production shifts into *g*, leaving excess demand in *m*. The price of *m* therefore increases. We see, then, that an increase in the price of a tradable has led to an increase in the price of a non-tradable. One might ask what the overall effect is on the relative price of tradables to non-tradables, but a better question would be the effect on the overall deficit. From (7.5)

$$\frac{dG^D}{dp_g} = -\frac{dR}{dp_g}$$
$$= -\{t_g[q_{gg} + q_{gm}p_{mg}] - q_g + t_r[Q_{rm}p_{mg} + Q_{rg} + D_{rm}p_{mg}]\} \qquad (7.12)$$

The expression in (7.12) tells us to be careful of general equilibrium effects. The partial equilibrium effect on revenue is

$$t_g q_{gg} - q_g = q_g \left[ \frac{t_g}{p_g} \cdot p_g \frac{q_{gg}}{q_g} - 1 \right] \qquad (7.13)$$

Thus we require the supply elasticity to satisfy

$$\eta_g = p_g \frac{q_{gg}}{q_g} > \frac{p_g}{t_g}, \qquad (7.14)$$

and it is an empirical matter whether this will be satisfied in practice or not. If the producer price exceeds the unit tax, then we require the price elasticity of supply to exceed unity – a condition which may be difficult to satisfy in the short run. In addition, the term $q_{gm}p_{mg}$ works in the opposite direction, since we would expect production of *g* to decrease when $p_m$ increases. There are also conflicting effects to take account of in the market for the other traded goods. Assuming $Q_{rm} > 0$, $D_{rm} > 0$ and $Q_{rg} > 0$, if *r* is a subsidized import then the increase in the consumption of *r* increases the charge on the government. However, if $t_r > 0$ then government revenue will benefit.

To conclude, then, while there exist a $t_g$, $t_r$ combination which will exactly induce a determinate change in the relative price of tradables and non-tradables, in this more realistic setting of disaggregated markets and piecemeal policy reform the insights of the simple Salter–Swan model have to be modified and treated with caution.

## 4 Further modifications: income distribution considerations

There is another sense in which the simple Salter–Swan framework is too aggregative for policy analysis. The community indifference curve, which is needed to specify the demand side of the framework, is well known to rely on certain assumptions. Even from the point of view of accurate representation of demands, fairly stringent conditions on preferences are required. Moreover, the community indifference curves beg the role of income distribution in the evaluation of the outcomes of structural adjustment. The focus of the analysis is on the aggregate external deficit – the consequences for incomes of various groups in society are ignored. There are two clear reasons why this is unsatisfactory. First, if lump-sum taxation cannot be used to achieve the optimal distribution of income, we cannot be indifferent to distributional outcomes. In particular, the consequences for the poorest of the poor have been causing concern in a number of circles. Secondly, the Salter–Swan framework, like many others, is not sensitive to political economy considerations – changes in trade policy affect the standard of living of different groups, some of which may be powerful enough to set in motion processes of redressing the adverse effects on them. In what follows we will take up these issues in turn.

To set the scene, notice that any one of the three policy instruments $G$, $t_r$ and $t_g$, can be used to address the external deficit – indeed, combinations of these are possible as well. But these instruments are not distributionally neutral. To focus the discussion, let us concentrate on the choice between $G$ and $t_g$. From (7.5), there is a locus of $G$ and $t_g$ combinations which will give the same external deficit. After some manipulation, it can be shown that this locus satisfies

$$\frac{dp_g}{dG} = \frac{1 - \{R_m p_{mg} + R_G\}}{R_g + R_m p_{mg}}. \qquad (7.15)$$

If government revenue increases with $p_g$ and if the deficit increases with $G$, then (7.15) will be positive. A given reduction in the deficit can thus be attained by an increase in $p_g$, a reduction in $G$, or some combination of the two. But the effects of changes in $p_g$ and $G$ on income distribution can be very different.

Braverman and Kanbur (1987) model income distribution effects through the indirect utility functions of urban and rural residents:

$$V^U = V^U(p_r, p_m, W_s)$$
$$V^R = V^R(p_r, p_m, p_g). \qquad (7.16)$$

Then

$$\frac{dV^U}{dp_g} = V^U_{p_m} p_{mg}$$
$$= V^U_\eta D_m p_{mg} \qquad (7.17)$$

where $V^U_\eta$ is the marginal utility of income for the urban population. Since $p_{mg} > 0$, we find that the urban population is made worse off by an increase in $p_g$. In contrast, of course,

$$\frac{dV^R}{dp_g} = V^R_\eta q_g + V^R_\eta q_m p_{mg}, \qquad (7.18)$$

so that the rural sector benefits both from the initial increment in $p_g$ and from the subsequent increase in $p_m$.

The distributional consequences of restoring external equilibrium through increasing $p_g$ are thus very clear. What of the route of reducing $G$? Here we need

$$\frac{dV^U}{dG} = V^U_\eta + V^U_{p_m} p_{mG}$$
$$= V^U_\eta[1 - D_m p_{mG}]$$
$$= V^U_\eta \left[ 1 - \frac{p_m D_m}{G} \cdot \frac{G}{p_m} \cdot p_{mG} \right] \qquad (7.19)$$
$$\frac{dV^R}{dG} = V^R_\eta q_m p_{mG}. \qquad (7.20)$$

The rural sector is thus made unambiguously worse off with a lower $G$, as is the urban sector if the ratio of expenditure on $m$ to their total income is not too high.

We thus have a distributional trade-off for the *same* effect on the external deficit. The trade policy instrument makes only the urban sector worse off, while the demand management instrument makes both urban and rural sectors worse off. If the social welfare function gives a high enough weight to the welfare of the rural sector, the trade policy instrument is to be preferred.

A similar, though perhaps less sharp, trade-off can be shown as between the two trade policy instruments $P_r$ and $P_g$. Under certain conditions, an increase in either $t_g$ or $t_r$ will induce an improvement in the deficit.

Rural farmers lose because of the increase in the price of $r$, which they consume, but gain as a result of the consequent increase in the price of $m$, which they are net suppliers of. It is possible, therefore, for rural farmers to be made better off while urban workers are made worse off for any given reduction in the deficit brought about by an increase in $p_r$. The trade-off between $G$ and $p_r$ is thus similar to the trade-off between $G$ and $p_g$. Even between $p_r$ and $p_g$ there will be a distributional trade-off because the *magnitudes* of gains and losses are different as between the two instruments.

The choice between the alternative trade policy instruments – $p_g$ and $p_r$ – is thus seen to depend on income distributional outcomes. However, in both cases the urban sector is made worse off. It seems unlikely that this sector will not attempt to restore its standard of living through the political process. These political economy repercussions are modelled in Braverman and Kanbur (1987) in a very simple way. It is assumed that the urban sector can induce an increase in government expenditure $G$ to maintain its utility level at the *status quo ex ante*. Thus we require

$$V^{U}[p_r, p_m(p_r, p_g, G), G] = \bar{V}^{U} \tag{7.21}$$

so that the response of $G$ is endogenous:

$$\frac{dG}{dp_r} \quad \frac{D_r + D_m p_{mr}}{1 - D_m p_{mG}} \tag{7.22}$$

$$\frac{dG}{dp_g} \quad \frac{D_m p_{mg}}{1 - D_m p_{mG}}. \tag{7.33}$$

The effect on the deficit of the two policy instruments is thus

$$\frac{dG^{D}}{dp_r} = \frac{dG}{dp_r}\left[1 - \frac{\partial R}{\partial G}\right] - \frac{\partial R}{\partial p_r} \tag{7.24}$$

$$\frac{dG^{D}}{dp_g} = \frac{dG}{dp_g}\left[1 - \frac{\partial R}{\partial G}\right] - \frac{\partial R}{\partial p_g}. \tag{7.25}$$

These expressions are analysed in detail in Braverman and Kanbur (1987), but it should be clear that, even if we were only interested in the deficit, the two trade policy instruments would not be equivalent, since their political economy repercussions would be different.

## 5 Imperfect competition and returns to scale

As was seen in our discussion of the Côte d'Ivoire SAL agreement, rates of protection in industry have increasingly come under attack. In Côte d'Ivoire and elsewhere, there is a strong move to introduce trade liberalization, involving the reduction of industrial protection. The rationale for this is rooted in basic welfare economics, where it is argues that any departure from world prices for a small open economy is detrimental to social welfare.

There are several standard counters to the above argument. If there are government revenue needs which cannot be met through lump-sum taxation, then the second-best pattern of taxes may indeed involve some taxes on imports. Moreover, the above analysis is static. Infant industry protection arguments can be brought to bear on the question, leading perhaps to the conclusion that temporary protection may be good from the long-term point of view. However, alongside these standard ripostes there has recently developed a line of analysis which stresses imperfect competition and increasing returns to scale, both of which are likely to be present in the protected import-competing sectors of African countries. The literature is a recent one, but it has considerable potential (Krugman 1986; Srinivasan 1986; Rodrik 1987; Venables 1985).

Krugman (1986) focuses the literature on the question of trade policy by delineating three effects – the effect of trade policy on the monopoly power of domestic firms in their home market, the effect on the market power of foreign firms in the domestic market, and the effect of the market power of domestic firms in foreign markets. The last of these is discussed by Brander and Spencer (1983), but it is unlikely to be of relevance to the African context – the scenario they have in mind is Japanese/US rivalry or newly industrializing countries such as Taiwan and Korea in foreign markets. The second is also analysed by Brander and Spencer (1981); in this case the argument rests on the incidence of a tariff being divided between the foreign monopoly's rent and domestic prices. However, in this section we will focus on the first effect since this seems to be uppermost in the minds of advocates of trade liberalization in Africa – that opening up to international competition will weed out inefficiency and improve welfare.

The strongest counter to this argument for liberalization is that of scale economies. If as a result of opening up protected sectors the average size of firms falls, then with scale economies there will be a clear loss to society which has to be set against the other possible gains. Rodrik (1987) provides an excellent exposition of this argument using modern duality techniques. Let $E(p_1, p_1, \ldots, U)$ be the expenditure function for the representative consumer – the distributional considerations of the previous section are ignored – and let $c_i(w, x_i)$ be the unit cost function for a firm in industry $i$. Letting $C_i$ and $X_i$ be consumption and industry output, respectively, the equality of income and expenditure in equilibrium gives us

$$\mathrm{E}(.) = \sum_i [p_i - c_i(.)]X_i + \sum_i w_j v_j + \sum_i (p_i - p_i^*)M_i, \quad (7.26)$$

where $p_i$ and $p_i^*$ are domestic and world prices respectively, $M_i = C_i - X_i$ are imports, $v_j$ is the supply of the $j'^{\text{th}}$ factor and $w_j$ its return. Taking the total derivative of (7.26) with respect to some policy change such as liberalization, Rodrik (1987) shows that

$$E_U \mathrm{d}U = \sum_i (p_i - p_i^*)\mathrm{d}M_i + \sum_i (p_i - c_i)\mathrm{d}X_i + \sum_i n_i c_i \left[1 - \left(\frac{1}{\theta_i}\right)\right] \mathrm{d}x_i \quad (7.27)$$

where $\theta_i$ is the ratio of average cost to marginal cost of a typical firm in industry $i$, and $n_i$ is the number of identical firms in that industry.

The left-hand side of (7.27) is the change in social welfare measured in money terms. The right-hand side tells us that this change can be broken down into three separate parts, as shown by each of the three terms. The first term is the one from the standard welfare economics of a small open economy. The welfare loss is in proportion to the wedge between domestic and foreign prices – the larger this gap, the more should expansion of imports into this sector be encouraged. However, the second term runs counter to this, since it suggests that those industries with the largest excess profits (i.e. the largest $p_i - c_i$) should experience the largest increase in output. Rodrik (1987) combines the first two terms to show that the crucial comparison is between $p_i^*$ and $c_i$. If domestic costs exceed world prices, then resources should be moved out of the sector.

The most interesting term on the right-hand side of (7.27) is the third one, which brings in scale effects. For firms with increasing returns to scale, average costs exceed marginal costs, so the $1/\theta_i < 0$. Thus expansion of output in these sectors will improve welfare. Whether or not the most heavily protected sectors are those with strongest returns to scale is of course an empirical matter, to be judged on the evidence for each African country separately. But another question is that of entry and exit. To the extent that certain firms leave the industry after liberalization, the average size of each firm does not have to drop by as much. Using simulations for Turkey, Rodrik (1987) argues that, without this effect, trade liberalization may lead to welfare losses. This suggests that attention be paid to the institutional details of firm entry and exit from an industry: making these moves easier would be an important supplement to the trade policy components of structural adjustment programmes.

## 6 Conclusion

The object of this paper has been to discuss theoretical aspects of the trade policy components of structural adjustment programmes. This is a large topic and we have focused on certain key areas. Throughout, the purpose has been to check the validity of 'conventional' analysis in the face of certain modifications which reflect African reality. By and large, our modifications tell a cautionary tale. We motivated our discussion with reference to the structural adjustment process in Côte d'Ivoire and found that trade policy instruments – export taxes and import tariffs – loomed large in the policy dialogue. In the simplest of models an uncritical application of these instruments would be supported. But if (i) disaggregation is introduced, (ii) income distribution considerations appear or (iii) scale economies are allowed for, the conventional wisdom is not necessarily valid. This is the purpose of the theoretical analysis – to systematize, to caution and to warn. It is for empirical work to draw conclusions on the balance of the argument for specific country cases.

## References

Addison, T. and Demery, L. (1985), 'Macrostabilisation and poverty: A preliminary survey', Overseas Development Institute, London.

Addison, T. and Demery, L. (1987), 'Stabilisation and poverty: A macroeconomic framework', paper prepared for the World Bank SDA project seminar at the University of Warwick, November 1987.

Brander, J. and Spencer, B. (1981), 'Tariffs and the extraction of foreign monopoly rents under potential entry', *Canadian Journal of Economics*, 14, August.

Brander, J. and Spencer, B. (1983), 'International R & D rivalry and industrial strategy', *Review of Economic Studies.*

Braverman, A. and Kanbur, S. M. R. (1987), 'Urban bias and the political economy of agricultural price reform', *World Development*, 15.

Kanbur, S. M. R. (1987a), 'Measurement and alleviation of poverty: With an application to the impact of macroeconomic adjustment', *IMF Staff Papers*, 34.

Kanbur, S. M. R. (1987b), 'Structural adjustment, macroeconomic adjustment and poverty; A methodology for analysis', *World Developmen*t, 15.

Kanbur, S. M. R. (1987c), 'Poverty under structural adjustment: A conceptual framework and its application to Côte D'Ivoire', mimeo, World Bank, Washington DC.

Knight, J. B. (1976), 'Devaluation and income distribution', *Oxford Economic Papers*, 28, July.

Krugman, P. (1986), 'New trade, theory and the less developed Countries', mimeo, WIDER, Helsinki.

Rodrik, D. (1987), 'Imperfect competition, scale economics, and trade policy in developing countries', mimeo, Department of Economics, Harvard University, Cambridge, Mass.

Srinivasan, T. N. (1986), 'Recent theories of imperfect competition and international trade: Any implications for development strategy?', mimeo, Department of Economics, Yale University, New Haven, Conn.

Venables, A. (1985), 'International trade, trade and industrial policy and imperfect competition: A survey', CEPR Discussion Paper No. 74, Centre for Economic Policy Research, London.

8

# Import compression and trade policy

Timothy Besley and Paul Collier

## 1 Introduction

The defining feature of import compression is that an economy experiencing it is required to make a rapid and substantial reduction in import volumes. This was a common experience among African countries during the 1980s. Within this definition experiences vary by cause, by duration, and by response. The principal case we consider is that in which the cause of import compression is the 'discovery' of a foreign exchange liability. Such a debt discovery creates a liability for the government which is transmitted on to the economy through government responses, which may be various. The key durational distinction is between permanent and temporary compression. The former case might be represented by the discovery of a debt burden, the servicing of which was perpetual, so that foreign exchange available for other uses is permanently reduced by a constant amount. The latter might in the limiting case have no permanent effects but simply represent a rephasing of foreign exchange receipts about an unaltered mean. The classic instance of this would be a commodity price fluctuation. Most actual experiences are a blend of permanent and temporary features: a temporary negative shock reduces permanent income but reduces current income much more. Faced by an international credit constraint, current consumption must temporarily be reduced below permanent income. We distinguish between two classes of response to these variants of import compression.

Primarily, we investigate optimal responses for the economy. Under certain assumptions discussed below, these will be the actual responses of the economy if private agents are unconstrained by government controls. However, we also consider the more typical case in which the government has a prior commitment to particular interventions, the most important of which is the exchange rate.

The model that we have in mind is of a small open economy producing traded and non-traded goods. Traded goods can be disaggregated into their exportable and importable components. The price of non-traded goods in determined domestically. Such markets are assumed to clear continuously for most of the analysis. We will comment on the extension below. We believe, however, that the assumption of price flexibility is relevant for most of Africa. For formal accounts of the trade theory on which we draw here, see Dixit and Norman (1980) and Neary and van Wijnbergen (1986).

We are interested in economies which are subject to an international borrowing constraint. If we consider an economy with a representative consumer, then this implies that, taking any two time periods, the marginal valuation of a unit of consumption today divided by the marginal valuation of consumption tomorrow (one plus the shadow rate of interest) exceeds one plus the world interest rate. Indeed the difference between the shadow and actual rate of interest provides us with a convenient measure of the extent to which a country is credit constrained i.e. it is a measure of that country's intertemporal consumption distortion. Below, we shall say that the intertemporal consumption distortion has worsened if the shadow interest rate increases. This occurs when the country concerned experiences any shock which necessitates a lower first period consumption, due for example to increased debt servicing costs or a worsened terms of trade.

This is illustrated in Figure 8.1. We consider a consumer allocating a fixed budget between two time periods $t$ and $t + 1$. The optimal allocation with no borrowing constraint is $(C_t, C_{t+1})$ and utility is $U^*$. A credit constraint forces period $t$ consumption to be $\overline{C}_{t+1}$ with period 2 consumption. The shadow interest rate is defined as the interest rate that makes it just worthwhile to voluntarily consume $\overline{C}_t$ in period $t$, i.e. it gives the relative values of present and future consumption. It is easy to see from the diagram that the shadow interest rate will be higher the greater is $\overline{C}_t$ below $C^*_t$.

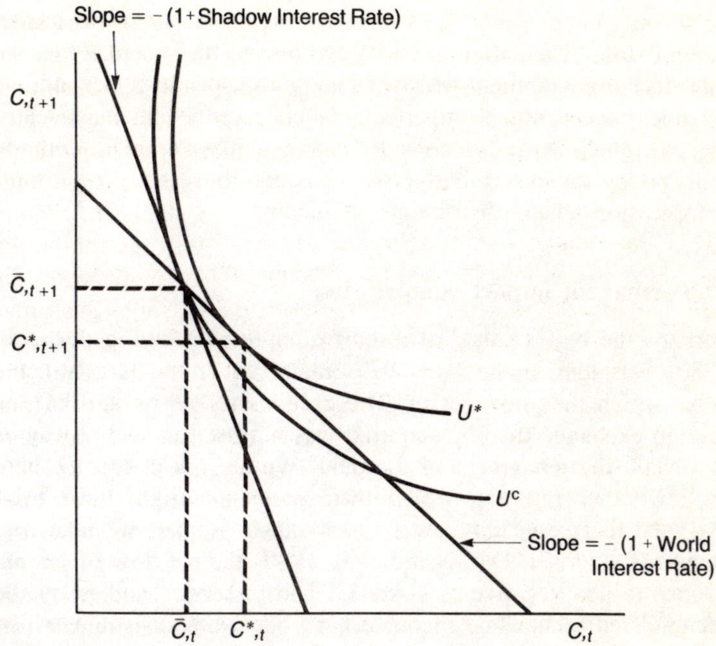


Figure 8.1 *A Credit-Constrained Consumer*

Hence anything which necessitates a further deduction in $\overline{C}_t$ increases the shadow interest rate.

Even though a country faces an international borrowing constraint, it does not follow that its investment level is inefficient. Provided that such funds as are available are intermediated perfectly by the financial system, then investors will discount at the consumer's rate of interest and will invest efficiently. This is important. In the absence of other distortions, it means that the allocation of resources attained will be Pareto efficient even though there is an international borrowing constraint. We do not believe that this best characterizes most economies in Africa. None the less, it does provide a very useful benchmark for our analysis. There are interesting questions regarding the adjustment of an efficient economy, which seem to us to be logically prior to questions concerning market imperfections. Our first task will therefore be to map out the adjustment of an efficient economy to import compression. Thereafter, we will complicate the model. First, we introduce a government which is taxing and spending. Second, we consider price rigidities, imperfect financial intermediation and learning by doing. Third, we consider changes in government controls induced by shocks. Finally, we consider the effects of import compression on the distribution of income.

## 2 Permanent import compression

Perhaps the major cause of import compression during the early 1980s was that in the late 1970s many governments contracted debts which they now regret. The grounds for regret are that the foreign exchange thereby acquired was not used in such a way as to sustain the repayment of the debt. We are not concerned here with whether rational, well-informed agents might have been expected to foresee this and so to avoid it. Rather, we take past decisions as given. During the early 1980s the net flow of private finance turned negative as countries had to service and repay the accumulated debts while encountering a borrowing constraint which prevented this from being financed by incurring new debts. We term this a *debt discovery* because at first sight, at least, it is analytically symmetrical to an oil discovery (the latter having been extensively analysed, see Neary and van Wijnbergen 1986). Whereas an oil discovery is the sudden acquisition of a foreign currency asset, a debt discovery is the sudden acquisition of a foreign exchange liability.[1]

Because of this symmetry, the outline of the first-best response is well understood. The reduction in (permanent) income causes a fall in the domestic demand for both tradable and non-tradable goods. However, since the debt is a first claim upon tradable goods output, the entire fall in income is made up of a reduced supply of tradable goods available for the economy. Hence, at the initial pattern of production, there is an excess demand for tradable goods and an excess supply of non-tradables. With flexible relative prices the latter therefore become cheaper, inducing a resource transfer into the tradable sector and moderating, but not eliminating, the fall in the demand for non-tradables. Even with this optimal switching of production and demand, the economy is worse off.

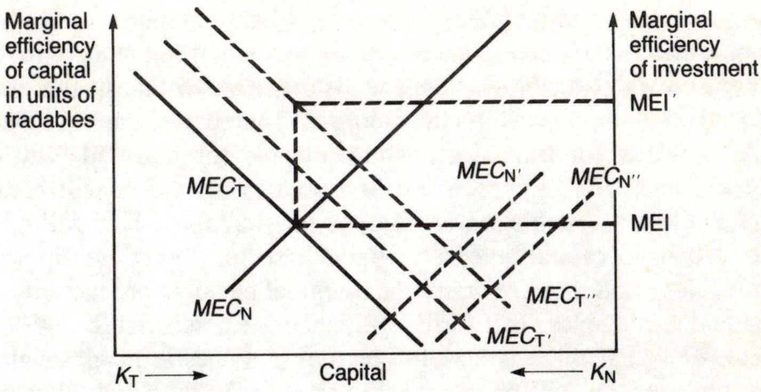


Figure 8.2 *The effect of a fall in the price of non-tradables on the marginal efficiency of investment*

However, without the contraction of non-tradables and expansion of tradables this welfare loss is accentuated.

*The effect of a debt discovery on investment*

So far the analysis has implied that the economy should instantly respond fully to the new optimal resource allocation: any delay merely incurs avoidable welfare losses. This baseline position may be altered once immobilities and adjustment costs are introduced. Capital, once installed, is usually either entirely sector specific or incurs high costs in being moved between sectors. Similarly, the skills embodied in the labour force are often sector specific.

The sectoral redeployment of capital between sectors, given that it is immobile once installed, can occur only by means of investment. In the absence of new investment, the marginal efficiency of capital rises in tradables without attracting capital from the non-tradables sector where it has fallen. Hence, the returns to investment rise as a result of the debt discovery even though the returns on the existing capital stock in aggregate fall.

This process is illustrated in Figure 8.2. The economy is initially in equilibrium at point E, capital being optimally allocated between sectors so that the marginal efficiency of investment is the same in the two sectors. The debt discovery raises the relative price of tradable goods. If capital goods are composed of some mixture of tradables and non-tradables (and there is less than perfect substitution), then the average price of capital goods will fall relative to the output of the tradable sector, and rise relative to that of the non-tradable sector. This shifts the marginal efficiency of capital schedule upwards for tradables and downwards for non-tradables, to $MEC_{T'}$ and $MEC_{N'}$ respectively. If labour is mobile, it will be attracted to the tradable sector from the non-tradable., This will raise the labour-to-capital ratio in the tradable sector (lowering it in non-tradables), and therefore raise the marginal physical productivity of capital in tradables. This further shifts the MEC schedules to $MEC_{T''}$ and $MEC_{N''}$. If there is a well-functioning domestic financial market, investment will be allocated to those projects which have the highest (risk-corrected) returns. Whereas in equilibrium these were to be found in both sectors, now they are entirely confined to the tradable sector. Hence, the MEI is the MEC in the tradables sector, and therefore rises from MEI to MEI′. Note that in the case of a positive windfall the MEI also rises. The symmetry is that the MEC schedules shift in opposite directions; the asymmetry is that in either case capital reallocation is required and investment is the process by which this takes place.

The adjustment process set out above was the standard sector-specific capital model: some factors such as labour are fully mobile, others such as capital are *ex ante* mobile, *ex post* immobile. In practice, labour is less than fully mobile; indeed, the extent of labour mobility is both a key variable and a key parameter in the adjustment process. The less mobile is labour then the less mobile is capital. This is because a key driving force attracting investment to the high-return sector is that labour is moving into it, thereby raising the marginal physical product of the existing capital stock in the sector. The less labour moves in, the less attractive is investment. Hence, labour mobility gears the whole adjustment process. The extent of their gearing depends in part upon how important is labour among the set of fully mobile factors: the fewer other factors that are mobile, the more crucial is labour mobility. Without it, the only incentive for investment is the rise in the price of tradable output relative to capital. Because of the increased returns to investment, the savings rate should increase. The converse of this is that consumption falls proportionately more than the decline in income. This is, of course, temporary, until the capital stock is expanded to the optimal level in the tradables sector. Thus, with a permanent shock such as a debt discovery, consumption should 'over-shoot' – falling by more than the percentage fall in permanent income and subsequently rising.

*The effect of debt discovery on imports of intermediate inputs*
So far we have considered the effect of a debt shock upon investment. We now consider its effect upon the volume of intermediate imports. We start with a very restrictive but simple model which nevertheless brings out some key issues in import compression. We assume that intermediate imports are used only in the tradable sector of the economy and are used in a fixed proportion, $a$, to output:

$$T = a \cdot I \,, \tag{8.1}$$

where

$T$ = the production of tradable goods valued at world prices
$I$ = the value of intermediate imports at world prices.

The economy's net output of tradable goods is therefore $(a-1)I$; in other words, the economy must export tradables to the value of $I$ to pay for the imported inputs, but it is free to absorb the remaining tradables and we will assume that prior to the debt shock it does so:

$$T^a_0 = (a - 1) \cdot I_0, \tag{8.2}$$

where

$T^a$ = the absorption of tradable goods through consumption or investment
$T^a_0$ = the value of $T^a$ in the pre-debt discovery period
$I_0$ = the value of $I$ in the pre-debt disvovery period

Upon the debt shock the capacity of the economy to make payments on its debt has as its absolute ceiling the economy's net output of tradable goods. This ceiling, $C$, which is reached once the economy's absorption of tradable goods is squeezed to zero, is given by:

$$C = (a - 1) \cdot I. \tag{8.3}$$

An important implication of this simple model is that, even with such a draconian commitment to debt payments, the volume of intermediate imports will increase as a result of the debt shock.

This is because, as we have seen, an appropriate response is for the production of tradables to increase (say to $T_1$). Intermediate imports therefore increase:

$$I_1 - I_0 = (T_1 - T_0)/a. \qquad (8.4)$$

In the above model intermediate goods were the only imports (since the economy acquired its other tradable goods through absorbing domestic production). Hence, in such an economy the appropriate response to a debt shock would give rise to import expansion not import compression (what gets compressed is the absorption of tradable goods). This gives rise to the apparent paradox that in order to maximize its payments on debt the economy must initially increase its borrowings to enable the extra imports to be financed. The rational external creditor in such an economy would therefore choose to extend further loans. If the creditor either refuses to extend further loans, or insists upon a more rapid repayment of debt than given by (8.3), he pays a cost in terms of lower future flows of repayments. For each \$1 repaid by means of compressing imports of intermediate goods, the creditor loses future annual repayments of $\$(a - 1)$. With real interest rates currently around 5 per cent, the rational creditor will therefore avoid import compression as long as $a > 1.05$. The coefficient $a$ tells us about value added by domestic firms at world prices. If $a$ is unity then the activity of the firm is useless: its output is worth only the same as its tradable inputs and so there is no value added. By extension, for all activities where $a$ is less than unity there is negative value added at world prices, so the economy augments its supply of tradable goods by closing the activity down. Parts of the industrial sector in Africa are so characterized. However, a critical value of 1.05 is, in fact, a very modest hurdle which is met once the share of value added in final output exceeds around 5 per cent. It would therefore be a mistake for the creditor in such an economy to restrict imports while there were tradable activities which passed this test and could otherwise be expanded. An indication that the activity could be expanded is if there is excess capacity. Thus, excess capacity can indicate that the economy is experiencing excessive import compression even from the viewpoint of the creditor. However, excess capacity can also indicate that the economy has undertaken investments in activities which have a share of value added in final output of below 5 per cent (for example, the share may be negative). Since the best that can be done with such investments is to abandon them, appropriate behaviour will give rise to excess capacity.

The above model has served to show that it is possible for the appropriate response to debt discovery to involve an increase in imports which a rational creditor would choose to finance. However, the model has made several extreme assumptions which we now discuss. First, the model assumed that all imports were intermediate goods, the economy acquiring other tradables through domestic production. More reasonably, the economy trades some of its net output of tradables. In this case, as absorption is reduced it is possible for total imports to fall even though imports of intermediate goods increase. Second, the model assumed that intermediate imports were used only in the tradable sector. More plausibly some are also used in the non-tradable sector. By contracting the non-tradable sector it is therefore possible for total imports of intermediate goods to be reduced even though intermediate imports for the tradable sector increase. Third, the model assumed that production involved fixed coefficients between intermediate imports and final output. There are, however, two processes by which the coefficient will fall as a result of debt discovery. Even if the coefficient is fixed in each firm, it will still differ between firms. Hence, as those firms which use imported inputs intensively contract relative to those which use them only a little, the average coefficient for the economy will fall. Further, within each firm there is likely to be scope for substitution between domestic factors of production and imported inputs: for example, in agriculture more frequent weeding is a substitute for the application of imported herbicides. Taken together, these processes imply that it is unlikely that the appropriate response to a debt discovery will be other than a contraction in imports. However, what remains valid is the result that it is inappropriate for tradable activities with positive value added at world prices to be constrained by a shortage of intermediate imports.

## 3 Temporary import compression

### *The effect on savings and investment*

So far we have considered only the case in which the negative shock is known to be permanent. In Africa most shocks have turned out to be temporary, although *ex ante* there is usually uncertainty as to their magnitude and duration. We therefore enrich the framework discussed in section 2 first by considering a known temporary negative shock and then by introducing uncertainty.

The appropriate response to a temporary negative shock follows from the theory of permanent income, a theory which has recently been extended by Deaton (1989) and Deaton and Laroque (1989) to include constraints upon borrowing. Deaton (1989) models the savings profile of an infinitely lived agent who is subject to temporary income shocks and borrowing constraints. He assumes that individuals have discount rates above the market interest rate. Were this not the case then, as Bewley (1977) has shown, agents would eventually accumulate enough assets for temporary shocks not to matter. In Deaton's model, agents sometimes find it optimal to run their savings to zero. Moreover, he finds that even relatively low levels of savings can lead to fairly substantial smoothing in the profile of the marginal utility of income.

During a temporary negative shock, both transient and permanent income fall and each gives rise to a change in behaviour. However, the consequences of a fall in permanent income have already been considered in our discussion of a debt discovery in section 2. Hence, we now abstract from the change in permanent income, considering a temporary negative shock which leaves permanent income unaltered. This leaves only the transient income effect: a temporary negative shock implies that transient income is negative and so the agent should dis-save. This involves either the decumulation of assets or the accumulation of debts. Most African countries are rationed in the world credit market and so do not have the option of choosing to increase debts, nor do most countries hold foreign financial assets. Hence, dis-saving involves the reduction of the domestic capital stock. In turn, this involves a reduction in gross investment. There is a close analogy here (though not complete symmetry) with the case of a temporary positive shock. Bevan *et al.* (1987, 1989a,b and 1990) show how a positive trade shock will give rise to an investment boom. They also disaggregate investment into its tradable and non-tradable components, introducing the concept of a *construction boom*, a rise in the relative price of non-tradable capital goods caused by an increase in investment. A pure temporary negative shock (i.e. one with no impact upon permanent income) can be expected to give rise to a construction slump, and this was indeed common to many African economies during the 1980s.

However, a construction slump is by no means inevitable as a response to a temporary negative shock. Recall that in response to a permanent negative shock investment should rise to assist the movement of resources into the tradables sector. In the case of a pure temporary negative shock with no impact upon permanent income, investment should fall. But both of these are extremely unlikely polar cases. Very few shocks are permanent and, since agents have finite lives, even temporary shocks will give rise to some change in permanent income almost regardless of the frequency distribution of expected events from which the shock is perceived to be a drawing. Hence, in the general case of a temporary negative shock which reduces permanent income, the response of investment is ambiguous because there are two offsetting effects.

The first arises because of a worsening of the intertemporal consumption distortion (i.e. a rise in the shadow interest rate). This is as a consequence of the reduction in consumption which a temporary negative shock entails. This acts like a rise in the interest rate and makes capital accumulation less attractive, no matter which sector is being considered. We refer to this as the intertemporal consumption effect of import compression. The second effect arises because of the desire to transfer capital to the traded goods sector. As we noted in section 2, this is motivated by sector specificity of capital. To combat the effects of import compression, resources must be transferred to the traded goods sector and this can be done only by investing in this sector. This we refer to as the resource transfer effect of import compression. The presence of these two competing effects explains why the effect upon capital accumulation is ambiguous. Whether there is an increased or reduced level of investment depends upon which is dominant.[2]

To summarize, a temporary positive external shock gives rise to a construction boom because two effects work in the same direction. The increase in permanent income to which the shock gives rise will change the relative price of non-tradables to tradables. As a result the initial capital stock is no longer optimally allocated. Since it cannot be moved (except at a cost), there is a premium upon capital mobility. Investment is the main process which enables capital to be relocated between sectors and so the returns to investment rise. The extra demand for investment is partly for capital such as buildings which cannot be imported and so, unless there is very easy substitutability between tradable and non-tradable capital, the investment boom will cause a construction boom. Since transient income increases during a temporary boom, savings also increase. Except in the special case of access to perfect world capital markets (which can be dismissed as far as most of Africa is concerned), an increase in savings will give rise to an increase in investment. Again, extra investment will partly take the form of non-tradable capital goods and so give rise to a construction boom. A temporary negative shock is not fully symmetrical. First, the fall in permanent income still gives rise to a change in the relative price of tradables to non-tradables. Although this is in the reverse direction, any change implies that the initial allocation of the capital stock is no longer optimal and so there is again an incentive to relocate capital by means of investment. This route from a trade shock to the construction sector thus tells us that a trade shock in either direction will stimulate the construction sector. However, transient income is now negative and so the economy dissaves. Here again there is to some extent an asymmetry because it is far harder for the economy to borrow in world capital markets during a negative shock than it is for it to acquire assets in the world capital market during a positive shock. Hence, whereas a substantial part of windfall savings can be in the form of foreign financial assets rather than investment, virtually all dissaving must take the form of a reduction in the domestic capital stock. The way of reducing the stock of non-tradable capital is not to pull buildings down but rather to let them fall down; that is, to cut back on maintenance and replacement, and these activities are largely undertaken by the construction sector. Hence, a negative temporary shock gives rise to two opposing effects on the construction sector, though empirically during the 1980s the net effect was a severe contraction.

*Uncertainty introduced*

Now consider the consequences of the uncertainty associated with the duration and magnitude of the negative shock. The work of Dixit (1989a,b,c) provides important insights into how uncertainty can interact with adjustment costs. The central idea is that, because it is costly to undo investment decisions once they have been implemented, in the presence of uncertainty it is better to remain liquid than to undertake an investment which, if outcomes were certain, would be only marginally attractive. One implication of Dixit's work is that even a pure temporary negative shock can give rise to permanent effects as a result of *hysteresis*.

Adjustment costs generate barriers to mobility. The cost of abandoning a half-finished investment project may be large. For example, half-completed buildings decay rapidly. Capital located in one sector may be non-fungible and hence it may be costly to uproot machines or turn over buildings to different uses. When this is true, the question of what is the optimal response is at once more interesting and more complex.

To examine the implications of adjustment costs under uncertainty, we shall review the analysis of this problem in Dixit (1989a). Dixit supposes that any investment project has sunk costs of entry and exit. He has a simple model in which the price of the good in which entry is being contemplated is uncertain but determines the pay-off to investing. The key to understanding Dixit's analysis is the idea that uninvested capital has an *option value*. Suppose that we are in a risky environment, in which an investment with capital cost $w$ per unit of time has sunk costs of entry $k$ and costs of exit $l$. If $\rho$ is the discount rate, the simplest argument suggests that if the return exceeds $w + \rho k$ the investment is worthwhile and if it is less than $w + \rho l$ it should be scrapped. Under uncertainty this argument is not valid. Suppose that the price of an exportable is just high enough to make the present value of a project equal to zero then, under uncertainty, it is always better to wait before investing. To see this, note that if at the end of the first period the price has risen, then the project now has positive value. If, on the other hand, the price has fallen, then no investment is made and the present value is still zero. Hence, waiting always has a positive expected value. The reason is that investment has an option value and it is not worth exercising the option until it is deeper in the money. Dixit shows that the solution to the optimal stochastic control problem determining the decision to invest has two trigger prices. The first is greater than $w + \rho k$ and is such that, if there is shock making the return to the project exceed this value, then investment is worthwhile. The second is below $w + \rho l$ and is such that a fall in the project return below this trigger price makes scrapping the project worthwhile. Dixit (1989a) shows that the difference between these two trigger prices is an increasing function of the sunk costs attached to entry and exit and the amount of uncertainty.

Turning now to the implications of this for temporary import compression, we can employ the insights from Dixit's work to consider the effect of either a temporary shock to the terms of trade or a temporary debt discovery. For small enough shocks, it may be rational for no projects to be abandoned; i.e. for there to be no cut in capital accumulation at all. Note, however, that in Dixit's model $\rho$ (the discount rate) is held fixed, and we would expect it to rise in the face of import compression because of the intertemporal consumption effect. This complicates the analysis somewhat but does not alter the general principles. Hysteresis is possible in this model because it may not be worthwhile abandoning projects undertaken when returns are abnormally high if returns fall again at a later date. Similarly, it may not be worthwhile resuming abandoned projects after a temporary negative shock. Hence the set of projects which an economy is pursuing at any point in time ought rationally to be related to the pattern of temporary shocks experienced in the past. Dixit's analysis also explains the rationality of 'weathering the storm' of temporary import compression by not abandoning projects which, although worthwhile when undertaken, would not be attractive if the decision whether or not to undertake them were made today.

## 4 The scope for policy intervention?

*Adjustments by governments*

In this section, we shall make the government directly liable for the discovered debt. The transmission of the income loss on to the economy now depends upon how the government chooses to meet this liability. Its basic choice is between increased taxation and reduced spending. Within the latter category it must choose between reducing capital and current spending. Our aim here is to look at the principles which govern these choices.

Consider a government currently intervening by levying taxes, and spending on both capital and consumption goods. Such interventions could be motivated by distributional concerns. However, it will suit our present purpose better to suppose that the government is spending on goods which would not otherwise be provided privately, the largest class of which are public goods. We will suppose that it is levying taxes from its citizens in order to finance these. If lump-sum taxation is infeasible, because of informational or social barriers, then this means that the model of the last section, in which the adjustments by the private sector coincided with the Pareto-efficient choices, will no longer be valid.

There are two interesting questions to be addressed in this framework. First, what is the optimal adjustment of public expenditures by the government to debt discovery and, second, how should tax policy be altered? Here, we will concentrate on the first of these issues. In particular, we are interested in the principles which guide the choice between cutting capital and current expenditures in the face of an import compression.

The introduction of the government raises the issue of how its objectives should be modelled. Since for the moment we are setting distributional considerations aside, the most natural assumption seems to be that the government is maximizing the welfare of a representative consumer and most of our analysis will labour under this assumption. This raises two difficulties. The first is that the conditions under which it is possible to aggregate so that the economy behaves as if it were motivated by the actions of a single economic agent are well known to be restrictive, in spite of the popularity of proceeding in this way (see Deaton and Muellbauer 1980, chapter 6). Second, it seems manifestly inappropriate as a behavioural model for many of the governments that we have seen in Africa. More typically, governments value the well-being of certain segments of their populations above that of others and seem to be prepared to sacrifice a good deal of economic efficiency in pursuing it. In spite of both of these reservations, we wish to preserve the spirit of the last two sections and try to find something resembling an ideal adjustment path from the perspective of economic efficiency.

We will begin by considering the case in which the government reacts to debt discovery by cutting public expenditures, i.e. we will assume taxes to be fixed. We shall refer to the value of a unit more of public expenditure at the margin as its *shadow price*. Supposing that the government supplies a single homogeneous good which can be used for either investment or consumption purposes, the rule for optimal public expenditure is that its shadow price be equated in both of its possible uses. Hence the response of the optimal mix of public expenditure between these two ends depends upon how the relative shadow prices of public investment and consumption change in the face of import compression. A crucial variable will be the shadow interest rate, which we argued above will rise in the face of import compression. Under our assumption of perfect internal financial intermediation, this will be the discount rate used for public projects. Hence, projects which yield returns in the future will be dispreferred relative to those with only current pay offs. This is the intertemporal consumption effect which we discussed above and implies a preference for cutting capital rather than current expenditures. There are other effects however, and it is to these which we turn now.

First, there are effects arising through changes in relative prices; specifically those of non-traded goods. These give rise to analogs of resource transfer effects. We would expect debt discovery to lower the price of non-traded goods, with the magnitude of this effect depending upon the marginal propensity to consume non-traded goods. Hence, there are motives to shift resources from the non-traded to the traded goods sector. The government will face similar motives, since we would expect the shadow price of public expenditure to increase relatively for those publicly provided goods used disproportionately by the traded goods sector. In more concrete terms, public projects intended to improve the infrastructure for the production of agricultural exportables should be enhanced in the face of debt discovery, relative to those which benefit non-tradables industries.

A second consideration concerns the complementarity and substitutability between public and private expenditures. If public and private projects are complements, and the resource transfer effect for private capital formation outweighs the intertemporal consumption effect, then it seems more likely that public sector capital spending, especially in the traded goods sector, should be maintained.

Hence, while the rise in the shadow interest rate makes it likely that public sector capital expenditure should rationally bear the brunt of adjustment to import compression, there are two main caveats: first, the effects arising because of relative price changes and second because of possible complementarities between public and private expenditures.

The above analysis has largely been concerned with how a fully decentralized market economy both should and would respond to import compression. Even if the government has no role to play in this process, it is important for the government to understand the changes that are at work in the economy. This is for two reasons. First, the government might itself have some view as to a desirable long-term development path. Resource reallocations which are first-best responses to the shock might run counter to some of these views. It is therefore vital that the government understands the adjustment process sufficiently to recognize these changes as desirable rather than attempting to impede them. That is, the government must achieve a more sophisticated understanding of the development path so as to realize that in the event of external shocks the ideal path is not straightforward. Second, all resource reallocations, however desirable, generate winners and losers. Losers typically lobby to prevent change. This lobbying does not occur in isolation; it is superimposed upon the continuous lobbying by those firms which have been unlucky in the normal course of business. Because of incomplete insurance and credit markets together with the disruption costs of bankruptcy, there is often a good case to be made for aiding the latter category of lobbyists to continue in business. By contrast, the former group, while they may warrant compensation, should not be helped to survive in a sector in which contraction is required. The government needs to understand optimal resource reallocation in order to distinguish between the two categories of lobbyist.

The virtues of a passive, or permissive, government policy should not be underestimated. However, there are some circumstances in which active responses are optimal. First, the government is very likely itself to be the major producer of non-tradable capital goods, notably infrastructure. In this case the optimal change in the output of this sector must be implemented by government decisions. The fact of public provision does not itself alter the optimal change in the output of the sector, which is determined as modelled above; it merely changes the mode of resource allocation from being market determined. The government therefore needs to know optimal resource reallocation in order to plan the response of the sector which it controls.

Second, there are possible imperfections in the market mechanism which may make the responses of private agents sub-optimal. The three most important in the present context are credit rationing, nominal rigidities (particularly in labour markets) and learning-by-doing externalities. We shall consider each of these in turn.

*Imperfect financial markets*

Even if there are imperfections in financial markets, it does not follow that the government can find Pareto-superior allocations by judicious interventions. To see this logic, consider the most widely cited source of credit market problems – imperfect information. As Jaffee and Russell (1976) have pointed out, two kinds of imperfect information problem are encountered. First, there are problems of adverse selection since lenders do not know borrowers' 'types'. Second, there are moral hazard problems since indebtedness reduces a borrower's incentive to make his/her projects successful. Both of these have implications for the way in which credit markets operate and may result in credit rationing (see Stiglitz and Weiss 1981). It does not follow, however, that the government can improve upon this allocation except in the implausible scenario in which it has better information about individual borrowers and their actions than do lenders. On the other hand, it is unlikely that the economy will be constrained Pareto efficient (see Greenwald and Stiglitz 1986). Economies with imperfect information typically have important non-convexities and externalities. Moreover, the experience of governments in Africa with credit policy reinforces the conclusion that, while credit markets typically do not work perfectly, government interventions bring their own set of problems with them.

Problems with imperfect financial intermediation imply that investment levels before import compression are not socially optimal. Contrary to immediate expectation, it is possible that investment levels may be too high relative to the social optimun in the presence of capital market imperfections induced by informational problems (see De Meza and Webb 1987). The main question is whether investment distortions are increased or reduced by import compression, i.e. is the wedge between the market and shadow price increased or reduced. This will determine how corrective policies, if they are employed, should be adjusted.

*Nominal rigidities*

Much of the literature on the Dutch disease has focused upon nominal rigidities, especially in labour markets (see Neary and van

Wijnbergen 1986, chapter 1). The focus of the problem is the involuntary unemployment to which import compression gives rise in the process of intersectoral relocation of resources. Under certain conditions, it may be optimal for governments to intervene in softening the adjustment process, i.e. allowing the process of resource transfer between sectors to take place more slowly. This may well apply in Francophone Africa where, because of low inflation, the downward nominal rigidity of wages gives rise to rigidity in the real wage. However, in much of Anglophone Africa inflation has been sufficiently rapid for a downward nominal rigidity to be compatible with a high degree of real wage flexibility.

If nominal rigidities are a problem, then the relative price of non-traded and traded goods may fail to fall, resulting in unemployment in the non-traded goods sector. There may, therefore, be a case to 'soften' the impact of import compression by slowing down the period of adjustment, e.g. by subsidizing the output of some non-traded goods.

*Learning by doing*

A further possible source of imperfections which might merit government attention concerns dynamic economies of scale, or learning by doing. Indeed, this was made the focus of the Dutch disease problem by van Wijnbergen (1984). He argued that the reason temporary resource-diverting shocks of the kind considered here are harmful is that learning by doing involves an externality, i.e. investors in some sectors fail to internalize the benefit which their being in that sector conveys on others who enter the industry later. Van Wijnbergen shows that the optimal subsidy to an industry with learning-by-doing externalities might increase when there is a temporary change in the terms of trade. This is an area in which the scope for government intervention both before and after import compression may be quite substantial. It ties in also with important recent work in growth theory by Lucas (1988) and Romer (1986), who emphasize externalities from growth in the form of knowledge production which results in increasing returns. This implies that the economy does not grow at an efficient rate without government intervention.

The difficulty in applying these ideas lies in identifying which industries are appropriate objects for subsidization on grounds of their bringing favourable externalities. There are also difficult questions concerning the appropriate time profile for subsidization. Delving into the political economy of the problem also suggests that subsidization on the general ground of there being favourable externalities for the rest of the economy creates vested interests which ultimately may tie the hands of policy-makers by limiting the scope for flexible policy-making.

## 5 Endogenous control regimes

So far we have considered only those responses to a negative temporary external shock which are appropriate. However, in some African economies responses have been inappropriate because of government commitments to the maintenance of particular policy instruments. We consider two key instruments: the nominal exchange rate and the nominal interest rate. If the exchange rate is maintained constant in the face of a negative shock then there will be excess demand for foreign exchange. The shortage of foreign exchange will lead to a tightening of trade restrictions, in Africa typically in the form of quotas. We refer to this as an *endogenous trade policy*. The inefficiency costs of trade restrictions are now well understood, and so it can be concluded that such a trade policy response to a negative shock is inappropriate. If the maximun interest rate that banks can charge remains constant then, as a result of dissaving, the temporary negative shock will give rise to a shortage of credit. In turn, the shortage of credit will lead to higher-risk projects being squeezed out of the loan market, which constitutes *endogenous financial repression*. Again, it is now well understood that financial repression is costly, so that such a response in inappropriate. To generalize from these two examples, if the government is committed to the maintenance of nominal policy instruments, a negative shock will give rise to shortages. The control systems which determine the allocation of shortages will then respond. We term this structure an *endogenous control regime*. These responses are unambiguously second best. The relevant question is not whether they are inferior to the use of the market, but by how much they are inferior. Were information free, the central bank, or whatever other government organization is determining the allocation, would simply have to work out the optimal response as indicated in the previous section, and allocate imports accordingly. The problem of non-market allocation is precisely that information is costly. Governments cannot afford full information, and private agents have an incentive to supply false information. Hence, government allocations will be in error.

Attempts to control the economy in a direct fashion have often resulted in the formation of parallel markets – most often as a vent for excess demand in official markets. These markets may lead to substantial changes in the resource allocation which a planner intends. Such effects are illustrated vividly by the experience of Ghana (see Azam and Besley 1989 for a more detailed discussion). Attempts to tax exporters (cocoa farmers) through lowering producer prices and to restrict imports (especially of consumer goods) through quantitative controls led to smuggling of cocoa to neighbouring Côte d'Ivore and Togo. The impact of import compression is then felt through price changes in informal markets. In the Ghanaian case, a reduction in imports would raise the parallel market price of consumer goods and thereby increase the premium to be gained by smuggling cocoa (since cocoa smuggling permits the acquisition of foreign exchange to acquire importables illegally). The net effect is that cocoa output sold through official channels is reduced and further cuts in quantities of imports are required. Such effects continue until a new equilibrium is reached in which parallel market prices for goods and foreign exchange are both higher than before and fewer transactions take place in offical markets.

This example reveals the importance of considering parallel market activities when governments operate quantitative restrictions. Such restrictions also give rise to lobbying activities on the part of those who feel disadvantaged in the allocation process. Compared with the first-best outcome described above, such activities are directly unproductive. However, in the context of an economy which is distorted by government controls, lobbying activity can actually be productive if those whose lobbying is most vociferous happen to have the highest shadow price for those goods which are rationed. A similar conclusion can be drawn about trade in parallel markets. Such markets typically use inefficient transactions technologies because of the need to evade detection when trading illegally. For example, smugglers may need to travel across country to cross the border rather than crossing at regular check points, with the consequence that transport costs are increased.

Hence parallel markets work inefficiently in comparison with the first best. However, *given the constraint of quantitative controls*, they increase the efficiency of resource allocation.

## 6 Import compression and income distribution

In this section we relax our assumption of a single representative consumer in order to incorporate distributional considerations into our analysis. A full examination of the issues is beyond the scope of this paper and some of them are taken up in Kanbur's contribution to this volume (Chapter 7). Our aim here is limited. We wish to identify only the main channels whereby import compression may have an effect.

Import compression will generally be associated with reductions in government expenditure. Two groups will lose from these reductions – the recipients and the suppliers of public goods. However, we will abstract from these effects, focusing upon the distributional consequences of relative price changes.

Five mappings determine the distributional consequences of import compression. First, there is the mapping from import compression onto relative prices of goods. This mapping depends upon the causes of import compression (debt discovery or a terms of trade deterioration), the policy response (exchange-rate depreciation or import restrictions), and the production process. We argued that, in the normal case, debt discovery met by exchange-rate depreciation will lower the demand for non-tradable goods. This will cause a reduction in their relative price in most but not all circumstances. One case in which relative prices are unaltered is that in which the economy produces both the tradable goods as well as the non-tradable under constant returns technology with two mobile and competitively priced factors. In this case factor prices are determined by the (given) terms of trade, and these factor prices in turn set the relative price of non-tradable goods. Hence, relative prices are unaltered by debt discovery except to the extent that the government increases indirect taxes differentially in order to finance the debt servicing. This case is something of a curiosum because of the high degree of factor mobility required.

In the case in which debt discovery is met by import restrictions, the price of importables rises relative to both exportables and non-tradables, but the price of exportables relative to non-tradables may rise or fall. The same relative price changes occur if import compression is the result not of debt discovery but of a deterioration in the terms of trade, whether or not the policy response includes import restrictions.

Second, there is the mapping from relative prices of goods to the relative prices of the factors which produce them. This mapping may take several forms depending upon how the production process is characterized. Clearly, in the debt discovery curiosum considered above, factor prices are unaltered. Now consider two variations to that model. First assume that the economy does not produce the importable good. This reduces the analysis to the standard two goods, two factors model. As the relative price of non-tradables declines owing to import compression, both the relative and the absolute returns to the factor used intensively in the production of the exportable good will rise. Alternatively, assume that there is one factor specific to each sector and one mobile factor. In the case of debt discovery met by depreciation, returns rise absolutely for the factor specialized in tradables production, fall absolutely for the factor specialized in non-tradables production, and may rise or fall for the mobile factor.

In the case of debt discovery met by import restrictions and a terms of trade deterioration, the domestic relative price of exportables falls as discussed above. The factor specialized in importables production gains higher returns. Recall that the change in the relative price of non-tradables and exportables is *a priori* ambiguous. The factor specialized in the production of the one of these whose relative price declines unambiguously loses. The factor specialized in the remaining sector, and the mobile factor, may either lose or gain.

Once intermediate imported inputs are introduced, it becomes possible that the factor specialized in the importables sector also loses from import compression even though the relative price of importables rises. This is because the output of the sector may fall as a result of scarcity of inputs. Demand for the specialized factor is consequently reduced, even though, were firms able to achieve their production plans, it would rise. This case is probably particularly pertinent to the emergence of spare capacity and the decline in the profitability of the import-substitute manufacturing sector in much of Africa during the 1980s.

The third mapping is from relative prices of goods onto rents.

If the policy response to import compression is first best, i.e. exchange-rate depreciation, then rents will not be generated. However, when the response is to restrict imports through quantity rationing (QR), then rents are created as a result of the gap between the c.i.f. price of imports and their domestic retail price. If the economy already had some QRs prior to import compression, then it is *a priori* ambiguous whether the total value of rents will increase or fall as a result of the tightening of QRs: the increased element of rent per unit of imports is qualitatively offset by the lower volume of imports. Considering an economy which starts from no QRs and progressively tightens them up to the limit of zero imports, the value of rents will first rise and eventually fall back to zero. The beneficiaries of rents are those agents able to gain access to imports at c.i.f. prices (or equivalently to foreign exchange at the official exchange rate). Three types of agent have an advantage. Among producers, those firms which have a high import content relative to value added will have the largest 'legitimate' claim for foreign exchange. The second type of agent to benefit is firms which distribute imports. Finally, public employees responsible for the allocation of foreign exchange have an opportunity to acquire the rents. This distribution of the rents from trade controls is unfortunate because in each case rewards are giving the wrong signals to the economy. Producers with a high import content alreay command excessive resources if the exchange rate is over valued, without being additionally rewarded by rents. Distributors of imports have less work to do as a result of import compression, yet their acquisition of rents can make the sector more rather than less attractive for entrants. Public employees responsible for the allocation of foreign exchange are precisely the decision-takers who should be undertaking a regime switch from the second best of import controls to the first best of depreciation, yet they are a group who will lose rents as a result.

The fourth mapping is from factor prices (and rents) to household incomes. Were all households to be endowed with a common ratio of factors, then clearly factor price changes would not affect the personal distribution of income. In much of Africa, exportables, importables and non-tradables tend to be produced by factors owned by different social groups, so that changes in factor prices indeed give rise to powerful redistributions. The sector-specific capital and land of the export sector is usually owned by regionally concentrated peasant households, so that benefits will accrue to spatially (and therefore commonly tribally) distinct groups of households. The sector-specific capital of the import-substitute sector is frequently owned either by the state or by a racial minority (Asian in East Africa, Lebanese in West Africa). The non-tradables sector is frequently dominated by household production (informal services in urban areas, food in rural areas), and so the ownership of factors specialized in these activities tends to be highly concentrated among a subset of households.

The fifth mapping is from the change in relative prices of goods onto changes in the cost of living. Because households differ in their expenditure patterns, even common changes in nominal income will give rise to different changes in real income as the cost of living rises differentially. In general, the fall in non-tradables prices relative to importables might favour the poor, whose consumption pattern is skewed towards food (usually non-tradable) and away from imported consumer durables. However, there are two qualifications to this. First, many peasant households will be net sellers of food, so that their expenditure pattern is very different from their consumption pattern. Such households stand to lose from the fall in the relative price of the good which they are selling. Second, because peasant households are production units, whereas the households of urban wage-earners are only consumption units, the expenditure pattern of peasant households includes farm inputs which often have a high import content. Hence, although the consumption pattern of peasants is skewed against those goods whose price is rising, their expenditure pattern may be skewed in its favour.

The conjunction of these five mappings determines how import compression will alter the distribution of household living standards. No *a priori* generalization as to the net effect appears justified. The distributional consequences can be expected to differ depending upon whether import compression takes the form of debt discovery or terms of trade deterioration, whether the policy response is first or second best, and the specific characteristics of the production process and the patterns of expenditure. However, just because no analytic generalization can be reached does not mean that the distributional effects are either modest or unresearchable. The appropriate technique for analysis becomes a computable general equilibrium model.

## 7 Conclusion

A negative external shock (temporary or permanent) is clearly a misfortune for an economy. However, the magnitude of the decline in living standards can be mitigated or exacerbated depending upon the responses by all the actors involved. In this paper, we have focused on resource movements into the tradable goods sector in response to the discovery of a foreign exchange liability. For the case of capital goods, we have emphasized the importance of mobility costs. If capital is immobile once installed, then a temporary negative shock might actually imply that investment should be increased. In the case of intermediate goods, we have emphasized the folly of import compression through allowing shortages of intermediate inputs to reduce the output of tradable goods. Creditors who restrict intermediate inputs in this way are acting against their own long-tern interest as much as that of the countries to which have lent.

There is no panacea for an economy which experiences import compression. There are, however, appropriate and inappropriate responses by government. These involve redeployment of government resources which are complementary to private sector resource flows. They may also involve using instruments intended to even out the burden of import compression across groups of agents. This is a difficult political economy problem whence the insights obtained from thinking about the most efficient path of adjustment will surely be useful.

## Notes

1 An alternative source of import compression arises as a consequence of an adverse terms of trade movement. This is considered further below.

2 If the shock is not a debt discovery but a deterioration in the terms of trade, the above analysis must be complicated. Tradables must be disaggregated into their importable and exportable components. There are now two domestic relative prices which can change – that between exportables and importables and that between non-traded and importables. One would expect both of these to fall, implying a flow of resources to the importables sector. The change in the relative price of exportables and non-traded goods is *a priori* ambiguous, and with it the direction of resource flows between the non-traded and export sectors. The central difference with the debt discovery case, therefore,

is that now there is no presumption that it is desirable for the export sector to be expanded. Hence, while there is still an intertemporal consumption effect, the resource transfer effect is somewhat more complicated in this case. On the other hand, the same basic story is possible in which the need to transfer resources to importables can necessitate a rise in capital accumulation. However, since there may be no resource transfer motive in the direction of exportables, one would expect that the possibility of increased capital accumulation would be less likely when a terms of trade shock is a cause of import compression.

Since many governments in Africa raise substantial revenues from export taxation, a terms of trade shock raises similar issues to a debt discovery; the government must either find new sources of tax revenue or cut its expenditures. There may also be an effect if the government absorbs tradables in producing its output. There is a further difference from the debt discovery case in so far as the change in the relative price of exportables affects the relative shadow prices of different types of government expenditures. This complicates the analysis somewhat, although we shall not pursue this in any detail here.

## References

Azam, J. P. and Besley, T. J. (1989), 'General equilibrium with parallel markets for goods and foreign exchange: Theory and application to Ghana', *World Development*, 17.

Bevan, D., Collier, P. and Gunning, J. W. (1987), 'Consequences of a commodity boom in a controlled economy: Accumulation and redistribution in Kenya 1975–83', *World Bank Economic Review*, pp. 489–515.

Bevan. D., Collier, P. and Gunning, J. W. (1989a), *Controlled Open Economies: A Neo-Classical Approach to Structuralism*, Oxford University Press, Oxford.

Bevan. D., Collier, P. and Gunning, J. W. (1989b), 'Economic policy in countries prone to temporary trade shocks', in M. Fg. Scott and D. Lal (eds), *Public Policy and Economic Development*, Oxford University Press, Oxford.

Bevan. D., Collier, P. and Gunning, J. W. (1990), 'The theory of construction booms: the new macroeconomics of temporary external shocks', in S. Lall and V. N. Balasubramanyam (eds), *Current Issues in Development Economics*, London, MacMillan.

Bewley, T. (1977), 'The permanent income hypothesis: A theoretical formulation', *Journal of Economic Theory*, 16, December.

Deaton, A. S. (1989), 'Saving in developing countries: Theory and review', Woodrow Wilson School, Research Program in Development Studies Discussion Paper No. 144.

Deaton, A. S. and Laroque, G. (1989), 'On the behavior of commodity prices', mimeo.

Deaton, A. S. and Muellbauer, J. N. J. (1980), *Economics and Consumer Behaviour*, Cambridge University Press, Cambridge.

De Meza, D. and Webb, D. (1987), 'Too much investment: A problem of asymmetric information?', *Quarterly Journal of Economics*, 102.

Dixit, A. (1989a), 'Entry and exit decisions under uncertainty', *Journal of Political Economy*, 97.

Dixit, A. (1989b), 'Hysteresis, import penetration and exchange rate pass-through', *Quarterly Journal of Economics*., 104, February.

Dixit, A. (1989c), 'Intersectoral capital relocation under price uncertainty', *Journal of International Economics*, 26, May.

Dixit, A. and Norman V. (1980), *Theory of International Trade*, Cambridge University Press, Cambridge.

Greenwald, B. and Stiglitz, J. E. (1986), 'Externalities in economies with incomplete markets and imperfect information', *Quarterly Journal of Economics*, 101, May.

Jaffee, D and Russell, T. (1976), 'Imperfect information, uncertainty and credit rationing', *Quarterly Journal of Economics*, 90, pp. 657–66.

Lucas, R. (1988), 'On the mechanics of economic development', *Journal of Monetary Economics*, 22, July.

Neary, J. P. and van Wijnbergen, S. (1986), *Natural Resources and the Macro-Economy*, Cambridge University Press, Cambridge.

Romer, P. (1986), 'Increasing returns and long run growth', *Journal of Political Economy*, 94.

Stiglitz, J. E. and Weiss, A. (1981), 'Credit rationing in markets with imperfect information', *American Economic Review*, 71.

van Wijnbergen, S. (1984), 'Dutch disease: A disease after all?', *Economic Journal*, 94, March.

9

# International trade and economic development in Tanzania

Benno J. Ndulu and Nguyuru H. I. Lipumba

## 1 Introduction and background

The growth and development of African economies in general and Tanzania in particular have been influenced significantly by both the external trade environment and domestic policies geared towards utilizing opportunities of trade and responding to constraints to trade. The domestic policies involved include exchange rates, tariff structure, export taxation, import controls and foreign exchange allocation systems, wage policies, pricing policies (especially for agricultural commodities) and adjustment policies to external conditions. The most important external factors are the prices of primary commodities, which for most small economies have to be taken as given. The barter terms of trade since the end of the coffee boom of 1977 have sharply deteriorated in the wake of slow-growing export demand. Commodity prices continued to deteriorate after the end of the major post world war recession in 1980–83, although there was a slight recovery from 1987 through early 1989 (IMF 1989).

In the specific case of Tanzania, akin to the general picture of the African economies, economic conditions have deteriorated and reached a crisis dimension, particularly since the end of the 1970s. Both external and internal factors have contributed to the current crisis (Lipumba 1984). The aggregate export volume has been falling since it peaked in 1972. The net barter terms of trade were improving in 1970–77 but have deteriorated sharply since then.

The export basket is still concentrated in commodities that have a low growth rate of demand in world markets.

Domestic policies have not favoured production for export. Real producer prices have generally declined (United Republic of Tanzania 1987). Overvalued exchange rates have not only reduced earnings of exporters, but also induced resources, including labour of young people, to move out of production for export because of higher relative prices of importables, home goods and services. Established industries are highly import dependent and have high unit costs (Skarstein and Wangwe 1986). The high cost of domestic manufactured goods has worsened the domestic terms of trade for agriculture.

The poor performance of the export sector – both the decrease in export volumes of traditional exports and the failure to develop new export goods, particularly from the manufacturing sector – is one of the major causes of the persistent shortage of foreign exchange and of the balance of payments crisis in Tanzania. Given the scarcity of foreign exchange and overvalued exchange rate, an administrative mechanism of allocating foreign exchange has become predominant over the past fifteen years.

The objective of this paper is to analyse factors that have influenced the trade performance and their impact on economic development. After this introduction, the second section of the paper provides an analytical description of the pattern and structure of trade since independence. Section 3 discusses the determinants of export performance, focusing on agricultural exports, which accounted for 80 per cent of the merchandise exports of Tanzania over the past twenty-five years. The determinants of manufactured exports and the export of services are also discussed. In section 4, the structure and determinants of imports are examined. Section 5 analyses the role of exports in the economic growth of Tanzania. Section 6 discusses policy reforms and conclusions.

## 2 Pattern and structure of trade

Tanzania inherited a typical colonial economy, dependent on primary exports. In 1960, primary exports (mainly agricultural products) accounted for almost one-third of the total GDP and 50 per cent of monetary GDP. Compared with most other African economies, exports were well diversified, although three commodities (sisal, cotton and coffee) contributed over 57 per cent of the total

Table 9.1 *Trend growth rates of volume of Tanzania's major exports, 1960–1984 (%)*

| | *1960–66* | *1966–72* | *1972–84* | *1960–84* |
|---|---|---|---|---|
| Coffee | 13.4 | −1.11* | −0.20* | 2.56 |
| Cotton | 13.9 | −3.97* | −4.75 | −0.01* |
| Sisal | −0.04* | 0.80* | −13.46 | −9.23 |
| Cashew nuts | 10.4 | 6.84 | −19.60 | −4.12 |
| Tea | 10.1 | 6.36 | 3.42 | 6.61 |
| Tobacco | 32.0 | 11.16 | −0.02* | 13.10 |

*Note:*
*Not statistically significant at 5%.

*Source:* Computed using data from Bank of Tanzania; *Tanzania. Twenty Years of Independence* (1984) and *Economic and Operations Report* (various issues), Dar-es-Salaam.

export value. Since then, export growth has varied a great deal and the commodity concentration has remained high.

*Export growth rates*

During the first five years of independence, Tanzania's external trade was in a persistent surplus because of a high growth rate of agricultural exports, particularly cotton, coffee and cashew nuts. Between 1960 and 1966 the volume of cotton, coffee and cashew-nut exports grew at annual average rates of 13.4, 13.9 and 10.4 per cent, respectively (Table 9.1); 1966 was a particularly good year. Since 1966, overall export growth stagnated and exports as a percentage of GDP decreased. Over the years 1960–67, export earnings financed 100 per cent of imports and Tanzania even recorded a net capital outflow. In the 1970s, a trade deficit emerged because of the low growth of exports and an increased capital inflow, mainly in the form of aid and concessionary loans. Table 9.2 shows exports and imports, as well as the trade deficit, as a percentage of GDP.

*Commodity Concentration*

The composition of exports has not been transformed significantly, but the relative importance of leading exports has changed. Sisal was the main export item in the 1960–64 period, when it accounted

Table 9.2 *Tanzania's exports and imports of goods and services as a percentage of GDP, 1966–85*

| *Year* | *Export ratio* | *Import ratio* | *Import gap ratio* |
|---|---|---|---|
| 1966 | 32.5 | 31.1 | –1.4 |
| 1967 | 30.6 | 29.5 | –1.1 |
| 1968 | 28.3 | 30.6 | 2.3 |
| 1969 | 28.3 | 27.8 | –0.5 |
| 1970 | 28.8 | 32.9 | 4.1 |
| 1971 | 29.3 | 36.9 | 7.6 |
| 1972 | 30.3 | 34.1 | 3.8 |
| 1973 | 27.8 | 35.1 | 7.3 |
| 1974 | 24.9 | 41.5 | 6.6 |
| 1975 | 21.9 | 36.7 | 4.8 |
| 1976 | 24.7 | 28.7 | 4.0 |
| 1977 | 20.9 | 27.4 | 6.5 |
| 1978 | 16.4 | 34.1 | 17.7 |
| 1979 | 17.4 | 30.6 | 13.2 |
| 1980 | 14.7 | 30.8 | 16.1 |
| 1981 | 14.4 | 24.6 | 10.2 |
| 1982 | 9.4 | 21.2 | 11.8 |
| 1983 | 8.9 | 17.2 | 8.3 |
| 1984 | 10.0 | 20.9 | 10.9 |
| 1985 | 6.6 | 20.7 | 14.1 |

*Source:* Computed using data from Bank of Tanzania *Economic and Operations Report* (various years), Dar-es-Salaam, and United Republic of Tanzania, *Economic Survey* (various years), Dar-es-Salaam.

for 31 per cent of the total. After a drastic fall in sisal prices in 1965, cotton became the dominant export. However, cotton production stagnated between 1966 and 1972 and decreased later on. Coffee emerged as the largest export article after 1967 and its share reached a peak of 35.6 per cent during the coffee boom of 1977.

The overall commodity concentration decreased between 1960 and 1971. The three leading exports – sisal, cotton and coffee – accounted for 57.7 per cent of the total in 1960. This share dropped to 40.9 per cent and 22.7 per cent in 1966 and 1971 respectively. (The trend decrease of the share of the three exports is statistically significant.) The decrease in concentration of the three main exports is only partly explained by the fall of the sisal share (caused by the fall in its price). Diversification of the export basket was being carried out, and other crops such as cashew nuts, tobacco and tea increased their share. It should be noted, however, that a number of export products which were important in the first half of the 1960s disappeared from the export basket by the 1970s. These include oil seeds, hides and skins, and meat and meat preparations. From 1971 to 1986, export concentration did not decrease. Indeed, in 1974 and 1977, the export share of the three main exports increased to 36.3 per cent and 50.2 per cent, respectively. This increase was caused by exceptionally high prices of sisal in 1974 and of coffee in 1977.

*Non-agricultural exports*

Tanzania's leading non-agricultural export article in the 1960s and early 1970s was diamonds. They accounted for 11.2 per cent of total exports in 1966 but only 4.2 per cent in 1976. Diamonds' contribution to total exports has decreased significantly because of a fall in mined output, caused partly by exhaustion of diamond-bearing rock and partly by the deterioration of mining equipment.

Manufacturing exports, broadly defined to include processed agricultural products, increased from a negligible amount in 1960 to 21.5 per cent in 1971. In the late 1960s and 1970, the important industrial exports were chemicals, mainly petroleum products (with low value added because they depended on crude petroleum imports), beverages and food, such as processed coffee, made tea, and meat and meat preparations. Textile exports became important in 1970s, accounting for an average of 3.5 per cent of total exports in 1970–78. The contribution of textiles to total exports reached a peak slightly above 8 per cent in 1979/80. At that time the government pushed exports at the expense of domestic consumption in order to alleviate the balance of payments crisis that had become acute at the beginning of 1979, after the Uganda war and the second increase in oil prices. Industrial exports, however, could not be increased when industrial output fell because of capacity underutilization.

*Share of World Trade*

Tanzania's shares of the world markets in various products generally increased in the 1960s and decreased or stagnated from the early 1970s. Between 1960 and 1966, Tanzania more than doubled its world market share of cotton and increased its share of coffee

Table 9.3 *World market share of Tanzania's exports of coffee, cotton, sisal, tabacco and tea by value, 1970–85 (%)*

| *Year* | *Coffee* | *Cotton* | *Sisal* | *Tobacco* | *Tea* |
|---|---|---|---|---|---|
| 1970 | 1.41 | 1.37 | 33.88 | 0.64 | 0.86 |
| 1971 | 1.16 | 1.22 | 29.27 | 0.64 | 0.83 |
| 1972 | 1.64 | 1.49 | 24.37 | 0.55 | 1.02 |
| 1973 | 1.62 | 1.15 | 21.02 | 0.52 | 1.04 |
| 1974 | 1.21 | 1.35 | 21.13 | 0.76 | 1.11 |
| 1975 | 1.52 | 0.93 | 31.56 | 0.61 | 1.07 |
| 1976 | 1.82 | 1.44 | 29.36 | 1.10 | 1.59 |
| 1977 | 1.79 | 1.08 | 29.99 | 0.84 | 1.08 |
| 1978 | 1.53 | 0.90 | 32.14 | 0.76 | 1.20 |
| 1979 | 1.21 | 0.89 | 26.94 | 0.48 | 1.25 |
| 1980 | 1.15 | 0.62 | 23.01 | 0.34 | 1.14 |
| 1981 | 1.78 | 1.06 | 30.56 | 0.42 | 1.06 |
| 1982 | 1.43 | 0.88 | 29.04 | 0.41 | 1.12 |
| 1983 | 1.34 | 0.79 | 15.30 | 0.26 | 1.09 |
| 1984 | 1.48 | 0.66 | 20.02 | 0.31 | 1.02 |
| 1985 | 0.99 | 0.40 | 7.93 | 0.33 | 1.01 |

*Source:* Computed from data in UNCTAD, *World Commodity Trade Statistics*, 1986, 1987, Geneva.

by 70 per cent. Since 1966, its volume share of cotton has decreased. Only in the case of tea has the share continued to grow. Table 9.3 shows the world market shares by value of the five leading agricultural exports for the 1970–1985 period, while Table 9.4 shows their corresponding trend growth rates relative to world volumes. The share in sisal exports decreased from 34 per cent in 1970 to below 8 per cent in 1985. The shares of coffee and tea exports did not increase in the 1970s and 1980s.[1] The lower gowth rates of these exports from Tanzania account for their stagnant or falling shares.

*Import Structure*

The composition of imports by end use has experienced a significant transformation since the early 1960s (Table 9.5). In 1960, consumer goods accounted for half of total imports, while capital goods accounted for 30 per cent and intermediate imports for 20 per cent.

Table 9.4 *Trend growth rates of world and Tanzanian exports of coffee, cotton, sisal, tobacco and tea by volume, 1970–84 (%)*

| | *World* | *Tanzania* |
|---|---|---|
| Coffee | 1.31 | 1.03[a] |
| Cotton | 0.58[a] | –4.43 |
| Sisal | –9.30 | –13.87 |
| Tobacco | 1.99 | 1.68[a] |
| Tea | 2.41 | 4.43 |

*Note:*
[a] Not statistically significant

*Source:* Computed from data in UNCTAD, *World Commodity Trade Statistics*, 1986, Geneva.

Table 9.5 *Classification of Tanzania's imports by end use, 1960–84 (%)*

| | *Consumer goods* | *Intermediate goods* | *Capital goods* |
|---|---|---|---|
| 1960 | 50.5 | 20.0 | 29.5 |
| 1967 | 36.6 | 40.7 | 23.7 |
| 1970 | 30.0 | 40.4 | 29.6 |
| 1973 | 30.4 | 45.8 | 23.8 |
| 1974 | 37.0 | 42.2 | 20.8 |
| 1975 | 31.4 | 41.4 | 27.2 |
| 1976 | 20.7 | 49.1 | 29.6 |
| 1977 | 18.6 | 41.4 | 40.0 |
| 1978 | 19.4 | 40.4 | 40.2 |
| 1979 | 14.6 | 40.4 | 45.0 |
| 1980 | 20.4 | 37.9 | 41.6 |
| 1981 | 16.2 | 34.8 | 48.9 |
| 1982 | 17.2 | 39.0 | 43.6 |
| 1983 | 16.9 | 42.8 | 40.0 |
| 1984 | 17.9 | 42.4 | 39.6 |
| 1985 | 16.2 | 40.1 | 43.5 |
| 1986 | 20.0 | 32.55 | 47.2 |

*Source:* Computed using data from United Republic of Tanzania, *Economic Surveys* (various issues), Dar-es-Salaam.

Import-substituting industrialization led to a decrease in the share of consumer goods. By 1970 consumer goods accounted for 30 per cent while the share of intermediate goods had increased to 40 per cent. In the 1970s, particularly after the adoption of the Basic Industry Strategy, the share of capital goods increased to a peak of almost 50 per cent in 1981. The share of consumer goods continued to decrease.[2]

## 3 Tanzania's export performance and its causes

Tanzania's 'revealed' trade orientation, based on both export and import shares, shows a high degree of openness between 1966 and 1980, before contraction in the post-1980 period (Table 9.2). The high share of imports during 1966–80 was a result of high levels of investment, especially infrastructural and industrial, both requiring significant imports of capital goods. The share of exports, however, indicates a declining trend, with an acceleration starting in 1975 when the export performance faltered badly.

### *Trade policy*

The trade regime in Tanzania seems to have been heavily influenced by the export performance and the 'availability' of foreign exchange. Until 1973, when export growth was high, the trade regime was largely liberal. The nationalization of import–export trade in 1967 did not lead to the use of quantitative restrictions. Tariffs on imports were the main measures used to restrict trade. The 1973–75 balance of payments crisis led to an extensive use of import controls (Green *et al.* 1980). The coffee boom of 1976–77 improved the balance of payments position and the availability of foreign exchange, and quantitative trade restrictions on imports were temporarily relaxed. The war with Uganda in 1978–79 and the second oil price increase in 1979 initiated another balance of payments crisis which led to the intensification of import controls. The worsening foreign exchange shortage caused severe shortages of all goods, including essential consumer goods, which reduced the incentives to produce for the market. The economic collapse was characterized by severe import strangulation. A crackdown on the large parallel market that had developed as a result of extensive price control did not ease the widespread shortages of essential commodities.

In 1984, the government adopted a policy of permitting foreign-exchange-funded imports, which were sold at market-clearing prices. This policy had the effect of dramatically increasing the availability of all kinds of goods, including low-priced, used clothes for low-income groups, basic and luxury consumer goods, spare parts and transport equipment. In addition to the import liberalization, the shilling was devalued and producer prices increased. A more active exchange-rate adjustment policy was adopted during the implementation of the Economic Recovery Programme 1986–89. The overall effect of the trade liberalization measures and exchange-rate adjustment was to increase economic activity. Non-traditional exports and some annual export crops such as cotton have responded positively to the higher producer prices that are a result of the devaluation. Official export earnings, however, have not increased significantly, partly because of difficulties in marketing agricultural exports and partly because of an increase in parallel market exports, which largely finance their own funded imports.

In the remainder of this section, we will attempt to identify the reasons for Tanzania's variable and deteriorating export performance since independence. Special effort will be made to disentangle the effects on export earnings growth of exogenous factors (not under the control of the Tanzanian government) and factors that are endogenous, i.e. the very trade policies that have been pursued. Export performance will be measured in terms of real export earnings or the import purchasing power of exports. Real export earnings, in turn, will be decomposed so as to make possible the estimation of relative shares that are explained by export volume changes and relative price changes. The period of analysis covers 1960 (one year before independence) to 1985. The average annual changes for each of the variables mentioned over a specified period are measured, using estimated functions relating each of the variables exponentially to time with a constant capturing the effects of other factors. This technique will be used for both analysis of growth rates of real export earnings and decomposition of its factors.

*Volume* v. *price effects*

Over the whole period 1960–85 real export earnings showed a negative trend growth of 3.35 per cent annually (Table 9.6); 91.4 per cent of this negative growth is explained by a decline in the

Table 9.6 *Purchasing power of Tanzania's exports, 1960–85 (%)*

| *Period* | *Growth rate of real export earnings* | *Quantity growth rate* | *Barter terms of trade* | *Variation of real exports explained by volume* | *Variation of real exports explained by TOT* |
|---|---|---|---|---|---|
| 1960–85 | –3.35 | –3.05 | –0.30* | 91.0 | 9.0 |
| 1960–72 | 3.03 | 2.97 | 0.05* | 98.0 | 1.7 |
| 1972–85 | –8.88 | –6.20 | –2.70 | 69.8 | 30.4 |
| 1977–85 | –11.92 | –6.76 | –5.15 | 56.8 | 43.2 |

*Note:*
* Not statistically significant.

*Source:* Trend growth rates have been estimated using data from UNCTAD, *Handbook of International Trade and Development Statistics*, 1980, 1986, Geneva.

volume of exports, at an average annual rate of –3 per cent, and 8.6 per cent by a decline in the barter terms of trade, at a rather insignificant average rate of –0.3 per cent annually. The export performance for the period as whole is thus totally dominated by an export quantity decline.

This development, however, is not uniform for the period of analysis. A time-series path for all three variables demarcates export performance into two major periods. The 1960–72 period was characterized by a rather robust 3 per cent annual growth rate of real export earnings, spurred by an export quantity growth rate of almost 3 per cent annually, barter terms of trade remaining more or less constant (Table 9.6). The 1972–85 period, however, saw Tanzania's real export earnings nose-dive at an annual average rate of –8.9 per cent. The export volume declined at a rate of –6.2 per cent and the barter terms of trade declined at an annual rate of –2.7 per cent. In fact, if one considers the post-1977 period (featuring the collapse of export commodity prices and the second oil shock), the relative shares of export quantity and barter of trade in the decline of real export earnings were 56.8 per cent and 43.2 per cent, respectively. While the real export earnings rate of decline accelerated to –11.9 per cent annually, the export quantity and the barter terms of trade rates of annual decline were about the same (at –6.8 and –5.2 per cent).

The main conclusion from the above analysis is that Tanzania's export growth has been predominantly supply constrained. That is, factors affecting the production of export commodities, rather than a decline in world market prices, explain the drop in real export earnings. This observation is paramount to the understanding of export performance in Tanzania. Although this assertion holds true for the period as a whole, the export performance since 1977 has been characterized by the increased role played by the barter terms of trade in accelerating the rate of decline of real exports (see Table 9.6). During this period, as we shall see, the decline in world market prices contributed significantly to the volume deceleration via the production incentive structure. Moreover, in the case of a commodity like sisal, which used to be a main export item, the decline in quantity was prompted by the decrease in world market demand as close substitutes were developed. World production of sisal showed a declining trend, though Tanzania's exports of sisal declined faster, resulting in a reduced share of the world market.

The decline in export volume has many possible explanations. Domestic policies that determine the cost of production of exports are, of course, of utmost significance. In this respect, pricing policies, marketing of products, exchange-rate policy and the structure of protection play important roles. Below, we attempt an aggregate explanation of export quantity performance due to domestic policies; more disaggregate explanations will follow subsequently.

*Export volume and the real exchange rate*

At the aggregate level, export quantity variations over the 1960–86 period are explained to more than 90 per cent by the two (domestic policy) variables: (i) the real exchange rate and (ii) the real prices of food crops, the main competitors for resources within the agricultural sector (Table 9.7, first row). The real exchange rate, measured by the purchasing power parity, is taken as a summary statistic to reflect the extent of taxation of the export sector and, hence, its relative profitability vis-à-vis the non-export sector. This taxation may originate either in domestic underpricing of export commodities because of overvaluation, or in protection given to the non-export sector (with income transfer effects from the export sector).

Table 9.7 *Determinants of Tanzania's exports, regression results (OLS), 1960–86*

| *Dependent variable* | *Intercept* | *Independent variables* | | *Statistical coefficients* | | |
|---|---|---|---|---|---|---|
| | | *(1)* | *(2)* | $\bar{R}^2$ | *F* | *DW* |
| *QUXIN* | 10.23 | 0.55 *RER* | −1.35 *RELP* | 0.92 | 104 | 1.58 |
| | (8.29) | (9.98) | (−5.14) | | | |
| *RMFX* | −3.44 | 1.95 *RER* | 0.48 *RGMF* | 0.65 | 20 | 1.13 |
| | (−1.78) | (5.48) | (2.04) | | | |
| *RSEXP* | −2.87 | 0.57 *RER* | 1.05 *DWGT* | 0.64 | 17 | 1.33 |
| | (−1.70) | (4.07) | (5.40) | | | |

*Notes:*
1. All values are in natural logarithms.
2. *t*-values in brackets.

*Abbreviations:*
*QUXIN* = export quantity index;
*RMFX* = real manufactured exports;
*RSEXP* = real export of services;
*RER* = real exchange rate;
*RELP* = real price of food crops (deflated by non-food consumer price index);
*RGMF* = real gross manufactured output;
*DWGT* = dead weight tonnage through Tanzanian ports.

The results strongly suggest that export sector taxation has been a major disincentive to the production of exports. The coefficient on the real exchange rate parameter has the expected sign and it is statistically significant at the 1 per cent level. The largest impact on export volume however, seems to stem from the substitution of agricultural resources between export crop production and production of food through their relative prices. Frank Ellis (1982) and Ødegaard (1985) emphasized this factor for the 1970s. In view of the dominance of agricultural exports, the impact of this variable on total export volume is quite pronounced. Taking agricultural exports alone, the results do seem to suggest (at minimum) a one-to-one substitution between export crops and food crops given relative profitability change within agriculture. Moreover, as pointed out above, a significant potential for a shift in resource use between other non-export sectors and agriculture exists given the estimated coefficient on the real exchange rate. This would probably cause a shift in the agricultural production frontier in the longer run via induced investments.

Having looked at the broad explanatory factors of export performance, we now turn to a disaggregated level. Two broad groups are distinguished: agricultural exports, accounting for 80 per cent of total export earnings, and non-agricultural exports, comprising manufactures and services.

*Agricultural export volume and producer prices*

An analytical model of agricultural export production is presented below, endogenizing five main export crops: coffee, cotton, sisal, tea and tobacco. These crops accounted for 50 per cent of total export earnings on the average between 1966 and 1984 (period of analysis) and 62 per cent of the total value of agricultural exports. It is our belief that the extent of coverage of these crops, and variations in their characteristics, is broad enough to enable some general insights and conclusions.

The model treats Tanzania as a small country, exporting whatever it can at the ruling world market prices.[3] All fluctuations in world supply and demand for particular commodities are transmitted through fluctuations in prices. A single exception may hold for sisal, where Tanzania's share of world supply was around 20 per cent in the 1980s.[4] The main determinant of exports of the commodities under study is taken to be production. Although some of the supplies find their way into domestic industrial use, these have averaged less than 30 per cent of production. The proportion of total production exported has averaged 88 per cent for coffee, 74 per cent for cotton, 67 per cent for sisal, 70 per cent for tobacco and 80 per cent for tea (United Republic of Tanzania, *Economic Survey*, 1986). Local sales of these have been by and large subsidized and are taken to be exogenous.

Production of export crops, in turn, is postulated to be depenent on (i) the price received by the producer, (ii) the price of competing agricultural activities represented broadly by a food price index, (iii) internal agricultural terms of trade represented by deflating crop prices by the non-food consumer price index (CPI) and (iv) weather. The choice of food CPI for competing food crops in most of the equations, rather than a weighted average of official producer prices for food crops, is premised on the fact that it reflects more closely the open market producer prices which dominate the food market. Where one particular food crop is dominant in the area where there is production of the specific export crop under surveillance, the price of this particular food crop, rather than the general food price index, was used. Weather, entered as a dummy (1 for bad and 0 otherwise), was derived on the basis of weather assessment for particular crops as contained in the *Crop Production Statistics Bulletins* from the Ministry of Agriculture. The production equations were thus specified using Nerlovian supply response models (Nerlove 1958) as follows:

$$Q_i = f(P_i/CPNF,\ PA/CPNF,\ W), \quad i = 1, \ldots, 5 \qquad (9.1)$$

where

$P_i$ = own price
$PA$ = price of competing crop
$CPNF$ = consumer price index for non-food items
$W$ = weather

Time has been included in the equations for tea, sisal and tobacco to capture specific institutional and crop attributes of a long-term nature. The details for these are discussed together with results later on.

The price paid to producers is expected to be the key determinant of export supply. This price will thus receive special treatment in the model, i.e. by endogenizing the producer price setting behaviour. This is done at two levels, the nominal and the real. Producer prices are often treated as exogenous policy variables premised on the ability of governments to insulate producers from fluctuations in the world market by driving a variable wedge between world market and domestic producer prices.

It is questionable, however, whether governments do in fact have the ability to support a prolonged divergence between the producer prices path and that of world market prices, in the form of either growing subsidies (where producer prices rise faster), or falling official exports (when producer prices lag behind world market prices). The major way of driving a wedge between nominal prices paid to producers and world market prices has been to overvalue the local currency, which is to tax export producers. On the subsidy side, starting in 1975 by switching from the treatment of producer prices as residuals, the Tanzanian government also took into account cost-of-production and cost-of-living increases facing agricultural producers in setting producer prices. This was made possible by absorbing into the budget whatever losses the official marketing agencies incurred in the process. Nominal producer price is thus assumed to be dependent on the world market price, exchange rate, marketing margins and non-food cost of living index:

$$P_i = f(Pw_i, E, MA_i, CPNF) \tag{9.2}$$

where

$P_i$ = nominal producer price for crop *i*
$Pw_i$ = world market price for crop *i*
$E$ = official exchange rate (shs/dollar)
$MA_i$ = marketing margins for crop *i*
$CPNF$ = non-food CPI.

It is thus hypothesized that nominal producer prices will move together with world market prices – with the nomial exchange rate assuming effective pass-through – and cost of production. They will move inversely with marketing margins.

In view of the fact that most rural households producing export crops also produce a significant proportion of the food they consume, producer prices, which enter into the supply functions of export crops, will be in real terms. The deflator used is the non-food cost of living index. Real producer prices will thus constitute a bridge equation which is definitional (i.e. an identity). However, an analysis of variations of real producer prices, related to variations of their components, will be undertaken to derive relative shares of explanation of variations. The results of the empirical test of the above model are presented in Table 9.8, starting with nominal price determination, through the bridge equations for real producer prices, to supply responses.

The results suggest that world market pass-through to nominal producer prices is the highest for coffee, sisal, and tea. In the case of coffee, for example, producers are paid in two instalments, before and after the coffee is sold in the export market. After the sales, producers are paid the difference between anticipated and realized prices (not of relevant margins). The coefficients on the exchange-rate parameter for these crops are also high, as they are expected

Table 9.8 *Nominal producer price block: Tanzania, 1966–84*

| *Crop* | *Constant* | *World market price ($)* | *Exchange rate* | *Marketing margin* | *Cost of living index* | *Statistical coefficients* | | |
|---|---|---|---|---|---|---|---|---|
| | | | | | | $R^2$ | *F* | *DW* |
| Coffee | –5.6196 | 0.785 | 0.9914 | –0.2288 | 0.3490 | 0.980 | 220.4 | 1.67 |
| | (–10.115) | (8.2855) | (3.936) | (5.554) | (4.565) | | | |
| Cotton | –4.7693 | 0.3316 | 0.4993 | –0.0955 | 0.5910 | 0.988 | 383.8 | 1.15 |
| | (–5.403) | (1.850) | (1.699) | (1.554) | (4.857) | | | |
| Sisal | –0.1071 | 0.8174 | 0.8415 | –0.00012 | 0.2797 | 0.998 | 2389.9 | 2.04 |
| | (0.155) | (10.461) | (1.946) | (1.031) | (2.152) | | | |
| Tobacco | –1.2611 | 0.0344 | 0.2844 | –0.0464 | 0.0656 | 0.998 | 1560.5 | 2.176 |
| | (1.831) | (0.224) | (1.0814) | (0.554) | (9.068) | | | |
| Tea | –0.9041 | 1.0779 | 1.0516 | –0.3644 | 0.3445 | 0.975 | 134.22 | 1.98 |
| | (9.672) | (5.9783) | (2.787) | (3.154) | (3.573) | | | |

*Notes:*
1. The functional relationship is in double log form.
2. *t*-values in brackets.

to be given the dominant pass-through effect of world market prices. For these crops, the world market prices are the most dominant explanatory variables, not only in the magnitudes of elasticities, but also in statistical significance. Cotton and tobacco are fairly well insulated from world market prices through domestic producer price fixation.

For the predominantly peasant-produced annual crops, cotton and tobacco, nominal producer price determination seems to be statistically (in terms of significance) influenced by cost-of-production considerations in the sense of 'fair' pricing. In the case of cotton, which is wholly grown on smallholder farms, the elasticity coefficient on cost of production is the highest; for tobacco, it is the second highest (after the exchange rate). The overall high statistical significance of cost of production bears out the govenment's deliberate policy, especially since 1975, to (partly) compensate for cost increases through budget-supported increases in prices to producers. In the cases of coffee, sisal and tea, cost compensation was effected through reductions in margins, especially export tax cuts since late 1970s, while in the cases of cotton and tobacco, most likely in the form of budgetary subsidies to the marketing agencies. As can be discerned from Table 9.8, marketing margins are statistically insignificant in explaining the determination of nominal producer prices of cotton and tobacco.

As pointed out earlier, the link between the nominal producer price block in the model and the production block is through 'bridge equations' for real producer prices. Table 9.9 provides an analysis of the variation in real producer prices by looking at the variations in its components – nominal producer prices and the deflator, non-food CPI (CPNF). The method used is akin to the one used previously in analysing the variation in the purchasing power of exports. Trend gowth rates are estimated separately for real producer prices, nominal producer prices and CPNF for each crop and results presented for three time periods, 1966–84, 1966–78 and 1978–84.

For the period 1966–84 as a whole, real producer prices showed a declining trend at annual average rates ranging from –1.19 per cent for sisal to –4.32 per cent for tobacco. Although nominal producer prices increased at annual trend rates ranging from 7.81 per cent for tobacco to 10.94 per cent for sisal, this increase was more than swamped by the trend rate of inflation (12.13 per cent) for the period. Nominal producer prices thus failed to keep pace

Table 9.9 *Analysis of variation in real producer prices: Tanzania, 1966–84*

| *Crop* | *Annual change in real producer prices (%)* | *Annual change in nominal producer prices (%)* | *Annual change in non-food CPI (%)* |
|---|---|---|---|
| *1966–84:* | | | |
| Coffee | –2.42 | 9.71 | 12.13 |
| Cotton | –2.22 | 9.91 | 12.13 |
| Sisal | –1.19* | 10.94 | 12.13 |
| Tea | –2.99 | 9.15 | 12.13 |
| Tobacco | –4.32 | 7.81 | 12.13 |
| *1966–78:* | | | |
| Coffee | 2.16 | 10.27 | 8.10 |
| Cotton | –1.38 | 6.72 | 8.10 |
| Sisal | 4.37* | 12.47 | 8.10 |
| Tea | –0.59* | 7.51 | 8.10 |
| Tobacco | –3.17 | 4.94 | 8.10 |
| *1978–84:* | | | |
| Coffee | –8.71 | 16.34 | 25.05 |
| Cotton | –6.53 | 18.52 | 25.05 |
| Sisal | –15.56 | 9.50 | 25.05 |
| Tea | –12.22 | 12.83 | 25.05 |
| Tobacco | –6.73 | 18.33 | 25.05 |

*Note:*
* Statistically insignificant trend growth rate.

with the inflation rate in general. The trend variations in real producer prices for the period 1966–84, however, hide significant differences between the sub-periods prior to 1978 and after 1978, when the rate of inflation accelerated and the barter terms of trade declined significantly.

The period 1966–78 was characterized by low rates of inflation (8.1 per cent annually) and rates of annual increase of nominal producer prices for coffee and sisal that exceeded the inflation rate. Real producer prices for coffee and sisal had positive growth rates; that of tea was more or less constant, while cotton and tobacco had negative growth rates. The post-1978 period, however, was characterized by steep declines of real producer prices, ranging from an annual rate of −6.53 per cent for cotton to −15.56 per cent for sisal. Although there was a general acceleration of the rate of increase of nominal producer prices, the three-fold increase in the rate of inflation was the main explanatory factor.

Table 9.10 presents supply responses for the various crops to the factors included in the model. Own real price elasticities are the highest for annual crops, cotton and tobacco, and the lowest for the slow-responding perennial crops, coffee, tea and sisal. With the exception of tea, whose supply response was dominated by increased yields over time as the spurt of plantings in the late 1960s matured, all other crops have own price elasticities that are statistically significant at 5 per cent or less.

The price elasticity for competing crops is the highest for cotton, which is an annual crop. It was followed by sisal, although a perennial crop, mostly likely due to extensive diversification from sisal as prospects for world market recovery became increasingly grim. In all cases except sisal (a drought-resistant crop), weather had the expected negative effect, and the coefficient is statistically significant. The largest impacts were on the annual crops, cotton and tobacco.

Time was included in the equations for tea, sisal and tobacco in order to capture the role of various institutional and biological factors. In the case of tea, as explained above, the 1970s experienced an increase in the supply of tea as trees planted in a spurt in the late 1960s matured and continued to increase yields irrespective of price movements. As for sisal, an output decline beyond what could be justified by expected continued weakness of the market was brought on by neglect as the estates became nationalized or passed on to the village communes. Tobacco received improvement support through a World Bank programme, which led to an expansion of acreage in new areas and possibly an increase in yields in the traditional growing areas.

*Non-agricultural exports*

The share of non-agricultural exports in Tanzania's total export earnings increased from an average of 26 per cent during 1964–66 to 40 per cent in the 1979–85 period. Within this group, exports of non-factor services were by far the most dominant for the entire 1964–86 period. The second-largest group of non-agricultural exports comprises manufactured goods.

Table 9.10 *Export crop production block for Tanzania*

| *Crop* | *Constant* | *Own real price* | *Competing crop*[a] | *Weather*[b] | *Time*[c] | *Statistical coefficients* | | | |
|---|---|---|---|---|---|---|---|---|---|
| | | | | | | $R^2$ | $F$ | $P^d$ | *DW* |
| Coffee | 3.22 | 0.43 | –0.24 | –0.13 | — | 0.97 | 137.3 | –0.27 | 1.91 |
| | (18.72) | (5.22) | (–2.92) | (–3.32) | | | | | |
| Cotton | 9.29 | 0.73 | –1.25 | –0.23 | — | 0.94 | 83.3 | 0.52 | 2.03 |
| | (5.60) | (5.22) | (–2.92) | (3.32) | | | | | |
| Sisal | 8.62 | 0.24 | –1.07 | –0.04 | –0.08 | 0.97 | 122 | — | 1.394 |
| | (5.46) | (2.98) | (–2.50) | (–0.74) | (–11.92) | | | | |
| Tobacco | 4.17 | 2.72 | –0.08 | –0.28 | 0.14 | 0.73 | 12.48 | — | 1.68 |
| | (2.99) | (4.75) | (–0.39) | (–3.58) | (5.54) | | | | |
| Tea | 5.68 | 0.25 | –0.63 | –0.07 | 0.06 | 0.80 | 16.97 | 0.88 | 1.51 |
| | (3.13) | (1.33) | (–1.33) | (–1.82) | (–2.38) | | | | |

*Notes:*

[a] Competing crop for coffee and tobacco is maize, given the dominance in growing areas of maize as a food crop (Kilimanjaro, Arusha, Mbeya, Ruvuma for coffee and Ruvuma and Tabora for tobacco).

[b] Weather is a dummy (1 = bad, 0 = good) based on the Ministry of Agriculture's weather assessment of crops (*Crop Statistics Bulletin*).

[c] The time trend for tea reflects a burst of planting in the 1960s and early 1970s which increased yield in maturity irrespective of prices. The time trend for tobacco captures the increase of acreage over time due to World Bank programme. The time trend for sisal captures the increasing neglect of sisal estates from changes in ownership.

[d] Equations with $\rho$ were estimated using maximum likelihood iterative procedure to correct for autocorrelation, otherwise OLS.

*Services.* The share of services in non-agricultural exports has fluctuated widely, from 38 to 78 per cent. On the average, services accounted for over 55 per cent during 1964–86. The two major contributors to exports of services are international transport and tourism. While the trade flows to and from neighbouring countries depend on their respective external trade volumes, the portion that flows through Tanzania depends partly on the efficiency and capacity of Tanzania's transport sector.

Earnings from tourism are dependent not only on supportive infrastructural services, but also on the ruling exchange rate. An overvalued currency escalates the cost to tourists of staying in Tanzania relative to other countries. This reduces the number of tourists visiting the country as well as the period of stay and hence earnings, given the high elasticity of demand for such luxurious services. In view of the effective competitiveness of its neighbour to the north in a similar tourist attraction, relative regimes of exchange-rate policy become absolutely important.

Given the factors explained above, we tested for their statistical significance in the determination of the volume of earnings from the export of services. This was done for the period 1966–84 and the results are shown in Table 9.7 above. The results suggest that both trade volumes and real exchange rates are statistically significant in explaining the volume of export of services. The two factors in combination explain 64 per cent of the variation in export earnings from services.

*Manufactures.* The key determinants of the volume of manufactured exports are production of manufactures and trade policy: manufactured output determines the base for exporting; trade policy influences the relative profitability between selling in the domestic market and exporting given the cost of production. In view of the high import dependence of the manufacturing sector, output is very sensitive to the availability of foreign exchange, both for the expansion of the sector through investment and for capacity utilization. Several studies have indicated this sensitivity (Wangwe 1983; Ndulu 1986; Skarstein and Wangwe 1986). Import capacity and its allocation have largely influenced the volume of production and the extent of utilization of available capacity.

The relative profitability of domestic and external markets for locally manufactured commodities depends heavily on the trade policy pursued. Given that local firms earn shillings, it does not matter to them whether they earn these through selling in the domestic or in the external market. The market that offers high profitability will be favoured by these producers. While taxes on competitive imports provided the basis for the attractiveness of the domestic market over the period up to 1978, the post-1978 period was characterized by significantly increased attractiveness of the domestic market through the overvalued shilling. This trend means significantly reduced incentives for the export of manufactures.

In order to determine the relative significance of the two factors described above in influencing the level of manufactured exports, a test was carried out for the period 1966–86, using OLS. The results are reported in Table 9.7 above and they vindicate the importance of the two factors in explaining the performance of manufactured exports. In combination, the two factors explain 65 per cent of the variation, and each one separately is statistically significant. The very high elasticity of manufactured exports with respect to the real exchange rate demonstrates the crucial role trade policies play in determining relative profitability and hence the level of exports.

## 4 Growth and structure of imports

The trend growth rate of the volume of imports for the period 1960–85 was 1.9 per cent. However, there are significant differences during the periods 1960–72, 1972–77 and 1977–85. While the volume of imports grew at an average rate of 6.5 per cent over the period 1960–72, the growth rate turned a negative 3.5 per cent during 1972–77 and a negative 5.6 per cent over the years 1977–85.

### *Determinants of imports*

For 'behavioural' purposes, imports are classified into consumer, intermediate and capital goods. While import capacity is the common determinant for all import categories, there are specific additional factors explaining each of them separately.

*Consumer imports* are assumed to be determined by a demand shift variable in addition to import capacity. Thus, aggregate consumer expenditure enters as an explanatory factor in the determination of the demand for consumer imports. Table 9.11 presents the estimated consumer import demand function for the period 1966–84, which takes the above factors into account. The high and

Table 9.11 *Determinants of Tanzania's imports, regression results (OLS), 1966–84*

| *Dependent* | *Intercept* | *Independent variables* | | | *Statistical coefficients* | | |
|---|---|---|---|---|---|---|---|
| | | *(1)* | *(2)* | *(3)* | $R^2$ | *F* | *DW* |
| *CONIMP* | −12.38 | 0.57 *CONS* | 1.69 *EXPO*(−1) | — | 0.83 | 44 | 1.63 |
| | (−2.05) | (1.28) | (7.06) | | | | |
| *INTIMP* | −4.79 | 0.74 *GDP* | 0.34 *EXPO*(−1) | 0.32 *FORIN* | 0.80 | 23 | 1.79 |
| | (−1.35) | (2.62) | (2.39) | (4.47) | | | |
| *KAPIMP* | −1.05 | 1.00 *FCF* | 0.29 *DWAR* | — | 0.90 | 80 | 2.36 |
| | (−1.08) | (8.58) | (3.84) | | | | |

*Notes:*
1. All values are in natural logarithms.
2. t-values in brackets.

*Abbreviations:*
*CONIMP* = real imports of consumer goods;
*INTIM* = real intermediate goods imports;
*KAPIMP* = real capital goods imports;
*CONS* = real aggregate consumption expenditure;
*EXPO*(−1) = real lagged export earnings;
*GDP* = real output;
*FORIN* = real foreign resources inflows;
*FCF* = real fixed capital formation;
*DWAR* = dummy for Kagera war.

statistically significant elasticity of consumer imports with respect to lagged export earnings is explained by the government policy of treating consumer imports as residual claims, depending on export earnings during the post-1973 period. For the earlier period, consumer imports varied with the export earnings without import restrictions.

*Intermediate imports* are also constrained by the supply of foreign exchange from both exports and foreign resource inflows. In addition, the level of production is assumed to be a derived demand shift factor. Whereas during periods of non-constrained availability of foreign exchange the demand shift factor is dominant, during periods of foreign exchange scarcity the import capacity becomes dominant. We thus expect both availability of foreign exchange and demand shift factors to explain the level of intermediate imports. The estimated intermediate import function for the period 1966–84 is presented in Table 9.11. As expected, both demand shift factors and import capacity are statistically significant in explaining variations in intermediate goods imports.

*Capital goods imports* are assumed to be derived from demand for investment goods (as the share of imports in capital formation has averaged 70 per cent over the period under study). Because of the underdeveloped capital goods producing sector, these imports are largely not competitive with domestic production. However, availability of foreign exchange in times of scarcity constrains capital formation and, hence, capital goods imports (see Lipumba *et al.* 1988). A dummy variable for the period 1978–81 is included in the estimated function to control for a sudden increase in the import of military transport equipment in connection with the Kagera war. The estimated demand function for capital imports for the period 1966–84 is presented in Table 9.11. As expected, there is an almost one-to-one relationship between capital imports and fixed capital formation. This is indicative of the low competitiveness of capital imports and fixed complementarity to locally produced capital goods (mainly non-traded construction).

## 5 The savings–investment process, import capacity and growth

In less developed economies, the critical importance of import capacity in the realization of the savings–investment process has been documented in several studies (Chenery and Bruno 1962; Chenery and Strout 1966; Weisskopf 1972; Michapolous and Jay 1973). The essence of the story is that investment requires capital goods that are not domestically produced and therefore domestic savings cannot be transformed into investment goods unless foreign exchange is made available. Apart from augmenting domestic savings, a net capital inflow thus plays a crucial role in bridging the gap between one's own import capacity (exports) and that required for realization of investment from savings.

The importance of import capacity for growth is not restricted to the savings–investment process alone. Ram (1985), for instance, confined the analysis of the impact of import capacity on growth to the link between imports and *investments*. However, Helleiner (1986), among others, has shown the critical importance of intermediate import strangulation on limiting the effectiveness of investment on growth through *capacity underutilization*. Apart from the total import capacity, its allocation between capacity expansion and utilization is of significant importance, particularly in the industrial sector (Ndulu 1986).

In the particular case of Tanzania, we investigated the relative importance of export and non-export income in the generation of aggregate domestic savings. In view of the critical role of import capacity in the realization of savings, one would expect the response of the domestic savings process to be more sensitive to the income component which permits the importation of capital goods. Following Maizels (1968), Lee (1971) and Stein (1979), a function relating savings to non-export and export income was estimated for the period 1967–84. The results are presented in Table 9.12 (row 1).

As the results show, the domestic savings process is dominated by export income. The marginal propensity to save out of export income is greater than one and statistically significant. This is not to say that all export income is saved at the margin, but the availability of foreign exchange from exports enables savings from non-export income to be realized. As pointed out above, it is not only export earnings and the enhancement of the import capacity that facilitate the domestic saving process, but also net capital inflows. We thus investigated the relative importance of the two components of import capacity on this process. The result is presented in Table 9.12 (second row).

Table 9.12 *Determinants of Tanzania's savings and growth, regression results (OLS), 1967–84*

| *Dependent variable* | *Intercept* | *Independent variables* | | | *Statistical coefficients* | | |
|---|---|---|---|---|---|---|---|
| | | *(1)* | *(2)* | *(3)* | $R^2$ | *F* | *DW* |
| *SAVS* | –1904.56 | 0.07 *YNEX* | 1.05 *EXPO* | — | 0.92 | 97 | 1.28 |
| | (–2.59) | (3.64) | (4.33) | | | | |
| *SAVS* | –740.79 | 0.08 *YNEX* | 0.82 *EXPO* | 0.49 *NEFI* | 0.92 | 70 | 1.37 |
| | (–2.43) | (3.82) | (2.92) | (1.50) | | | |
| *RGCF* | –5024.78 | 0.39 *YNEX* | 0.64 *RIMCP* | — | 0.56 | 18 | 2.18 |
| | (–2.71) | (5.94) | (4.54) | | | | |
| *GGDP* | –0.61 | 0.09 *ICPGDP*(–1) | –3.53 *DWE* | 0.02 *ITPKAP* | 0.79 | 21 | 2.25 |
| | (–0.63) | (3.00) | (–6.50) | (1.71) | | | |

*Notes:*
1. All values are in natural logarithms.
2. t-values in brackets.

*Abbreviations:*
*SAVS* = domestic savings;
*RGCF* = real gross capital formation;
*GGDP* = growth rate of gross domestic production (%);
*EXPO* = export income from merchandise and service;
*NEFI* = net foreign inflows;
*RIMCP* = real import capacity;
*YNEX* = real non-export gross domestic product;
*ICPGDP* = ratio of import capacity to gross domestic product;
*DWE* = dummy for weather;
*ITPKAP* = ratio of intermediate to capital goods imports.

These results show that Tanzania's own generated import capacity dominates the domestic saving process. The smaller and less significant contribution of net foreign inflows in inducing domestic savings can be explained partly by the smaller flexibility of its use to specific and predominantly public sector projects. The catalytic role of net foreign inflows to domestic savings is mainly confined to public savings, which, at the margin, has used the additional available external resources to increase public consumption. As Weisskopf (1972) notes, 'foreign savings seem to have substituted for domestic savings'. Net foreign inflows by and large leave *private* incomes unchanged and hence have negligible impact on private savings.

On the investment side, import capacity plays a more direct and significant role. The import content of investment has been estimated to average 70 per cent (Roemer *et al.* 1975). The ratio of imported capital goods to fixed capital formation is also around 70 per cent for the 1966–84 period (United Republic of Tanzania, *Economic Surveys*, 1970–84, *National Accounts* 1984). Net capital inflows additively augment the capacity to import these capital goods over and above the own import capacity generated by exports. Domestic capital goods are complementary to a large extent and predominantly in the form of construction. This component of capital goods is mainly financed by savings from non-export income.

The relationship between real gross capital formation as the dependent variable and real import capacity and real non-export income as the independent variables was tested. The result is given in Table 9.12 (third row). The statistically significant coefficients on import capacity and non-export income validate the expected complementary roles of imported capital goods and domestic capital goods in the investment process. The relative contributions of import capacity and non-export income seem to bear out the average contribution of imported and domestic capital goods pointed out above.

The traditional approach of linking investment to growth has been through fixed incremental capital–output ratios (ICOR). This assumes constancy at reasonable levels of capacity utilization and availability of complementary factors of production. However, the experiences of less developed countries in general, and Tanzania in particular, have shown wide variations in ICOR because of variation in capacity utilization rates and the non-availability of complementary infrastructure. A significant reason for low capacity imports stemming from general import strangulation and an unbalanced allocation of import capacity in favour of capacity expansion relative to capacity utilization (Gulhati and Datta 1983; Wangwe 1983; Helleiner 1986).

The growth performance of economies with predominantly rainfed agriculture tends to show wide weather-induced fluctuations. The growth performance of Tanzania was related to import capacity, weather and the allocation of import capacity between intermediate and capital goods imports. The result is presented in Table 9.12 (row 4). Although the results show that growth is dominated by weather vagaries, import capacity and its allocation are also part of the explanation of the growth variations. Based on this analysis, the importance of the export performance in the savings–investment process and growth cannot be overrated.

## 6 Trade policy implications and concluding remarks

The empirical analysis in this paper has corroborated the importance of international trade in economic development. The income from exports has a larger impact on domestic savings and, hence, growth. The availability of foreign exchange from exports that can easily be allocated to finance intermediate imports leads to a high capacity utilization, particularly of the industrial sector, which has a positive impact on the level and growth of output.

The policy lessons that can be learnt from the above analysis are that the real exchange rate in general, and the incentives to produce for exports in particular, are important for promoting exports, which are necessary for economic growth. During the 1970s and the first half of the 1980s, policy-makers neglected the use of active exchange-rate policy and allowed the real producer prices of the major export crops to decrease. The drastic fall in the volume of exports is largely explained by the lack of adequate incentives to produce for export. Since 1984 and particularly after 1986, domestic policy has been adjusted to increase incentives for export production. These policies need to be sustained and improved. Trade liberalization measures should include imports financed by officially held foreign exchange so as to remove distortions and inefficient use of scarce resources. To achieve this objective, trade and exchange-rate policies will complement each other.

The poor export performance is largely the result of misconceived domestic policies. This does not, however, imply that Tanzania has not been affected by adverse external shocks, or been uninterested in the developments of the global trading system. Tanzania is a large country with diverse climate and soil that can support production of various types of crop. Positive and sustained incentives for export production by smallholder farmers is likely to lead not only to a high growth of exports but also to a more diversified export basket. Tanzania's export basket is dominated by commodities for which demand in the world market is not increasing (Table 9.4). Both the (world market) price and the income elasticities of demand are very low (see Behrman 1979), which is reflected in declining real prices. Hence the need to diversify to promote the production of exports that have better price prospects. Tanzania then has the potential of increasing exports of a wide range of agricultural products.

Over the somewhat longer term, appropriate reforms in the industrial sector can lead to an increase in the production and export of manufactured goods. A global trading system that guarantees market access in industrialized countries for goods that can be competitively produced in Tanzania is necessary for the export-promoting policies to succeed. It is therefore in Tanzania's interests that the multilateral trade negotiations roll back protectionism in the industrialized countries, extend reciprocity to the newly industrialized countries and confine special and differential treatment to the poorest countries.

## Notes

1 The natural conditions in Tanzania are favourable to the production of high-quality coffee and tea. Unfortunately, the quality of coffee and tea has declined to the extent that, while Tanzania's share of tea exports by volume has increased, the share by value has decreased.

2 The increase in the share of capital goods at a time when a shortage of consumer goods was acute is partly explained by the fact that the foreign capital inflow was tied to investment expenditures that could not be switched to finance imports of consumer or intermediate goods.

3 One may mention the quota restriction of coffee, but so far Tanzania has never failed to sell supplies in excess of the quota, albeit at lower prices.

4 However, if one unifies all natural hemp fibre (also jute and abaca) and the close substitutes (synthetic fibres), one would have strong doubts whether Tanzania's supply variation would have a perceptible influence on world market prices for sisal.

## References

Behrman, J. (1979), 'International integrated commodity programme', in W. R. Cline (ed.), *Policy Alternatives for a New International Economic Order: An Economic Analysis*, Praeger (for Overseas Development Council), New York.

Chenery, H. B. and Bruno, M. (1962), 'Development alternatives in an open economy: The case of Israel', *Economic Journal*, 72, March.

Chenery H. B. and Strout, A. M. (1966), 'Foreign assistance and economic development', *American Economic Review*, September.

Ellis, F. (1982), 'Agriculture price policy in Tanzania', *World Development*, No. 4.

Green, R. H., Rwegasira, D. G. and van Arkadie, B. (1980), *Economic Shocks and National Policy Making: Tanzania in the 1970s*, Institute of Social Studies, The Hague.

Gulhati, R. and Datta, G. (1983), 'Capital accumulation in Eastern and Southern Africa: A decade of setbacks', World Bank Staff Working Paper No. 562, Washington DC.

Helleiner, G. (1986), 'Outward orientation import instability and African economic growth: An empirical investigation', in Sanjaya Lall and Frances Stewart, *Theory and Reality in Development*, Macmillan, London.

Helleiner, G. (1988), 'Trade strategy in medium term adjustment', United Nations University, Tokyo.

IMF (1989), *Primary Commodities: Market Developments and Outlook*, International Monetary Fund, Washington DC.

Lee, J. K. (1971), 'Exports and the propensity to save in LDCs', *Economic Journal*, June.

Lipumba, N., (1984), 'Economic crisis in Tanzania', in N. Lipumba *et al.* (eds), *Stabilization Policies in Tanzania*, University of Dar-es-Salaam.

Lipumba, N. (1988), 'Domestic supply constraints versus market access: International trade and economic development in Tanzania', in John Whalley (ed.), *The Small among the Big*, University of Western Ontario, London, Ontario.

Lipumba, N. *et al.* (1988), 'A supply constrained macroeconometric model of Tanzania', *Economic Modelling*, 5, October.

Maizels, A. (1968), *Exports and Economic Growth of Developing Countries*, Cambridge University Press, Cambridge.

Michapolous, C. and Jay, K. (1973), 'Growth of exports and income in the developing worlds', AID Discussion Paper No. 28, Washington DC.

Ndulu, B. J. (1986), 'Investment output growth and capacity utilization in an African economy: The case of the manufacturing sector in Tanzania', *East African Economic Review*, 2, June.

Nerlove, H. (1958), *The Dynamics of Supply: Estimation of Farmers' Response to Price*, Johns Hopkins University Press, Baltimore, Md.

Ødegaard, K. (1985), 'Cash crops versns food crop production in Tanzania: An assessment of the major post-colonial trends', Economic Studies No. 33, University of Lund.

Ram, Rati (1985), 'Exports and economic growth: Some additional evidence', *Economic Development and Cultural Change*, 33.

Roemer, M. *et al.* (1975), 'The range of strategic choices in Tanzania industry', *Journal of Development Economics*, 3.

Skarstein, R. and Wangwe, S. (1986), *Industrial Development in Tanzania: Some Critical Issues*, Scandinavia Institute of African Studies, Uppsala; Tanzanian Publishing House, Dar-es-Salaam.

Stein, L. (1979), *The Growth of East African Exports and Their Effect on Economic Development*, Croom Helm, London.

United Republic of Tanzania (1987), 'Agricultural price policy recommendation', Marketing Development Bureau, Ministry of Agriculture, Dar-es-Salaam.

Wangwe, S. (1983), 'Industrialization and resource allocation in a developing country', *World Development*, 2.

Weisskopf, T. (1972), 'The impact of foreign capital inflows on domestic saving in underdeveloped countries', *Journal of International Economics*, February.

10

# An analysis of Nigeria's trade with special reference to import demand

Joe U. Umo

## 1 Introduction

International trade is perhaps the single most important set of economic activities that has shaped the Nigerian economy since the turn of the century. Important economic and socio-political landmarks in the country's recent history can be traced directly or indirectly to major events in international trade activities:

(1) Trade in primary commodities like palm oil, cocoa, cotton, groundnut, rubber, etc., constituted the major means by which the country could earn foreign exchange up to the time of political independence in 1960. Indeed, it was the huge sterling reserves built through primary commodity exports in the 1950s that enabled the country to construct the socioeconomic infrastructure on which the new nation started its post-independence development journey.

(2) Efforts at modernizing the economy can be traced to the heavy importation of raw materials and machinery which fuelled the import-substitution industrialization strategy in the 1960s and 1970s.

(3) Changes in the commodity composition of trade which started in the mid-1960s were substantially to alter the structure of the national economy. More specifically, the emergence of petroleum as the key export not only precipitated the demise of the primary exports but also worsened the precarious external dependence of the economy.

Oil exports alone accounted for over 95 per cent of the country's foreign exchange earnings, and import dependence on several key areas like food and raw materials ranged between 80 and 90 per cent.

(4) The vulnerability of the Nigerian economy to global recession and the attendant collapse of the oil market in recent years can be directly traced to Nigeria's trade profile. The problems that have cropped up in the foreign trade sector include the accumulation of short-term trade arrears and the associated debt crisis, balance of payment deficits, an overvalued currency, smuggling, etc. On the domestic front, the economy has remained seriously depressed, with over 3 million people currently unemployed. Agriculture, which was the mainstay of the economy in the 1960s, has equally been depressed. It is increasingly unable to employ and feed Nigerians. Industries operate at about 20 per cent of their installed capacity because of shortages of imported raw materials following the foreign exchange crunch.

This sketch is intended to show that, like all open economies, Nigeria's economic fortune (or misfortune) depends critically on international trade issues. Despite this acknowledgement, it is unfortunate that only scanty analytical and empirical knowledge exists in the country for rational policy guidance in this area. A few studies that have been attempted have focused mainly on import demand (Olayide 1968; Ajayi 1985; Fajana 1977; Mouka 1982) and only partially on export supply (Umo 1981). To the best of our knowledge, there is no comprehensive study of Nigeria's trade problems in the context of development policy. It is therefore apparent that a systematic study of the whole sector seems imperative.

This study modestly aims at examining the key components of Nigeria's external trade in a development context. A rather unusual combination of two methodological approaches – formal and informal – was adopted for this study. The formal one undertook the conventional procedures of descriptive analysis of Nigeria's trade profiles (section 2); and the estimation of import functions (section 3). The second (informal) approach involved carrying out a National Policy Dialogue on Trade and Development (NAPOD) in Nigeria. The conference, which took place in late November 1987, drew participants from a cross-section of the policy community, including scholars, senior civil servants, government and private sector officials. Although the deliberations of the NAPOD have been put together in another monograph (Umo 1987), the results of some of the salient issues raised are synthesized in the discussion of the policy implications of the whole study which conclude this paper (section 4).

## 2 Descriptive analysis of Nigeria's trade profile

To put Nigeria's analytical and empirical trade issues in perspective, a background descriptive analysis of some key variables seems in order. The main variables of interest here include aggregated and disaggregated exports, aggregated and disaggregated imports, spatial trade patterns and balance of payments profile covering the study period (1960–86).

*Exports*

Nigeria's aggregate exports stood at ₦331.3 million in 1960 when the country gained its political independence from Britain. They then grew to reach their highest peak of about ₦14 billion in 1980, from where they slumped to ₦8.6 billion in 1985. Nigerian export trade actually entered the billion Naira range from 1970; and based on the 1960 value, the increase by 1980 was over forty-one-fold. The trend growth rates of exports and the major components over the three and a half decades spanned by this study are shown on Table 10.1.

The main features of Table 10.1 can be summarized as follows:

(1) Nigeria's total exports experienced the highest growth rate (27 per cent) in the 1970s and had their worst shortfall (–8.6 per cent) in the first seven years of the 1980s (see row 5).

(2) Export of mineral fuels (row 3) was reasonably robust, averaging 27 per cent during the study period and reaching a peak of 50 per cent in the 1960s. Evidently, export performance was influenced by the crude oil components, given its fluctuations in line with total exports.

(3) Exports of food and live animals declined by 70 per cent in the 1960s and recovered to merely 11 per cent in the 1970s.

(4) It is significant that the export of crude materials has been on

Table 10.1 *Growth trends of some Nigerian exports, 1960–86*

| *Export categories* | *Growth trends by periods* | | | |
|---|---|---|---|---|
| | *1960–85* | *1960–70* | *1970–80* | *1981–86* |
| Food and live animals | 0.06<br>(7.81) | –0.70<br>(–2.70) | 0.11<br>(4.52) | 0.025<br>(0.775) |
| Crude materials | –0.09<br>(–11.88) | –0.031<br>(–2.36) | –0.65<br>(–1.78) | –0.179<br>(3.96) |
| Mineral fuels | 0.27<br>(11.1) | 0.50<br>(4.26) | 0.32<br>(8.32) | –0.091<br>(–2.66) |
| Manufactured Goods | 0.06<br>(0.38) | 0.26<br>(3.9) | –0.14<br>(–1.12) | –0.25<br>(–1.86) |
| Total exports | 0.17<br>(15.05) | 0.063<br>(4.21) | 0.27<br>(8.90) | –0.086<br>(–2.62) |

*Note:*
1. *t*-values in brackets.

*Source:* Author's estimates from semi-log functions on time.

the decline (–9 per cent per annum) throughout the entire period. This same trend characterized the export of manufactured goods since the 1970s (row 4).

*Oil* v. *non-oil exports*

Given the importance of both oil exports and non-oil exports for the current economic policy, the most significant feature of Nigeria's export trend is that, while oil export revenue rose sharply between 1970 and 1973, that of non-oil revenue correspondingly fell sharply from 1967. The policy problem of raising non-oil export revenue, which constitutes the core of the current export promotion strategy, will be addressed in the later sections of this study.

*Imports*

Aggregate Nigerian imports increased from ₦431.7 million in 1960 to ₦756 million in 1970; and reached their highest peak of ₦12.6 billion in 1981. Since 1981, imports have been declining both absolutely and in relative terms.

Table 10.2 *Growth trends of some Nigerian imports, 1960–86*

| *Import categories* | *Growth trends by periods* | | | |
|---|---|---|---|---|
| | *1960–85* | *1960–70* | *1970–80* | *1981–86* |
| Total imports | 0.16 (12.03) | 0.91 (0.68) | 0.29 (9.32) | –0.116 (–1.55) |
| Foods and live animals | 0.18 (12.19) | –0.026 (–0.63) | 0.24 (16.13) | — |
| Chemicals | 0.16 (10.51) | 0.098 (10.84) | 0.15 (1.83) | 0.068 (0.48) |
| Machinery and transport equipment | 0.14 (5.45) | –0.03 (–0.20) | 0.30 (7.79) | 0.165 (–1.69) |

*Note:*
1. *t*-values in brackets.

*Source:* Author's estimates from semi-log functions of import categories on time.

The trend growth rates for aggregate imports and the major components are shown on Table 10.2. It is clear from the table that in the 1960s and 1970s import growth rates were in general explosive. The sharp increase (29 per cent) in the 1970s can be accounted for by the heavy importation for post civil war reconstruction activities and the availability of oil revenue. It is equally obvious that the sharp declines in imports since the beginning of the 1980s are attributed to the economic difficulties resulting from the collapse of oil revenues.

In terms of the component import categories in Table 10.2, it is important to note the following two points:

(1) Food imports registered the highest growth rate (34 per cent) in the 1970s. This was followed only by imports of machinery and transport equipment, which stood at 30 per cent during the same decade. The 1970s can plausibly be referred to as the 'age of import boom' in Nigeria.

(2) The high import dependency of the economy can be demonstrated by the fact that the average growth rates of different

import categories were quite robust for the period spanned by our study. These included food and live animals (18 per cent), chemicals (16 per cent) and machinery and transport equipment (14 per cent).

*Spatial profiles of Nigeria's trade*

Nigeria became a colonial territory largely through trade, which was spearheaded by the Royal Niger Company. It is therefore no accident that Britain remained Nigeria's main trading partner during the colonial period and the early post-colonial period.

During the first few years of the first decade of independence (1960–70), there was no fundamental change in this direction of trade. In 1960, for instance, the United Kingdom accounted for 43 per cent of Nigeria's imports, while Western Europe, Japan and the United States accounted for 26, 13 and 5.4 per cent, respectively, of Nigeria's imports.

The geographical spread of its export trade was broadly similar to that of imports during the first decade of political independence. However, towards the end of this first decade, trade with the United Kingdom declined somewhat: exports fell to 30 per cent in 1970, while they rose from 21 per cent to 32 per cent for Western Europe. Export trade with Japan also declined during the first decade of independence, while it increased considerably for the US (from 5 per cent in 1960 to 15 per cent in 1970).

A percentage ranking of the volume of both exports and imports amongst Nigeria's trading partners between 1970 and 1985 shows the following:

(1) Western Europe and US, with a combined average of about 70 per cent of export business, overtook Britain, which was Nigeria's traditional export buyer. This can be attributed to the fact that, with the dominance of crude petroleum in Nigeria's trade commodity composition, Western Europe and USA are becoming increasingly important as Nigeria's export markets.

(2) Western Europe maintained a lead (41 per cent) as Nigeria's import market, followed by the United Kingdom (23 per cent) and US (12 per cent).

(3) Nigeria's export trade with West Africa was only 2 per cent while imports remained a mere trickle of 0.4 per cent.

(4) Both import and export trade with the Commonwealth stood at 4 per cent;
(5) Nigeria was becoming important as a Japanese export market (10 per cent) and less so as an import market (1.5 per cent).

*Balance of payments profile*

For expositional convenience, the main categories of Nigeria's balance of payments (BOP) to be presented here include the capital account balance, the current account balance, the services account balance and the overall balance. Table 10.3 depicts the broad trends of these components of the BOP account. It is clear from the table that virtually all the components of the balance of payments were stable from 1960 to early 1970. Interesting gyrations started from the early 1970s.

The overall balance, which is the most comprehensive BOP concept often settled by reserves and appropriate liabilities, had only about three years of substantial surpluses: 1974, 1979 and 1980 respectively. The intervening periods were characterized by deficits, which have shown some improvement since 1983.

The capital account balance progressively maintained a surplus, reaching its peak of ₦3.5 billion in 1982, but thereafter sliding until it slumped into a deficit by 1985. This shows the movement of long-term investment into Nigeria.

The current account balance almost moved in sympathy with the overall balance. This is because trade balance, especially the short-term trade arrears component, has a lot to do with the overall balance. This in particular explains why this balance had been progressively in deficit, reaching its highest of –₦4.9 billion in 1982. Since 1984 it has moved into a marginal surplus.

It is interesting to note that Nigeria's invisibles account has consistently and progressively been in deficit since 1970. It seems obvious that the invisibles account and other components of the trade account constitute the main drains in Nigeria's BOP account. The implications for trade and development policy will be drawn in the last section of this paper.

## 3 Nigerian import models

In this section, attempts will be made to develop and estimate import models for Nigeria, based on time-series data from 1960 to

Table 10.3 *Nigeria's balance of payments (summary), 1960–85*

| *Year* | *Balance of trade* | *Services account balance* | *Transfer payments* | *Current account balance* | *Capital account balance* | *Errors + omissions* | *Overall Balance* | *Reserve movement* |
|---|---|---|---|---|---|---|---|---|
| 1960 | –101.0 | –36.2 | NA | –137.2 | 64.6 | –0.8 | –73.4 | NA |
| 1965 | –5.6 | 127.6 | 5.4 | –127.4 | 132.0 | 19.2 | –23.8 | NA |
| 1970 | 173.0 | –268.0 | 45.0 | –50.0 | 49.2 | 47.4 | 46.6 | 158.7 |
| 1971 | 285.0 | –516.2 | 1.8 | –229.4 | 293.4 | 53.4 | 117.4 | 282.5 |
| 1972 | 477.5 | –785.9 | –14.3 | –322.7 | 269.2 | 3.7 | –44.8 | 248.5 |
| 1973 | 1,166.9 | –1,078.8 | –35.4 | 52.7 | 144.8 | 23.1 | 220.4 | 383.2 |
| 1974 | 4,439.3 | –1,314.7 | –62.1 | 3,062.5 | –5.9 | 45.6 | 3,102.2 | 3,452.3 |
| 1975 | 1,487.1 | –1,367.7 | –76.8 | 42.6 | 141.1 | –26.2 | 157.5 | 3,564.0 |
| 1976 | 1,293.5 | –1,455.0 | –97.8 | –259.3 | –50.6 | –30.0 | –339.9 | 3,063.9 |
| 1977 | 1,553.9 | –2,082.7 | –118.7 | –647.5 | 150.4 | –30.1 | –527.2 | 2,746.6 |
| 1978 | –741.7 | –1,474.6 | –170.6 | –2,386.9 | 1,111.9 | –18.6 | –1,293.6 | 1,266.1 |
| 1979 | 2,967.4 | –1,724.4 | –233.5 | 1,009.5 | 813.2 | 46.2 | 1,868.9 | 3,080.4 |
| 1980 | 6,132.7 | –3,462.2 | –315.2 | 2,355.3 | 97.4 | –50.5 | 2,402.2 | 5,485.9 |
| 1981 | –703.5 | –2,948.4 | –346.5 | –3,998.4 | 929.5 | 48.1 | –3,020.8 | 3,036.2 |
| 1982 | –1,810.2 | –2,799.9 | –289.4 | –4,879.5 | 3,470.9 | 10.3 | –1,398.3 | 1,393.3 |
| 1983 | –647.3 | –2,092.8 | –285.8 | –3,025.9 | 2,832.2 | –51.1 | –244.8 | 244.8 |
| 1984 | 2,299.7 | –1,781.6 | –253.8 | 264.3 | 132.5 | 34.7 | 431.5 | –362.1 |
| 1985 | 3.320.6 | –2,034.0 | –379.0 | 907.6 | –1,211.4 | –1.0 | –301.8 | 304.8 |

*Sources:* Central Bank of Nigeria, *Bulletin*, vol. 7, no. 1, January/March, 1972; *Annual Report and Statement of Accounts* (various issues).

1985, to illustrate some of the characteristics of the external sector. As oil exports constitute about 97 per cent of total exports, an export model has not been considered of much relevance in this analysis.

*Import demand model*

As was noted earlier, attempts at studying the determinants of import demand in Nigeria, though useful in terms of the price and incomes questions probed, failed to account for environmental factors that affect demand for imports. Besides, since most of the study periods pre-date Nigeria's oil boom era, some interesting empirical issues that emerged during and after the oil boom era might not have been considered. The modelling efforts here will make an attempt to take these factors into account.

The aggregate demand for Nigeria's import is therefore specified as:

$$\log MP_t = \log a_0 + a_{1_{it}} \log REP_t + a_{2it} \log REY + a_{3_{it}} \log NEX_t + U_{it}, \quad (10.1)$$

where

$MP_t$ = real import demand at time $t$;
$REP$ = relative import price $P_m/P_y$ (i.e. price index of imports, $P_m$ deflated by Nigeria's price index, $P_y$, for time $t$);
$REY$ = real per capita income;
$NEX$ = net external influence, proxied by capital inflow at time $t$; and
$U_t$ = stochastic error terms.

The disaggregated version of (10.1), which takes account of different SITC import contents, will be estimated as:

$$\log MP_{it} = \log b_{0_{it}} + b_{1_{it}} \log REP_{it} + b_{2_{it}} \log REY_{it} + b_{3_{it}} \log NEX_{it} + U_{it}, \quad (10.2)$$

where all $i$'s refer to the component levels of imports and other variables remain as defined previously.

A brief theoretical discussion of (10.1) in terms of the independent variables is given as follows:

*Relative price (REP)* REP is measured as the ratio of import price to domestic price index. For well-known reasons of income and substitution effects for normal goods, we expect $a_1 < 0$ and $a_2 < 0$.

*Real per capita income (REY)* With the exception of a rare case of commodity inferiority, we expect $a_2 < 0$. However, Khan (1974, p. 221) has noted that $a_2$ can be negative for a reason other than that of commodity inferiority. This is expected to be the case where import-substituting industrialization (ISI) leads to an excess supply of domestic import substitutes; hence the expected reduction in demand following any given increase in income. Since the ISI strategy has failed to generate excess supply in Nigeria (Odejide 1983; and Fabayo 1983), it is plausible that the *a priori* expectation in respect of the sign of $a_2$ will hold.

*Net external influence (NEX)* The impact of external environmental factors in an open economy hardly needs emphasis. The current economic difficulties faced by many less developed countries have made the recognition of external influences an analytical imperative. David Wheeler (1984), for instance, has used foreign aid as one of the vector elements to proxy environmental variables in his study of the sources of African economic stagnation.

In the above model we intend to capture external influences on imports by using net capital inflows as a proxy. Although Nigeria has not been aid-dependent since 1960, capital inflow seems a plausible surrogate since it serves the same resource gap function as aid. NEX grew at an average rate of 11 per cent during the period under study, although this declined to 7 per cent between 1981 and 1985. The *a priori* sign of NEX is ambiguous since the circumstances under which it would have positive or negative impact on imports depend on a complex set of internal and external variables impinging on it.

*Some theoretical assumptions*

The specifications of (10.1) or (10.2) are based on the following assumptions, following Khan (1974) and Umo (1981).

First, importers are assumed to be at their demand frontier. This is to avoid the possibility of perverse disequilibrium behaviour. Second, the adjustment lags in import propensity are extremely short. Third, the import supply function is assumed to be infinitely elastic, and, fourth, domestic prices and incomes are taken as exogenous.

The first two assumptions allow us to estimate model (10.1) in static terms. The last two allow us to estimate (10.1) as a reduced form using OLS for calibration.

*The methodology and data* The trade and balance of payment functions were all estimated with OLS using the relevant data covering 1960–85. The data sets and the sources include the Nigerian Federal Office of Statistics, Nigerian Trade Summary, National Accounts Publications, Central Bank of Nigeria's *Annual Reports and Statements of Accounts*, etc.

The sources of these data are reasonably reliable since trade documentation is one of the areas where the Federal Office of Statistics has been doing an excellent job since independence. The supplementation by the Central Bank statistical collections further strengthens their reliability.

A couple of methodological problems are worth noting. The first is the aggregation problem involved in the use of the import value as the dependent variable, as well as other regressors, in (10.1). It does appear, however, that the aggregation problem here is not as damaging as it may look. Theoretically, it can be justified by reference to Hicks' composite goods theorem (Patinkin 1965, pp. 411–16), which justifies aggregation on grounds of complementarity in consumption. A good proportion of Nigeria's imports include raw materials and machinery, which are complementary imputs in domestic production given the ISI strategy. In any case, the disaggregated parameter estimates are likely to reveal certain facts which might have been buried under aggregation.

The second methodological problem is the use of NEX as the external influence proxy. Since this is essentially an inflow of foreign capital, collinearity problems with real income (REY) can be expected. The true situation on this will, however, be revealed by the empirical results.

*The results* The results of our estimates for both aggregate and disaggregated import demands are shown in Table 10.4. The main highlights can be summarized as follows:

(1) Both the relative price (REP) and per capita income (REY) parameters are correctly signed (in terms of *a priori* expectations) and statistically significant in the aggregate import functions (equation 1). The external influence proxy (NEX) is positive but statistically insignificant.

(2) With the exception of a few cases in respect of disaggregated models (equations 2–7), the behaviour of the REP, REY

Table 10.4 *OLS estimates of import trade models for Nigeria (1960–85) with cochrane–orcut correction*

| *No. of equation* | *Dependent variable* | *Constant* | *Independent variables* | | | *Regression statistics* | | | |
|---|---|---|---|---|---|---|---|---|---|
| | | | *REP* | *REY* | *NEX* | $\overline{R}^2$ | *SEE* | *DW* | ρ |
| 1 | MP (Total imports) | 3399 (5.122) | –0.175 (–4.412) | 0.722 (6.204) | 0.054 (0.695) | 0.94 | 0.30 | 1.75 | 0.299 |
| 2 | MF (Import of food & live animals) | 0.930 (1.8.13) | –0.256 (–8.470) | 0.717 (8.501) | 0.843 (1.138) | 0.96 | 0.27 | 1.98 | 0.024 |
| 3 | MM (Import of crude materials) | 5.429 (4.037) | –0.004 (0.78) | 0.158 (1.057) | –0.016 (0–.355) | 0.96 | 0.23 | 1.76 | 0.950 |
| 4 | MTR (Import of Machinery & Transport Equipment) | 2.484 (1.551) | –0.168 (–1.807) | 0.752 (2.952) | 0.041 (0.165) | 0.60 | 0.93 | 2.08 | –0.121 |
| 5 | MC (Import of chemicals) | –0.927 (–0.714) | –0.450 (–0.584) | 0.743 (3.353) | 0.453 (2.705 | 0.78 | 0.63 | 2.04 | 0.184 |
| 6 | MRT (Import of raw materials) | 2.484 (4.124) | –0.139 (–3.888) | 0.652 (6.256) | 0.053 (0.713) | 0.93 | 0.28 | 1.78 | 0.240 |
| 7 | MFU (Import of mineral fuels) | 2.429 (2.038) | –0.151 (–2.120) | 0.471 (2.235) | –0.231 (–1.720) | 0.69 | 0.52 | 1.80 | 0.337 |

*Notes:*

1. All variables are in natural logarithms.
2. *t*-values are in brackets.
3. REP = relative price; REY = relative real income; NEX = net external influence (capital inflow).

and NEX parameters remained consistent with the aggregate function.

(3) It is noteworthy that the price and income elasticities for Nigerian imports are consistently below unity, with the former exhibiting much lower elasticity coefficients than the latter. This elasticity behaviour seems to reflect 'habit persistence', which has been reported for other African countries (Wheeler 1984).

(4) The behaviour of NEX is rather unstable throughout the estimates, hence one cannot make a categorical statement about the net impact of external influence on Nigeria's import behaviour. It is significantly positive for the import of chemicals (MC), while it is significantly negative for the import of mineral fuels (MFU). This behaviour can only be traced to the peculiarity of each of the products.

(5) The regression statistics in general show that the import demand models were reasonably robust.

*Tests for structural stability* Given the structural changes and shocks that the Nigerian economy has been experiencing, it became necessary to test for the stability of our statistical relationship for the import functions.

The Chow test (Chow 1960, pp. 591–605; Dutta 1975, pp. 173–8) was chosen for this purpose, and the two sub-samples include the pre-oil boom era (1960–73) and the oil boom era (1974–86). The results of the test for import function show that the import relationship is consistently stable at both 99 per cent and 95 per cent levels of significance.

It will be noted that export instability was more pronounced in Nigeria (see Table 10.1 and Obadan 1984) while import behaviour has been consistently stable, possibly because of 'habit persistence' parameters noted earlier. It should also be noted that a substantial component of Nigeria's import was debt-financed; hence import behaviour became relatively insensitive to the declining export fortunes.

## 3 Conclusions and policy implications

The study has attempted to analyse Nigeria's trade profile as well as estimate import functions. Some conclusions and policy implications emerge which should be compared and contrasted with the salient issues that emerged from the National Policy Dialogue on Trade and Development (NAPOD), conducted as a supplement to this study (see section 1).

The analysis of Nigeria's trade profiles has demonstrated, among other things, the following features, with the associated policy implications:

(1) Nigeria's monocultural export status, based on crude petroleum (approximately 97 per cent of export revenue), has hardly diminished. The current policy thrust has been to diversify the export base of the economy through the structural adjustment programme (SAP). Given the long-standing structural impediments and distortions facing the domestic economy, especially on the supply side, the programme of export diversification (into non-oil, semi-processing and manufacturing) may require a much longer time span to yield significant impacts than allowed for by SAP, which is conceived as a medium-term programme.

Besides, the full potential of the energy sector itself, as was noted during the NAPOD, is yet to be fully exploited for national development. In the light of the promising energy resource picture uncovered, it has been shown that, if successful upstream exploitation of the energy sector is achieved, Nigeria may emerge more as a gas-endowed than as an oil-endowed economy (Olorunfemi 1987). In this circumstance, the future still holds strong prospects for energy exports for Nigeria.

(2) Nigeria's trade profile is also characterized by high import dependency (about 29 per cent annual growth trend in the 1970s) with concentrations on machinery, raw materials and food items. Despite the attempts at import reduction by the use of nominal exchange-rate policies, from the average of \$15 billion between 1980 and 1982 to about \$6 billion annually in 1982–86, import demand still exerts severe pressures on the dwindling foreign exchange reserves. The current policy thrust has also been to pursue import reduction via local raw material sourcing by import-substituting firms. Supporters of this approach at the NAPOD advocated an effective protection strategy for viable industries whose social

benefits had been found to be positive during Nigeria's post-independence industrialization period (Sagagi 1987). Although the backward integration efforts so far advocated can also solve domestic employment problems, it requires strong creativity and indigenous technological capability to yield the expected results. Meanwhile, Nigeria's indigenous technological resources are fragile and the complexities of trade in technology are yet to be analytically probed.

(3) Nigeria's trade relations with the industrialized countries have continued to expand, compared with its intra-African trade, which has remained negligible (under 3 per cent). The policy of trade liberalization, which is an important component of SAP, was extensively discussed at the NAPOD. Given its adverse impact on uncompetitive domestic firms and the worsening unemployment situation, the need to adopt a cautious and selective approach was emphasized (Omoruyi 1987). Analysis of an increasingly protectionist stance by the industrialized market economies (Ubogu 1987) and significant trade potentials existing in the West Africa sub-region (Nwane 1987) suggest the need to examine trade strategies that would exploit trade potentials in the African sub-region.

(4) Estimates of the import function show that Nigeria's import demand is both price and income inelastic, thereby confirming the existence of 'habit persistence' parameters (Wheeler 1984).

(5) At the policy level, these empirical features raise doubts about the potency of expenditure-switching components of SAP in the Nigerian context. The weak productive capacity of the economy for sustaining purchases of non-tradables had led many policy-makers to advocate selective export promotion so as to serve local needs for food and raw materials (Obadan 1987). The need to enhance domestic productive capacity also underscores the advocacy of efficient import substitution through a meaningful programme based on backward integration (Sagagi 1987).

(6) Observations of the trends in exports show that the terms of trade are negatively related to aggregate exports, that Nigerian domestic export capacity is weak and that the real exchange rate has an unstable impact on export trends.

(7) If the hypothesis of transitory income effects with respect to

the terms of trade is plausible (Umo 1982), a regime of trade policy emphasizing quotas would undermine the growth-boosting impacts which can be expected from a short-term positive shock associated with the terms of trade (Besley and Collier, this volume). The importance of developing domestic productive capacity as a precondition for a successful export drive has also been noted by a growing number of economists (Kravis 1970; Jung and Marshall 1987). The policy implication raised in the NAPOD in this connection is for the domestic export supply response to be enhanced by establishing export free zones (Obadan 1987) and relaxing supply constraints, preferably via research and development (Abudu 1978). The intention is to increase the efficiency and speed of the export supply response, which has been found to be sluggish in the Nigerian economy.

(8) Attempts to realign the once overvalued exchange rate have been made by floating the Nigerian Naira in what is now called IFEM (Inter Bank Foreign Exchange Market). The divergence between demand for and supply of foreign exchange has averaged at a factor of about $54 million weekly. Consequently, the Naira value has been depreciating along an unstable path. The almost unanimous call to find a realistic and stable value for the Naira (made at NAPOD) is of policy relevance. This remains a factor in the inflationary pressures, estimated to be approaching an annual rate of 50 per cent in 1988.

(9) The analysis of the balance of payments (BOP) profile has shown that short-term trade arrears and deficits in invisibles constitute the main drains on Nigeria's external accounts. The policy issues raised by these results include the following:

(10) An improved efficiency in balance of payments management seems to be what is needed more urgently to reduce the negative impact of short-term trade arrears in the BOP. In the same vein, more effective allocation and management of the nation's invisible tradables like shipping, communication and consultancy could drastically cut down on the drains on the invisibles account (Umo 1988).

(11) The food import drain also reflects domestic policy failure and serious managerial lapses in the agricultural sector, since

the nation is richly endowed with resources that could enable it to achieve self-sufficiency in food production.

(12) Apart from the elements of the policy dialogue cited above, two additional policy issues which generated considerable debate at the NAPOD related to counter-trading. The analysis of counter-trade in Nigeria (Sonoiki 1987) indicates, among otherthings, the following facts:

(i) 4–10 per cent global trade is of the counter-trade variety involving straight barter, counter-purchases, buy-back, offset and switch-trading arrangements, etc.

(ii) both the developed and developing countries engage in counter-trade for various socioeconomic reasons perceived as advantageous to individual participants; and

(iii) counter-trading is in general shrouded in secrecy. Given these features the need to pull counter-trade from the international parallel market category seems an interesting issue to explore.

(14) Attempts to analyse the relationship between external debt problems and the balance of payments (Fajana 1987) suggest that self-reliance in trade policy orientation could offer a potential solution. Specifically, the NAPOD participants advocate strategies of selective export promotion and import substitution based on sensitivity to local availabilities and requirements. In effect, this approach raises the question of the degree of trade-off between domestic and foreign requirements during the process of liberalization in the African context. Failure to strike an optimal balance could seriously jeopardize both growth and development goals.

## Note

1 The invaluable comments of the participants in the seminars on Trade and Development in Sub-Saharan Africa, held during the course of the study (1987–89) at Nairobi, are gratefully acknowledged.

## References

Abudu, F. (1987), 'Import compression and local sourcing of raw materials in Nigeria', in Joe U. Umo (ed.), *Papers on Trade and*

*Development in Nigeria*, monograph, Department of Economics, University of Lagos.

Ajayi, S. I. (1985), 'Econometric analysis of import demand function for Nigeria', *Nigerian Journal of Economic and Social Studies*, 17, pp. 169–82.

Besley, Timothy and Collier, Paul (1989), 'Import compression and trade policy', this volume.

Chow, Gregory L. (1960), 'Test of equality between sets of coefficients in two linear regressions', *Econometrics*, 28, pp. 591–605.

Dutta, M. (1975), *Econometric Methods*, South-West Publishing Company, Cincinnati.

Fabayo, Ademola (1983), 'Two decades of import substituting industrialisation in Nigeria – A stock taking', *Ife Social Science Review*, 6, pp. 40–55.

Fajana, F. O. (1977), 'Demand shortage, A case study of selected food import trade', *Nigerian Journal of Economic and Social Studies*, March, pp. 109–20.

Fajana, F. O. (1987), 'Nigeria's post independence external debts and balance of payments problems: A policy perspective', in Joe U. Umo (ed.), *Papers on Trade and Development in Nigeria*, monograph, Department of Economics, University of Lagos.

Jung, W.S. and Marshall, P. J. (1987), 'Exports, growth and causality in developing countries', *Journal of Development Economics*, 18, pp. 1–12.

Khan, M. S. (1974), 'Import and export demand in developing countries', *IMF Staff Papers*, 21, November.

Kravis, I. B. (1970), 'Trade as a handmaiden of growth – Similarities between the 19th and 20th centuries', *Economic Journal*, 80, pp. 850–72.

Mouka, Aethelbirth (1982), 'An econometric study of Nigeria's demand for imports 1960–79', unpublished M.Phil. thesis, University of Lagos, July.

Nwane, S. S. O. (1987), 'Export diversification and promotion: Policies and problems in Nigeria', in Joe U. Umo (ed.), *Papers on Trade and Development in Nigeria*, monograph, Department of Economics, University of Lagos.

Obadan, M. I. (1984), 'Instability in Nigeria's export earnings', *Nigerian Journal of Political Economy*, 2, pp. 20–39.

Obadan, M. I. (1987), 'Export diversification and promotion: Policies and problems in Nigeria', in Joe U. Umo (ed.), *Papers on Trade and Development in Nigeria*, monograph, Department of Economics, University of Lagos.

Odejide, A. F. (1983), 'Import substitution as a strategy of industrial development in Nigeria', *Ife Social Sciences Review*, 6, pp. 32–9.

Olayide, S. O. (1968), 'Import demand model: An econometric analysis of Nigeria's import trade', *Nigerian Journal of Economic and Social Studies,* November, pp. 303–19.

Olorunfemi, M. A (1987), 'Nigeria's petroleum industry and trade policies; An analysis of post independence experience', in Joe U. Umo (ed.), *Papers on Trade and Development in Nigeria*, monograph, Department of Economics, University of Lagos.

Omoruyi, E. S. (1987), 'Structural Adjustment Programme, Second Foreign Exchange Market (SFEM) and trade policies in Nigeria', in Joe U. Umo (ed.), *Papers on Trade and Development in Nigeria*, monograph, Department of Economics, University of Lagos.

Patinkin, Don (1965), *Money, Interest and Prices*, Harper & Row, New York.

Sagagi, Muhammed (1987), 'Effective protection and economic performance of the Nigerian manufacturing sector', in Joe U. Umo (ed.), *Papers on Trade and Development in Nigeria*, monograph, Department of Economics, University of Lagos.

Sonoiki, J. O. (1987), 'Counter-trade in Nigeria: An analysis of quantum, implications and problems for trade policy', in Joe U. Umo (ed.), *Papers on Trade and Development in Nigeria*, monograph, Department of Economics, University of Lagos.

Ubogu, Roland E. (1987), 'Impacts of external economic and trade policies on Nigeria's trade performance (1960–1986)', in Joe U. Umo (ed.), *Papers on Trade and Development in Nigeria*, monograph, Department of Economics, University of Lagos.

Umo J. U. (1981), 'Import demand and export supply elasticities for African countries: A comparative analysis', *Journal of Business and Social Studies*, 5, pp. 43–54.

Umo, J. U. (1982), 'Econometric tests of some stylized savings hypotheses for members of West African Economic Community (ECOWAS)', *West African Economic Journal*, 2, pp. 1–15.

Umo, J. U. (1987), *Papers on Trade and Development in Nigeria*, edited monograph, Department of Economics, University of Lagos.

Umo, J. U. (1988), 'Domestic resource mobilisation in Africa: The case of human capital in Nigeria', paper presented at Conference on *Economic Policy Research Centre for Africa*, Nairobi, 1–3 August.

Wheeler, David (1984), 'Sources of stagnation in sub-Saharan Africa', *World Development*, 12, pp. 1–23.

11

# Trade, trade management and development in Zimbabwe

Rob Davies

## 1 Introduction

Zimbabwe became independent in April 1980, ninety years after it had been colonized. The fifteen years preceding independence had seen a range of international trade and financial sanctions imposed after the settler regime in Southern Rhodesia had unilaterally declared independence (UDI) from Britain. Although sanctions had not been completely effective, they did enforce a period of relative autarky on the economy. This relative autarky was accompanied by some *de facto* import substitution and the diversification of the economic base.[1] After 1980, with independence and the removal of sanctions, the foreign sector became more open, with expansion of imports and exports as well as increased capital inflows. Subsequent balance of payments difficulties, however, led to the tightening of strict quantitative restrictions on imports and tighter controls over invisible outflows. Although some of these have been relaxed, many are still in operation, but they are increasingly recognized as requiring reform and restructuring; there is a growing debate centred on the liberalization issue. The government commissioned a trade liberalization study in 1988 and has subsequently stated its commitment to reform of the system, although the precise content of these reforms is not yet known.

The main concern of this paper is the administered foreign exchange regime and the implications of using import quotas as a macroeconomic instrument for balance of payments control. A secondary concern is the impact that the liberalization of the trade regime has had on the direction and commodity composition of trade. After reviewing the performance of the economy and the importance of trade in section 2, the paper outlines the main features of the foreign exchange management system and the evolution of government views on trade policy in section 3. It then looks at changes in the country and commodity pattern of Zimbabwe's trade in section 4. In section 5, a decomposition technique is used to identify the main sources of movements in the balance of trade. Finally, the paper examines some of the potential consequences of the trade management system (section 6); the question of import compression through policy controls is given special consideration.

It should be noted at the outset that the statistical analysis is conducted with relatively simple methods. The use of more sophisticated econometric techniques is prohibited by the fact that consistent time-series trade data are available only for the seven post-independence years 1980–86.

## 2 Performance of the economy and the role of trade

The pre-independence period can be divided into two phases, one of expansion up to 1974, and one of stagnation and decline between 1975 and 1979 (see Table 11.1). Between 1970 and 1974, there was real growth in the economy: gross national income (GNI) per capita grew despite wide fluctuations; inflation was below 6.0 per cent per annum (except 1974); and the proportion of the population employed in the formal sector expanded. After 1975, per capita GDP and GNI declined, the inflation rate accelerated and the proportion of the population employed in the formal sector began to decline. The turnaround in 1975 has variously been attributed to the escalating war of liberation, the drying-up of the 'easy' stages of import substitution, and the impact of the 1974 oil price rise (Stoneman 1982; Davies 1980).

Independence saw a reversal in the post-1975 downward trend. In 1980 and 1981, real GDP grew by over 10 per cent, leading to increases in per capita income of almost 8 per cent per annum. However, inflation remained high and formal employment was static. The post-independence boom collapsed in 1982; the economy went into a period of stagnation and decline from which, except for a brief upturn in 1985, it has not fully recovered. This turnaround

Table 11.1 *Selected economic indicators for Zimbabwe, 1970–86 (%)*

| *Year* | *Growth Rates* | | *Inflation measured by GDP deflator* | *Employment as a proportion of population* | *Ratio of imports to GDP (mp) (1980 prices)* | *Ratio of exports to GDP (mp) (1980 prices)* |
|---|---|---|---|---|---|---|
| | *GDP (fc) (1980 prices)* | *GNI (mp) per head (1980 prices)* | | | | |
| 1970 | 6.7 | –0.7 | 1.5 | 16.1 | 30.5 | 25.1 |
| 1971 | 8.8 | 4.4 | 5.7 | 16.2 | 31.7 | 27.5 |
| 1972 | 8.2 | 11.0 | 5.4 | 16.7 | 29.0 | 30.4 |
| 1973 | 2.4 | –0.2 | 6.0 | 16.9 | 30.4 | 30.1 |
| 1974 | 5.9 | 10.5 | 16.5 | 17.1 | 30.9 | 24.8 |
| 1975 | –0.1 | –2.3 | 6.3 | 16.7 | 29.2 | 28.4 |
| 1976 | –0.8 | –4.6 | 9.4 | 15.9 | 21.5 | 29.8 |
| 1977 | –7.5 | –8.8 | 8.0 | 15.1 | 21.0 | 29.0 |
| 1978 | –0.8 | –4.8 | 10.0 | 14.3 | 19.7 | 30.9 |
| 1979 | 1.4 | 0.5 | 15.8 | 13.8 | 19.1 | 30.7 |
| 1980 | 10.4 | 7.7 | 9.5 | 13.7 | 23.5 | 26.4 |
| 1981 | 10.2 | 7.9 | 13.6 | 13.7 | 26.4 | 22.7 |
| 1982 | 1.4 | 0.8 | 12.4 | 13.7 | 27.3 | 22.5 |
| 1983 | –4.3 | –1.8 | 18.3 | 13.2 | 22.5 | 23.4 |
| 1984 | 2.6 | –3.7 | 10.8 | 12.8 | 22.9 | 23.0 |
| 1985 | 8.9 | 8.3 | 12.2 | n.a. | 22.7 | 22.8 |
| 1986 | 0.2 | n.a. | 12.5 | n.a. | 24.0 | 26.4 |

*Notes:*
GDP (fc) = gross domestic product at factor costs
GDP (mp) = gross domestic product at market prices
GNI (mp) = gross national income at market prices

*Sources:* Central Statistical Office, *National Income and Expenditure Report 1987*, Harare, Tables 1.1 and 1.2; *Quarterly Digest of Statistics*, Harare, September 1987, Tables 11.1 and 11.2.

and the subsequent failure to expand was partly due to domestic drought and a recession in the world economy. Increasingly, however, the stagnation has come to be attributed to foreign exchange shortages; the performance of the foreign trade sector is thus at the centre of the question of overall development performance and strategy.

As Table 11.1 indicates, trade plays a relatively important part in the Zimbabwean economy. Between 1970 and 1986, imports averaged 25.4 per cent and exports 26.7 per cent of GDP in constant price terms. However, there are noticeable structural changes in both indices. In the case of imports, the main break came in 1976. In the wake of the first oil shock, there was significant import compression and the propensity to import had not recovered, despite some relaxation in the years 1980–82. For exports, the structural break came at independence, the export ratio declining significantly between 1979 and 1981. However, both exports and imports have been rather volatile. The coefficient of variation of the export/GDP ratio fell from 7.4 per cent before independence to 6.7 per cent after. For imports, the coefficient of variation was 18.9 per cent before independence and 7.3 per cent after. It will be argued later that much of this variation in the import ratio stems from the management of the trade system.

Zimbabwe operates a managed floating exchange rate. The rate is determined against a basket of currencies, using undisclosed trade weights. Table 11.2 presents some estimates of the nominal and effective exchange rates for the period 1980–87. It can be seen that both the nominal and the real effective exchange rates appreciated immediately after independence. In December 1982, however, there was a 20 per cent nominal devaluation, followed by a further 10 per cent in January 1983. During the period of the IMF stand-by credit (March 1983 to April 1984), the authorities attempted to ensure that the real rate did not appreciate against the major trading partners. Subsequently, there has been a regular depreciation in both nominal and real terms. Zimbabwe thus appears to have been successful in preventing the domestic currency from becoming overvalued, or, rather, in avoiding an increase in the degree of overvaluation. A severe foreign exchange shortage in the economy remains, and there is still a system of managed foreign exchange allocation. It is thus widely argued that the removal of quantitative restrictions would lead to a large devaluation, signifying that the Zimbabwean dollar is still overvalued.

Table 11.2 *Zimbabwe's exchange-rate movements, 1980–87*

| *Year* | *Nominal effective exchange rate*[a] | *Real effective exchange rate*[b] |
|---|---|---|
| 1980 | 100.0 | 100.0 |
| 1981 | 101.8 | 103.6 |
| 1982 | 99.8 | 103.2 |
| 1983 | 78.5 | 94.0 |
| 1984 | 70.2 | 95.1 |
| 1985 | 60.9 | 83.4 |
| 1986 | 53.6 | 78.7 |
| 1987 | 50.4 | 77.6 |

*Notes:*

[a] The nominal effective exchange rate is an index of nominal rates weighted by shares of trade. The weights used here are the shares in total trade for the period 1981–86. The formula used is:

$$NEEP_t = \frac{\sum_i e_i^t w_i^t}{\sum_i e_i^0 w_i^0},$$

where $i$ = £, R, DM, SF, FF and US\$

$w = (M_i + X_i) / \sum_i (M_i + X_i)$

except $w_{US\$} = 1 - \sum w_i$ for $i \neq$ US\$

[b] Real effective exchange rates are the nominal effective rates adjusted by an index of domestic prices to world prices. Here the domestic price index is the GDP deflator and the world price is an index of GDP deflators in the trading partners weighted by trade shares.

*Sources:* CSO, *Quarterly Digest of Statistics*, September 1988, Harare; IMF, *International Financial Statistics*.

## 3 Foreign exchange management and the evolution of trade policy

When sanctions against Rhodesia were imposed after UDI, an extensive system of direct management of foreign trade and exchange was introduced. In its essential features, this system has continued to the present.

*Foreign exchange allocation*

At the centre of the system is the procedure for allocating foreign exchange. For each six-month quota period, the Reserve Bank forecasts expected global foreign exchange receipts, based upon projected export earnings, expected aid inflows, viable borrowing levels, and other factors. From this figure are deducted commitments for debt servicing, for expected invisible requirements, and for known long-term payments. The balance is then available for distribution among importers. The allocation between competing demands is done through the Ministries of Trade and Commerce and of Industry and Energy. There are more than thirty headings under which the allocations are made; these include certain ministries, parastatals, specific products (such as oil and switchgear), specific sectors (such as mining), and more general categories, the main two of which are commercial imports and industrial imports. Many of the general headings receive a fixed share of the foreign exchange available, within broad minimum and maximum absolute amounts, so that allocation among them is quite automatic. This is to ensure that adequate foreign exchange is allocated to 'essential' users, such as oil importers and export industries. This process means that allocations for commercial and industrial imports tend to be residuals. When there are cuts in the amount of foreign exchange being allocated, these categories tend to adjust the most.

Allocations to individual users within the commercial and industrial categories are made by using a combination of fixed shares and ad hoc allocations. Regular users of foreign exchange have quotas which fix their share of what is available. However, both regular and new users are able to make ad hoc applications for additional foreign currency. New users can apply for a regular allocation on the grounds that they can buy the imports more cheaply than an existing user. It is also possible to enter the system by demonstrating that one will be able to ensure a substantial net saving of foreign exchange. Users who have received several successive ad hoc allocations are also eligible to apply for regular allocations.

Within this broad system, there are a number of committees (including the government and the private sector) that deal with foreign exchange allocations to long-term investment projects. Over the years, a number of criteria have been developed with regard to these projects. Although they include general issues such as employment creation, in practice the committees place most emphasis on a project's ability to generate or save foreign exchange in the future. This is a necessary, but not sufficient, condition for a project to be approved.

*Import licences*, which primarily serve a monitoring purpose, are automatically given to recipients of foreign exchange. It is possible for those who have legitimate access to foreign exchange outside Zimbabwe (e.g. through gifts) to obtain a 'no-currency-involved' import licence. Although the controls on visible imports have been fairly tight, those on invisible ones have tended to be operated at a macro rather than a micro level. Thus, payments for transport, insurance, commission, etc., have been controlled at the micro level by rule-of-thumb criteria based on the normal ratio between these and the value of the visible trade to which they relate. At the same time, there have been periodical macro constraints on some outflows, such as dividends, rents and royalties.

There is no system of *export licences*, but exporters are required to complete export documents certified through authorized foreign exchange dealers to ensure that foreign exchange receipts are repatriated to the general pool. Dealings in foreign exchange can be undertaken only through authorized dealers, namely the commercial banks.

*Modification in the allocation system*

The inherited system for the allocation of foreign exchange has been modified in several ways since independence. The most immediate post-independence modification was the special treatment of black businessmen who were not in the system before the independence. This was an attempt to offset the inherent racial discrimination implied by a system which is heavily biased towards the status quo. Of greater significance have been several reforms which have provided alternative channels of access to foreign currency for users: commodity import programmes (CIPs), funded by bilateral and multilateral donors; the establishment of an export revolving fund and its subsequent expansion into an export promotion programme; and the growth of counter-trading and barter arrangements. All these have led to a reduction in the proportion of imports going through the traditional allocating system. This proportion declined from 92 per cent of total imports in 1980 to 56 per cent in the 1984-86 period (Ministry of Finance, Economic Planning and Development 1987, p. 10).

There is some evidence that the firms which receive imports

through the alternative channels have their traditional allocations reduced, if not removed completely. It also appears that entry into one of these supernumerary programmes is not determined by the same criteria as those used in the traditional system. This applies particularly to CIPs, where it is possible for importers to make the initial contact with the donor. It thus seems that these alternative channels substitute for, rather than complement, the traditional system, implying that the government's direct control of the pattern of imports has been reduced since independence.[2]

In practice, the modifications amount to the introduction of an ad hoc system of multiple exchange rates. The export promotion programme incorporates two important incentives to exporters. First, there is a 9 per cent export incentive bonus to exporters of manufactured goods; in effect this is equivalent to a 9 per cent devaluation as far as the price of export goods is concerned. In some cases, exporters have used this bonus to reduce the prices quoted to foreign customers. Second, in 1987 a system was introduced whereby most exporters are entitled to use 25 per cent of *incremental* export earnings to import inputs for production for the domestic market. In the case of barter and counter-trade, the effective price received for the bartered experts is lower than the normal export price, again implying an effective devaluation. Finally, the 'tied' nature of most CIPs implies that firms participating in the programmes pay a higher price for their imports than would otherwise be the case, which amounts to an effective devaluation as regards imports.[3] However, since the local importers pay for the imports in local funds to the government for general development purposes, the differential between the official exchange rate and the effective exchange rate accrues to the government.

*An evolving trade policy*

In general, the various modifications of the trade system have been introduced in response to the perceived shortage of foreign exchange. The government has wished to retain the control implied by the system, but has also wanted to provide incentives to exporters. The evolution of the government's views on trade policy emerges clearly from an examination of several official statements by the Zimbabwean government. In the earliest of these, *Growth with Equity* (Zimbabwe 1981), it was apparent that the government's standpoint on foreign trade policy could not be characterized as either export led or import substituting. On the one hand, the importance of enhancing the capacity of the economy to earn foreign exchange was stressed at several points; on the other, further import substitution was explicitly called for. In the subsequent *Transitional National Development Plan 1982/83–1984/85* (TNDP; Zimbabwe 1982), the government's objectives appeared to have moved away from the import-substituting industrialization of the past:

> Government will encourage and give necessary and appropriate assistance in terms of export incentives, design, equipment, availability of imported inputs, research, and manpower development to enterprises in order to promote rapid growth of exports. This will involve formulation of a general export/foreign exchange policy to replace current policies based primarily on import substitution. (Zimbabwe 1982, para 4.43)

The TNDP also pointed to the need to reduce the heavy dependence of the manufacturing sector on imported inputs. In the course of its discussion, it was said:

> Because of the failure to promote industries in which the economy has a long-term comparative advantage – principally raw material processing and/or employing labour-intensive production methods – manufacturing has become a substantial net user of foreign exchange. The past import-substitution industrialisation has brought significant benefits to the economy, but at substantial costs. It has resulted in economic inefficiency and inequity arising from deterioration in terms of trade between manufacturing and agriculture and has caused relative capital intensity of the sector and thus failing [sic] to generate larger volumes of employment. (Zimbabwe 1982, para 13.3)

The successor of the TNDP, the *First Five-year National Development Plan 1986–1990* (Zimbabwe 1986), indicated an intention to intensify export promotion, but made no statement concerning import substitution. However, it did state that 'Zimbabwe will examine possibilities of establishing industries that will produce intermediate, capital and consumer goods to meet its requirements and some of the requirements of SADCC [Southern African Development Co-ordinating Conference] and PTA [Preferential Trading Area] member countries' (Zimbabwe 1986, para 2.5).

These plans demonstrate the evolution of the plan drafters' attitude that import substitution is inherently problematical and that export promotion is desirable. The reforms made to the foreign exchange management outlined above, and particularly the introduction of the various export promotion schemes, reflect this evolution. However, at the same time, the government has not been willing to dismantle the system of administered foreign exchange allocation, which is the main source of protection for the import-substituting industries and which may also impose serious costs on the export industries.

## 4 The direction and composition of trade

Since independence, there have been two main *exogenous* factors influencing Zimbabwe's trading patterns: (i) the removal of sanctions and (ii) the emerging regional co-operation with the implications this has for relations with South Africa. The main *endogenous* influence is likely to have been the operation of the foreign exchange management system itself and particularly the impact of CIPs. Unfortunately, reliable data on the direction of trade before independence do not exist, so the relative importance of these forces cannot be fully analysed in econometric terms. There are, however, several observations that can be made on a more qualitative basis.

*Effects of the removal of sanctions*

Although Zimbabwe has maintained the system of controls of trade that it inherited from the time before the independence, the removal of sanctions could be seen as a relative liberalization of the trade regime. It is an interesting question what impact this had on the direction and commodity composition of trade. *A priori* it might be expected that conventional comparative advantage factors would have been strengthened. As far as the *direction of trade* is concerned, it could be argued that sanctions led to increased dependence on a few countries, in which case their removal would lead to a greater diversification of trading partners. On the other hand, it might be that the sanctions required trading with any countries that were willing to ignore them, regardless of cost; in this case, their removal would lead to a relative concentration as the comparative advantage reasserted itself.

It is equally difficult to make *a priori* judgements about the expected effect of sanctions removal on the *commodity composition* of trade. One line of argument could run as follows. Sanctions provided an incentive to switch production in the economy from primary (traditional) to manufactured goods. The exchange rate was kept overvalued in the sense that foreign exchange was rationed and at a premium. Non-market export promotion measures were undertaken, so that the question of whether a particular product was exported depended not so much on the domestic production costs as on sanction-breaking efforts. In other words, there was an implicit shadow exchange rate which was used when trying to promote exports.

The problem with this argument is that the main divergence between the official and the shadow exchange rate probably was at the social rather than the private level. There does not seem to have been any mechanism whereby the social premium was internalized so as to compensate exporters for exporting below private costs. Nevertheless, intuitively one would expect that the removal of sanctions would encourage a shift back to more traditional exports in which the comparative advantage was clearer. This would show up as an increase in the commodity concentration of exports. Against this would be the fact that certain industries established under the import-substituting regime might have become competitive at an international level. In this case one would not expect to see a complete reversion; rather, it would take place at the margin.

*Expected effects of regional co-operation and links with the South African Union*

The Southern African Development Co-ordinating Conference (SADCC) was established in 1980, partly to combat South Africa's economic dominance in the sub-region. It has concentrated its efforts on infrastructural development until recently; any impact it has had on trade has been due to the *indirect* effect of these developments rather than to trade-oriented policies. The Eastern and Southern African Preferential Trading Area (PTA) has been much more concerned with facilitating intraregional trade, both through reduction of trade barriers and through the establishment of clearing-house facilities to mitigate the problems of shortages of hard foreign currency. Most of its significant reforms have come into effect only since 1985 and are not yet reflected in available statistics.

Trade relations between Zimbabwe and South Africa since independence have been rather unstable. South Africa has used trade as part of its armoury of weapons periodically to destabilize Zimbabwe – one of the front-line states – squeezing both trade and trade routes. On the Zimbabwean side, there is a firm commitment to reduce trade with South Africa. This commitment is supported by some of Zimbabwe's other trading partners, which are seeking ways to help Zimbabwe realize this intention; this is a main motive for some of the CIPs.[4] Nevertheless, there is a trade agreement between the two countries, which facilitates preferential exports from Zimbabwe to South Africa.

*De facto changes in trade patterns*

The data on the direction trade by region for the period 1981–86 are presented in Table 11.3. We can see that there is no significant trend in the concentration, as measured by the Gini–Hirschman Index, in either exports or imports. For both, the indices fell in 1982, indicating less concentration, but then rose again in 1983 and 1984. They declined once more in 1985 and remained low in 1986; however, given that this was five years after independence, it is debatable whether this is a result of the sanctions removal or of other forces.

The most noticeable change of export partners in the period is the declining importance of South Africa and the rising importance of the European Community. South Africa's share of exports fell by 9.5 percentage points between 1981 and 1986 from 21.9 per cent to 12.4 per cent. The European Community's share rose by an almost equivalent amount over the same period, from 26.4 per cent to 35.6 per cent. The share of the SADCC and the whole of sub-Saharan Africa (including the SADCC) has remained virtually constant. There have been slight upward trends in exports to Eastern Europe and to other developing countries, but from very low levels.

The import pattern has not changed as noticeably as the export pattern. There has been a decline in the share of imports coming from South Africa and this, as is the case with exports, has essentially been supplanted by a rising share from the European Community.

Overall, therefore, the main post-independence trend has been the substitution of the European Community for South Africa. This is in part a reflection of both the European Community's and Zimbabwe's policies towards South Africa, which have reinforced a trend that was probably inevitable after the removal of sanctions against Rhodesia and the restoration of more 'normal' trading relations. However, the collapse of the Rand, which has meant that the Zimbabwean dollar has depreciated less relative to it than to

Table 11.3 *Direction of Zimbabwe's trade, 1981–86*

| | *1981* | *1982* | *1983* | *1984* | *1985* | *1986* |
|---|---|---|---|---|---|---|
| *Exports classified by region* | | | | | | |
| (percentage share of total exports) | | | | | | |
| Sub-Saharan Africa (excl. SADCC) | 4.0 | 4.9 | 4.0 | 3.7 | 4.5 | 7.2 |
| SADCC | 9.2 | 9.2 | 9.5 | 10.6 | 10.2 | 8.8 |
| South Africa | 21.9 | 17.1 | 18.8 | 18.4 | 10.9 | 12.4 |
| European Community | 26.4 | 30.0 | 30.3 | 31.1 | 35.1 | 35.6 |
| East Europe | 1.2 | 0.3 | 2.8 | 2.5 | 4.7 | 4.0 |
| United States | 7.9 | 7.9 | 6.7 | 6.2 | 8.1 | 5.7 |
| Other developing contries | 7.7 | 7.9 | 10.9 | 10.9 | 8.8 | 10.2 |
| Other low-income countries | 3.8 | 0.9 | 1.1 | 2.7 | 4.8 | 3.6 |
| Middle-income countries | 2.0 | 1.7 | 1.6 | 1.5 | 1.3 | 1.9 |
| Upper middle-income countries | 11.6 | 15.0 | 11.8 | 10.8 | 10.5 | 9.5 |
| High-income oil exporters | 0.8 | 0.7 | 1.0 | 0.4 | 0.0 | 0.3 |
| Other, not elsewhere specified | 3.4 | 4.4 | 1.6 | 1.1 | 1.1 | 0.6 |
| | 100.0 | 100.0 | 100.0 | 100.0 | 100.0 | 100.0 |
| Gini–Hirschman Index | 0.240 | 0.210 | 0.238 | 0.240 | 0.208 | 0.207 |
| No. of countries buying more than 0.1% of exports | 50 | 49 | 57 | 58 | 58 | 61 |
| *Imports classified by region* | | | | | | |
| (percentage share of total imports) | | | | | | |
| Sub-Saharan Africa (excl. SADCC) | 1.9 | 0.9 | 0.9 | 0.0 | 0.1 | 0.2 |
| SADCC | 5.9 | 6.7 | 7.3 | 6.5 | 5.5 | 7.8 |
| South Africa | 27.5 | 22.1 | 24.5 | 19.3 | 18.9 | 21.4 |
| European Community | 25.7 | 31.0 | 28.2 | 26.5 | 25.3 | 27.9 |
| East Europe | 0.3 | 0.4 | 0.8 | 1.2 | 2.2 | 1.9 |
| United States | 7.3 | 9.6 | 9.5 | 9.3 | 10.1 | 8.3 |
| Other developing countries | 11.3 | 11.9 | 10.2 | 11.2 | 9.7 | 12.9 |
| Other low-income countries | 1.7 | 0.7 | 1.0 | 0.6 | 2.8 | 1.6 |
| Middle-income countries | 0.0 | 0.2 | 0.0 | 1.6 | 0.0 | 0.0 |
| Upper-middle-income countries | 5.2 | 4.7 | 5.2 | 6.5 | 5.8 | 7.0 |
| High-income oil exporters | 0.0 | 0.0 | 0.0 | 0.0 | 0.0 | 0.1 |
| Returned exports | 0.3 | 0.3 | 0.2 | 0.2 | 0.3 | 0.3 |
| Other, not elsewhere specified | 13.0 | 11.6 | 12.3 | 17.1 | 19.2 | 10.5 |
| | 100.0 | 100.0 | 100.0 | 100.0 | 100.0 | 100.0 |
| Gini–Hirschman Index | 0.283 | 0.264 | 0.269 | 0.271 | 0.211 | 0.244 |
| No. of countries supplying more than 0.1% of imports | 37 | 35 | 39 | 37 | 40 | 38 |

*Source:* Compiled from statistics provided by the Central Statistical Office.

Table 11.4 *Concentration of Zimbabwe's commodity exports, 1975–86*

| *Year* | *Number of commodities accounting for more than 0.1% of Exports* | *Gini – Hirschman Index* |
|---|---|---|
| 1975 | 60 | 0.221 |
| 1976 | 56 | 0.224 |
| 1977 | 56 | 0.216 |
| 1978 | 59 | 0.221 |
| 1979 | 59 | 0.209 |
| 1980 | 67 | 0.235 |
| 1981 | 58 | 0.283 |
| 1982 | 61 | 0.281 |
| 1983 | 57 | 0.265 |
| 1984 | n.a. | n.a. |
| 1985 | 69 | 0.282 |
| 1986 | 71 | 0.291 |

*Sources:* CSO, *Statement of External Trade*, Harare, various dates; data provided by CSO.

European currencies, has provided additional stimuli to trade with Europe rather than with the SAU. Direct actions by South Africa have also had an impact, particularly on the side of exports.

Zimbabwe exports a relatively diversified range of commodities. Table 11.4 gives some estimates of the standardized Gini–Hirschman Index of *commodity concentration*. It can be seen that this has risen in the post-independence period, suggesting that export concentration has increased. Nevertheless, the indices are low by international standards.[5] Furthermore, if one looks at the number of exports which account for more than 0.1 per cent of total commodity exports (excluding gold), one sees that the number has risen from an average of fifty-eight in the five years preceding independence to an average of sixty-four per year since then. In 1986, seventy-one commodities met this criterion, suggesting some diversification. The picture is thus one of the important commodities increasing their share of export earnings, simultaneously with a greater number of less significant commodities being exported.

*Dominant exports and imports*

Between 1975 and 1986, tobacco was consistently the single biggest export item. The relative importance of asbestos has been declining, that of gold has been rising, while maize exports fluctuate depending on the agricultural season. Overall, Zimbabwe's exports are dominated by primary products: the only manufactured goods that feature among the top twenty export goods in any of the years 1975–86 are clothing, telecommunication products, footwear, and furniture.

Table 11.5 shows exports classified according to whether they are primary exports (SITC 0+1+2+3+4+67+68) or 'non-traditional' (SITC 5+6+7+8−67−68). There has really not been any discernible trend in the share of these two categories; while the value of 'non-traditional' exports has increased in nominal terms, it has not done so in constant price terms. Indeed, there was a sharp fall in the performance of 'non-traditional' exports in 1982 and 1983. This was due primarily to difficulties over the renegotiation of the trade agreement with South Africa, which was an important market for manufactured exports. Table 11.6 shows a breakdown of traditional and non-traditional exports by major *destination*. This clearly shows that the shift in the direction of trade from South Africa to the European Community has primarily involved non-traditional exports. However, the relative importance of the SADCC countries as a market for Zimbabwe's non-traditional exports has also increased.

Imports classified by broad SITC heads are given in Table 11.7. There are some fluctuations in the share of fuel imports, caused in 1982 by an important volume drop through South African destabilization and, in 1986, by a price drop. The second panel of this table shows shares for imports, excluding fuel. It appears that most of the imports are concentrated in SITC groups 5, 6, and 7. Most of these imports are capital goods and intermediate inputs; direct importation of consumer goods has almost been squeezed out of the system.

## 5 Sources of change in the balance of trade

Zimbabwe's current account balance deteriorated substantially in the early 1980s. The balance of trade has fluctuated since 1980, moving from a small surplus to a growing deficit in 1982 and 1983

Table 11.5 *Zimbabwe's primary and non-traditional exports, 1975–86*

| *Year* | *Shares in total* | | | *Current price totals* | | | *Constant price totals* | | |
|---|---|---|---|---|---|---|---|---|---|
| | *Primary exports (%)* | *Non-traditional exports (%)* | *Residual (%)* | *Primary exports (Z$m.)* | *Non-traditional exports (Z$m.)* | *Residual (Z$m.)* | *Primary exports (1980 Z$m.)* | *Non-traditional exports (1980 Z$m.)* | *Residual (1980 Z$m.)* |
| 1975 | 80.2 | 13.5 | 6.3 | 407.9 | 68.5 | 32.3 | 718.1 | 120.5 | 56.9 |
| 1976 | 82.1 | 12.3 | 5.6 | 449.1 | 67.2 | 30.6 | 757.3 | 113.3 | 51.6 |
| 1977 | 81.7 | 11.2 | 7.1 | 431.6 | 59.3 | 37.4 | 699.5 | 96.1 | 60.6 |
| 1978 | 80.6 | 11.0 | 8.4 | 485.5 | 66.4 | 50.6 | 739.0 | 101.1 | 77.0 |
| 1979 | 77.7 | 10.8 | 11.4 | 542.9 | 75.6 | 79.8 | 719.1 | 100.1 | 105.7 |
| 1980 | 83.6 | 11.6 | 4.8 | 658.1 | 91.5 | 37.9 | 658.1 | 91.5 | 37.9 |
| 1981 | 82.5 | 11.4 | 6.2 | 732.6 | 101.0 | 54.7 | 663.0 | 91.4 | 49.5 |
| 1982 | 84.2 | 9.4 | 6.4 | 678.2 | 75.8 | 51.7 | 632.1 | 70.6 | 48.2 |
| 1983 | 86.2 | 8.8 | 5.0 | 900.6 | 92.0 | 51.7 | 726.9 | 74.3 | 41.7 |
| 1984 | 81.0 | 14.9 | 4.1 | 1,029.3 | 188.8 | 52.0 | 650.2 | 119.3 | 32.8 |
| 1985 | 86.9 | 11.3 | 1.8 | 1,342.3 | 174.9 | 28.1 | 712.1 | 92.8 | 14.9 |
| 1986 | 87.1 | 11.9 | 1.0 | 1,480.2 | 202.2 | 17.4 | 770.9 | 105.3 | 9.1 |

*Sources:* CSO, *Statement of External Trade*, Harare, various dates; *Quarterly Digest of Statistics*, Harare, September 1988.

Table 11.6 *Destinations of Zimbabwe's traditional and non-traditional exports, 1981–86*

| *Year* | *SADCC* | *South Africa* | *EC* | *US* | *Japan* | *Other* | *Total* |
|---|---|---|---|---|---|---|---|
| *Traditional exports: '000 Z$* | | | | | | | |
| 1981 | 46,699 | 73,546 | 186,810 | 36,499 | 11,903 | 178,014 | 533,471 |
| 1982 | 44,330 | 46,850 | 177,641 | 34,929 | 8,150 | 168,270 | 480,170 |
| 1983 | 55,515 | 81,435 | 236,064 | 16,575 | 24,425 | 171,430 | 585,444 |
| 1984 | 32,447 | 105,056 | 290,990 | 23,910 | 16,725 | 247,898 | 717,026 |
| 1985 | 64,122 | 96,389 | 410,829 | 44,689 | 21,341 | 288,694 | 926,064 |
| 1986 | 86,899 | 154,372 | 450,338 | 17,494 | 20,218 | 315,248 | 1,044,569 |
| *Percentage shares* | | | | | | | |
| 1981 | 8.8 | 13.8 | 35.0 | 6.8 | 2.2 | 33.4 | 100.0 |
| 1982 | 9.2 | 9.8 | 37.0 | 7.3 | 1.7 | 35.0 | 100.0 |
| 1983 | 9.5 | 13.9 | 40.3 | 2.8 | 4.2 | 29.3 | 100.0 |
| 1984 | 4.5 | 14.7 | 40.6 | 3.3 | 2.3 | 34.6 | 100.0 |
| 1985 | 6.9 | 10.4 | 44.4 | 4.8 | 2.3 | 31.2 | 100.0 |
| 1986 | 8.3 | 14.8 | 43.1 | 1.7 | 1.9 | 30.2 | 100.0 |
| *Non-traditional exports: '000 Z$* | | | | | | | |
| 1981 | 42,643 | 118,631 | 85,733 | 33,271 | 13,008 | 61,310 | 354,596 |
| 1982 | 38,513 | 90,967 | 92,841 | 28,650 | 17,399 | 58,604 | 326,974 |
| 1983 | 47,759 | 110,535 | 121,618 | 52,110 | 40,553 | 67,689 | 440,264 |
| 1984 | 87,074 | 127,123 | 152,370 | 55,069 | 49,435 | 82,973 | 554,044 |
| 1985 | 95,914 | 70,156 | 204,806 | 81,117 | 50,098 | 117,190 | 619,281 |
| 1986 | 110,233 | 56,719 | 232,546 | 79,896 | 57,350 | 118,451 | 655,195 |
| *Percentage shares* | | | | | | | |
| 1981 | 12.0 | 33.5 | 24.2 | 9.4 | 3.7 | 17.3 | 100.0 |
| 1982 | 11.8 | 27.8 | 28.4 | 8.8 | 5.3 | 17.9 | 100.0 |
| 1983 | 10.8 | 25.1 | 27.6 | 11.8 | 9.2 | 15.4 | 100.0 |
| 1984 | 15.7 | 22.9 | 27.5 | 9.9 | 8.9 | 15.0 | 100.0 |
| 1985 | 15.5 | 11.3 | 33.1 | 13.1 | 8.1 | 18.9 | 100.0 |
| 1986 | 16.8 | 8.7 | 35.5 | 12.2 | 8.8 | 18.1 | 100.0 |

*Source:* Statistics provided by the Central Statistical Office.

Table 11.7 *Zimbabwe's imports classified by SITC group, 1980–86 (%)*

| *SITC* | *1980* | *1981* | *1982* | *1983* | *1984* | *1985* | *1986* |
|---|---|---|---|---|---|---|---|
| 0 Food | 3.4 | 1.5 | 1.0 | 2.0 | 6.7 | 3.6 | 1.6 |
| 1 Beverages | 0.5 | 0.2 | 0.2 | 0.3 | 0.2 | 0.3 | 0.5 |
| 2 Crude materials | 3.2 | 3.3 | 3.5 | 3.9 | 3.0 | 3.5 | 5.9 |
| 3 Fuels | 24.0 | 20.8 | 16.5 | 21.2 | 20.6 | 24.0 | 15.2 |
| 4 Oils and fats | 0.8 | 0.8 | 0.6 | 1.1 | 0.9 | 1.1 | 1.1 |
| 5 Chemicals | 13.4 | 13.9 | 11.6 | 14.3 | 16.5 | 16.4 | 15.9 |
| 6 Manufactures | 18.4 | 19.3 | 14.5 | 14.2 | 15.8 | 15.0 | 14.5 |
| 7 Machinery & equipment | 26.0 | 32.2 | 40.7 | 34.5 | 30.0 | 29.2 | 37.8 |
| 8&9 Misc. manufactures | 10.3 | 7.9 | 11.4 | 8.5 | 6.3 | 6.9 | 7.4 |
| Total | 100.0 | 100.0 | 100.0 | 100.0 | 100.0 | 100.0 | 100.0 |
| *Shares excluding fuel:* | | | | | | | |
| 0 Food | 4.5 | 1.9 | 1.2 | 2.6 | 8.4 | 4.7 | 1.9 |
| 1 Beverages | 0.6 | 0.3 | 0.2 | 0.4 | 0.3 | 0.4 | 0.6 |
| 2 Crude materials | 4.2 | 4.1 | 4.2 | 4.9 | 3.8 | 4.6 | 6.9 |
| 4 Oils and fats | 1.1 | 1.1 | 0.8 | 1.4 | 1.1 | 1.5 | 1.3 |
| 5 Chemicals | 17.7 | 17.6 | 13.8 | 18.1 | 20.8 | 21.5 | 18.8 |
| 6 Manufacture | 24.2 | 24.4 | 17.4 | 18.1 | 19.8 | 19.8 | 17.1 |
| 7 Machinery and equipment | 34.2 | 40.6 | 48.7 | 43.7 | 37.8 | 38.4 | 44.6 |
| 8&9 Misc. manufactures | 13.5 | 10.0 | 13.7 | 10.8 | 7.9 | 9.1 | 8.7 |
| Total | 100.0 | 100.0 | 100.0 | 100.0 | 100.0 | 100.0 | 100.0 |

*Source:* CSO, *Quarterly Digest of Statistics*, September 1988, Harare, Table 11.6.

and back to surplus again in recent years (see Table 11.8). The question arises what has caused these movements.

*Volume* v. *barter terms of trade effects*

Svedberg decomposed the income terms of trade (ITT) to identify internal and external influences on the export performance of sub-Saharan countries (Svedberg, Chapter 2 in this volume). Zimbabwe's income terms of trade developed differently during three distinct periods: 1966–73, when they were rising; 1973–79 when they were falling; and 1979–87 when they rose again. These developments can be decomposed into changes in the net barter terms of trade and changes in export volumes. Table 11.9 sets out this decomposition for each of the three periods. Following Svedberg, we would then conclude that the main source of change in the ITT was *internal* in the first period, *external* in the second period, and in the third period internal and external factors contributed equally. How-

Table 11.8 *Zimbabwe's current external transactions, 1975–86 (current prices)*

| *Year* | *Exports of goods and services (Z$m.)* | *Imports of goods and services (Z$m.)* | *Visible and invisible balance (Z$m.)* | *Net factor income from abroad (Z$m.)* | *Net transfers from abroad (Z$m.)* | *Current account balance* | |
|---|---|---|---|---|---|---|---|
| | | | | | | *Total (Z$m.)* | *As % of GNP* |
| 1975 | 590 | 613 | –24 | –46 | –18 | –88 | –4.5 |
| 1976 | 617 | 533 | 84 | –59 | –19 | 6 | 0.3 |
| 1977 | 610 | 558 | 52 | –48 | –13 | –9 | –0.4 |
| 1978 | 675 | 593 | 82 | –42 | –16 | 25 | 1.1 |
| 1979 | 798 | 803 | –5 | 255 | –15 | 235 | 8.5 |
| 1980 | 1,043 | 1,146 | –103 | –47 | –6 | –157 | –4.6 |
| 1981 | 1,118 | 1,442 | –325 | –115 | 1 | –439 | –10.2 |
| 1982 | 1,141 | 1,450 | –309 | –194 | –30 | –533 | –10.7 |
| 1983 | 1,345 | 1,542 | –197 | –248 | –9 | –454 | –7.6 |
| 1984 | 1,708 | 1,673 | 35 | –195 | 57 | –103 | –1.6 |
| 1985 | 2,101 | 2,015 | 86 | –284 | 39 | –159 | –2.1 |
| 1986 | 2,559 | 2,202 | 358 | –384 | 41 | 15 | 0.2 |

*Source:* CSO, *National Income and Expenditure Report 1987*, Harare, Table 1.9.

Table 11.9 *Decomposition of Zimbabwe's income terms of trade, 1966–87*

| *Period* | *Average annual percentage changes in:* | | |
|---|---|---|---|
| | *Net barter terms of trade* | *Export volumes* | *Income terms of trade* |
| 1966–73 | 0.85 | 7.73 | 8.58 |
| 1973–79 | –7.55 | –0.18 | –7.73 |
| 1979–87 | 3.38 | 3.18 | 6.56 |

*Source:* Estimated from CSO, *Quarterly Digest of Statistics*, September 1988, Harare, Tables 11.1 and 11.2.

ever, as Svedberg notes, this method, particularly the attribution of volumes to internal factors, has to be treated with caution.

*Further decomposition*

An alternative method is to decompose the balance of trade, drawing on Worswick (1956). The method allows the influence of changes in the import and export prices and volumes on the balance of trade to be separated statistically. This can be extended to identify the impact of domestic economic growth and of import controls. The method gives some idea of the relative quantitative importance of alternative sources of change in the balance of trade.[6] Table 11.10 shows the basic decomposition for the period 1967–87.

Focusing on the post-independence period, it may be noted that, in the period of increasing balance of trade deficits (1980–82), import volume was the main contributory factor. If, over these three years, nothing else had changed, the balance of trade would have been worsened by some Z$500 million, simply because of the increased volume of imports. This negative impact on the balance of trade was offset to some extent by improved export prices, resulting mainly from the removal of sanctions and the export discount that these entailed.

In the subsequent period (1983–87), the improvement in the balance of trade stemmed from several sources. Improved export prices contributed Z$810.3 million in extra earnings; a greater export volume contributed Z$592.7 million, mainly concentrated in the last

Table 11.10 *Decomposition of changes in Zimbabwe's balance of trade, 1967–87 (current prices, Z$m.)*

| *Year* | *Actual change in trade balance* | *Export volume effect* | *Import volume effect* | *Export price effect* | *Import price effect* |
|---|---|---|---|---|---|
| 1967 | –17.2 | 6.5 | –18.2 | –6.1 | 0.6 |
| 1968 | –16.1 | –0.1 | –22.7 | 4.0 | 2.7 |
| 1969 | 46.1 | 26.4 | 11.4 | 12.8 | –3.8 |
| 1970 | –7.6 | 1.8 | –26.3 | 26.1 | –9.2 |
| 1971 | –16.0 | 47.3 | –32.3 | –15.8 | –15.2 |
| 1972 | 66.7 | 57.3 | 1.5 | 1.6 | 6.3 |
| 1973 | 6.1 | 8.1 | –22.2 | 31.9 | –11.7 |
| 1974 | –87.6 | –78.7 | –17.5 | 120.8 | –112.2 |
| 1975 | 77.1 | 70.9 | 22.3 | 29.2 | –45.3 |
| 1976 | 124.7 | 22.7 | 140.1 | 23.4 | –61.5 |
| 1977 | –32.0 | –50.0 | 34.0 | 23.4 | –39.4 |
| 1978 | 42.9 | 22.8 | 37.4 | 35.7 | –53.0 |
| 1979 | –39.2 | 15.5 | 3.0 | 90.9 | –148.6 |
| 1980 | –66.6 | –38.7 | –220.7 | 232.2 | –39.4 |
| 1981 | –145.8 | –33.9 | –212.3 | 96.4 | 4.0 |
| 1982 | –67.4 | 25.7 | –68.2 | –29.0 | 4.1 |
| 1983 | 202.0 | 55.4 | 209.1 | 126.4 | –188.9 |
| 1984 | 163.7 | –48.0 | –4.1 | 350.8 | –135.0 |
| 1985 | 96.7 | 65.3 | –49.0 | 277.2 | –196.8 |
| 1986 | 180.9 | 341.5 | –127.6 | 33.3 | –66.3 |
| 1987 | 99.8 | 178.5 | 137.8 | 22.6 | –239.1 |

*Source:* Calculated from CSO, *Quarterly Digest of Statistics*, September 1988, Harare, Tables 11.1 and 11.2. For notes on decomposition see Appendix.

two years. As against this, rising import prices cost an extra Z$826.1 million. Over the whole period, compressed import volumes contributed a net Z$166.2 million to the improvement of the balance of trade. Import volumes fluctuated considerably, however. There was a period of import compression in 1983 (subsequent to the relaxation immediately after independence), followed by varying degrees of expansion in 1984–86, and renewed compression in 1987. This is an indication of the 'stop–go' policies of the authorities allocating the foreign exchange.[7]

*World price* v. *exchange rate change*
The price indices used are those for exports and imports measured in Zimbabwean dollar prices. They are therefore influenced by movements in the exchange rate. The effects of these movements would net themselves out on the whole *if trade were in balance*. To put it differently, in such a case there should be no difference between the balance of trade measured in domestic currency and that measured in foreign currency. However, there will be a difference in the movements, as measured in these two ways, when trade is not in balance. This is shown in Table 11.11.

It is noticeable that the negative effects of falling world *export prices* have been offset by the exchange-rate depreciation. Thus, whereas Table 11.10 gives the impression that export prices have been generally rising, the decomposition in Table 11.11 shows that this is true only in Zimbabwean dollar terms. In fact, the apparent improvements in the price of Zimbabwe's exports have come from the continually depreciating dollar *only*.

The *world prices* of Zimbabwe's *imports* fell between 1981 and 1983, fluctuated mildly in 1983, 1984, and 1985 fell again in 1986, and then rose again in 1987 to the 1983–85 level. There were thus significant impacts on the balance of trade in 1983, 1986 and 1987. However, the depreciating value of the Zimbabwean dollar had a negative impact on the balance of trade (measured in Zimbabwean dollar terms), outweighing any positive impact from falling import prices, so that the import price effect in Table 11.10 appears to be strongly negative. It seems that much of the price effect identified from the decomposition in Table 11.10 has, in fact, arisen from the declining value of the Zimbabwean dollar.

*Volume effects*
There was an order-of-magnitude shift in *export volume* in 1986, reflecting the impact of the various export promotion schemes introduced (see Table 11.10). The *import volume* fluctuated much more violently than the export volume, particularly after 1980. Large negative effects in 1980 and 1981 probably represent the substantial relaxation of import controls during that period. By 1983, there is an equally great positive effect, representing the import compression which occurred when the authorities reacted to the deteriorating balance of payments situation. It is probable that the depreciation of the Zimbabwean dollar in 1982 contributed to this contraction in

Table 11.11 *Decomposition of price effects in Zimbabwe, 1980–87*

| *Year* | *World export price effect (Z$m.)* | *Export exchange-rate effect (Z$m.)* | *World import price effect (Z$m.)* | *Import exchange-rate effect (Z$m.)* | *Net exchange-rate effect (Z$m.)* | *World export price (1980=100)* | *World import price (1980=100)* |
|---|---|---|---|---|---|---|---|
| 1980 | | | | | | 100.0 | 100.0 |
| 1981 | 112.5 | –16.1 | –10.3 | 14.3 | –1.8 | 112.6 | 101.3 |
| 1982 | –48.5 | 19.5 | 24.5 | –20.4 | –0.9 | 107.1 | 98.9 |
| 1983 | –136.4 | 262.8 | 104.7 | –293.5 | –30.8 | 95.2 | 91.4 |
| 1984 | 214.9 | 136.0 | –9.5 | –125.5 | 10.5 | 111.1 | 92.1 |
| 1985 | 55.3 | 221.9 | –13.4 | –183.4 | 38.5 | 114.8 | 93.0 |
| 1986 | –211.2 | 244.5 | 130.7 | –197.0 | 47.5 | 102.9 | 85.6 |
| 1987 | –155.2 | 137.8 | –134.9 | –104.2 | 33.6 | 97.8 | 92.2 |

*Sources:* Tables 11.2 and 11.10.

Table 11.12 *Decomposition of import volume effect in Zimbabwe, 1967–86*

| *Year* | *Import ratio effect (Z$m.)* | *Income level effect (Z$m.)* |
|---|---|---|
| 1967 | 3.8 | 14.4 |
| 1968 | 18.7 | 4.0 |
| 1969 | −33.4 | 22.1 |
| 1970 | −15.6 | 41.9 |
| 1971 | 9.5 | 22.8 |
| 1972 | −22.9 | 21.4 |
| 1973 | 13.2 | 9.0 |
| 1974 | 6.7 | 10.7 |
| 1975 | −26.5 | 4.2 |
| 1976 | −136.8 | −3.3 |
| 1977 | −10.8 | −23.2 |
| 1978 | −27.0 | −10.5 |
| 1979 | −18.1 | 15.1 |
| 1980 | 137.9 | 82.8 |
| 1981 | 98.8 | 113.5 |
| 1982 | 32.5 | 35.7 |
| 1983 | −222.7 | 13.6 |
| 1984 | 24.9 | −20.8 |
| 1985 | −16.1 | 65.1 |
| 1986 | 85.5 | 42.1 |

*Sources:* Table 11.10 and CSO, *National Income and Expenditure Report 1987*, Harare, Tables 1.1 and 1.2.

import volumes. In 1986, however, there was a substantial negative effect, which was rapidly reversed in 1987. These fluctuations vividly illustrate the 'stop–go' nature of the management of imports. They give a strong impression of over- and undershooting by the authorities in their attempts to balance trade over the short term by using quantitative restrictions as macroeconomic instruments for balance of payments management.

Some further insights into this process can be gained from the decomposition of the import volume effect provided in Table 11.12. Here the effects on import volumes of changing levels of national income have been separated from those of changing import ratios (average propensity to import). In 1980, the primary cause of the increasing import bill was a rise in the import ratio, a reflection not only of the removal of sanctions, but also of a relaxation of import controls on the part of the authorities. This relaxation was motivated by a perceived need to increase imports for reconstruction and refurbishment in the aftermath of the sanctions and the liberation war. It was also perceived that there would be large inflows of foreign capital, following pledges of assistance from foreign donors in the wake of independence. In 1981, the growth in the economy combined with import relaxation contributed further to the expansion of import volumes.[8]

In 1983 there was a sharp compression of imports as the authorities reacted to the worsening balance of trade. This compression continued through 1985, to be decidedly reversed in 1986. It may be argued, therefore, that there are significant fluctuations in the import volume that stem from the trade management regime to a considerable extent.

## 6 Import demand and import compression

A partial adjustment model may be used to capture the impact of the control regime on import demand. Let the desired level of imports, $M^*$, be a function of a measure of output, $Y$:

$$M^* = kY \tag{11.1}$$

This function may be regarded as 'structuralist' in that $k$ is not determined by relative prices; it could be assumed that some exchange-rate mechanism keeps relative domestic and world prices constant. Assume that there is *incomplete* adjustment of actual imports. $M$, to the desired level of imports in each period. Thus

$$M = v(M^* - M_{-1}) + M_{-1} \tag{11.2}$$

By substitution

$$M = vkY + (1 - v)M_{-1} \tag{11.3}$$

The adjustment coefficient, $v$, would capture the constraints on adjustment which, in a quantitatively restricted regime, would primarily be imposed by the authorities through the import allocation system.

The appropriate measure of $Y$ is debatable. The use of capacity output implies that aggregate demand would not constrain the model in the absence of import compression, so that it is only the import shortage which determines capacity utilization. Alternatively, $Y$ may be regarded as some form of expected income. Here the idea would be that producers anticipate being able to produce and sell a certain level of output; given the structural characteristics of the economy, this determines a certain level of imports they would wish to obtain. In practice, the choice of measure for $Y$ was determined by the fact that there is no adequate measure of full-capacity output for Zimbabwe. Current GDP was therefore used as a measure of expected ouptput.

Finally, since import compression would shift the import demand function down, a dummy variable was used to capture the major import compression episodes (1975–79; 1982–86). An OLS estimate for the period 1967–86 was undertaken. This gave:

$$M = \underset{(-0.50)}{45.33} + \underset{(4.23)}{0.135Y} + \underset{(4.36)}{0.553M_{-1}} - \underset{(-4.99)}{184.0D} \qquad (11.4)$$

Adjusted $\bar{R}^2 = 0.81$ $F(3, 16) = 28$
Durbin h stat = −1.57

The coefficients on the variables are all significant at the 1 per cent level. The fact that the constant term is not significantly different from zero accords with the model specification, as does the sign on the dummy. The Durbin h statistic is not significant at the 5 per cent level, suggesting there is no serial correlation. The results thus appear to be reasonably good econometrically.

The results also accord with intuitive expectations; they imply that $k = 0.302$ and $v = 0.447$, which seems plausible. They signify that the desired level of imports is about 30 per cent of GDP and that actual imports adjust only half-way towards the desired level in any one year. The coefficient on the dummy may be interpreted as the downward shift in absolute import demand under import compression. Since the mean level of imports for the period was Z$840 million (constant 1980 prices), this suggests that, in the periods of import compressions, imports were on an average 20 per cent below the desired level.

## 7 Consequences of the trade management regime

In an import-dependent production system such as Zimbawe's, one would expect that policy-induced fluctuations in import volumes will translate into fluctuations in production. This hypothesis is supported by perceived periodic shortages, not only in imported, but also in domestically produced commodities. However, this does not show up in single-equation regressions between GDP and aggregate import levels. There are several reasons for this. First, shifts in the composition of aggregate imports mean that the production – import relationship may be obscured. If compression falls on capital goods rather than on intermediates, it will not lead to a fall in current production. Secondly, given other factors, which also contribute to output fluctuations (notably alternating droughts and exceptionally rainy seasons), and given structural and other policy changes in Zimbabwe during the period under review (price controls, minimum wages, changing patterns of government expenditure, changed patterns of support for peasant agriculture, investment controls, ambiguities in government policy on foreign investment, disinvestment by multinationals, and political instability in the Southern African region), it is difficult to isolate particular causal factors.

Bevan, Collier and Gunning (1989) have used a 'Dutch disease' type of model to examine the impact of the coffee boom on the Kenyan economy. One of the interesting results that emerges from this model is that, when a boom is initiated by the export sector, the existence of rigid quantitative controls on imports will lead to the *contraction* of the export sector itself. This argument may be generalized to apply to any attempts to control a balance of trade deficit through import quotas, as is the case in Zimbabwe.

Assume that there is a balance of trade deficit running at a certain level, being financed by borrowing or reserves, and that there is a quota on imports. Then, in year 0,

$$Y_0 = A_0 + X_0 - M_0, \tag{11.5}$$

where

$A$ = domestic absorption
$X$ = exports
$M$ = imports
$Y$ = GDP
$X_0 < M_0$
and $M_0 = M$.

Now assume that the authorities attempt to reduce the deficit by cutting import quotas to $M_1$ ($<M_0$). Then in the first round

$$Y_1 = A_0 + X_0 - M_1 \quad (11.6)$$

Since $M_1 < M_0$, $Y_1$ must be greater than $Y_0$, i.e. income rises in the short run. There will thus be an increase in domestic demand. How can this increased demand be accommodated? Assuming that the import quotas are effective, there are only two sources of goods to meet it. First, goods previously exported could be switched to domestic consumers. Second, more non-tradable (domestic) goods could be produced if there is unutilized capacity.

The first option is feasible in Zimbabwe where exports of food, basic consumer goods and light capital goods are significant. If this switching does occur, there will be a contraction of exports (although production in the exportables sector will not necessarily decline). If there is no export switching, the demand for domestic goods will rise. This will raise prices of domestic goods, as long as there is an upward-sloping supply curve in the domestic goods sector. This price increase will cause resources to shift from the export sector, causing it to contract.[9]

The tightening of the quota in order to reduce the deficit will thus lead to a contraction of exports, causing the deficit to increase again. The picture is complicated by the existence of price controls. However, where price controls do not cover all goods and are not completely effective, as is the case in Zimbabwe, the income effects on the demand for uncontrolled goods will be exaggerated and are likely to strengthen the above argument. It should be noted, though, that this model is entirely demand driven. It therefore *complements* the traditional supply-driven import compression model, where exports may contract because of lack of required imported inputs.

## 8 Summary and conclusions

A main focus of the previous sections has been on the use of import quotas as a macroeconomic instrument for controlling the balance of trade. It has been argued that the policy of the Zimbabwean government is to use quotas and maintain tight quantitative controls over the import side of the balance of trade while simultaneously providing incentives for exporters to increase exports. It has been demonstrated that changes in the import ratio – which have been ascribed to import compression by policy-makers have been the most important source of change in the balance of trade.

As we have seen, there are several potentially adverse effects which the import quota system might have. First, it transmits exogenous shocks to the domestic economy fairly quickly. Indeed, since cuts in quotas are based on anticipated foreign exchange availability, it is *anticipated* shocks that are transmitted to the system. Second, there seems to have been under- and overshooting by the authorities – what has been depicted above as a stop–go policy. Third, adjustment to exogenous shocks through quotas effectively means that all the burden of adjustment is on incomes; no substitution effects are allowed to work themselves out. This must necessarily make the costs of adjustment higher than they would otherwise be.

It could also be argued that the system suffers from the fact that many of the reforms which have been outlined above have been introduced on an ad hoc basis. The story is typical of the evolution of control regimes. After the initial set of controls has been introduced, more reforms are introduced to offset some of their undesired side-effects. These reforms in turn breed other offsetting reforms. After some time, it is not at all clear whether the system as a whole would not operate more efficiently – better achieve whatever objectives the government may have – without the initial controls and their related reforms. Indeed, it is not clear what the effects of the system taken as a whole are.

Zimbabwe's trade management regime is not a pure quota one; however, the exchange rate has moved considerably. Furthermore, the reforms made implicitly recognize the potentially negative effects of export quotas on export performance. Export incentive bonuses shift the relative incentive structure back to exports. Allowing exporters to retain some of their incremental export earnings for importing inputs for domestic production is designed to achieve the same end. However, if the quota system has raised the profitability of the domestic market substantially, the export promotion scheme could have the effect of encouraging inefficient exporting. Firms will be willing to export at a loss, knowing that they will be able to make it up when they use the foreign exchange bonus to increase domestic sales.

It thus appears that, although the Zimbabwean trade management regime has been modified in certain ways to avoid the extreme anti-export bias of a pure quota system, contradictions remain within it. However, an important theoretical and political question concerning the concept of import compression is raised by the previous discussion. Import compression has been mainly regarded as a problem of quantitative restrictions of imports. Would a regime which placed greater emphasis on price adjustments have performed better? In the pure quota model, there is no room for price and substitution effects: everything is concentrated on income effects. But the alternative to quantitative restrictions is to allow the effects to work through the exchange rate, depreciation bringing about the desired external balance. Clearly such an adjustment entails a form of import compression – devaluation works through both relative prices and income effects. A devaluation will entail a reduction in the volume of imports, which will affect the level of domestic production. The difference between the two alternatives is that the responses to relative price changes will, to the extent that the substitution is possible, lead to changes in the patterns of production that should reduce the costs of adjustment. Import compression in the quantitative restriction version automatically imposes a greater cost in terms of national income forgone.

## Appendix: Decomposition of balance of trade

Decomposition based on:

$$\Delta BOT \equiv \overset{\text{Export volume effect}}{P'(X' - X)} - \overset{\text{Import volume effect}}{Q'(M' - M)}$$

$$+ \overset{\text{Export price effect}}{X(P' - P)} - \overset{\text{Import price effect}}{M(Q' - Q)}$$

$$X(P' - P) \equiv \overset{\text{World export price effect}}{XR'(P'_w - P_w)} + \overset{\text{Export exchange-rate effect}}{XP_w(R' - R)}$$

$$M(Q' - Q) \equiv \overset{\text{World import price effect}}{MR'(Q'_w - Q_w)} + \overset{\text{Import exchange-rate effect}}{MQ_w(R' - R)}$$

where:

$P'$ ≡ unit value index of exports in year 1
$P$ ≡ unit value index of exports in year 0 (= 1)
$Q'$ ≡ unit value index of imports in year 1
$Q$ ≡ unit value index of imports in year 0 (=1)
$X'$ ≡ value of exports in year 1 measured in year 0 prices
$X$ ≡ export volume (index)
$M'$ ≡ value of imports in year 1 meansured in year 0 prices

$M$ ≡ export volume (index)
$R'$ ≡ exchange rate (Z$ per unit of foreign currency) in year 1
$R$ ≡ exchange rate in year 0 (= 1)
$P_w'$, $Q_w'$ ≡ world prices of exports (imports) in year 1 (= $P/R$)
$P_w$, $Q_w$ ≡ 1
ΔBOT change in balance of trade.

## Notes

I would like to thank my colleagues in the Rockefeller Project and in particular Peter Svedberg, Ravi Kanbur, Jonathan Frimpong-Ansah and Tim Besley for their comments and assistance on earlier drafts. I would also like to thank Jorn Rattso, Mike Walton, Kalle Moene, Mats Lundahl and my colleagues at the University of Zimbabwe for suggestions and criticisms at various stages; I am sure the paper would have been better if I had listened to it all. Thanks also to the Rockefeller Foundation for funding.

1 The impact of this period on industrial structure in Zimbabwe has been most extensively dealt with in Riddell (1988).

2 Of course, this does not imply that the allocation is responding more to market signals. Rather, it means that the influence exerted by lobbies, always inherent in a managed system, has increased.

3 In practice, it is difficult to estimates the devaluation equivalent of these programmes since participants are trading off the higher price they pay for imports against the non-availability of imports they would otherwise face.

4 The long-term *economic* sense of this strategy – which amounts to voluntary trade diversion – can be questioned.

5 For example. UNCTAD (1989, Table 4.5) reported indices for 1985 of 0.372 for Côte d'Ivoire, 0.359 for Tanzania, 0.340 for Kenya, 0.544 for Ghana and 0.943 for Nigeria. Among the developing countries at that time, only Argentina (0.184), Brazil (0.122), Thailand (0.154), Korea (0.193) and India (0.153) had indices less than 0.200, while only ten developed economies had indices greater than 0.200.

6 Essentially, the method entails asking what the value of exports would have been in 1980 if the same *volume* had been exported as in 1979 but at the 1980 *price*. This gives an export price effect. The export volume effect is next derived by asking what the value would have been if the 1979 price had been obtained but the 1980 volumes had been exported. This gives the export volume effect. The same reasoning can then be applied to imports to get the equivalent import effects. For imports it may be asked what the value of imports would have been if the 1979 ratio of imports to GDP had been obtained with the

1980 level of GDP and vice versa. The method suffers particularly from the fact that index numbers are being used, so there are some cross-effects through the weighting system. The method and the problems related to it are dealt with at greater length in Davies (1988), who also gives detailed references for the sources of the figures.

7 In the context of a more general discussion of macroeconomic policies, Kadhani and Green analysed the sources of the deterioration in the current account over the period 1981–83 (Kadhani and Green 1985). They divided the effects into three categories: external conditions (barter terms of trade, interest rate, recession, weather, transport), domestic policy, and capital rehabilitation shocks. They saw that most of the deterioration in 1981 came from domestic policy effects, which were mainly concentrated on output growth. By 1983, however, external shocks dominated, mainly in the form of terms of trade deterioration and international recession.

8 This impression is strengthened by the fact that the coefficient of variation for the import/GDP ratio is considerably higher than that for the export/GDP ratio.

9 It may be argued that resources could shift from the import-substituting sector rather than the export sector. However, the reduced import quotas will, if they have any effect at all, cause a rise in the price of import-substituting products. Depending on the relative strength of this effect, resources will move from exportables to both importables and non-tradables.

## References


Bevan D. L., Collier, P. and Gunning, J. W. (1989), 'Fiscal response to a temporary trade shock: The aftermath of the Kenyan coffee boom', Applied Economics Discussion Paper No. 68, Institute of Economics and Statistics, Oxford.

Davies, R. J. (1980), 'Foreign trade and external economic relations', in C. F. Stoneman (ed.), *Zimbabwe's Inheritance*, Macmillan, London, pp. 195–219.

Davies, R. J. (1988), 'A statistical analysis of changes in Zimbabwe's balance of trade, 1979–1986', mimeo, Department of Economics, University of Zimbabwe.

Kadhani, X. and Green, R. H. (1985), 'Parameters as warnings and guide posts: The case of Zimbabwe', *Journal of Development Planning*, 15, pp. 195–244.

Ministry of Finance, Economic Planning and Development (1987), *Annual Review of Zimbawe 1986*, Harare, Government Printer.

Riddell, R. C. (1988), *Industrialisation in Sub-Saharan Africa: country case study: Zimbabwe*, Overseas Development Institute, London.

Stoneman, C. F. (1982), 'Industrialisation and self-reliance in Zimbawe', in M. Fransman (ed.), *Industrialisation and Accumulation in Africa*, Heinemann, London.

UNCTAD Geneva. (1989), *Handbook of Intemational Trade and Development Statistics*, Geneva.

Worswick, G. D. N. (1956), 'Components of a change in the balance of trade', *Review of Economic Studies*, 23, pp. 76–82.

Zimbabwe (1981), *Growth with Equity: an Economic Policy Statement*, Harare: Government Printer, February.

Zimbabwe (1982), *Transitional National Development Plan 1982/83–1984/85: Volume 1*, Harare: Government Printer, November.

Zimbabwe (1986), *First Five-year National Development Plan 1986–1990: Volume 1*, Harare: Government Printer.

12

# A study of Ghana's trade performance

Philip K. Quarcoo

## 1 Introduction

The main aim of this study is to explain the interrelationships between growth, the underlying key economic indicators and trade performance in Ghana in the post-independence period.

The qualitative part of the analysis includes a review of the main features characterizing the various trade policy regimes over the period. It highlights the key macroeconomic indicators and how these relate to the pattern of trade and trade policies. This part also presents the findings of a trade policy dialogue involving consultations and interviews with senior trade officials on Ghana's policy stance as it participates in multilateral trade negotiations, especially the Uruguay Round of the General Agreement on Tariffs and Trade (GATT).

The export-led growth hypothesis of outward-looking development examined by Balassa (1980, 1982), Bhagwati (1986) and others appears to throw some light on both the positive and negative growth phases of Ghana's past experience. When exports growth was positive (1950s, 1984–88), income growth was also positive, but during periods when exports growth turned negative (1972–83), the growth trend in income was also negative. This experience seems to provide a classic demonstration of the characteristics and implications of 'outward-oriented' development vis-a-vis 'inward-oriented' development as hypothesized by Balassa, Bhagwati *et al.* The second part of this study attempts to develop a theoretical framework with which to illustrate and measure this transmission mechanism between the growth indicators and trade, especially export performance. This includes the specification and estimation of a trade sector macroeconomic model for policy analysis and evaluation.

The model is used to identify both internal and external determinants of Ghana's trade performance. By way of illustrating the transmission mechanism, an attempt is made to incorporate in the model some of the main elements of the monetary approach to the balance of payments as developed by Johnson (1972), Mundell (1968) and Polak (1957). This transmission mechanism on how domestic credit creation affects the balance of payments and hence income growth has been extensively investigated and also applied to Chana by Franco (1979) and by Teal and Giwa (1985). It is shown that increases in domestic credit increase real balances and raise domestic expenditures, which increase imports and worsen the balance of payments but raise the price level. The feedback effects of these on income growth in the long run can, however, only be determined empirically.

The study has four main sections. Section 2 examines Ghana's past growth path leading to the current Economic Recovery Programme. Section 3 presents the pattern of trade including the colonial trade pattern, the commodity structure and the direction of trade. In section 4 an outline of Ghana's trade policies is reviewed covering trade policy, exchange-rate policy and participation in multilateral trade negotiations. Section 5 presents the trade sector macroeconomic model of Ghana, including model specification, estimation and evaluation.

## 2 Ghana's past growth path and the Economic Recovery Programme

After almost two decades of secular deterioration in the key economic indicators, there has been a significant turn-around, starting in 1984 and continuing to the present. The profile of Ghana's growth path over the past three decades is presented in Table 12.1.

The country attained independence in 1957 in the midst of high economic performance characterized by export-led growth in which it produced 30 per cent of the world's cocoa, 10 per cent of its gold and had an accumulation of about US$500 million in reserves. By

Table 12.1 *Selected key economic indicators for Ghana: average real growth rate (% per annum), 1955–86*

| *Indicator* | *1955–60* | *1960–65* | *1966–70* | *1971–80* | *1981* | *1982* | *1983* | *1984* | *1985* | *1986* |
|---|---|---|---|---|---|---|---|---|---|---|
| Real GNP | 4.4 | 3.5 | 4.5 | 0.7 | –2.9 | –6.5 | –4.4 | 8.5 | 5.3 | 4.2 |
| Real GNP per capita | 1.8 | 0.9 | 2.2 | –1.6 | –5.9 | –9.4 | –7.4 | 5.1 | 2.0 | 0.9 |
| Consumer Price Index | 1.9 | 10.9 | 4.3 | 34.8 | 116.5 | 22.3 | 121.9 | 40.2 | 19.5 | 33.5 |
| Exports of goods and non-factor services | 8.8 | –0.8 | 0.3 | –5.4 | –8.8 | –17.8 | –26.[illegible] | 9.2 | 6.6 | n.a. |
| Imports of goods and non-factor services | 12.3 | 4.7 | –1.5 | –1.3 | –13.5 | –38.3 | –10.5 | 5.3 | 23.4 | n.a. |
| Agriculture | 6.5 | n.a. | 5.5 | 1.3 | –2.6 | –5.4 | –7.0 | 9.7 | 0.2 | 5.9 |
| Industry | 6.6 | n.a. | 7.5 | –1.1 | –16.1 | –16.9 | –1[illegible].8 | 8.6 | 17.9 | 0.7 |

*Sources:* for values computed covering 1955–60 – R. Szereszewski in Birmingham *et al.* (196[illegible]); for all other values computed – World Bank; *World Tables*, 1976, 1980, 1984, 1988.

the early 1960s, the political leadership had reversed this development strategy. The new strategy involved a 'big push' capital investment effort centred around an industrialization drive emphasizing import substitution, active state participation and a less open economy (Killick 1978). Such a strategy closely followed prescriptions of the contemporary mainstream development economists such as Nurkse (1953), Scitovsky (1954), Lewis (1955), Myrdal (1957), Hirschman (1958) and others.

*The post-independence period*

The period 1960–65 witnessed the very heavy inflow of capital goods imports for the rapid industrialization and mechanization of agriculture that the new development strategy called for. The investments could not generate the high returns expected but rather depleted the accumulated foreign exchange reserves from about US$350 million in 1960 to only about US $50 million by 1965. There is therefore a wide consensus among students of Ghana's political economic history that later deterioration in economic performance over the 1970s and early 1980s had its roots in the policies of the immediate post-independence period.

The period also saw the emergence of a trade policy regime involving import quotas, foreign exchange rationing, administrative pricing and wage controls. Capital and raw material imports expanded to feed the import-substituting industries and there was drastic reduction in the share of consumer goods imports. Exports performance stagnated with negative growth in earnings generating deficits even on the trade balance. By early 1966 the preconditions for political instability had been created by the worsening economic instability. A joint military and police administration took power in February 1966.

*The period 1966–71*

The government of the second administration handed over power to a civilian regime in October 1969, designated here as the third administration. The regime survived only until January 1972 when it was overthrown in the second military coup. Both regimes of the period 1966–71 followed liberal and economic stabilization policies to remove the distortions in production brought about by the previous trade and exchange-rate policies. Following a devaluation 1967, exports experienced a moderate 0.3 per cent growth, while imports declined by an average of 1.5 per cent over the period. The positive external balance, combined with significant growth in agriculture and industry, resulted in 2.2 per cent per capita income growth with a mild inflation of 4.3 per cent, compared with an average 10.9 per cent inflation rate in the previous period.

*The period of economic decline (1971–83)*

The decade of the 1970s and the early 1980s saw a decline in most of the key economic indicators, accompanied by political instability and uncertainties. The new military government of the fourth administration reversed the exchange-rate policy of the previous government and reintroduced restrictive trade policies.

This government lasted until June 1978 when it was overthrown in a palace coup to establish the fifth administration. But this administration could not survive long, as in July 1979 it was toppled by a group of young military officers to become the sixth administration. Within four months of seizing power the new military government voluntarily handed over power to a civilian government in September 1979. This seventh administration lasted only two years, when it was overthrown in another military coup on New Year's Eve, 1981. The military regime of the eighth administration governs Ghana to the present day.

As illustrated in Table 12.1, over the 1971–83 period, real GNP and per capita income declined. Inflation accelerated rapidly, reaching triple digit levels in 1977, 1981 and 1983. Value added in agriculture and industry declined as strong disincentives developed against production and in favour of retail trade. But perhaps the single most critical element leading the decline in economic performance was the sharp negative growth rates of exports[1] and of imports. The decline in exports, in addition to negligible capital inflows, reduced available foreign exchange, which forced down the level of imports, creating chronic and acute shortages of raw materials and spare parts and reducing capacity utilization below 15 per cent during the period.

The spiralling inflation combined with exchange controls implied overvaluation of the domestic currency. The real effective exchange rate appreciated over twelve-fold during 1972–82. The strong disincentives against production and exports tended to pull resources towards retail trade, hoarding, smuggling and other rent-seeking activities.

Major exogenous shocks played a part in the economic problems of the period. These include the drought and desertification of 1975–77 and 1981–83, the oil price shocks of 1973–74 and 1979–80, global recession and inflation, the 'new protectionism' of industrial countries, deterioration in barter terms of trade and the debt problem. There were also major deficiencies in domestic policy. These included direct and indirect distortions in export producer prices, high effective protection rates beyond the infant industry stage, absence of cost recovery strategies in health, education and public utilities, overextension of the parastatal sector, greater reliance on controls and administered allocative mechanisms, and negative real interest rates in the financial system.

*The Economic Recovery Programme (1984–88)*
The policy package that may be credited with the dramatic turnaround in economic performance, as illustrated in Table 12.1, is the Economic Recovery Programme (ERP). The evidence is quite convincing and portrays positive growth rates of all indicators from 1984 and beyond, in contrast with the negative rates of the immediate past. The centre-piece of this reform programme is the market-determined and liberalized exchange-rate system. This has produced higher real producer prices for exportables and has dampened consumer import demand, with anticipated improvements in the trade and current accounts balances.

The ERP has so far undergone two main phases. The period 1984–86 characterized the short-term stabilization phase, during which contractionary fiscal and monetary policies were combined with drastic depreciation of the local currency to redress the chronic budget and balance of payments deficits and the inflationary spiral. The period 1986 and beyond corresponds to the medium-to long-term phase, during which structural adjustment and growth policies are superimposed to eliminate internal and external structural imbalances and to achieve sustained growth and development. This period has been characterized by rehabilitation of the main infrastructure in transport, agriculture, mining and industry, initiation of cost recovery measures in health, education and state enterprise in general, as well as by the current comprehensive 'Programme of Action for Mitigating the Social Costs of Adjustment's (PAMSCAD).

Between 1984 and 1988, Ghana achieved an annual average GNP growth rate of 6 per cent and reduced inflation from 122 per cent in 1983 to some 20 per cent in 1988. The positive response of the economic indicators to ERP has been aided by provision of quick disbursing concessional finance (from bilateral and multilateral sources) for the rehabilitation of the economic and social infrastructure. Despite the presence of PAMSCAD, the retrenchment, cost recovery measures in health and education, malnutrition and other social costs of adjustment continue to provide major social and political implications.

## 3 **The pattern of trade in Ghana**

*Export commodity composition*

The primary commodity export structure inherited from the colonial period dominates Ghana's exports to the present day. Some diversification has been attempted, but the main export products remain cocoa, minerals and timber. Table 12.2 presents Ghana's export commodity shares over the period 1955–85.

As shown in Table 12.2 the share of total cocoa exports averaged well over 60 per cent during the three decades. On the world market Ghana's share of world cocoa supply was more than 40 per cent in the 1920s. By 1970 it was still high at 33 per cent, but by 1981 that share had declined to a little over 16 per cent.

Mineral products represent the second most important export group, with their share in Ghana's total exports ranging between 10.6 per cent in 1970 and 26 per cent in 1983. Among the mineral products, gold has the largest share, corresponding on average to about 50 per cent of the share of all minerals over the entire period. Timber, which is the other traditional export product, has had a declining share, particularly during the 1980s owing to the government's concern over deforestation and desertification.

The recent attempts at diversification include processing of cocoa beans into cocoa paste, butter and powder and the sale of electricity from the Akosombo hydroelectric scheme to the neighbouring countries of Côte d'Ivoire, Togo and Benin. New non-traditional exports, such as small manufactures in the form of wood and textile fabrics, have also contributed to exports. The share of all these items in total exports is summed together in the 'Others' category. Aluminium production and exports based partly on the country's bauxite deposits, by Valco, in an export free zone, constitute an important dimension of export diversification. By

Table 12.2 *Ghana's export commodity shares (% of total value), 1955–85*

| *Commodity* | *1955* | *1960* | *1965* | *1970* | *1875* | *1980* | *1981* | *1982* | *1983* | *1984* | *1985*[a] |
|---|---|---|---|---|---|---|---|---|---|---|---|
| *All cocoa* | 68.5 | 59.0 | 66.6 | 70.9 | 69.4 | 71.8 | 62.2 | 65.1 | 61.3 | 67.5 | 63.0 |
| – cocoa beans | 67.4 | 58.1 | 61.1 | 64.3 | 60.1 | 64.2 | 56.4 | 59.8 | 55.1 | 62.2 | 52.2 |
| – cocoa products (paste, butter, powder) | 1.1 | 0.9 | 5.5 | 6.6 | 9.3 | 7.6 | 5.8 | 5.3 | 6.2 | 5.3 | 10.5 |
| *Timber* (sawn wood, logs) | 8.4 | 13.9 | 11.0 | 8.0 | 9.1 | 3.1 | 5.0 | 2.5 | 3.6 | 3.7 | 4.9 |
| *Minerals* (gold, diamonds, manganese, bauxite) | 21.1 | 24.6 | 19.5 | 10.6 | 13.2 | 17.2 | 22.4 | 19.0 | 26.0 | 18.2 | 16.1 |
| *Others* (electricity, refined oil, manufactures) | 2.0 | 2.5 | 2.9 | 10.5 | 8.3 | 7.9 | 10.5 | 13.4 | 9.1 | 10.6 | 16.0 |

*Note:*
[a] Provisional estimate.

*Sources:* Central Bureau of Statistics, *Economic Survey* (various issues), Accra; Central Bureau of Statistics, *Statistical Yearbook* (various issues), Accra; United Nations, *Yearbook of International Trade Statistics* (various issues), Accra; Government of Ghana (1985) for values covering 1980–85.

convention, however, these are excluded from merchandise trade and included rather under 'invisibles' in the balance of payments, as an export of services.

*Import commodity structure*

Table 12.3 illustrates the 'big push' development strategy in the immediate post-independence period. Trade policy encouraged the importation of manufactured goods, machinery and transport equipment between 1956 and 1966 and severely restricted food imports from 1961 to 1965.

During the period of the second and third administrations (1966–71), the 'big push' strategy was abandoned in favour of liberal trade and exchange-rate policies. The structure of imports over the period of economic decline (1971–83) reflects the impact of the shortage of foreign exchange. The share of manufactured goods, in particular, declined steeply from 23 per cent in 1975 to about 11 per cent in 1982. The share of food imports also declined from 12 per cent in 1976 to 7 per cent in 1981. On the other hand, the share of the fuel bill rose in 1982 to about six times the level in 1971. There was some relief in 1983, with both a steep decline in imports of oil and increases in consumer prices. The inauguration of ERP also brought in needed capital goods imports for infrastructure rehabilitation.

*Direction of trade*

The geographical pattern of trade inherited from the colonial period underwent some transformation over the three decades up to the present (Tables 12.4 and 12.5). The dominant share of the United Kingdom and the European Community countries of Western Europe is clearly evident for both Ghana's exports and imports. After independence, however, the share of the UK declined steadily as Ghana tried to diversify its trading partners.

The government of the first administration pursued a policy of non-alignment, which was translated into counter-trade with centrally planned economies (CPEs). This explains the dramatic rise in the share of CPEs in both Ghana's exports and imports during 1961–65. After the overthrow of the first administration, the share of imports particularly declined to negligible proportions by 1982, with a mild recovery up to 1986. The share of exports to CPEs also declined, but recovered around 1975 and again in 1985 as Ghana

Table 12.3 *Ghana's import commodity shares (% of total value by SITC group, 1956–83*

| *SITC* | | *1956* | *1960* | *1961* | *1965* | *1966* | *1970* | *1971* | *1975* | *1976* | *1980* | *1981* | *1982* | *1983* |
|---|---|---|---|---|---|---|---|---|---|---|---|---|---|---|
| 0 | Food and live animals | 15.9 | 16.2 | 18.6 | 11.1 | 15.6 | 19.0 | 14.1 | 11.5 | 12.0 | 7.8 | 7.1 | 9.9 | 11.1 |
| 1 | Beverages and tobacco | 4.8 | 2.9 | 2.5 | 0.7 | 1.0 | 0.9 | 1.0 | 0.7 | 1.2 | 1.4 | 0.9 | 0.4 | 2.5 |
| 2 | Crude materials | 0.4 | 0.3 | 0.6 | 1.0 | 0.9 | 2.2 | 2.8 | 3.1 | 3.4 | 1.8 | 1.8 | 1.1 | 2.5 |
| 3 | Minerals, fuels and lubricants | 5.7 | 5.2 | 4.6 | 4.2 | 4.2 | 5.8 | 6.1 | 16.6 | 14.9 | 26.7 | 30.3 | 35.6 | 10.1 |
| 4 | Animal fats and vegetable oils | 0.1 | 0.2 | 0.3 | 0.9 | 1.1 | 0.9 | 1.2 | 1.1 | 1.2 | 0.9 | 0.9 | 0.3 | 1.1 |
| 5 | Chemicals | 7.0 | 7.3 | 7.3 | 6.3 | 6.6 | 16.0 | 16.2 | 13.9 | 15.7 | 15.5 | 11.9 | 11.0 | 10.3 |
| 6 | Manufactured goods | 36.7 | 30.7 | 31.6 | 34.1 | 30.7 | 24.1 | 22.4 | 22.9 | 18.9 | 12.3 | 11.3 | 10.8 | 16.2 |
| 7 | Machinery & transport equipment | 19.2 | 26.0 | 23.5 | 32.7 | 32.7 | 25.8 | 29.7 | 25.1 | 27.3 | 29.7 | 27.3 | 20.8 | 32.5 |
| 8&9 | Miscellaneous | 10.2 | 11.2 | 11.0 | 9.0 | 7.2 | 5.3 | 6.5 | 5.1 | 5.4 | 3.9 | 8.5 | 8.9 | 13.7 |

*Sources:* for values covering 1956–70 – Central Bureau of Statistics, *Economic Survey*; *Quarterly Digest of Statistics* (various issues), Accra; Leith (1974); for values covering 1970–83 – World Bank (1987a), Statistical Appendix, Table 3.03.

Table 12.4 *Ghana's exports: percentage share by country/region, 1956–86*

| *Country/region* | *1956* | *1960* | *1965* | *1970* | *1975* | *1976* | *1980* | *1982* | *1984*[a] | *1986*[a] |
|---|---|---|---|---|---|---|---|---|---|---|
| United Kingdom | 34.6 | 31.3 | 20.8 | 24.1 | 17.7 | 17.6 | 16.8 | 1[illegible].3 | 13.9 | 15.8 |
| EC (excluding UK) | 32.3 | 33.4 | 27.8 | 24.3 | 26.2 | 27.8 | 25.6 | 23.3 | 23.1 | 22.0 |
| United States & Canada | 19.4 | 15.9 | 18.6 | 20.2 | 13.9 | 18.8 | 7.9 | 13.8 | 8.9 | 20.8 |
| Centrally planned economies (USSR, China, Yugoslavia & Eastern Europe) | 2.4 | 7.2 | 21.3 | 16.3 | 26.2 | 21.3 | 16.6 | 9.3 | 26.9 | 20.3 |
| Japan | n.a. | 0.8 | 2.3 | 6.9 | 8.7 | 7.1 | 7.4 | 7.2 | 12.1 | 7.7 |
| Africa | n.a. | n.a. | 0.9 | 1.0 | 3.1 | 2.4 | 0.4 | 1.7 | 0.9 | 0.5 |
| Rest of the world (S. America, Australia, rest of Asia, etc.) | 11.3 | 11.4 | 8.3 | 7.2 | 4.2 | 5.0 | 25.3 | 21.4 | 14.2 | 12.9 |

*Note:*
[a] Provisional estimates – derived from partner countries.

*Sources:* for estimates covering 1980–86 – IMF, *Direction of Trade Statistics Yearbook 1987*; for estimates covering 1965–80 – Central Bureau of Statistics, *Quarterly Digest of Statistics* (various issues), Accra; for estimates covering 1950–62 – Tony Killick in Birmingham *et al.* (1966), Table 14.6, p. 338.

Table 12.5 *Ghana's imports: percentage share by area of origin, 1956–86*

| *Country/region* | *1956* | *1960* | *1965* | *1970* | *1975* | *1976* | *1980* | *1982* | *1984*[a] | *1986*[a] |
|---|---|---|---|---|---|---|---|---|---|---|
| United Kingdom | 48.9 | 38.0 | 25.8 | 24.1 | 17.1 | 18.8 | 21.8 | 14.4 | 19.5 | 20.9 |
| EC (excluding UK) | 18.8 | 25.5 | 21.4 | 21.8 | 23.2 | 25.6 | 19.8 | 16.0 | 22.1 | 27.8 |
| United States & Canada | 5.6 | 8.3 | 10.5 | 21.3 | 20.8 | 20.6 | 13.1 | 16.3 | 12.1 | 12.6 |
| Centrally planned economies (USSR, China, Eastern Europe) | 2.0 | 4.4 | 26.3 | 8.5 | 4.4 | 4.0 | 2.3 | 0.8 | 6.0 | 4.4 |
| Japan | 10.1 | 8.3 | 4.3 | 6.2 | 6.5 | 5.2 | 3.8 | 2.5 | 5.4 | 4.2 |
| Africa (Nigeria) | n.a. | n.a. | 2.8 | 4.8<br>(0.6) | 16.5<br>(6.8) | 14.4<br>(9.7) | 23.1<br>(20.3) | 29.5<br>(20.3) | 18.6<br>(8.7) | 11.8<br>(3.7) |
| Rest of the world (S. America, Australia, rest of the Asia, etc.) | 14.6 | 15.5 | 8.9 | 13.3 | 11.5 | 11.4 | 16.1 | 20.7 | 16.3 | 18.3 |

*Note:*
[a] Provisional estimates – derived from partner countries.

*Sources:* for estimates covering 1980–86 – IMF, *Direction of Trade Statistics Yearbook 1987*; for estimates covering 1965–80 – Central Bureau of Statistics, *Quarterly Digest of Statistics* (various issues), Accra; for estimates covering 1950–62 – Tony Killick in Birmingham *et al.* (1966), Table 14.6, p. 338.

diverted some of its primary exports, particularly cocoa and timber, towards bilateral partners and away from slumping world prices. The evidence shows that products were not in high demand in Ghana and hence Ghana's trade balance with CPEs was generally in surplus.

Ghana's trade with Africa has not improved significantly despite several attempts at political and economic integration. As most African countries are primary commodity exporters like Ghana, the bulk of its exports cannot find a ready market. On the other hand, the rise in Ghana's imports originating from some African countries is accounted for largely by oil imports from Nigeria, rising from 5 per cent in 1970 to about 17 per cent in 1975 and to about 30 per cent in 1982.

## 4 Ghana's trade policies

*Trade policy*

Restrictive trade policies were first introduced in 1961 with specific quotas for a selected list of commodities and for all invisibles. These restrictions were enforced with increasing severity during the second half of the first administration (1961–66) as well as during the fourth administration (1972–78) and the first part of the eighth administration (1982–83).

The partial liberalization in the period 1967–71 introduced once again the non-restrictive open general licence (OGL) and progressively expanded the range of goods included.

Despite the increasing use of nominal exchange-rate policies during the 1980s, trade policy predominates, and prohibits, restricts or regulates imports into Ghana consistent with foreign exchange availability determined by annual foreign exchange budgets.

Two kinds of import licence exist. These are: (a) Specific Licence with sub-categories 'G' and 'A', and (b) Special Lincence 'S' category. The 'G' licence is reserved for imports of government institutions. The 'A'licence permits the holder to bid for foreign exchange at the auction. The 'S' licence is issued for imports of any goods (except those on a prohibited list) financed from importers' own foreign exchange resources. In addition to import quotas, tariffs are extensively used to compress imports.

*Exchange-rate policy*
A key element in Ghana's ERP, however, continues to be the phased elimination of restrictive trade policies. The process was begun in 1983 with massive exchange-rate adjustments. This has been followed since September 1986 with the introduction of the foreign exchange auction system for importers holding specific licence 'A' category. In April 1988 foreign exchange bureaus were introduced to buy and sell foreign exchange of all denominations on the open market. By December 1988, there were about 100 such bureaus and a significant decline in the informal black market.

Liberalization has also been extended to the tariff system since May 1987. Duties on raw materials and capital goods, previously set at 20–30 per cent, were unified at 20 per cent. Raw materials for pharmaceuticals as well as all spare parts, accessories and lubricants were given a concessionary rate of 10 per cent. All import duties and purchase taxes were abolished on commercial vehicles, railway engines and coaches, motorcycles and bicycles. Also abolished was the 10 per cent sales tax on goods imported under the special 'S' import licence. In addition, tariff rates were lowered on all 'non-luxury' consumer goods from 30 to 25 per cent.

*Global trade negotiations and policies*
Ghana's current trade liberalization stance is consistent with the goals and objectives of a global transparent trading system as currently pursued in the Uruguay Round or multilateral trade negotiations (MTN) under the aegis of the General Agreement on Tariffs and Trade (GATT).[2]

In order to review the trade policy stance of Ghana as it participates in the Uruguay Round as well as in other MTNs in general, a trade policy dialogue was held in Accra with key trade officials in February 1988. The dialogue took the form of consultations and interviews with senior government officials of the Ministries of Finance, Economic Planning and Trade and Tourism. In addition to GATT, the dialogue also reviewed Ghana's membership and active participation in the ACP/EC Lomé Conventions, UNCTAD and the Global System of Trade Preferences (GSTP).

Ghana joined the GATT in October 1957 by British sponsorship. Since then it has maintained a permanent mission in Geneva and has participated in three GATT negotiations – the Dillon Round

(1960–61), the Kennedy Round (1964–67) and the Tokyo Round (1973–79). In all these Ghana has enjoyed most favoured nation (MFN) status and has remained a 'free rider' as it has never negotiated bound tariffs but has benefited from tariff cuts derived from negotiations among industrial member countries. Ghana has also relied on gains from the Generalized System of Preferences (GSP) which the benefactors provide but can withdraw at any time without notice. By virtue of the so-called *Enabling Clause* which issued out of the Tokyo Round, Ghana also enjoys special and differential treatment of its exports in the markets of contracting parties without the need for reciprocity.

It was emphasized that Ghana's position on the main issues for negotiation during the Uruguay Round is similar and consistent with the general position of the ACP (Africa, Caribbean and Pacific) group of countries in the Lomé III Convention. The most important issue, of course, has been the demand for elimination of tariff and non-tariff barriers on tropical products. This issue has been tentatively resolved at the Montreal mid-term review meeting. The status of negotiations on tariff escalation on processed and semi-processed tropical products remains unclear. Other critical issues for Ghana on the agenda but not yet resolved include non-tariff barriers (NTBs) of various forms: multifibre arrangements (MFA), voluntary export restraint (VER), orderly marketing arrangements (OMA), anti-dumping and countervailing duties (CVD), health and safety standards, among others. Ghana has supported negotiations strengthening the GATT safeguard codes during the mid-term review. This has included strengthening the dispute settlement mechanism of GATT, expansion of its rules to the new areas of services, investment and intellectual property rights (patents, copyrights) as well as non-tariff barriers on trade in goods.

At the present, Ghana and other ACP countries enjoy special and differential treatment at two main levels. First, within the GATT framework, they are free riders on all tariff concessions among other contracting parties by virtue of the MFN principle. In addition, they benefit from GSP concessions by Group of Seven industrial countries within GATT that wish to extend those preferences. Secondly, as members of the Lomé Convention, Ghana and ACP countries are accorded all Lomé preferences including Stabex and Sysmin.

In view of the present structure of special and differential preferences, across-the-board tariff reductions as envisaged in the Uruguay Round negotiations are likely to erode the MFN, GSP and Lomé preferences enjoyed by Ghana and its ACP partners. Herein lies the conflict faced by these countries as they actively participate in the current Uruguay Round negotiations. The conflict also applies in different forms to the US/Canada free trade pact launched in January 1989 as well as to the anticipated 1992 single European market. The major question is whether GATT would eventually prevail within a global transparent trading system or whether it would become extinct in a world dominated by trading blocs and preferential trading areas surrounded by protective barriers.

For Ghana, the main preoccupation remains product and export diversification in order to take advantage of present and future trade concessions. Lomé III preferences permit access to EC markets for semi-processed and processed manufactures from ACP countries. Similar concessions will be granted within the GATT framework if agreement is reached to reduce or eliminate tariff escalation during the final two years of the Uruguay Round negotiations.

## 5 A trade sector macroeconomic model for Ghana

As noted in previous sections, the responsiveness of trade performance and the overall economic structure to relative price incentives at the inception of the liberal regime was dramatic. Apart from price variables, other underlying factors that explain variations in trade patterns include production capacity, import capacity, the real exchange rate, domestic credit and domestic expenditures, among others. In view of the interrelationships between trade and overall economic performance, the analysis of the determinants of Ghana's trade performance in this section is carried out within the framework of a trade sector macroeconomic model.

*Model specification*

The presentation which follows was inspired by the models of Project LINK, particularly the Prototype Model (Kwack, Demirors and Walker 1987) and the macroeconomic model of Ghana (Altshuler 1987). It also draws on elements from other country and cross-country models such as May (1985), World Bank (1983), and Aghevli and Khan (1980), among others.

The complete model has five main blocks, including twenty stochastic equations and six identities. The formal model is presented in Appendix 1 followed by variable definitions in Appendix 2 and the estimated stochastic equations in Appendix 3.

The first sub-model on domestic expenditures and prices involves some of the key elements in the transmission mechanism between trade and overall economic activity. There are six endogenous variables is this sector: consumption, investment, tax revenue, exports and imports on national accounts basis, and the price level. The national income identity closes the sector. Private real consumption is specified as a function of current and lagged GDP, real money balances, and the inflation rate lagged one period.[3] Real investment is explained by raw material imports, real domestic credit and the capital stock lagged one period, and the lagged dependent variable. The prevalence of credit rationing explains why the quantity variable (bank credit) and not the price variable (bank lending rate) is the relevant determinant of investment. A single tax revenue function is assumed and is related to two-period lags of nominal GDP. Exports and imports on national accounts basis are specified as functions of up to two lagged values of the corresponding exports and imports variables on balance of payments basis.

The final stochastic equation in the first sub-model is the GDP implicit price deflator, which is the only price endogenously determined in this model. All unit export and import prices are externally determined by world demand and supply factors. Determinants of the GDP price deflator or of inflation follow specification of traditional inflation theories of demand pull and cost push as well as structuralist and rational expectations theories. In this study, movements in the GDP price index are explained by current and lagged domestic credit, current and lagged consumer price index (PC) and the price of imported manufactured products. The domestic credit variable captures the effects of budget deficits and monetary accommodation. The PC reflects domestic labour cost pressures and its lagged value is a proxy for price expectations.

The second sub-model on production determines the basis for export supply equations in the next sub-model. Gross domestic product is the sum of outputs (value added) in four main producing sectors: cocoa, timber and other agriculture, mining, and the rest[4]. Outputs in the first three sectors are determined by supply conditions and the rest is deduced as a residual.

Cocoa output is the dominant export product (see Table 12.2) and is specified as a function of three main variables: (i) a six-period polynomial lag distribution on the relative producer price of cocoa (PPCB) over the consumer price index (PC), (ii) the relative producer price of cocoa in Ghana vis-á-vis Côte d'Ivoire (PSIC) measured at the black market exchange rate, and (iii) a weather-related variable represented by up to two-period lags on rainfall in the main cocoa-producing regions of Brong Ahafo and Ashanti. The relative real producer price (PPCB/PC) has generally been adopted as a proxy variable (Bateman 1971; May 1985) to capture average production capacity of available tree stock.[5] The producer price is assumed exogenous as it is, by and large, determined generally as a residual from the world price after taxation, marketing and other resource costs are accounted for. The relative price variable PSIC was developed by May (1985) as a proxy for cocoa smuggling to neighbouring countries of Côte d'Ivoire and Togo whenever their producer prices are higher (see Appendix 4). The observed series on cocoa production are lower than actual production by the amount of smuggling, and PSIC is expected to capture that effect.

Output of timber and other agriculture is specified as a function of population and a five-period polynomial distribution lag on the relative unit export price of timber deflated by PC. The population variable is a proxy reflecting labour supply constraints in the sector. Output of the mining sector is also specified following a polynomial distributed lag relation on the relative unit export price of manganese (as a proxy) deflated by PC. Finally, output in the residual category is determined as the difference between GDP and the sum of the outputs of cocoa, other agriculture and mining.

The third sub-model explains determinants of merchandise exports. The disaggregation of exports corresponds to the four sectoral outputs of GDP: exports of cocoa beans, timber and other agriculture, minerals, and residual exports (see Table 12.2 above). For cocoa beans, some of the product goes into exports, others into domestic manufacturing of cocoa paste, powder and chocolate, while a significant amount is smuggled. Similarly, apart from exports, part of the other sectoral outputs are for domestic processing, while the remainder, particularly minerals, are also smuggled outside of the country. A general export supply relation has therefore been adopted where each export supply is specified simply as a function of the corresponding expected sectoral output. A proxy variable for expected sectoral output is approximated by the fitted or forecast value. The residual export supply is expressed as a function of residual output and the price of residual exports.

The fourth sub-model represents the import sub-sector. Real merchandise imports are decomposed into four SITC class categories: food products (0 + 1), raw materials and intermediate products (2 + 4), oil products (3) and manufactured or capital goods including miscellaneous items (5 to 9) (Table 12.3 above). There is a fifth imports function representing net invisibles (service) imports over exports. Following traditional demand theory, income and relative price variables are expected to be the main determinants. The relevant real income variable is domestic expenditures (DE), which excludes net exports from national income (Aghevli and Khan 1980). The relative price variable adopted is the real exchange rate, which reflects purchasing power parity and cost considerations. It is defined as the nominal exchange rate index adjusted by the relative consumer price index of trading partners vis-á-vis that of Ghana.[6] Specification of each import function incorporates combinations of the basic and specific determinants. The specification also allows for the difference between desired and actual imports by employing the partial adjustment hypothesis, which introduces the lagged dependent variable as an explanatory variable in some of the import functions.

The following are the specific import functions. Food imports are explained by the real exchange rate, the lagged dependent variable and a dummy variable to capture shocks of trade restrictions (1975–77). Intermediate goods imports are determined by the current and lagged values of domestic expenditures, the real exchange rate and lagged real domestic credit. Oil imports are a function of the unit price of petroleum imports, the lagged real exchange rate and the lagged dependent variable. Imports of manufactured goods are determined by current and lagged values of domestic expenditures, the lagged real exchange rate and the lagged dependent variable. Finally, net service imports are explained by the value of import trade.

The fifth block of the model represents the balance of payments identities. It puts together the third and fourth sub-models to define total imports, exports and the balance of payments. From these, the

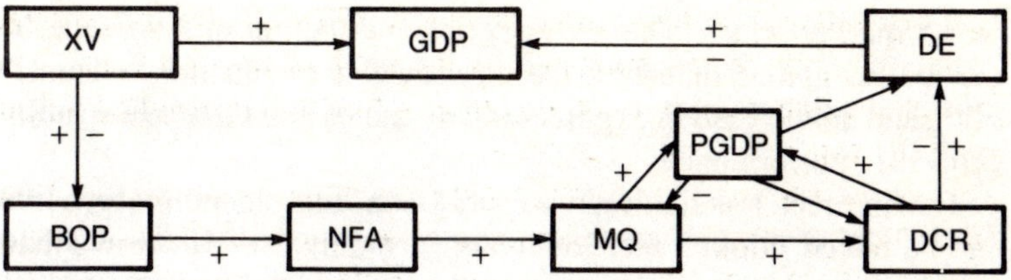


Figure 12.1 *Export-led growth*

trade balance, current account balance and the capital account can easily be deduced.

The sixth and final sub-model deals with the consolidated balance sheet of the monetary system, which also plays a role in linking trade performance to overall economic activity. This sub-model represents the monetary survey and contains two stochastic equations. The real demand for money, broadly defined, is specified as a function of GDP, current and lagged values of both the inflation rate and domestic credit as well as the lagged dependent variable. The net foreign assets variable represents an accumulation of past overall balances on balance of payments. The change in net foreign assets of the banking system is then set as a function of the overall balance of payments as well as current and lagged values of real money balances.

The model presented above incorporates the transmission mechanism between trade performance and overall economic performance. This is illustrated in the flow chart of Figure 12.1, which demonstrates the outward-oriented strategy of export-led growth. It shows that an initial export boom will improve GDP directly but will also have an indirect impact which is indeterminate, *a priori*, through a chain reaction linking the balance of payments to other monetary aggregates back to GDP.

The direct positive link between export boom and economic growth depends on the critical determinants of export performance. The key element from the analysis above is producer price incentives and elimination or relaxation of supply constraints. First, this requires linkage between world prices and their corresponding domestic producer prices at market-determined exchange rates. It also requires elimination of export taxes and reduction of marketing, transactions and other resource costs to increase the share of producer prices in world market prices. The net effect of a reduction in these supply constraints and associated price incentives is a reduction in smuggling and an increase in exports directly increasing GDP and overall economic performance.

The indirect link between export boom and economic growth can be traced through the flow chart in Figure 12.1. It shows that an initial export boom will improve the balance of payments, which would increase the net foreign assets of the banking system. To maintain balance in the monetary system this will increase the real money supply and domestic credit. But the price level will also increase and this will have a depressing effect on the real money supply, real domestic credit and real domestic expenditures. If the price effect is less than the monetary effect, then exports growth will translate into income growth unambiguously through this indirect channel. On the other hand, if the price effect is stronger, then, even with exports growth, income growth may not necessarily be positive but may be neutral or even negative through this indirect transmission mechanism. Thus, on the whole, the net direct and indirect effects of an export boom cannot be determined *a priori*, especially in periods of high domestic credit expansion and accompanying inflationary consequences.

The data on macroeconomic aggregates over the period 1961–83 provide ample evidence of accumulating budget deficits, monetary accommodation, rapid domestic credit creation and accelerating inflation. The dominance of this on trade and overall economic performance has also been depicted in the model presented above. It shows the transmission mechanism on how domestic credit creation affects the balance of payments, and hence income growth. This is illustrated in the flow chart of Figure 12.2.

Expansion in domestic credit may be autonomous or induced by passive monetary accommodation to government budget deficits. Either way, the credit expansion will increase real money balances, which will stimulate consumption expenditures through the real balance effect (Patinkin 1965). This will raise domestic expenditures and aggregate demand, increasing imports, and, under a fixed exchange regime, worsen the balance of payments as postulated by Johnson (1972), Mundell (1968) and others. But this transmission mechanism ignores the inflationary consequences of credit creation highlighted in the model presented above. Credit and monetary expansion will also increase the price level and, if this effect

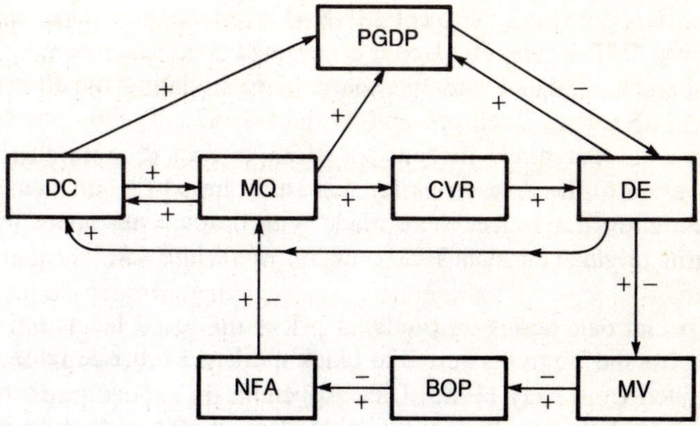


Figure 12.2 *Credit creation and the balance of payments*

outweighs the real balance effect, domestic expenditures will decline, imports will decline and the balance of payments may improve. Compounding these initial effects are the indirect feedback effects from the balance of payments through net foreign assets back to the monetary stock and credit creation. Teal and Giwa (1985) came up with a similar conclusion in their review of the Ghana experience over the period 1955–80. This link between credit creation and the balance of payments in Ghana can, therefore, be determined not *a priori* but rather through empirical investigation.

*Sources of data*

Most of the base data on national accounts, the balance of payments and unit export and import price indices were obtained from IMF, *International Financial Statistics Yearbook*, 1984–88 editions. Data on decomposition of exports into commodity classes and imports into SITC class categories were obtained from Central Bureau of Statistics, *Statistical Yearbook, Quarterly Digest of Statistics* and *Economic Survey* (Accra, various issues). To achieve consistency with the series on balance of payments, percentage shares of the export and import class categories were calculated and applied to the total merchandise exports and imports values to yield the dollar or cedi equivalents.

Output data by industrial origin corresponding to the export commodity classes as well as capital stock series were obtained from data sources of Project LINK (United Nations, *Documentation for DRPA Data Bank of World Development Statistics*).[7] This database as updated was the source for estimating the Prototype Model (Kwack, Demirors and Walker 1987). The output series from this source are in constant 1975 cedis and were therefore converted to the data series for this study based on constant 1980 cedis. Cross-references were made with output data series by industrial origin at constant 1980 cedis from World Bank, *World Tables 1987*.

Special data series on producer prices on cocoa beans for Côte d'Ivoire and Togo converted at black markert exchange rates were obtained from May (1985) (See Appendix 4).

The sample period for available data on the output series is 1966–82 and this predetermines the sample for estimating the export sector sub-model. Similarly the available sample for estimating the import sector sub-model terminates in 1982. On the other hand, GDP and other national accounts data at constant 1980 cedis are available over the period 1955–83. As the main focus of this study is the trade sector, the sample period adopted for the econometric analysis which follows has therefore been restricted to 1967–83, less two periods for *ex post* forecasts.

*Model estimation and regression results*

The functional forms of the equations estimated were either linear or log-linear. The imports and exports equations, in particular, were all estimated in log-linear form to permit direct estimation of income and price elasticities. Most of the equations were estimated by two-stage least squares.[8]

Short-run/long-run dynamic behaviour is accounted for in all specifications by introducing various lag structures. The simplest are one- or two-period lags of explanatory variables in various equations. The production equations were all estimated with polynomial distributed lags of up to six periods on the relative price variables. In addition, where it can be justified, generalized first- or second-order autoregressive error processes were fitted to eliminate the presence of significant autocorrelation.[9]

The overall results are quite satistactory. In general, the null hypothesis of constant parameters was not rejected in most cases; in the few cases where it was rejected there was evidence of measurement errors in the observed values over the forecast period. Overall, the tests for autocorrelation, autoregressive conditional heteroscedasticity and normality yielded generally satisfactory results. The model as estimated is thus valid and can therefore be adopted for applied policy simulation and forecasting. A brief evaluation of each of the five sub-models now follows.

Real consumption is shown to be positively related to current GDP and real money balances but negatively related to lagged GDP and expected inflation. The long-run marginal propensity to consume is approximately 0.85, which is plausible. Real investment is a non-linear function and is positively related to intermediate goods imports and lagged real domestic credit but negatively related to the capital stock lagged one period. The presence of the lagged dependent variable implies that the partial or stock adjustment hypothesis applies and that actual investment is different from the desired. Total tax revenue is positively related to nominal GDP lagged up to two periods. Exports and imports on national accounts basis are positive functions of current and lagged values of their balance of payments counterparts.

As expected, the GDP price deflator is very well explained by the current and one-period lags on domestic credit and the consumer price index as well as by the current price on imported manufactured goods. The almost perfect fit is verified by the $R^2$ and F-test statistics and the underlying distribution is approximately normal, while the diagnostic tests indicate the presence of no significant autocorrelation.

Output of cocoa beans is explained by the real producer price following a six period, third-order polynomial distributed lag, the relative producer price in Ghana vis-á-vis Côte d'Ivoire, as well as the amount of rainfall in the main cocoa producing area of Brong Ahafo. The results indicate a mean lag of 2.5 years, representing the average response time of cocoa supply to a change in the real producer price. As this is a log-linear relation, the sum of coefficients in the distributed lag relation (equal to 0.18) represents the long-run price elasticity, which confirms the low responsiveness of supply price found in other studies (Bateman 1971; World Bank 1983a; May 1985). The coefficient for PSIC is significant and has the correct sign, validating the hypothesis that significant amounts of smuggling occur when the producer price is higher in neighbouring countries. Finally, favourable weather in the form of rainfall, though not very significant, changes soil moisture levels and takes up to two years to affect cocoa supply.

Both the outputs of other agriculture (including timber) and mining are each explained by five-period distributed lags on their relative supply prices. The mean lag or average response time to price change is approximately two years for both sectors, while supply response is highly inelastic for other agriculture (0.06) and fairly inelastic for mining (0.41). Changes in population, a proxy for labour supply, are also shown to be significant in explaining supply of timber and other agriculture.

The three main export commodity relations are explained by their respective expected sectoral outputs. As diagnostic correlogram tests revealed residual autocorrelation, first- and second-order autoregressive error processes were fitted to improve upon the specifications. This part of the regression experiments was performed with the MicroTSP software package, which has built-in algorithms for the purpose. Equations for cocoa exports and exports of minerals were each explained by second-order autoregressive structures, while the equation for other agriculture was explained by the first-order structure. Finally, residual exports were explained by the unit price on these exports. As price indices are unavailable for Ghana's residual exports of manufactures, electricity, refined oil and others, a proxy representing unit export price of all developing countries was adopted. A first-order autoregressive structure was fitted to this export relation as well.

As expected, import demands in the various SITC commodity class categories are generally explained with satisfactory test statistics by the level of economic activity (represented by domestic expenditures) and the cost of imports (represented by the real exchange rate). The presence of the lagged dependent variable among regressors for food imports, petroleum imports and manufactured goods imports confirms the hypothesis that the desired imports in these cases are different from their actual realized counterparts.

The specific import relations are the following. Food imports are negatively related to the real exchange rate and a dummy variable representing trade restrictions, but positively related to the lagged dependent variable. Trade restrictions during the fourth administration took the form of import licensing and elimination of open general licences (1975–77) under which food items were imported. This explains the negative sign for the dummy variable. Imports of intermediate goods are positively related to the current and lagged domestic expenditures and real domestic credit but negatively related to the real exchange rate, as expected, with very satisfactory diagnostic text statistics. Petroleum imports are negatively related to the oil price shocks and the lagged real exchange rate but positively related to the lagged dependent variable. Diagnostic tests revealed the presence of first-order serial correlation but full sample regression without forecasts indicated (AR F = 2.21) no significant autocorrelation. The imports of manufactured goods variable is positively related to current domestic expenditure but negatively related to lagged domestic expenditure and the real effective exchange rate.[10] The net invisibles imports variable is shown to be positively related to the value of total imports as expected, with fairly satisfactory test statistics.

Two endogenous variables were estimated for the final sub-model on the monetary sector. The first is demand for real money balances, which is shown to be positively related to GDP and the current and lagged values of domestic credit but negatively related to expected prices in the long run. This demand for money specification is in line with Friedman's restatement of the Quantity Theory of Money. It also satisfies the partial adjustment hypothesis in view of the presence of the lagged dependent variable among the explanatory variables. The monetary sector includes also the relation for the change in net foreign assets (NFAD). As expected, NFAD is positively related to the balance of payments and the long-run value of real money balances. All the diagnostic test statistics for the variables in this sub-model are fairly satisfactory, suggesting the validity of these equations also for policy simulation and forecasting.

*Policy implications*

This study has considered two separate but related economic hypotheses to determine whether they are consistent with Ghana's economic history and performance. The main hypothesis is that exports act as an engine of growth, and hence that economic performance in Ghana can be enhanced through an export-led growth strategy. The second related hypothesis states that domestic monetary expansion and credit creation lead ultimately to deterioration in the balance of payments and that there is a definite link between Ghana's domestic credit policy and the adverse external balances that were observed.

Application of the findings in this study to Ghana's past economic history suggests important policy implications. During the liberal regime, exports act as an engine of growth and exports growth is associated with overall economic growth. In addition, during this period, domestic credit creation has a direct effect on the balance of payments, a phenomenon also noted by Teal and Giwa (1985). This is because, in a liberal regime with exports growth and relaxation in the foreign exchange constraint, domestic credit expansion is on the decline, which can be linked to improvement in the balance of payments to validate the theory.

On the other hand, in a regime of restrictive trade policy, an export growth strategy can achieve some initial income growth, but the inflationary consequences may be so large that growth may be suppressed. Domestic credit expansion during such a regime will also have a more direct effect on inflation than on the balance of payments. This finding was demonstrated in Figure 12.2 and was similarly noted by Teal and Giwa. Thus, in a restrictive regime, exports growth may not, on balance, lead to growth in income.

The model developed in this study would validate the above conclusions. The sample period for the empirical analysis was 1967–83, which lies wholly in the restrictive regime as has been defined. Thus, solution of the model and application of the regression results in a simulation experiment can validate the conclusions for the restrictive trade policy regime. If data were obtained to cover the periods depicted here as corresponding to a liberal regime, it is expected that the model will also simulate quite satisfactorily the conclusions associated with the liberal regime.

It is therefore clear from the foregoing policy conclusions that the ideal state for promoting economic growth is the liberal regime. But what are the main features of such a regime? Perhaps part of the answer can be found in the policy package of the current Economic Recovery Programme (ERP). The key elements are: a market-determined exchange rate; deregulation and removal of import licensing, price and exchange controls; producer price incentives for cocoa and other export commodities; export retention accounts in foreign exchange; lastly, rehabilitation of the transport, energy, mining and financial sectors, as well as commercialization of public sector enterprises.

The ERP acknowledges the significance of the cocoa sector as part of its export-led growth strategy by the elaborate provisions made for this sector in the form of producer price incentives, retention of accounts, marketing reforms and general rehabilitation. It is expected that over the medium term the producer price will continue to rise up to about 55–60 per cent of f.o.b. world price, while at the same time the share of the Ghana Cocoa Board will decline from the current 25 per cent to about 15 per cent. Despite this priority treatment for cocoa, it is anticipated that the share of cocoa in total exports will decline from 67 per cent in 1986 to about 52 per cent by 1995. Among non-cocoa exports, gold is expected to increase in importance rapidly as rehabilitation of the mines progresses.

However, continued dependence on primary commodity exports must not remain the long-term strategy of the export-led growth policy. Overextension of the cocoa sector can lead to depressed prices on the world market, given similar structural adjustment programmes in Nigeria for cocoa and the aggressive production strategies in Malaysia and Indonesia. Over the medium term, Ghana expects to increase its exports to about 300,000 metric tons. Côte d'Ivoire is currently producing over 600,000 metric tons. Brazil is a major producer and so can Nigeria become once again. The implication is that, as a long-range policy, the export drive in Ghana should be accompanied by a major diversification effort. This diversification should be based not on continued primary commodity diversification, but rather on diversification into light manufactures. This is the kind of strategy upon which Hong Kong, South Korea, Taiwan and others graduated to become the so-called newly industrialized countries which have been experiencing the fastest growth rates in income.

It is at this stage that it becomes more critical for Ghana to participate actively in MTNs such as the current Uruguay Round of the GATT or UNCTAD VII. Full knowledge and understanding of the issues on the agenda of these MTNs is most essential. Only by such active participation can Ghana and other African countries make positive contributions to expand market access for all developing countries in a free and transparent global trading system.

## Appendix 1: A trade sector macroeconomic model for Ghana, The complete model

I. *Domestic expenditures and prices*

1. $CVR = CVR\ [GDP, GDP(-1), M2R, PCD(-1)]$
2. $IVR = IVR\ [MM, DCR(-1), K(-1), IVR(-1)]$
3. $TRV = TRV\ [GDPV(-1), GDPV(-2)]$
4. $XNAV = XNAV\ [XVC(-1)]$

5. $MNAV = MNAV\ [MVSVC(t)];\ t = 0, -1, -2$
6. $PGDP = PGDP\ [DC + DC(-1), PMRG, PC, PC(-1)]$
* $GDPV = CV + IV + GV + XNAV - MNAV + EONAV$

II. *Production*

7. $$YCA = YCA \left[ \mathrm{PDL}\left(\frac{\mathrm{PPCB}}{\mathrm{PC}}\right), PSIC, RBR(-2) \right]$$
8. $$YRAG = YRAG \left[ \mathrm{PDL}\left(\frac{\mathrm{PXTM*NER}}{\mathrm{PC}}\right), POP \right]$$
9. $$YMIN = YMIN \left[ \mathrm{PDL}\left(\frac{\mathrm{PXXM*NER}}{\mathrm{PC}}\right) \right]$$

* $YR = GDP - YCA - YRAG - YMIN$

III. *Exports*

10. $XCBC = XCBC\ (YCAS)$
11. $XTMC = XTMC\ (YRAGS)$
12. $XMINC = XMINC\ (YMINS)$
13. $XR = XR\ (PXR)$

IV. *Imports*

14. $MF = MF\ [REER, MF(-1), DM]$
15. $MM = MM\ [DE, DE(-1), REER, DCR(-1)]$
16. $ML = ML\ [PML, REER(-1), ML(-1)]$
17. $MRG = MRG\ [DE, DE(-1), REER(-1), MRG(-1)]$
18. $NMSV = NMSV(MV)$

V. *Balance of payments identities*

* $MV = MFV + MMV + MLV + MRGV$
* $XV = XCBV + XTMV + XMINV + XRV$
* $BOP = XV - MV - NMSV + KA + EOBP$

VI. *Monetary sector: monetary survey*

19. $MQ = MQ\ [GDP, PGDP, PGDP(-1), DC, DC(-1), MQ(-1)]$
20. $NFAD = NFAD\ [BOP, MQ, MQ(-1)]$
* $NFA + DC = M2 + OIN$

* denotes identities

## Appendix 2: Variable definitions

*BOP* = balance of payments, nominal (US$)
*CVR* = real private consumption expenditures: nominal *CV* deflated by *PC*
*CV* = private consumption expenditures, nominal (cedis)
**DC* = domestic credit, nominal (cedis)
*DCR* = real domestic credit: nominal *DC* deflated by *PGDP*
*DE* = real domestic expenditures: nominal *DEV* deflated by *PGDP*
*DEV* = domestic expenditures, nominal (cedis): sum of *CV*, *IV* and *GV*
**DM* = dummy variable for trade restrictions: 1975–77, 1981–82
**EOBP* = errors and omissions in balance of payments, nominal (US$)
**EONAV* = statistical error in national income accounts, nominal (cedis)
*FX* = foreign exchange available, nominal (US$): sum of *XV* and *KA*
*GDP* = real gross domestic product: nominal *GDPV* deflated by *PGDP*
*GDPV* = Gross domestic product, nominal (cedis)
**GV* = government consumption expenditures, nominal (cedis)
*IV* = gross investment expenditures, nominal (cedis)
*IVR* = real gross investment expenditures: nominal *IV* deflated by *PGDP*
**K* = real capital stock, index (1980 = 1.00)
**KA* = capital account in balance of payments, nominal (US$)
*MF* = real imports of food products, SITC (0 + 1): nominal *MFV* deflated by *PMF*
*MFV* = imports of food products, SITC (0 + 1), nominal (US$)
*ML* = real imports of crude oil and Petroleum products, SITC (3): nominal *MLV* deflated by *PML*
*MLV* = imports of crude oil and petroleum products, SITC (3), nominal (US$)
*MM* = real imports of raw materials and intermediate products, SITC (2 + 4): nominal *MMV* deflated by *PMM*
*MMV* = imports of raw materials and intermediate products, SITC (2 + 4), nominal (US$)

*MNAV* = imports of goods and services (excluding factor payments), national accounts basis, nominal (cedis)
*MRG* = real imports of manufactured and capital goods, SITC (5 to 9): nominal *MRGV* deflated by *PMRG*
*MRGV* = imports of manufactured and capital goods, SITC (5 to 9), nominal (US$)
**M2* = money and quasi-money (broad money), nominal (cedis)
*M2R* = real balances: *M2* deflated by *PC*
*MQ* = real balances: two-year moving average of *M2* deflated by *PGDP*
*MV* = total merchandise imports at c.i.f., SITC (0 to 9), nominal (US$)
*MVSVC* = total merchandise and net invisible imports nominal (cedis): sum of *MV* and *NMSV* converted to cedis by *NER*
**NER* = nominal official exchange rate: amount of cedis per US$ 1.00
*NFA* = net foreign assets of the banking system, nominal (cedis)
*NFAD* = first difference or one-period change in *NFA*
*NMSV* = net invisibles (services) imports over exports, nominal (US$)
**OIN* = other items net: errors and omissions in monetary survey
**PC* = consumer price index (1980 = 1.00)
**PCD* = percentage change in *PC*, inflation index
*PGDP* = GDP implicit price deflator, index (1980 = 1.00)
**PMF* = unit value of imports of food products, SITC (0 + 1), index (1980 = 1.00)
**PML* = unit value of imports of crude oil and petroleum products, SITC (3), index (1980 = 1.00)
**PMM* = unit value of imports of raw materials and intermediate products, SITC (2 + 4), Index (1980 = 1.00)
**PMRG* = unit value of imports of manufactured and capital goods. SITC (5 to 9), index (1980 = 1.00)
**POECD* = weighted average consumer price index of OECD countries (1980 = 1.00)
**POP* = total population in thousands of persons
**PPCB* = producer price of cocoa beans in Ghana, index (1980 = 1.00)
**PSIC* = relative producer price of cocoa in Ghana vis-à-vis Côte d'Ivoire valued at Ghana's black market exchange rate
**PST* = relative producer price of cocoa in Ghana vis-à-vis Togo valued at Ghana's black market exchange rate

**PXTM* = unit value of timber and other agricultural exports (other than cocoa beans), SITC (0 + 1), index (1980 = 1.00)
**PXXM* = unit value of exports of mineral products, index (1980 = 1.00)
**PXR* = unit value of rest of exports, SITC (5 to 9), index (1980 = 1.00)
**PWCB* = world price of cocoa beans, index (1980 = 1.00)
**RBR* = annual rainfall in inches, Brong Ahafo region of Ghana
**REER* = real exchange-rate index (1980 = 1.00): *NER* Index adjusted by ratio of *POECD* to the domestic *PC*
*TRV* = total government net tax revenue over transfer payments, nominal (cedis)
*XCBC* = real exports of cocoa beans: nominal *XCBV* converted into cedis, deflated by *PC*
*XCBV* = exports of cocoa beans, nominal (US$)
*XMINC* = real exports of mineral products: nominal *XMINV* converted into cedis, deflated by *PGDP*
*XMINV* = exports of mineral products, nominal (US$)
*XNAV* = exports of goods and services (excluding factor payments), national accounts basis, nominal (cedis)
*XR* = rest of real exports, SITC (5 to 9): nominal *XRV* deflated by *PXR*
*XRV* = rest of exports, SITC (5 to 9), nominal (US$)
*XTMC* = real exports of timber and other agricultural products: nominal *XTMV* deflated by *PXTM*
*XTMV* = exports of timber and other agricultural products, nominal (US$)
*XV* = total merchandise exports, nominal at f.o.b. (US$)
*XVC* = total merchandise exports, nominal (cedis), i.e. *XV* converted to cedis by *NER*
*YCA* = output of cocoa industry in cedis, real
*YMIN* = output of mining and quarrying industry in cedis, real
*YR* = rest of output: refined oil, electricity, manufacturing, utilities, construction and service industries in cedis, real
*YRAG* = rest of agricultural output (other than cocoa): food, timber, livestock and fishing in cedis, real
YCAS, *YMINS*, *YRS* and *YRAGS* are fitted or forecast values of their respective variables
PDL = polynomial distributed lag relation

* denotes exogenous variables

## Appendix 3: A trade sector macroeconomic model of Ghana (1967–83), estimates of behavioural equations

*Note:* Absolute values of *t*-statistics in parentheses:

( ) for *t*-statistics based on least squares standard errors

[ ] for *t*-statistics based on heteroscedastic consistent standard errors

(*) accompanying test statistics denotes unsatisfactory diagnostic tests

$\rho(j)$ represents adjustment coefficients of order *j* in autoregressive structural transformations

SUM { } In equations A12.7–A12.9, these expressions refer to the distributed lags over several periods on the logarithm of the relevant variable. 'SUM' represents the sum of all terms in the distributed lags in each case; and A(I), B(I) and C(I) represent the six, five or four individual coefficients respectively, where I takes the period values 0, … 4, 5 or 6. The bracketed terms under these coefficients are the corresponding *t*-statistics. This model follows the format of Kwack, Demirors and Walker (1987).

Sample range is 1967–83 less two-period forecasts unless otherwise stated.

I. *Domestic expenditures and prices*

$$CVR = -4124.4324 + 1.3160\,GDP - 0.4714\,GDP_{t-1}$$
(0.3320) (2.6921) (1.0561)
[0.2132] [1.7377] [0.6244]

$$+\,1.5144\,M2R - 11597.5890\,PCD_{t-1} \qquad \text{(A12.1)}$$
(3.9445) (2.4837)
[2.6809] [0.8702]

$R^2 = 0.854$; DW = 2.135; F = 14.56
CHOW F = 1.22; AR F = 0.22; ARCH F = 0.01
Normality $X^2 = 0.718$

$$\ln IVR = 238.9546 + 0.6865 \ln MM + 2.2049 \ln DCR_{t-1}$$
(2.2836) (1.2767) (1.8023)
[3.0196] [0.9056] [1.2717]

$$-26.5561 \ln K_{t-1} + 0.3132 \ln IVR_{t-1} \qquad \text{(A12.2)}$$
(2.2700) (1.0953)
[3.2494] [0.2860]

$R^2 = 0.609$; DW = 1.926; F = 3.90
CHOW F = 3.26; AR F = 0.08; ARCH F = 0.0
Normality $X^2 = 0.345$

$$TRV = 353.9512 + 0.1419\ GDPV_{t-1} - 0.0865\ GDPV_{t-2} \qquad \text{(A12.3)}$$

(4.2724) (3.5528) (1.4557)

[2.4617] [1.0660] [0.4356]

$R^2 = 0.9523$; DW = 1.459; F = 119.47

CHOW F* = 8.14; AR F = 0.31; ARCH F = 2.28

Normality $X^2 = 0.089$

$$XNAV = 308.2675 + 0.9900\ XVC_{t-1} \qquad \text{(A12.4)}$$

(1.4594) (5.9636)

[1.4785] [2.9213]

$R^2 = 0.7323$; DW = 1.238; F = 35.56

CHOW F* = 88.38; AR F = 3.94; ARCH F = 0.26

Normality* $X^2 = 12.521$

$$MNAV = 126.8385 + 1.3514\ MVSVC + 0.7562\ MVSVC_{t-1}$$

(1.7341) (6.7476) (2.5928)

[1.0943] [5.8064] [1.4970]

$$- 0.8470\ MVSVC_{t-2} \qquad \text{(A12.5)}$$

(3.1122)

[1.1938]

R2 = 0.9799; DW = 2.001; F = 179.10

CHOW F* = 378.95; AR F = 0.02; ARCH F = 0.22

Normality $X^2 = 1.127$

$$PGDP = 0.00393 + 0.00002\ DC - 0.00000622\ DC_{t-1} + 0.0696\ PMRG$$

(0.8077) (6.4534) (1.3204) (3.5789)

[0.3379] [1.0000] [0.3108] [1.1828]

$$+ 0.6246\ PC + 0.2072\ PC_{t-1} \qquad \text{(A12.6)}$$

(23.5596) (3.6338)

[2.2540] [0.5539]

$R^2 = 0.9999$; DW = 2.233; F = 33153.27

CHOW F* = 69.83; AR F = 0.14; ARCH F = 0.01

Normality $X^2 = 0.195$

## II. *Production*

$$\ln YCA = 7.3210 + 0.5188 \ln PSIC + 0.7446 \ln RBR_{t-2}$$

(13.1299) (1.7891) (1.0286)

$$+ \text{SUM}\ \{I = -5 \text{ TO } 0\text{: } A(I)^* \ln(PPCB/PC)\} \qquad \text{(A12.7)}$$

$A(0) = -0.4784$ (1.3692) $A(1) = -0.0348$ (0.2305) $A(2) = 0.1843$ (2.3864)

$A(3) = 0.2381$ (3.4356) $A(4) = 0.1858$ (2.3923) $A(5) = 0.0867$ (1.2556)

3RD DEGREE PDL CONSTRAINED AT FAR END
SUM COEFF = 0.1817 MEAN LAG = 2.5

$R^2 = 0.7646$; DW = 2.0166; F = 7.1456

Sample range: 1966–82; TSLS estimates

ln *YRAG* = 6.5973 + 1.3936 ln *POP* + SUM[*I* = –4 TO
(24.8638) (5.6457)

0: *B*(*I*)* ln[(*PXTM**NER*)/*PC*]) (A12.8)

*B*(0) = 0.1350 (1.6854) *B*(1) = 0.0712 (1.8705) *B*(2) = –0.0285 (0.4456)

*B*(3) = –0.0736 (1.3751) *B*(4) = –0.0459 (0.6744)

4TH DEGREE PDL CONSTRAINED AT BOTH ENDS
SUM COEFF = 0.0583 MEAN LAG = 2.0

$R^2 = 0.8472$; DW = 2.1316; F = 9.2436
ρ(1) = 0.4524, ρ(2) = –0.5415

Sample range: 1966–82; TSLS estimates

ln *YMIN* = 6.1971 + SUM(*I* = –4 TO 0: *C*(*I*)* ln[(*PXXM**NER*)/*PC*])
(52.0990) (A12.9)

*C*(0) = 0.1209 (1.9243) *C*(1) = 0.1886 (3.7498) *C*(92) = 0.1005 (2.0933)

*C*(3) = –0.0337 (0.8555) *C*(4) = –0.1038 (1.9174)

3RD DEGREE PDL CONSTRAINED AT FAR END
SUM COEFF = 0.2725 MEAN LAG = 2.0

$R^2 = 0.9535$; DW = 2.0551 F = 40.9725
ρ(1) = 0.4064, ρ(2) = –0.6832

Sample range 1967–82; TSLS estimates

III. *Exports*

ln *XCBC* = –10.1250 + 2.5824 ln *YCAS* (A12.10)
(1.7583) (3.2488)

$R^2 = 0.7006$; DW = 2.0704; F = 0.3621
ρ(1) = 0.5798, ρ(2) = –0.3672

ln *XTMC* = –40.7474 + 2.6954 ln *YRAGS* (A12.11)
(0.2150) (1.9915)

$R^2 = 0.7244$; DW = 1.7029; F = 17.0888
ρ(1) = 0.9935

$$\ln \text{XMINC} = -8.9877 + 2.3187 \ln YMINS \qquad \text{(A12.12)}$$
$$(5.6174) \quad (9.6553)$$

$R^2 = 0.9252$; DW = 1.9925; F = 49.5028
$\rho(1) = 0.6812$, $\rho(2) = 0.6926$

$$\ln XR = 6.2341 = 0.6402 \ln PXR \qquad \text{(A12.13)}$$
$$(16.8523) \quad (2.1571)$$

$R^2 = 0.8762$; DW = 1.6381; F = 46.001
$\rho(1) = 0.8136$

IV. *Imports*

$$\ln MF = 3.4203 - 0.1681 \ln REER + 0.3831 \ln MF_{t-1}$$
$$(2.9623) \quad (2.3425) \qquad (1.7766)$$
$$[2.7263] \quad [2.7538] \qquad [1.6202]$$
$$- 0.1662\, DM \qquad \text{(A12.14)}$$
$$(1.7766)$$
$$[1.4513]$$

$R^2 = 0.6555$; DW = 2.713; F = 6.98
CHOW F = 0.01; AR F = 4.93; ARCH F = 0.35
Normality $X^2 = 0.749$

Sample period: 1967–82 with 1 forecast

$$\ln MM = -15.5963 + 1.1969 \ln DE + 0.7716 \ln DE_{t-1}$$
$$(5.3256) \quad (2.7058) \qquad (1.7272)$$
$$[2.9880] \quad [1.7734] \qquad [1.6280]$$
$$- 0.2451 \ln REER + 0.8829 \ln DCR_{t-1} \qquad \text{(A12.15)}$$
$$(4.6236) \qquad (2.8940)$$
$$[3.3609] \qquad [2.0006]$$

$R^2 = 0.9233$; DW = 1.855; F = 30.10
CHOW F* = 13.39; AR F = 0.04; ARCH F = 0.88
Normality $X^2 = 0.794$

Sample period: 1967–82 with 1 forexast

$$\ln ML = 2.7038 - 0.0979 \ln PML - 0.3229 \ln REER_{t-1}$$
$$(2.9212) \quad (1.8063) \qquad (3.2249)$$
$$[2.5648] \quad [2.2479] \qquad [3.3421]$$
$$+ 0.60623 \ln ML_{t-1} \qquad \text{(A12.16)}$$
$$(4.19075)$$
$$[3.7614]$$

$R^2 = 0.7619$; DW = 3.143; F = 11.74
CHOW F = 4.56; AR F* = 10.17(2.21); ARCH F = 0.11
Normality $X^2 = 1.169$

Sample Period: 1967–82 with 1 forecast

$$\ln MRG = 1.0045 + 1.0929 \ln DE - 0.7098 \ln DE_{t-1}$$
(0.5269) (3.1508) (1.6887)
[0.4397] [2.2415] [2.0526]

$$- 0.1293 \ln REER_{t-1} + 0.5615 \ln MRG_{t-1} \qquad \text{(A12.17)}$$
(1.9972) (2.6467)
[1.7491] [2.4047]

$R^2 = 0.8980$; DW = 1.537: F = 22.00
CHOW F* = 15.39; AR F = 0.81; ARCH F = 0.04
Normality $X^2 = 0.330$
Sample period: 1967–82 with 1 forecast

$$\ln NMSV = 1.5903 + 0.5048 \ln MV \qquad \text{(A12.18)}$$
(2.5399) (5.1172)
[1.6995] [3.5180]

$R^2 = 0.6680$; DW = 1.754; F = 26.19
CHOW F = 0.01; AR F = 0.08; ARCH F = 0.10
Normality* $X^2 = 2.846$

V. *Monetary sector*

$$\ln MQ = -5.94009 + 0.2660 \ln GDP = 7499 \ln PGDP$$
(3.9160) (1.5744) (2.9837)
[1.8450] [0.7874] [1.6162]

$$+ 0.2108 \ln PGDP_{t-1} + 0.2166 \ln DC + 1.3246 \ln DC_{t-1}$$
(0.9567) (1.0713) (2.0123)
[0.5927] [0.6098] [1.0017]

$$+ 0.8004 \ln MQ_{t-1} \qquad \text{(A12.19)}$$
(3.7039)
[2.1120]

$R^2 = 0.960$; DW = 2.383; F = 31.73
CHOW F = 1.86; AR F = 0.04; ARCH F = 0.44
Normality $X^2 = 0.752$

$$NFAD = -138.5031 + 1.3270\, BOP + 0.0993\, MQ - 0.0830\, MQ_{t-1}$$
(0.6822) (2.6253) (2.5546) (1.9306)
[0.4832] [1.8556] [0.9490] [1.0611]
(A12.20)

$R^2 = 0.609$; DW = 1.603; F = 5.71
CHOW F = 1.807; AR F = 0.0 ARCH F = 0.08
Normality $X^2 = 1.595$

Sample period: 1967–82 with 1 forecast

## Appendix 4: Black market exchange rates and cocoa prices: Ghana, Ivory Coast, and Togo, 1960–81

| *Year* | *Black market rates* | | | *Cocoa prices* | | | | | *PST* | *PSIC* |
|---|---|---|---|---|---|---|---|---|---|---|
| | *US/cedi* | *CFA/US* | *Cedi/CFA* | *Ghana (credis/mt)* | *Togo (CFA/mt)* | *Ivory Coast (CFA/mt)* | *Togo (cedis/mt)* | *Ivory Coast (cedis/mt)* | | |
| 1960 | 1.40 | 245.38 | 0.003 | 220.46 | 100,000 | 94,736 | 291.09 | 275.77 | 0.75735 | 0.79943 |
| 1961 | 1.40 | 245.08 | 0.003 | 220.46 | 95,000 | 94,921 | 276.88 | 276.65 | 0.79642 | 0.79690 |
| 1962 | 1.40 | 245.00 | 0.003 | 220.46 | 58,000 | 69,805 | 169.10 | 203.51 | 1.30375 | 1.08327 |
| 1963 | 1.79 | 245.00 | 0.002 | 216.78 | 60,000 | 69,993 | 137.01 | 159.82 | 1.58227 | 1.35637 |
| 1964 | 1.72 | 245.05 | 0.002 | 198.42 | 65,000 | 70,185 | 154.22 | 166.52 | 1.28663 | 1.19158 |
| 1965 | 1.53 | 245.00 | 0.003 | 181.88 | 70,000 | 70,126 | 187.35 | 187.69 | 0.97078 | 0.96904 |
| 1966 | 0.47 | 245.05 | 0.009 | 151.56 | 40,000 | 59,144 | 351.04 | 519.04 | 0.43175 | 0.29200 |
| 1967 | 0.60 | 247.55 | 0.007 | 197.67 | 55,000 | 70,513 | 368.76 | 472.77 | 0.53604 | 0.41811 |
| 1968 | 0.57 | 245.70 | 0.007 | 247.91 | 70,000 | 70,158 | 497.64 | 498.96 | 0.49817 | 0.49686 |
| 1969 | 0.57 | 247.68 | 0.007 | 278.55 | 80,000 | 73,298 | 571.68 | 523.78 | 0.48725 | 0.53180 |
| 1970 | 0.61 | 277.48 | 0.006 | 293.80 | 88,000 | 82,269 | 523.12 | 489.05 | 0.56163 | 0.60076 |
| 1971 | 0.57 | 278.25 | 0.006 | 300.47 | 93,000 | 84,511 | 583.81 | 530.52 | 0.51467 | 0.56637 |
| 1972 | 0.61 | 261.41 | 0.006 | 360.92 | 93,000 | 85,182 | 588.03 | 538.60 | 0.61378 | 0.67011 |
| 1973 | 0.67 | 247.88 | 0.006 | 385.04 | 93,000 | 92,838 | 564.19 | 563.21 | 0.68246 | 0.68365 |
| 1974 | 0.58 | 243.38 | 0.007 | 484.47 | 95,000 | 125,770 | 675.92 | 894.85 | 0.71676 | 0.54140 |
| 1975 | 0.67 | 219.88 | 0.007 | 577.90 | 115,000 | 175,230 | 783.56 | 1,193.94 | 0.73753 | 0.48403 |
| 1976 | 0.52 | 220.75 | 0.009 | 679.15 | 120,000 | 176,970 | 1,055.54 | 1,556.65 | 0.64342 | 0.43629 |

(*cont.*)

| *Year* | *Black market rates* | | | *Cocoa prices* | | | | | *PST* | *PSIC* |
|---|---|---|---|---|---|---|---|---|---|---|
| | *US/cedi* | *CFA/US* | *Cedi/CFA* | *Ghana (credis/mt)* | *Togo (CFA/mt)* | *Ivory Coast (CFA/mt)* | *Togo (cedis/mt)* | *Ivory Coast (cedis/mt)* | | |
| 1977 | 0.19 | 248.00 | 0.022 | 976.78 | 130,000 | 198,110 | 2,795.70 | 4,260.43 | 0.34939 | 0.22927 |
| 1978 | 0.14 | 239.88 | 0.031 | 1,601.40 | 150,000 | 250,340 | 4,632.04 | 7,730.57 | 0.34572 | 0.20715 |
| 1979 | 0.10 | 233.75 | 0.042 | 3,308.10 | 200,000 | 262,890 | 8,347.46 | 10,972.32 | 0.39630 | 0.30149 |
| 1980 | 0.06 | 204.31 | 0.078 | 3,936.30 | 220,000 | 279,160 | 17,232.23 | 21,866.14 | 0.22843 | 0.18002 |
| 1981 | 0.06 | 236.00 | 0.068 | 5,333.50 | 220,000 | 300,000 | 14,914.72 | 20,338.25 | 0.35760 | 0.26224 |
| 1982 | 0.03 | 291.50 | 0.134 | 12,133.00 | 225,000 | 300,000 | 30,203.59 | 40,271.45 | 0.40171 | 0.30128 |

*Sources:* Black market rates were obtained from *Pick's Currency Yearbook* (various issues). Because black market activity was negligible in Ghana 1960–62, and in the CFA countries 1960–70, the official rates from the IMF, *International Financial Statistics* were used for those years.

Cocoa prices for Ghana and the Ivory Coast were obtained from the data used for World Bank (1982). For Togo, different World Bank Country Economic Memoranda were used. The cocoa price for Togo in 1962 is an estimate.

Taken from May (1985), Table B3, p. 129.

## Notes

1 Svedberg (Chapter 2, this volume) demonstrates that over the period 1970–85 the sharp decline in export revenue amounts to a 7.7 per cent decline per year in the income terms of trade, decomposed into 1.8 per cent decline in the barter terms of trade and a massive 5.9 per cent decline in export volume. Thus, both the deteriorating terms of trade and volume contraction contributed to poor export performance during the period.

2 See GATT (1987a,b).

3 The lagged inflation rate is a proxy for inflationary expectations. It may also represent a proxy for the real return on lending in the unorganized money markets, which reflects the real opportunity cost of consumption but also of investment expenditures. See Wijnbergen (1981), Quarcoo (1979). As the unorganized market rates are not available in the statistics, the inflation rate is a useful proxy.

4 Cocoa represents output of cocoa beans. Other agriculture includes timber (logs and sawn wood), food, livestock and fish products. Mining covers gold, manganese, diamonds, bauxite and other metals. The rest of output includes cocoa products, other manufactured products, electricity, refined oil, construction, utilities and other miscellaneous activities.

5 In the absence of actual tree stock data, Bateman's (1971) original formulation adopted as proxy a weighted sum of the product of past real producer prices less planting costs, a farmer effort coefficient and a tree yield coefficient. In addition to the tree stock variable he also introduced a survival variable and a gammalin (insecticide) variable. The weighted sum of these was then assumed to measure the average production capacity. The six-period polynomial distributed lag relation adopted in this study captures the cycle of planting and first harvests, a formulation similar to that used in the LINK Project (Altshuler 1987).

6 Formally the measure of the real exchange rate, *REER* , adopted is defined by:

$$REER_t = \frac{NER_t}{NER_0} \cdot \frac{POECD_t}{PC_t},$$

where

$NER_t$ = nominal exchange rate in period $t$
$NER_0$ = nominal exchange rate in base period, i.e. 1980
$POECD_t$ = weighted consumer price index for OECD countries
$PC_t$ = consumer price index for Ghana.

7 This database as well as other documentation on Project LINK were kindly provided by Itsuo Kawamura, Projections and Perspectives

Studies Branch, Department of International Economics and Social Affairs, United Nations.

8 The main software used for estimating the model was PC-GIVE, version 5.0, developed at the Institute of Economics and Statistics, University of Oxford (Hendry 1988). A second software, MicroTSP, version 6.0, from Quantitative Micro Software, California (Lilian 1988), was also employed in estimating some selected functional relationships. The results are presented in Appendix 3.

9 Adjustment coefficients of order *j* are denoted by ρ(*j*) in regression results for the autoregressive structures. Various diagnostic tests were carried out in order to validate the model. They include robust heteroscedastic consistent standard errors (HCSE) to determine the degree of heteroscedasticity present, CHOW F tests of parameter constancy to determine stability of parameter estimates over forecast periods, Lagrange multiplier to test for presence of autocorrelation (ARF) where the DW statistic is invalid if not all explanatory variables are non-stochastic or the lagged dependent variable is included among explanatory variables, ARCH F test for autoregressive conditional heteroscedasticity to determine presence of autocorrelated squared residuals, and the normality $X^2$ test.

10 The evidence seems to suggest the presence of heteroscedasticity in some degree to the extent where the forecasting capability is impaired somewhat as reflected by the relatively poor Chow test.

## References

Aghevli, B. B. and Khan, M. S. (1980), 'Credit policy and the balance of payments in developing countries', in W. L. Coates and D. R. Khatkhate (eds), *Money and Monetary Policy in Less Developed Countries*, Pergamon Press, New York.

Altshuler, Clive (1987),'A macroeconomic model of Ghana', *Policy Modelling for African Economies*, UN/DIESA/PPS – Project LINK, United Nations, New York.

Balassa, Bela (1980), 'The process of industrial development and alternative development strategies', World Bank Staff Working Paper No. 438, Washington, DC.

Balassa, Bela *et al.* (1982), *Development Strategies in Semi-Industrial Economies*, Johns Hopkins University Press, Baltimore, Md.

Bateman, Merril J. (1971), 'Cocoa Projects 1971–1975', mimeo, prepared for the IBRD-Ghana Mission.

Bhagwati, Jagdish (1978), *Foreign Trade Regimes and Economic Development: Anatomy and Consequences of Exchange Control Regimes*, Ballinger for NBER, Cambridge, Mass.

Bhagwati, Jagdish (1986),'Export promoting trade strategy: Issues and evidence', Development Policy Issues Series Report, VPERS7, Office of the Vice President, Economics and Research, World Bank, Washington DC.

Birmingham, W., Neustadt, I. and Omaboe, E. N. (eds) (1966), *A Study of Contemporary Ghana: Vol. 1 – The Economy of Ghana*, Allen & Unwin, London.

Economic Commission for Africa (ECA) (1987), 'Declaration of African Ministers Responsible for Trade and Development Preparatory to UNCTAD VII', E/ECA/TRADE/70, ECA, Addis Ababa, March.

Franco, Robert G. (1979), 'Domestic credit and the balance of payments in Ghana', *Journal of Development Studies*, 15.

GATT (1987a), '1987 Consultation with Ghana', Background Paper, GATT Secretariat, BOP/W/109, Geneva, October.

GATT (1987b), '1987 Consultation with Ghana under Article XVIII: 12(b)', Statement by Ghana under Simplified Procedures for Consultations, BOP/276, Geneva, October.

Government of Ghana (1985), *Progress of the Econmic Recovery Programme 1984–86 and Policy Framework 1986–88*, Report Prepared for the Third Meeting of the Consultative Group for Ghana, Paris (November 1985), Accra, October.

Government of Ghana (1986), *Commercial and Industrial Bulletin*, Accra, 10 October.

Government of Ghana (1987), *Commercial and Industrial Bulletin*, Accra, 8 May.

Hendry, David F. (1988), *PC-GIVE, Version 5*, Institute of Economics and Statistics, University of Oxford.

Hirschman, Alberto (1958), *The Strategy of Economic Development*, Yale University Press, New Haven, Conn.

IMF, *International Financial Statistics Yearbook*, Washington DC, various issues.

IMF, *Balance of Payments Statistics Yearbook*, Washington DC, various issues.

IMF, *Direction of Trade Statistics Yearbook*, Washington, DC, various issues.

Johnson, Harry G. (1972), 'The monetary approach to balance of payments theory', *Journal of Financial and Quantitative Analysis*, III.

Killick, Tony (1978), *Development Economics in Action: A Study of Economic Policies in Ghana*, Heinemann, London.

Krueger, Anne O. (1978), *Foreign Trade Regimes and Economic Development: Liberalization Attempts and Consequences*, Ballinger for NBER, Cambridge, Mass.

Kwack, S. Y., Demirors, U. and Walker, D. O. (1987), 'The Prototype Model', Chapter 7 in *Policy Modelling for African Economies*, UN/DIESA/PPS – Project LINK, United Nations, New York.

Leith, J. Clark (1974) *Foreign Trade Regimes and Economic Development: Ghana*, Colombia University Press for NBER, New York.

Lewis, W. Arthur (1955) *The Theory of Economic Growth*, Allen and Unwin, London.

Lilian, David M. (1988) *MicroTSP*, Quantitative Micro Software, Irving, California.

May, Ernesto (1985), 'Exchange controls and parallel market economies in sub-Saharan Africa: Focus on Ghana', World Bank Staff Working Paper No. 711, Washington DC.

Mundell, Robert A. (1968), *International Economics*, Macmillan, New York.

Myrdal, Gunnar (1957), *Economic Theory and Under-Developed Regions*, Methuen, London.

Nurkse, Ragnar (1953), *Problems of Capital Formation in Underdeveloped Countries*, Blackwell, Oxford.

Patinkin, Don (1965), *Money, Interest and Prices: An Integration of Monetary and Value Theory*, 2nd edition, Harper & Row, New York.

Polak, J. J. (1957), 'Monetary analysis of income formation and payments problems', *IMF Staff Papers*, VI, November.

Quarcoo, Philip K. (1979), 'Credit allocation in segmented capital markets of underdeveloped economies', *Savings and Development*, No. 3.

Scitovsky, Tibor (1954), 'Two concepts of external economies', *Journal of Political Economy*, April.

Teal, F. and Giwa, Y. M. (1985),'Domestic credit and the balance of payments in Ghana: A comment', *Journal of Development Studies*, 21, November.

United Nations, *Yearbook of International Trade Statistics*, New York, various issues.

United Nations (1987), *Documentation for Development Research and Policy Analysis (DRPA) Data Bank of World Development Statistics*, United Nations, New York.

UNCTAD (1987), *Problems of Protectionism and Structural Adjustment: Restrictions on Trade*, TD/B/1126, Part I. Report by the UNCTAD Secretariat, Geneva.

Wijnbergen, Sweder van (1981), 'Short-run macro-economic adjustment policies in South Korea: A quantitative analysis', World Bank Staff Working Paper No. 510, Washington DC, November.

World Bank (1972), *Current Economic Situation and Prospects of Ghana, Volume 1: Main Report*, and *Volume 5: Interest Rates*, Report No. AW-32a, Washington DC. March.

World Bank (1982) 'Analysis of the world cocoa market', World Bank Staff Commodity Working Paper No. 8, Washington DC.

World Bank (1983a), 'Ghana: The cocoa sector', Background Paper No. 1 of 4, Working Paper of West Africa Programs Department I, Division B, Washington DC.

World Bank (1983b), Ghana: *Policies and Program for Adjustment, Volume I: Main Report* and *Volume II: Statistical Appendix*, Report No. 4702-GH, Washington, DC, October.

World Bank (1987a) *Ghana: Policies and Issues of Structural Adjustment*, Report No. 6635-GH, Washington DC, 1987.

World Bank (1987b), *World Development Report 1987*, Oxford University Press, New York.

13

# Non-traditional exports in Côte d'Ivoire

Allechi M'Bet

## 1 Introduction

Much has been written about the 'Ivorian miracle' and its basis in the traditional export crops of cocoa and coffee. Thus Herman Kahn (1979, p. 422) observes that:

'The Ivory Coast's economic progress has been largely led by export agriculture. In remarkable contrast to the experiences of many other LDCs, the government does allow the profits from exports sales to trickle down to even the smallest farmers, promoting grassroots economics initiative and integration into the mainstream of the nation's economic development.

In the 1980s, with a decade of stagnant or declining world prices for Côte d'Ivoire's traditional exports and large fluctuations around this trend, heavy reliance on export agriculture began to look suspect. As the President, Felix Houphouet Boigny, noted in his message to the nation in 1987: 'We have been denouncing for many years the deterioration of the terms of trade; but as long as we are not able to process all or part of our raw materials into manufactured or semi-manufactured products, we will be wasting our time denouncing the situation.'

The tension between making the best of the current situation by expanding traditional exports versus diversification into non-traditional, perhaps non-agricultural, areas is of course present in other developing countries. As many developing countries have discovered, however, such diversification is not easy and has its own costs.

In contrast to the several studies on Côte d'Ivoire's traditional exports, little work seems to have been done on exploring trends in behaviour of non-traditional exports. This paper is a first step in that direction. It does not attempt to be comprehensive or complete; its object, rather, is to open up an area of debate which seems to have been neglected in the analytical work on Côte d'Ivoire. The plan of the paper is as follows. Section 2 presents a descriptive analysis of Ivorian exports, focusing on the non-traditional sector but keeping in sight the context provided by development in the traditional sector. Section 3 presents a start in the econometric analysis of non-traditional exports, while section 4 concludes the paper with a discussion of policy implications – particularly in light of the Uruguay Round of the General Agreement on Tariffs and Trade (GATT).

## 2 Côte d'Ivoire's exports: patterns of evolution

In order to examine the evolution of the commodity composition of Ivorian exports, we have first of all to adopt a classification scheme. Since our focus is on traditional versus non-traditional exports we start by clarifying this distinction. Following the classification tradition in Côte d'Ivoire, coffee, cocoa and timber are treated as traditional exports while those remaining are grouped together under the non-traditional heading.

Table 13.1 presents a first look at traditional exports. In the early 1960s traditional exports accounted for around 80 per cent of all exports, this being made up of contributions of (around) 40 per cent, 20 per cent and 20 per cent by coffee, cocoa and timber, respectively. In the 1970s the share of non-traditional exports in total exports fell to around 65 per cent and in the early 1980s this had fallen to around 55 per cent. The share of traditional exports in GDP has fluctuated considerably but does not show a clear trend. The reason for this is that, although traditional exports have fallen as a share of total exports, total exports have risen as a share of GDP. Within the traditional exports category, the dominance of coffee has been reduced by an increasing share of cocoa. Timber, however, which reached a peak as a share of traditional exports in 1973, has been declining in importance.

Table 13.1 *Côte d'Ivoire's exports of coffee, cocoa and timber as a share of total traditional exports, of total exports and of GDP, 1960–85*

| *Product* | *1960* | *1961* | *1962* | *1963* | *1964* | *1965* | *1966* | *1967* | *1968* | *1969* | *1970* | *1971* |
|---|---|---|---|---|---|---|---|---|---|---|---|---|
| Coffee as a % of traditional exports | 56.00 | 53.45 | 49.92 | 51.97 | 50.98 | 49.95 | 51.89 | 44.49 | 46.76 | 34.85 | 46.25 | 46.79 |
| Cocoa as a % of traditional exports | 26.19 | 25.99 | 27.82 | 23.95 | 23.35 | 21.06 | 22.56 | 24.28 | 25.31 | 30.44 | 28.65 | 24.47 |
| Timber as a % of traditional exports | 17.79 | 20.54 | 22.25 | 24.06 | 25.66 | 28.98 | 25.54 | 31.21 | 27.91 | 34.69 | 25.09 | 28.73 |
| Coffee as a % of total exports | 18.02 | 42.37 | 39.71 | 43.03 | 43.34 | 37.83 | 39.43 | 31.67 | 34.18 | 25.51 | 33.16 | 33.31 |
| Cocoa as a % of total exports | 22.46 | 20.60 | 22.13 | 19.83 | 19.85 | 15.95 | 17.14 | 17.29 | 18.51 | 22.28 | 20.54 | 17.42 |
| Timber as a % of total exports | 15.26 | 16.28 | 17.70 | 19.92 | 21.81 | 21.74 | 19.41 | 22.22 | 20.41 | 25.39 | 17.98 | 20.45 |
| Traditional exports as a % of total exports | 85.75 | 79.26 | 79.55 | 82.80 | 85.01 | 75.74 | 75.99 | 71.19 | 73.11 | 73.20 | 71.68 | 71.18 |
| Coffee as a % of GDP | 13.24 | 12.66 | 11.39 | 12.49 | 13.23 | 10.80 | 11.71 | 9.22 | 10.98 | 8.25 | 10.40 | 9.58 |
| Cocoa as a % of GDP | 6.19 | 6.15 | 6.35 | 5.75 | 6.06 | 4.55 | 5.09 | 5.03 | 5.94 | 7.20 | 6.44 | 5.01 |
| Timber as a % of GDP | 4.21 | 4.86 | 5.08 | 5.78 | 6.66 | 6.26 | 5.76 | 6.47 | 6.55 | 8.21 | 5.64 | 5.88 |
| Traditional exports as a % of GDP | 23.65 | 23.68 | 22.83 | 24.03 | 25.95 | 21.63 | 22.58 | 20.72 | 23.48 | 23.67 | 22.49 | 20.48 |
| Total exports as % of GDP | 27.58 | 29.88 | 28.69 | 29.02 | 30.59 | 28.55 | 29.71 | 29.11 | 32.12 | 32.33 | 31.37 | 28.77 |

*Sources:* Computed by the author from IMF, *International Financial Statistics*, Washington DC; Direction des Douanes (Ministère de l'Economie et des Finances); *Statistiques économiques et monetaires de la BCEAO* (various issues).

Let us turn now to the non-traditional exports. These can in turn be divided into two categories – new primary products (bananas, pineapples, cotton and rubber) and manufactured and semi-manufactured products. Our focus in this paper is on the latter. Table 13.2, however, does provide some data on the evolution of exports of the new primary products. It shows that the individual product share of new primary products is fairly small but that this share is on the rise. Their share in GDP was about 1.60 per cent from 1966 to 1982 and rose to 3.72 per cent in 1985. Their share in total exports has been variable. It increased during the 1960s to reach 6.45 per cent in 1972, declined thereafter to a record low of 2.67 per cent in 1977, and then started an increase, rising to 6.62 per cent in 1985. The magnitude of the diversification task is shown by the case of cotton, in which Côte d'Ivoire moved from no cotton

| *1972* | *1973* | *1974* | *1975* | *1976* | *1977* | *1978* | *1979* | *1980* | *1981* | *1982* | *1983* | *1984* | *1985* |
|---|---|---|---|---|---|---|---|---|---|---|---|---|---|
| 39.53 | 33.07 | 10.89 | 42.80 | 49.81 | 54.41 | 38.02 | 56.53 | 33.70 | 30.69 | 39.55 | 40.09 | 27.83 | 37.82 |
| 24.84 | 22.11 | 79.50 | 33.04 | 26.78 | 27.06 | 46.64 | 39.45 | 41.49 | 50.62 | 42.42 | 40.91 | 60.19 | 54.27 |
| 35.61 | 44.80 | 9.60 | 24.15 | 23.39 | 18.51 | 15.33 | 4.01 | 24.80 | 18.67 | 18.01 | 18.99 | 11.96 | 7.90 |
| 25.83 | 21.74 | 17.68 | 24.23 | 33.82 | 37.53 | 25.00 | 31.13 | 20.50 | 17.56 | 20.35 | 20.01 | 15.48 | 21.06 |
| 16.22 | 14.54 | 17.93 | 18.71 | 18.19 | 18.66 | 30.68 | 21.73 | 25.24 | 28.97 | 21.83 | 20.42 | 33.48 | 30.22 |
| 23.27 | 29.45 | 15.60 | 13.67 | 15.88 | 12.77 | 10.08 | 2.20 | 15.08 | 10.68 | 9.27 | 9.48 | 6.65 | 4.40 |
| 65.32 | 65.75 | 51.22 | 56.63 | 67.90 | 68.97 | 65.77 | 55.07 | 60.83 | 57.23 | 51.46 | 49.91 | 55.62 | 55.69 |
| 7.63 | 7.33 | 6.98 | 7.39 | 11.91 | 12.90 | 7.35 | 8.56 | 6.09 | 5.23 | 6.12 | 6.38 | 6.12 | 8.90 |
| 4.79 | 4.90 | 7.08 | 5.70 | 6.40 | 6.41 | 9.02 | 5.97 | 7.50 | 8.62 | 6.57 | 6.51 | 13.23 | 12.78 |
| 6.88 | 9.93 | 6.16 | 4.17 | 5.59 | 4.39 | 2.96 | 0.60 | 4.48 | 3.18 | 2.79 | 3.02 | 2.63 | 10.86 |
| 19.32 | 22.16 | 64.11 | 17.27 | 23.92 | 23.71 | 19.34 | 15.14 | 18.07 | 17.04 | 15.48 | 15.92 | 21.98 | 31.30 |
| 29.57 | 33.70 | 39.48 | 30.50 | 35.23 | 34.37 | 29.40 | 27.50 | 29.71 | 29.77 | 30.90 | 31.90 | 39.52 | 56.20 |

production to 210,000 tons per year. This puts it third behind Egypt and Sudan, but the share of cotton in total exports has never gone above 4 per cent.

These products are 'new' to Côte d'Ivoire but they are still primary products, open to the vagaries of weather, of global fluctuations and of downward global trends in prices. As in many developing countries, in the area of non-traditional exports the emphasis is on manufactured and semi-manufactured products. But these two can be subdivided into relevant categories. Table 13.3 considers processed coffee, processed cocoa, plywood, other processed food products (canned fish, canned fruits, etc), processed industrial products (chemicals, etc) and manufactured items (fabric made from cotton, etc). Table 13.4 further develops some contrasts by comparing some selected primary products with their respective semi-manufactured products.

Table 13.3 reveals that the percentage share of processed coffee and cocoa has increased steadily since 1966 when Côte d'Ivoire

Table 13.2 *Côte d'Ivoire's exports of new primary products as a share of total exports and of GDP, 1960–85*

| *Product* | *1960* | *1961* | *1962* | *1963* | *1964* | *1965* | *1966* | *1967* | *1968* | *1969* | *1970* |
|---|---|---|---|---|---|---|---|---|---|---|---|
| Bananas as a % of total exports | 3.28 | 4.39 | 6.07 | 6.13 | 4.26 | 4.08 | 3.60 | 3.79 | 2.98 | 2.34 | 2.46 |
| Pineapples as a % of total exports | 0.25 | 0.19 | 0.21 | 0.22 | 0.26 | 0.29 | 0.39 | 0.54 | 0.58 | 0.50 | 0.60 |
| Rubber as a % of total exports | . . | . . | . . | . . | 0.25 | 0.47 | 0.84 | 0.69 | 0.60 | 0.76 | 0.91 |
| Cotton as a % of total export | 0.0025 | 0.008 | 0.02 | 0.10 | 0.08 | 0.21 | 0.43 | 1.10 | 1.38 | 1.32 | 1.24 |
| New primary exports as a % of total exports | . . | . . | . . | . . | 4.86 | 5.06 | 5.35 | 6.14 | 5.55 | 5.13 | 5.22 |
| New primary exports as a % of GDP | . . | . . | . . | . . | 1.48 | 1.45 | 1.60 | 1.79 | 1.78 | 1.66 | 1.63 |

*Source:* see Table 13.1.

Table 13.3 *Côte d'Ivoire's manufactured and semi-manufactured products as a share of total exports and of GDP, 1960–85*

| *Product* | *1960* | *1961* | *1962* | *1963* | *1964* | *1965* | *1966* | *1967* | *1968* | *1969* | *1970* |
|---|---|---|---|---|---|---|---|---|---|---|---|
| Processed coffee as a % of total exports | . . | . . | . . | . . | . . | . . | 0.61 | 0.80 | 0.90 | 1.11 | 1.44 |
| Processed cocoa as a % of total exports | . . | . . | . . | . . | . . | . . | 2.23 | 3.09 | 4.05 | 4.86 | 4.01 |
| Other processed food products as a % of total exports | 1.45 | 1.16 | 1.50 | 1.60 | 1.61 | 1.87 | 5.24 | 6.67 | 7.40 | 8.19 | 8.87 |
| Other industrial products as a % of total exports | 1.24 | 1.38 | 6.15 | 4.30 | 4.94 | 8.12 | 4.79 | 6.75 | 5.85 | 6.10 | 4.90 |
| Processed (ply) wood as a % of total exports | 1.70 | 1.22 | 1.77 | 1.96 | 2.58 | 5.04 | 4.08 | 3.93 | 3.25 | 3.24 | 4.39 |
| Manufactured (semi) products as a % GDP | . . | . . | . . | . . | . . | . . | 5.04 | 6.18 | 6.89 | 7.60 | 7.41 |

*Source:* see Table 13.1.

started transforming these two products. The percentage share of processed cocoa, however, is greater than that of processed coffee. Similarly, from 1960 to 1985 one observes a continuous increase in the share of other processed food products in total exports. The highest share was in 1975 with 14.74 per cent of total exports. This share of other processed food products is overall greater than the combined share of processed coffee and cocoa in total exports.

Turning to Table 13.4, exports of processed cocoa as a share of exports of cocoa bean those are greater than of processed coffer as a share of coffee bean exports. The figures in 1966 were 13.02 per cent and 1.54 per cent respectively. Such shares are on the rise, to

| *1971* | *1972* | *1973* | *1974* | *1975* | *1976* | *1977* | *1978* | *1979* | *1980* | *1981* | *1982* | *1983* | *1984* | *1985* |
|---|---|---|---|---|---|---|---|---|---|---|---|---|---|---|
| 2.34 | 2.47 | 1.58 | 1.03 | 1.18 | 0.80 | 0.61 | 0.79 | 0.66 | 1.58 | 1.14 | 0.84 | 0.70 | 0.58 | 1.11 |
| 0.71 | 1.38 | 1.09 | 0.89 | 1.22 | 0.70 | 0.51 | 0.77 | 0.80 | 1.72 | 1.61 | 1.29 | 1.21 | 1.18 | 1.93 |
| 0.88 | 0.70 | 1.03 | 0.63 | 0.67 | 0.75 | 0.58 | 0.68 | 0.84 | 0.89 | 0.92 | 0.93 | 1.36 | 1.27 | 1.03 |
| 1.35 | 1.89 | 1.67 | 1.17 | 1.42 | 1.41 | 0.95 | 1.53 | 1.92 | 2.19 | 2.61 | 2.41 | 4.00 | 2.87 | 2.53 |
| 5.30 | 6.45 | 5.39 | 3.73 | 4.51 | 3.67 | 2.67 | 3.78 | 4.24 | 6.40 | 6.29 | 5.49 | 7.29 | 5.92 | 6.62 |
| 1.52 | 1.91 | 1.81 | 1.47 | 1.38 | 1.30 | 0.91 | 1.11 | 1.16 | 1.90 | 1.87 | 1.65 | 2.32 | 2.34 | 3.72 |

| *1971* | *1972* | *1973* | *1974* | *1975* | *1976* | *1977* | *1978* | *1979* | *1980* | *1981* | *1982* | *1983* | *1984* | *1985* |
|---|---|---|---|---|---|---|---|---|---|---|---|---|---|---|
| 1.42 | 0.89 | 0.83 | 0.67 | 0.92 | 0.61 | 0.42 | 1.20 | 1.25 | 1.31 | 1.57 | 1.80 | 1.84 | 1.29 | 1.57 |
| 3.47 | 3.36 | 2.94 | 3.42 | 5.63 | 5.06 | 5.54 | 7.39 | 5.53 | 4.16 | 4.77 | 4.81 | 4.90 | 5.97 | 6.70 |
| 9.84 | 9.32 | 8.03 | 9.05 | 14.74 | 10.82 | 10.67 | 13.83 | 10.71 | 10.00 | 12.01 | 12.09 | 12.59 | 11.21 | 12.01 |
| 4.53 | 2.68 | 1.82 | 5.59 | 11.45 | 7.84 | 8.29 | 7.52 | 9.14 | 5.85 | 7.40 | 7.55 | 8.47 | 5.87 | 7.03 |
| 2.79 | 3.76 | 5.05 | 3.10 | 3.32 | 3.46 | 3.33 | 3.22 | 2.83 | 2.31 | 2.18 | 2.50 | 3.04 | 2.51 | 2.49 |
| 6.35 | 5.92 | 6.30 | 8.62 | 11.00 | 9.80 | 9.72 | 9.76 | 8.10 | 9.17 | 8.32 | 8.65 | 9.84 | 10.62 | 15.76 |

9.21 per cent for coffee and 24.02 per cent for cocoa in 1983. One possible explanation of the greater proportion of processed cocoa exports than of processed coffee exports is that, while processed coffee is in the form of instant coffee alone, processed cocoa takes the form of butter and of instant cocoa.

The structure and nature of cotton exports show an interesting pattern. As a percentage share of its raw material, more processed cotton is exported than for coffee and cocoa combined. In 1966, 55.52 per cent of processed cotton was exported against 88.86 per cent in 1972 and the share rose above 100 per cent between 1974 and 1979. This was due to imports of cheaper semi-processed

Table 13.4 *Evolution of selected Côte d'Ivoire primary products and their respective semi-manufactured products, 1960–85*

| *Product* | *1960* | *1961* | *1962* | *1963* | *1964* | *1965* | *1966* | *1967* | *1968* | *1969* | *1970* | *1971* |
|---|---|---|---|---|---|---|---|---|---|---|---|---|
| (1) Exports of processed coffee (instant coffee) (CFAfr m.) | n.a. | n.a. | n.a. | n.a. | n.a. | n.a. | 467 | 639 | 949 | 1,312 | 1,877 | 1,800 |
| (2) Exports of coffee beans (CFAfr m.) | 18,640 | 20,174 | 18,931 | 24,472 | 31,724 | 25,890 | 30,233 | 25,423 | 35,861 | 30,169 | 43,172 | 42,158 |
| (1) as % of (2) | n.a. | n.a. | n.a. | n.a. | n.a. | n.a. | 1.54 | 2.51 | 2.64 | 4.34 | 4.34 | 4.26 |
| (3) Exports of cocoa beans (CFAfr m.) | 8,718 | 9,809 | 10,553 | 11,281 | 14,530 | 10,915 | 13,144 | 13,878 | 19,417 | 26,350 | 26,742 | 22,049 |
| (4) Exports of processed cocoa (butter) (CFAfr m.) | n.a. | n.a. | n.a. | n.a. | n.a. | n.a. | 1,712 | 2,484 | 4,252 | 5,747 | 5,229 | 4,399 |
| (4) as % of (3) | n.a. | n.a. | n.a. | n.a. | n.a. | n.a. | 13.02 | 17.89 | 21.89 | 21.81 | 19.55 | 19.95 |
| (5) Exports of fabrics of cotton (CFAfr m.) | n.a. | n.a. | n.a. | n.a. | n.a. | n.a. | 186 | 330 | 601 | 802 | 1,430 | 1,456 |
| (6) Exports of raw cotton (CFAfr m.) | 1 | 4 | 10 | 57 | 63 | 145 | 335 | 887 | 1,450 | 1,571 | 1,616 | 1,718 |
| (5) as % of (6) | n.a. | n.a. | n.a. | n.a. | n.a. | n.a. | 55.52 | 37.20 | 41.44 | 51.05 | 83.49 | 84.74 |
| (7) Exports of transformed wood (plywood) (CFAfr m.) | 418 | 581 | 844 | 1,117 | 1,890 | 3,449 | 3,134 | 3,159 | 3,409 | 3,836 | 5,725 | 3,543 |
| (8) Exports of timber (CFAfr m.) | 5,924 | 7,755 | 8,438 | 11,330 | 15,968 | 15,022 | 14,883 | 17,839 | 21,411 | 30,025 | 23,417 | 25,889 |
| (7) as % of (8) | 7.05 | 7.49 | 16.18 | 9.85 | 11.83 | 22.95 | 21.05 | 17.70 | 15.92 | 12.77 | 24.44 | 13.68 |

*Source:* See Table 13.1.

cotton from neighbouring countries. Export possibilities, however, are not expanding; after a peak in 1977 (184 per cent), the share of processed cotton exported declined to 42.95 per cent in 1985.

## 3 Determinants of export supply: traditional *v.* non-traditional exports

The usual analysis of export supply in developing (and developed) countries seeks to test for the importance of price and capacity effects. The price elasticity of export supply is an important parameter from the policy point of view because many of the policy instruments available to governments work through their influence on price (e.g. producer prices, nominal exchange rates, etc.). In the non-traditional/semi-manufactured category, an important question is whether an export subsidy would indeed increase supply – or whether other factors are important. The focus of our interest is the *difference* between traditional and non-traditional exports. To that end we carry out a very simple analysis which estimates export supply functions for coffee, cocoa and 'industrial products'. Thus the new primary exports are excluded from the latter category,

| *1972* | *1973* | *1974* | *1975* | *1976* | *1977* | *1978* | *1979* | *1980* | *1981* | *1982* | *1983* | *1984* | *1985* |
|---|---|---|---|---|---|---|---|---|---|---|---|---|---|
| 1,246 | 1,599 | 1,982 | 2,365 | 2,421 | 2,228 | 6,341 | 6,687 | 8,709 | 10,822 | 13,463 | 14,698 | 15,362 | 20,744 |
| 36,045 | 41,511 | 51,607 | 61,702 | 132,757 | 198,165 | 131,142 | 166,542 | 136,118 | 121,103 | 152,172 | 159,474 | 183,382 | 277,657 |
| 3,45 | 3,85 | 3,84 | 3,83 | 1,82 | 1,12 | 4,83 | 4,01 | 6,39 | 8,93 | 8,84 | 9,21 | 8,37 | 7,47 |
| 22,645 | 27,759 | 52,329 | 47,637 | 71,397 | 98,799 | 160,907 | 116,231 | 167,596 | 199,716 | 163,220 | 162,731 | 396,610 | 398,409 |
| 4,699 | 5,628 | 9,981 | 14,334 | 19,885 | 29,365 | 38,783 | 29,617 | 27,667 | 32,940 | 35,971 | 39,094 | 70,715 | 88,409 |
| 20.75 | 20.27 | 19.07 | 30.09 | 27.85 | 29.72 | 24.10 | 25.48 | 16.47 | 16.49 | 22.03 | 24.02 | 17.82 | 22.19 |
| 2,347 | 1,799 | 3,538 | 5,277 | 5,931 | 9,334 | 8,410 | 11,223 | 11,367 | 14,615 | 14,733 | 15,249 | 14,843 | 14,331 |
| 2,641 | 3,205 | 3,423 | 3,640 | 5,565 | 5,073 | 8,046 | 10,298 | 14,592 | 18,007 | 18,038 | 31,922 | 34,019 | 33,360 |
| 88.86 | 56.13 | 103.35 | 144.97 | 106.57 | 183.99 | 104.52 | 108.98 | 77.89 | 81.16 | 81.67 | 47.76 | 43.63 | 42.95 |
| 5,257 | 9,640 | 9,051 | 8,462 | 13,617 | 17,632 | 16,889 | 15,188 | 15,343 | 15,089 | 18,739 | 24,229 | 29,813 | 32,825 |
| 32,417 | 56,224 | 45,524 | 34,824 | 62,357 | 67,586 | 52,878 | 11,812 | 100,170 | 73,676 | 69,318 | 75,535 | 78,855 | 58,032 |
| 16.18 | 17.14 | 19.88 | 24.29 | 21.83 | 26.08 | 31.93 | 12.80 | 15.31 | 20.48 | 27.03 | 32.07 | 37.80 | 56.56 |

which includes processed cocoa, coffee, timber, cotton and other industrial products. These are together labelled *INDQ*.

The following equations were estimated:

$$\ln XCOFFEE_t = \alpha_0 + \alpha_1 \ln\left(\frac{PCO}{PD}\right)_t + \alpha_2 \ln Q^*_t$$

$$\ln XCOCOA_t = \beta_0 + \beta_1 \ln\left(\frac{PCA}{PD}\right)_t + \beta_2 \ln Q^*_t$$

$$\ln XINDO_t = \gamma_0 + \gamma_1 \ln (RER)_t + \gamma_2 \ln Q^*_t$$

Where:

*XCOFFEE* = quantity supplied of coffee
*XCOCOA* = quantity supplied of cocoa
*XINDQ* = quantity supplied of industrial products
*PCO* = producer price for coffee
*PCA* = producer price for cocoa
*PD* = domestic price (here consumer price index was used)
*RER* = real exchange rate
$Q^*$ = domestic supply capacity variable. GDPA (gross domestic product originating in agriculture) was used for coffee and cocoa and GDPI (gross

Table 13.5 *Estimates of export supply equations for Côte d'Ivoire for cocoa, coffee and industrial products (OLS)*

| | *Constant* | *Log Relative price* | *Log $Q^*_t$* | *Adjusted $R^2$* | *DW* | *F* |
|---|---|---|---|---|---|---|
| | | $(PCA/PD)_t$ | Log GDPA | | | |
| Log $XCOCOA_t$ | 5.41 | 0.64 | 0.53 | 0.84 | 1.83 | 61.8 |
| | (9.11) | (2.70) | (11.01) | | | |
| | | $(PCO/PD)_t$ | Log GDPA | | | |
| Log $XCOFFEE_t$ | 9.60 | 0.46 | 0.21 | 0.56 | 1.60 | 15.5 |
| | (20.25) | (2.28) | (5.56) | | | |
| | | $RER_t$ | Log GDPI | | | |
| Log $XINDQ_t$ | –3.94 | 0.12 | 1.32 | 0.76 | 2.00 | 15.0 |
| | (–0.63) | (0.28) | (2.40) | | | |

*Note:*
1. t-values in brackets

*Source:* Computed by the author from data in previous tables.

domestic product of industrial product) was used for *XINDQ*. (GDPA is a series available in M'bet and Atsain 1990. GDPI was proxied by GDP – GDPA, and hence includes the small services output.)
$t$ = period (years).

The results obtained are presented in Table 13.5.

The results indicate that coffee and cocoa export supply respond positively to relative price and to domestic capacity. However, during the study period, cocoa export supply seemed to respond more strongly to the relative price. In addition, the gross domestic product originating in agriculture has a greater and more significant effect on the supply of cocoa than on that of coffee. For instance, a 10 per cent rise in the respective relative prices will increase the export supply of cocoa and coffee by 6.4 per cent and 4.6 per cent respectively. Overall, the effect of the domestic capacity is smaller than that due to relative price variation. This seems to indicate that export supply is determined above all by relative price incentives.

It is interesting to note that, for the supply of industrial products, domestic capacity is the most significant and most important determinant. The relative price has no significant effect, whereas a 10 per cent increase in domestic capacity will raise export supply of industrial products by 13.2 per cent.

These results clearly need to be confirmed by further work. More detailed specifications and further disaggregations can be attempted on the basis of the data base that has been put together for this paper. However, there seems to be a preliminary indication that non-traditional exports are *not* like traditional exports: the price factor is not as important in supply, whereas capacity *is* important. This suggests that policy should focus on non-price features such as export promotion campaigns rather than directly on export subsidies. When the increase in supply does come about, however, can it be sold on world markets?

## 4 Market access for non-traditional exports

While it is conventional wisdom that Africa has only a minor interest in the Uruguay Round of the GATT when compared with some of the newly industrializing countries, an examination of the Côte d'Ivoire experience cautions us against this view. While it is true that manufactured and semi-manufactured products account for only around 25 per cent of all exports, and that coffee/cocoa dominate the export sector, the trends show that a country like Côte d'Ivoire rightly has an interest in certain aspects of the GATT negotiations. Some non-traditional exports are on a trend increase and would perhaps have increased even faster were it not for the problem of market access. These comprise both tariff and non-tariff barriers.

Côte d'Ivoire is particularly interested in reducing barriers to processed goods from less developed countries. In fact, the scope for expansion of processed goods is greater than for primary commodities because the price elasticities of demand are greater for processed goods than for primary products. Protection is generally higher the further the goods are processed up the processing chain. According to Ray and Marvel (1984), the Pattern of higher effective rather than nominal tariff rates results from the common practice of maintaining a so-called 'cascading' tariff schedule, in which little or no protection exists for unprocessed raw material, low tariffs are applied to processed raw materials, with higher rates for parts and components, and the highest tariffs exist for finished manufactured goods.

Table 13.6 illustrates such patterns. The figures show clearly

Table 13.6 *Tariff escalation in selected tropical products*

| *Stage of processing* | *Product* | *Tariff before MTN* | *Tariff after MTN* |
|---|---|---|---|
| 1 | Coffee | 10.0 | 6.8 |
| 2 | Processed coffee | 13.3 | 9.4 |
| 1 | Cocoa beans | 4.2 | 2.6 |
| 2 | Processed cocoa | 6.7 | 4.3 |
| 1 | Natural rubber | 2.8 | 2.3 |
| 2 | Semi-processed rubber | 4.6 | 2.9 |
| 3 | Rubber articles | 7.9 | 6.7 |
| 1 | Semi-processed wood | 2.6 | 1.8 |
| 2 | Wood panels | 10.8 | 9.2 |

*Source:* Derived from Cable (1987).

that processed goods suffer from high protection and thus reduced market access.

Despite the reduction after multilateral trade negotiations (MTNs), a gap remains and processed goods face a high tariff wall. For instance, wood panels face a tariff rate five times higher than that for semi-processed wood. Similarly, processed cocoa and coffee face a tariff rate 1.5 times that for the raw products.

The significant decline of tariff rates achieved in previous MTNs also led to the emergence of non-tariff barriers (NTBs). Indeed, the GATT allows countries to impose several kinds of measure. They include safeguard, anti-dumping restrictions and countervailing duties. The report of the group on quantitative restrictions and other non-tariff measures of the GATT Secretariat enumerates more than forty categories of measure. For Côte d'Ivoire and other African countries, these NTBs have an unwanted and significant impact. As assessed by Nogues *et al.* (1986), the prevalence in sixteen industrial economies of NTBs is real and has far more negative impact than anticipated. Overall, 13 per cent of these countries' tariff lines are subject to NTBs and 27 per cent of their imports fall into these categories. The Tokyo Round tariff concession covered only about 18 per cent of the imports of the major developed countries.

Specifically for Côte d'Ivoire, cocoa powder and cocoa butter production could not expand as fast as it might have done (see Gbetibouo and Mehta 1988.

To conclude, then, the longer-term problem facing Côte d'Ivoire is a choice between two options: expanding production in traditional exports whose prices are likely to be on a downward trend, versus attempting to expand production in processed exports where it will continue to face severe market access problems. The role of international negotiations in easing the latter constraint is therefore extremely important.

## References


Cable, Vincent (1987), *Tropical Products in the Uruguay Round: A Handbook for a MTN*, World Bank.

Gbetibouo, Mathurin and Mehta, Kirti (1988), 'Cocoa Product Price Relationship', World Bank, Division working paper No. 1988-1.

Kahn, Herman (1979), *World Economic Development 1979 and beyond*, Morrow Quill, New York.

M'bet, Allechi and Atsain, Achi (1990), *A Comparative Study of the Political Economy of Agricultural Pricing Policies. Country Study: Côte d'Ivoire*, World Bank, RPO 673-74 (forthcoming).

Nogues, Julio *et al.* (1986), 'The extent of nontariff barriers to industrial countries' imports', *World Bank Economic Review*, 1.

Ray, Edward and Marvel, Howard (1984), 'The pattern of protection in the industrialized world', *Review of Economics and Statistics*, 66.

14

# Kenya's export performance

Nehemiah K. N'geno

## 1 Introduction

The postulate that trade is an important determinant of development dates back to the last century. This view, however, began to be challenged in the 1950s and the early 1960s.[1] One of the consequences of this challenge was that most post-independence developing countries (LDCs) adopted trade policies invariant to the theory of comparative advantage. These countries emphasised import-substituting industrialization (ISI) policies as a means of diversifying away from exports of raw materials. Ironically, to finance ISI projects, LDCs have had to intensify their position as exporters of raw materials and cash crops.

For most countries the first few years of ISI policies were successful. Once the 'easy phase' was passed, however, the high hopes of faster economic development, increased export of manufactures and less reliance on exports of raw materials began to fade. Many examples of such phenomena are to be found in sub-Saharan Africa, where most countries face economic stagnation and declining export growth. These countries are at the same time burdened with high external indebtedness and chronic balance of payments problems.[2]

Several arguments have been advanced to explain the economic crisis facing many LDCs. The export pessimists hold the view that LDCs cannot depend on export-led growth.[3] This group argues that the poor export performance of LDCs is a result of external factors

– mainly deteriorating barter terms of trade, as well as recessions and increased protectionism in the North. This argument has led to such policy recommendations as greater North–South dialogue, and the use of international agencies like the United Nations and GATT to negotiate for increased exports of LDC manufactures to developed countries (DCs), and greater South–South co-operation. While such policy recommendations have been received, at best, with indifference in the North, the view that the growth of LDC exports is limited by external factors persists.

The inward-looking ISI policies began to be questioned in the late 1960s and early 1970s. Several country studies, summarized in Little, Scitovsky and Scott (1970), Bhagwati (1978), Krueger (1978) and Balassa (1985), provide evidence which links poor export performance in LDCs to internal factors. In particular, these studies conclude that ISI policies are distortive, anti-export and hence in the long run anti-growth. This has led to recommendations of policies which aim to promote domestic production for export (EPP). These recommendations have in general called for less government involvement in the economy, relaxation of trade restrictions and exchange controls, and the maintenance of 'realistic' exchange rates.[4] The economic decline in many LDCs in the 1970s and 1980s has lent more weight to these policies.

The purpose of this paper is to shed some light on the determinants of Kenya's export performance. While some studies have categorized Kenya as one of the few sub-Saharan African countries reliant on export-led growth, few of them have provided an econometric analysis of the determinants of its exports. The aim of this study is to fill this gap. This study also examines Kenya's past trade and exchange policies and their role in export performance.

## 2 The Kenyan economy

### *Sectoral growth of GDP*

As shown by Table 14.1, the Kenyan economy is dominated by the agricultural sector. The relative importance of this sector has, however, been declining over the years. The share of the private monetary service sector in real GDP is high and has since 1979 supplanted agriculture as the leading sector. On the other hand, the share of the manufacturing sector has marginally increased over the

Table 14.1 *Shares of major sectors in Kenya's real GDP (1980 prices), 1964–85 (%)*

| *Year* | *Agriculture* | *Manufacturing* | *Private services* | *Government services* |
|---|---|---|---|---|
| 1964 | 42 | 9 | 30 | 12 |
| 1965 | 37 | 10 | 33 | 12 |
| 1966 | 40 | 9 | 32 | 12 |
| 1967 | 38 | 10 | 32 | 12 |
| 1968 | 36 | 10 | 33 | 14 |
| 1969 | 35 | 10 | 32 | 14 |
| 1970 | 35 | 10 | 33 | 14 |
| 1971 | 33 | 11 | 33 | 16 |
| 1972 | 34 | 11 | 32 | 16 |
| 1973 | 34 | 12 | 32 | 15 |
| 1974 | 33 | 12 | 34 | 14 |
| 1975 | 32 | 12 | 34 | 15 |
| 1976 | 36 | 11 | 32 | 14 |
| 1977 | 40 | 11 | 30 | 13 |
| 1978 | 35 | 12 | 32 | 14 |
| 1979 | 32 | 12 | 34 | 14 |
| 1980 | 31 | 13 | 36 | 15 |
| 1981 | 31 | 13 | 36 | 15 |
| 1982 | 31 | 13 | 36 | 15 |
| 1983 | 31 | 12 | 37 | 14 |
| 1984 | 30 | 13 | 38 | 15 |
| 1985 | 29 | 13 | 38 | 15 |

*Sources:* Kenya, *Statistical Abstract* (various issues); Vandermoortele (1985).

years. In fact, it would appear that this share has stabilized at about 13 per cent in the last few years.[5] The World Bank (1962, pp. 18-19) shows that during the 1950s the agriculture and manufacturing sectors contributed about 40 and 10 per cent of GDP respectively.[6] This suggests that, apart from the changes in the agricultural sector, the structure of the economy has not changed much since independence.

The development process in post-independent Kenya can be divided into three phases. Phase I (1964–73) is what can be called the development decade because it is associated with high economic growth. Phase II (1974–79) can be called the disruption period

Table 14.2 *Growth of Kenya's real GDP and its major components (annual growth rate)*

| | *1964–85* | *1964–73* | *1974–79* | *1980–85* |
|---|---|---|---|---|
| GDP[a] | 3 | 7 | 3 | –1 |
| Agriculture | 2 | 4 | 3 | –2 |
| Manufacturing | 5 | 9 | 3 | –1 |
| Private services | 4 | 7 | 2 | 1 |
| Government services | 4 | 10 | 2 | –1 |

*Note:*
[a] GDP at factor cost is used because the GDP components are valued at factor cost in the National Accounts.

*Source:* Table 14.1.

because during this period the economy experienced external shocks arising from the oil crises of 1973 and 1979 and the coffee boom of 1976–77. Phase III (1980–85) can be called the structural adjustment period because it coincides with a period in which stabilization and liberalization policies were used in an attempt to rejuvenate the economy.

The growth rate of real GDP and its various components for the different periods are given in Table 14.2. Over the period 1964–85, real GDP grew by 3 per cent per year, while agriculture and manufacturing grew at an annual rate of 2 and 5 per cent respectively; the two service sectors grew at about 4 per cent per annum. These do not appear to be spectacular growth rates for a country normally considered a success story in sub-Saharan Africa. However, a different picture emerges when economic performance during the different sub-periods is examined. During the development decade (1964–73) high real GDP growth rates were achieved, with manufacturing and government services leading the way at over 9 and 10 per cent per year, respectively. The second phase (1974–79) exhibits a less favourable picture. The growth of GDP during this period declined to less than half that of the previous period. Manufacturing growth fell by about two-thirds of the previous rates. The growth of private and government services also declined substantially.

The growth of GDP and its components (except for private services) was negative over the structural adjustment period (1980–85).

This result was largely due to the poor economic performance in 1980 and 1982. It should be noted that poor weather in 1980 and 1984, and the balance of payments crises of 1980 and 1982 contributed to the poor economic performance.

The more recent performances of the Kenyan economy are contained in Kenya (1988), which shows that real GDP grew by 4.8 per cent, 5.5 per cent and 4.8 per cent in 1985, 1986 and 1987, respectively. At the sectoral level it shows that agriculture grew in real terms by 3.7 per cent, 4.9 per cent and 3.8 per cent, while manufacturing grew by 4.5 per cent, 5.8 per cent and 5.7 per cent during the same years.

*Pattern and direction of trade*

Table 14.3 shows that the Kenyan economy is relatively open. Total merchandise trade has over the years been above 40 per cent of real GDP. The table also shows that the barter terms of trade have sharply declined in the 1980s. The openness of the Kenyan economy can easily lead to the usual claim that it will be prone to fluctuations in the international economy. Such a causal link is in fact inferred by Van der Hoeven and Vandermoortele (1987), who find a high correlation between Kenya's annual growth of real GDP and the terms of trade.

The commodity concentration of exports is shown by Table 14.4. During the colonial period coffee was the major export earner, as it is today. Together with sisal and tea, coffee contributed over 40 per cent of export earnings. This pattern of commodity concentration has not changed very much over the years. While the share of sisal has declined, those of tea and petroleum products have gone up.

The geographic concentration of exports is shown in Table 14.5. During the 1960s and early 1970s East African countries and the UK were the main markets for Kenya's exports. Together, these countries imported over 40 per cent of Kenya's exports. From the middle of the 1970s this concentration began to decline.

The decline in Kenya's exports to East African markets is attributable to the collapse of the East African Community in 1977, which reduced exports to Tanzania below 1 per cent of total recorded exports. However, it is evident that the decline of exports to the East African markets has to some extent been made up by increased exports to other African markets. N'geno (1985) has shown that this increase has mainly been to Rwanda and Burundi. The

Table 14.3 *Kenya's exports and imports as a percentage of real GDP (1980 constant prices) and barter terms of trade, 1964–85*

| *Year* | *Barter terms of trade* | *Exports* | *Imports* |
|---|---|---|---|
| 1964 | 147 | 21 | 23 |
| 1965 | 141 | 22 | 27 |
| 1966 | 141 | 21 | 28 |
| 1967 | 141 | 17 | 24 |
| 1968 | 147 | 17 | 25 |
| 1969 | 139 | 18 | 23 |
| 1970 | 150 | 18 | 26 |
| 1971 | 130 | 17 | 30 |
| 1972 | 123 | 18 | 26 |
| 1973 | 123 | 20 | 26 |
| 1974 | 108 | 22 | 35 |
| 1975 | 96 | 20 | 30 |
| 1976 | 112 | 23 | 28 |
| 1977 | 148 | 27 | 28 |
| 1978 | 118 | 19 | 32 |
| 1979 | 109 | 18 | 27 |
| 1980 | 100 | 19 | 36 |
| 1981 | 86 | 17 | 30 |
| 1982 | 82 | 16 | 26 |
| 1983 | 77 | 17 | 23 |
| 1984 | 90 | 19 | 27 |
| 1985 | 75 | 16 | 25 |

*Source:* Kenya, *Statistical Abstract* (various issues).

exports to the African markets are mostly petroleum, chemicals and manufactured goods. This contrasts sharply with exports to the developed countries, which are mainly agricultural goods and basic raw materials.

## 3 Protection and trade policies

This section outlines Kenya's trade policies, with emphasis on the post-independence period. To set the stage however, the colonial policies will be briefly sketched.

The purposes of colonial trade policies were mainly to collect revenue and to a lesser extent to protect domestic consumer goods

Table 14.4 *Kenya's major exports as a percentage of total exports, 1950–85*

| *Year* | *Coffee* | *Tea* | *Petroleum* | *Sisal* |
|---|---|---|---|---|
| 1950 | 17 | 6 | — | 20 |
| 1955 | 28 | 9 | — | 6 |
| 1960 | 21 | 9 | — | 9 |
| 1964 | 33 | 13 | 5 | 8 |
| 1965 | 30 | 13 | 10 | 5 |
| 1966 | 32 | 15 | 10 | 4 |
| 1967 | 29 | 14 | 14 | 2 |
| 1968 | 22 | 17 | 11 | 2 |
| 1969 | 27 | 18 | 12 | 2 |
| 1970 | 22 | 13 | 13 | 2 |
| 1971 | 18 | 13 | 14 | 1 |
| 1972 | 20 | 13 | 12 | 2 |
| 1973 | 22 | 11 | 10 | 3 |
| 1974 | 18 | 9 | 18 | 8 |
| 1975 | 16 | 11 | 23 | 3 |
| 1976 | 29 | 10 | 18 | 1 |
| 1977 | 43 | 15 | 15 | 1 |
| 1978 | 34 | 17 | 16 | 1 |
| 1979 | 29 | 16 | 18 | 1 |
| 1980 | 22 | 12 | 31 | 2 |
| 1981 | 21 | 12 | 31 | 2 |
| 1982 | 27 | 14 | 26 | 2 |
| 1983 | 25 | 20 | 20 | 2 |
| 1984 | 27 | 25 | 17 | 2 |
| 1985 | 30 | 25 | 14 | 2 |

*Source:* Kenya, *Statistical Abstract* (various issues).

industries. For these reasons tariffs were the major trade policy instruments and hardly any quantitative import controls existed. There were also no strong and effective measures to promote exports. Some of the policies used for this purpose included low export taxes and railway tariffs, and duty drawbacks and remissions. However, in 1958 import licensing began to be used for protection. Specific duties were also introduced not only to increase revenue collections but also for industrial protection.

Table 14.5 *Direction of Kenya's real exports (% of total by destination), 1960–86*

| *Year* | *United Kingdom* | *West Germany* | *US* | *Africa*[a] | *Tanzania* | *Uganda* | *Rest of Africa*[b] |
|---|---|---|---|---|---|---|---|
| 1960 | 11 | 12 | 7 | 31 | 15 | 11 | 5 |
| 1961 | 12 | 10 | 9 | 33 | 16 | 12 | 5 |
| 1962 | 12 | 12 | 6 | 33 | 17 | 12 | 5 |
| 1963 | 13 | 10 | 4 | 34 | 15 | 13 | 6 |
| 1964 | 16 | 9 | 6 | 37 | 17 | 16 | 4 |
| 1965 | 19 | 9 | 3 | 41 | 18 | 19 | 4 |
| 1966 | 17 | 9 | 6 | 38 | 15 | 17 | 6 |
| 1967 | 17 | 6 | 4 | 37 | 14 | 17 | 6 |
| 1968 | 15 | 6 | 5 | 37 | 15 | 15 | 8 |
| 1969 | 16 | 8 | 5 | 37 | 13 | 16 | 8 |
| 1970 | 15 | 6 | 6 | 37 | 14 | 15 | 8 |
| 1971 | 17 | 6 | 4 | 41 | 13 | 17 | 10 |
| 1972 | 12 | 7 | 4 | 30 | 12 | 12 | 6 |
| 1973 | 12 | 8 | 4 | 24 | 9 | 12 | 2 |
| 1974 | 12 | 8 | 3 | 24 | 8 | 12 | 3 |
| 1975 | 11 | 8 | 3 | 25 | 9 | 11 | 5 |
| 1976 | 8 | 12 | 5 | 20 | 7 | 8 | 5 |
| 1977 | 9 | 17 | 5 | 17 | 2 | 9 | 7 |
| 1978 | 8 | 14 | 4 | 15 | 0 | 8 | 7 |
| 1979 | 7 | 15 | 4 | 21 | 1 | 7 | 12 |
| 1980 | 11 | 11 | 3 | 24 | 1 | 11 | 12 |
| 1981 | 9 | 11 | 4 | 27 | 1 | 9 | 17 |
| 1982 | 10 | 11 | 6 | 26 | 1 | 10 | 15 |
| 1983 | 10 | 13 | 6 | 28 | 1 | 10 | 17 |
| 1984 | 8 | 13 | 5 | 25 | 1 | 8 | 16 |
| 1985 | 8 | 12 | 7 | 24 | 2 | 8 | 14 |
| 1986 | 7 | 14 | 9 | 22 | 3 | 7 | 11 |

*Notes:*

[a] African countries including Tanzania and Uganda.

[b] All African countries except Tanzania and Uganda.

*Source:* Kenya, *Statistical Abstract* (various issues).

*Post-independence policies*

The period preceding independence was one of high uncertainty. The reality of impending independence resulted in high capital flight and low capital formation. Kenya therefore entered the independence era under depressed economic conditions and urgent steps were necessary to rejuvenate the economy. The policies initially implemented were adopted from a World Bank mission, which recommended that Kenya protect the industrial sector by means of tariffs, duty drawbacks, quotas and subsidies. These ISI policies, as outlined in the first Development Plan (1966–70, p. 235), had the stated objectives of raising the standard of living for Kenyans; enhancing technical progress; increasing the domestic value added of domestic products; and promoting export-oriented industries. These policies were restated by the 1970–74 Plan, which advocated increased protection 'by use of import licensing, quantitative restrictions, and by duty drawbacks on imported raw materials' (p. 320).

Lack of adequate data on tariff and quantitative restriction (QR) limits the analysis of the extent of protection during the 'growth decade'. Studies by Reimer (1970) and Phelps and Wasow (1972) show that some industries (especially consumer goods) were highly protected. Sharpley and Lewis (1988) demonstrate that tariffs were lower in the 1970s than in the 1980s. It would appear that high economic growth reduced the need for high protection during most of the 'development decade'. Import licensing was also not excessively used as a means of protection. However, all that changed with Kenya's first balance of payments crisis in 1971, when a large number of imports were banned or placed under quota. It was also at this time that foreign exchange controls was introduced. While the use of these instruments before 1978 was mainly due to Kenya's inability to use tariffs independently as a result of the East African Community's common external tariff policy, their continued use reflects the fact that they are easy to use and yield desired results immediately. Of course, once put into place such policies create powerful interest groups who would not want to have them abolished.

*Attempts at trade liberalization*

Under the shadow of economic difficulties a shift in trade and industrial policies began to emerge in the early 1970s. This shift is apparent in the 1974–78 Development Plan, and in the introduction of export subsidies under the Local Manufactures (Export Compensation) Act of 1974.

The 1974–78 Plan called for an efficient industrial sector which could produce goods which were competitive in both quality and price in world markets. This was to be achieved by the creation of a liberal trade regime through uniform tariff protection and relaxation of import controls. Tariffs and import controls were to be eventually replaced by excise and sales taxes. However, production for export was to be encouraged by waiving these new taxes on the inputs of export-oriented industries.

The Local Manufactures Act introduced the most clear policy on export promotion. The subsidies introduced under the Act were to replace duty drawbacks, which had been criticized by exporters as costly and unpredictable. The Export Compensation Scheme was therefore meant to reduce administrative costs and to facilitate prompt payments to exporters. The scheme allowed exporters of eligible goods to claim 10 per cent of the f.o.b. value of the goods declared for export or 10 per cent of export earnings received in foreign currency, whichever was less. A further rule for eligibility was that the exported goods be wholly produced in Kenya; and, where imported inputs were used in production, their value should be less than 70 per cent of the ex-factory price of the goods.

The poor economic conditions in 1974 and 1975 and later in 1978 and 1979 made the trade liberalization policies difficult to implement. Import controls and bans were used in 1974–75 to deal with balance of payments crises arising from the oil shocks of 1973. A balance of payments deficit in 1978 also made the government use import controls, which included an import payment and deposit scheme.

*Structural adjustment and stabilization policies*

The economic crisis of the late 1970s and the fear of a protracted economic slowdown made the government seek external funds to finance development and balance of payments deficits. This led to the structural programme agreements between Kenya and the World Bank[7] and several standby agreements with the IMF.[8] The loans obtained under these programmes and agreements were conditional on implementation of policies aimed at liberalizing Kenya's economic system. Some of these policies have been articulated by the

1979–83 and 1984–88 Development Plans, the *Sessional Paper No. 4* of 1980 and 1982, various budget speeches, and the *Sessional Paper No. 1* of 1986 (Kenya 1986).

Under the structural adjustment programmes, trade and industrial policies were to be actively used to restructure the manufacturing sector. This was seen as necessary to make the sector more competitive. The growth of the industrial sector was also to be achieved through greater reliance on the private sector and foreign investments.

Several specific policies were to be used to achieve these objectives. These included reforms of tariff and import control systems and an array of export promotion measures.

Tariff 'rationalization' was to be carried out initially through reduction of duties on consumer goods and increases on those on intermediate and capital goods. Thereafter, all tariffs were to be gradually reduced. The use of quantitative restrictions as a means of protection was to be reduced. For example, more imports were to be placed on the open general licence list (the list with no restriction) and other less restrictive lists; and the 'non-objection certificates' were to be abolished.[9]

A variety of policies were to be used to promote exports. These included: review and modification of the export compensation scheme; maintenance of 'realistic' exchange rates; introduction of manufacture under bond; establishment of an export credit insurance and guarantee scheme; encouragement of increased production of non-traditional exports; attempts to seek new markets in Africa, the Middle East, the US, Japan and Eastern Europe; and increased government support for a liberal world trading system, including increased participation in regional and international co-operation.

The extent to which some of these policies have been implemented, together with their effectiveness, are discussed below. This is done selectively, since a detailed analysis of all the policies is beyond the scope of this paper.

*Tariff reforms* Under the 1980 liberalization programme a 10 per cent tariff surcharge was imposed on all imports. Tariff increases were also imposed on over 200 import items. The purpose of the tariff surcharge was to protect domestic industry from the effects of a relaxation of import controls, while tariff increases were a means of rationalization. The reforms begun in 1980 were continued in

Table 14.6 *Kenya's unweighted average tariff rates by SITC category,*[a] *1981/82–1986/87*

| *SITC category* | *1981/82* | *1982/83* | *1983/84* | *1984/85* | *1985/86* |
|---|---|---|---|---|---|
| Crude rubber | 37 | 40 | 37 | 32 | 29 |
| Cork and wood | 47 | 52 | 47 | 39 | 42 |
| Pulp and waste paper | 54 | 60 | 51 | 42 | 36 |
| Textile fibres | 39 | 42 | 38 | 37 | 37 |
| Metal ores | 35 | 38 | 33 | 28 | 24 |
| Chemicals | 39 | 43 | 39 | 38 | 30 |
| Medicines | 20 | 22 | 20 | 17 | 16 |
| Chemical products | 37 | 41 | 39 | 34 | 31 |
| Leather | 51 | 56 | 50 | 46 | 48 |
| Rubber manufactures | 46 | 64 | 55 | 54 | 54 |
| Textiles | 68 | 76 | 67 | 57 | 57 |
| Non-metallic minerals | 47 | 54 | 48 | 41 | 40 |
| Iron and steel | 28 | 34 | 31 | 27 | 28 |
| Non-ferrous metals | 42 | 46 | 41 | 32 | 31 |
| Metals | 49 | 55 | 49 | 42 | 42 |
| Machinery | 29 | 33 | 29 | 26 | 22 |
| Clothing | 100 | 111 | 102 | 89 | 89 |
| Footwear | 49 | 54 | 45 | 45 | 45 |
| Total average | 45 | 51 | 46 | 40 | 39 |

*Note:*

[a] These are only non-PTA tariff rates.

*Source:* Kenya, *Import Licensing Schedules* (various issues), Nairobi.

1981, with tariff increases of 2–90 per cent imposed on about 1,400 items. There was also tariff reduction on about twenty import items used mainly by export-oriented industries.[10]

The tariff increases of 1980 and 1981, as shown in Table 14.6, were followed by further increases at an average of 13 per cent in 1982. Tariffs were reduced in 1983 to about 1981 levels and the reductions continued in 1984. However, it is evident that the process of tariff reductions lost steam in subsequent years. With the exception of a few commodities, there were hardly any tariff reductions between 1984 and 1986. It is also evident that during this period there was little movement towards uniform tariffs.

*Import controls (QRs)* In the past, import controls have been in the form of quota restrictions, total bans, approval to import given only by specific government bodies, licence to import given to

Table 14.7 *End-use analysis of Kenya's imports as a percentage of total imports, 1960–86*

| *Year* | *Consumption* | *Intermediates* | *Capital* | *Intercap*[a] |
|---|---|---|---|---|
| 1960 | 34 | 39 | 27 | 66 |
| 1964 | 27 | 58 | 15 | 72 |
| 1965 | 26 | 61 | 13 | 74 |
| 1966 | 27 | 57 | 16 | 72 |
| 1967 | 22 | 56 | 22 | 78 |
| 1968 | 24 | 58 | 18 | 76 |
| 1969 | 23 | 60 | 18 | 78 |
| 1970 | 23 | 58 | 19 | 77 |
| 1971 | 24 | 56 | 20 | 76 |
| 1972 | 22 | 55 | 22 | 76 |
| 1973 | 18 | 62 | 21 | 83 |
| 1974 | 13 | 72 | 13 | 85 |
| 1975 | 15 | 67 | 18 | 85 |
| 1976 | 18 | 63 | 19 | 82 |
| 1977 | 15 | 61 | 25 | 86 |
| 1978 | 15 | 55 | 29 | 84 |
| 1979 | 15 | 63 | 22 | 85 |
| 1980 | 15 | 70 | 15 | 85 |
| 1981 | 20 | 58 | 22 | 80 |
| 1982 | 16 | 61 | 22 | 83 |
| 1983 | 17 | 61 | 22 | 83 |
| 1984 | 14 | 64 | 22 | 86 |
| 1985 | 14 | 64 | 21 | 85 |
| 1986 | 12 | 55 | 29 | 84 |

*Note:*

[a] INTERCAP is the percentage sum of capital and intermediate goods in total imports.

*Source:* Kenya, *Statistical Abstract* (various issues); Kenya (1962).

specific agents, and requirement of a 'non-objection certificate' from the domestic producers of the import-competing product. It has been stated before that originally controls were used for protection, but after the foreign exchange crises of 1971 the system began to be used to deal with balance of payments problems. This dual role of the system heightened protection of the industrial sector; but it would appear that it has not fulfilled some of its goals.

Together with tariffs, import controls were meant to encourage the processing of domestic raw materials and to develop intermediate and capital goods industries. Of course the other purpose was to promote import-substituting industries, particularly the consumer goods industries.

Table 14.7 shows that protection has been very effective in reducing the proportion of consumer goods in total imports from 34 per cent in 1960 to 14 per cent in 1985. However, it has failed to stimulate increased utilization of domestic resources. This is shown by the increase in imports of intermediates from 39 per cent in 1960 to 64 per cent in 1985. The percentage of intermediate and capital goods in total retained imports has increased over time, implying greater dependence of the industrial sector on imported inputs.

The most common import control instrument is the import licensing system.[11] The pervasiveness of this system in Kenya can be seen by the growth of the number of items under licence. In 1964, the number of licensed items stood at 69, but by 1972 the number had gone up to 228 and in 1975 had more than doubled to 472 (World Bank 1975). As the licensing system became a prominent trade policy instrument, these numbers (as shown by the Appendix) shot up to 2,689 in 1981 and have stayed above 2,700 since. Another important feature of this system is that imports considered essential are placed on less restrictive lists, while those considered non-essential, such as consumer goods, are put on restrictive lists or banned. As mentioned above, part of the liberalization process involved shifting more items to the less restrictive list. As the Appendix shows, this has not generally been the case.

Under the 1980 liberalization programme, import bans and requirements for 'non-objection certificates' were removed. Import controls were to be relaxed from 1981 by shifting 20 per cent of the items in the more restrictive Schedules IIA and IIB to the more liberal Schedule I each year.[12] This is reflected in the 1982 *Import Licensing Schedule*, which had 11 per cent more items in Schedule I than in 1981 (see the Appendix). As the Appendix shows, the licensing system had to some extent been liberalized by 1985. More items had been moved to the more liberal Schedule I A. However, the number of items in the more restrictive Schedule IIB, and indeed the total number of licensed items, has remained more or less the same over time.

## 4 Export promotion policies and export performance

In this section we analyse the role of the export compensation scheme and of exchange rates as instruments for export promotion. Other instruments which have been used for this purpose, for example duty drawbacks and sales tax rebates, will not be examined. This is because these instruments have not been actively used for policy purposes.

*Export compensation*

The contribution of export compensation to the promotion of exports has generally been considered to be minimal. Exporters have often claimed that the rate was too low, and that payments were not made promptly. The liberalization programme of 1980 set out to deal with some of these claims. Under the programme the basic rate, which had remained at 10 per cent since 1974, was raised to 20 per cent. However, this did not last long since the whole scheme was suspended in June 1982. When announcing the suspension of the scheme, the Minister of Finance argued that it was ineffective in promoting exports because claims were made by only four or five firms which were already competitive in world markets and therefore required no incentives. He also argued that the domestic value added requirement was often not applied and hence non-qualifying exports obtained compensation. The Minister pointed out that compensation increased between the fiscal years 1979–80 and 1980–81 even though during the same period export earnings from qualifying commodities declined by 7.8 per cent.[13]

When the scheme was reintroduced in December 1982, the basic rate had been reduced to 10 per cent, but an additional rate of 15 per cent was to be paid to exporters whose earnings increased over the previous year's earnings. But this new system created more problems than were first anticipated and in 1985 the incremental rate was abolished and the basic rate was raised back to 20 per cent.

*Exchange-rate regime*

One of the major planks of the liberalization policies of the 1980s was the use of a flexible exchange-rate regime to stimulate exports and as an alternative means of protection. Between 1975 and 1980 the Kenya shilling was pegged to the SDR: the rate of exchange was fixed at 1 SDR to KSh 9.60. This regime ended with the devaluations of February and September 1981 amounting to 23.7 per cent. There was a further devaluation of the shilling by 17.7 per cent in December 1982. This exchange rate was in force until May 1983 when the shilling was again devalued, by 2.6 per cent. After this devaluation the official exchange-rate policy became one of 'managed float' in which the shilling was allowed to fluctuate against the SDR within certain margins.

Overall, between 1980 and 1986 the shilling depreciated by 98 per cent against the SDR and 112 per cent against the dollar. Such substantial nominal devaluations, through expenditure-switching effects, should stimulate the growth of exports.

In analysing the impact of exchange rates on exports, a more appropriate indicator to use is the real effective exchange rate (REER) index. This index is obtained using trade-weighted average exchange rates deflated by the ratio of the domestic consumer price index (CPI) and the trading partners' wholesale price index (WPI).[14] From this definition, a decline in REER, with fixed nominal exchange rates, implies that the inflation rate in foreign markets is rising faster than the domestic inflation. This in turn implies a real devaluation of the domestic currency and therefore increased competitiveness.

Table 14.8 shows indices of nominal and real exchange rates. These indices have been derived using the value of exports as weights and 1980 as a base year. Trade weights are calculated as the share of Kenya's exports to its major trading partners – the UK, West Germany, the Netherlands, Japan, Italy, France and the US. Kenya's African trading partners are excluded because of lack of consistent exchange-rate data.

By construction, an increase in the nominal exchange rate index (NEER) implies a devaluation. Therefore, its increase from 1981 onwards reflects the devaluations of 1981–83 and the policy of managed float started in 1983. It is also evident that the REER was not overvalued in the 1960s and early 1970s, but began to be overvalued after 1972. The fact that REER was mostly greater than NEER before 1973 would seem to suggest that the exchange rate was undervalued. REER began to depreciate in 1978, partly owing to a decline in terms of trade after the coffee boom, and thereafter because of devaluations and a flexible exchange-rate policy. It is, however, clear that the depreciation of the real exchange rate since 1978 has not been consistent.

Table 14.8 *Kenya's nominal and real effective exchange rates (1980 = 100), 1960–86*

| *Year* | *NERX* | *RERX* |
|---|---|---|
| 1960 | 86.98 | 93.91 |
| 1961 | 86.57 | 94.54 |
| 1962 | 86.00 | 91.86 |
| 1963 | 87.41 | 91.79 |
| 1964 | 85.26 | 96.10 |
| 1965 | 84.34 | 92.40 |
| 1966 | 85.72 | 92.79 |
| 1967 | 85.23 | 83.50 |
| 1968 | 83.14 | 85.39 |
| 1969 | 82.01 | 88.94 |
| 1970 | 83.37 | 94.17 |
| 1971 | 83.41 | 96.97 |
| 1972 | 86.96 | 99.53 |
| 1973 | 86.53 | 103.05 |
| 1974 | 84.47 | 107.98 |
| 1975 | 89.01 | 103.69 |
| 1976 | 91.83 | 108.01 |
| 1977 | 90.95 | 104.61 |
| 1978 | 94.17 | 95.36 |
| 1979 | 98.11 | 99.67 |
| 1980 | 100.00 | 100.00 |
| 1981 | 102.92 | 100.84 |
| 1982 | 115.05 | 99.31 |
| 1983 | 129.85 | 103.73 |
| 1984 | 124.41 | 95.18 |
| 1985 | 142.87 | 98.61 |
| 1986 | 174.32 | 112.53 |

NERX: nominal effective exchange rates weighted by exports.
RERX: real effective exchange rates weighted by exports.

*Export performance*

In this paper we shall confine ourselves to the performance of non-oil exports, treating the behaviour of petroleum exports as being determined by factors exogenous to the Kenyan economy. Non-oil exports are divided into five categories: tea, coffee, foods, basic raw materials and manufactured goods.[15] Tables 14.9 and 14.10 show

Table 14.9 *Growth of real value of Kenya's exports (annual percentage change), 1964–85*

| *Commodity* | *1964–85* | *1964–73* | *1974–79* | *1980–85* |
|---|---|---|---|---|
| Tea | 6.99* | 8.78* | 15.74** | 16.73* |
| Coffee | 5.60* | 5.34* | 16.18 | 3.90* |
| Food | –0.85 | 8.12* | –8.26 | 8.26 |
| Basic raw materials | –1.02 | –0.79 | –12.09 | –7.25* |
| Manufactures | 1.86* | 3.92* | –2.71 | –5.05* |
| Non-oil exports | 3.86* | 5.17* | 6.65 | 6.27* |

*Notes:*
* Significant at 5% level.
** Significant at 10% level.

Table 14.10 *Growth of volume of Kenya's exports (annual percentage change), 1964–85*

| *Commodity* | *1964–85* | *1984–73* | *1974–79* | *1980–85* |
|---|---|---|---|---|
| Tea | 9.34* | 13.44* | 14.73* | 10.62* |
| Coffee | 4.59* | 5.81* | 3.69 | 4.63* |
| Food | 1.67 | 15.42* | –2.81** | 13.05 |
| Basic raw materials | 3.64 | –1.13* | –0.61* | –6.04* |
| Manufactures | 3.04* | 5.89* | 2.74* | –0.29* |
| Non-oil exports | 3.17* | 6.72** | 2.77 | 1.38* |

*Notes:*
* Significant at 5% level.
** Significant at 10% level.

the trends in the growth of real value and volume of exports, respectively. The real value of non-oil exports grew at positive rates in the period 1964–85. However, this growth was lower than in the three sub-periods (1964–73, 1974–79, 1980–85), which had almost similar growth rates. The similarity of export growth in these periods, despite steep declines in the real growth of some export categories in the 1974–79 and 1980–85 periods, is accounted for by the commodity booms. A 4 per cent negative growth in

1982 was due to a large decline in the values of basic raw materials and manufactures, while a 14 per cent positive growth in 1984 is explained by a tea boom. Overall, the export performance of manufactured and basic raw materials has been very poor since the early 1970s.

The growth of the volume of exports during the growth decade (1964–73) was much larger than in the following two periods. Again, the fact that the growth of export values far exceeded that of export volume reflects the influence of the commodity booms. A 14 per cent decline in the volume of exports in 1984 was the result of a decline in the export volume of food, tea and manufactures. The decline in the exports of the first two items was due mainly to the drought of 1984.

Looking at the growth rates of individual commodities, it is clear that coffee and tea are the major contributors to the favourable growth in non-oil exports. Except for the decline in the volume of tea in 1984, the two commodities have had positive and relatively high growth rates in both value and volume terms. But the growth of export values of the other commodities has generally lagged behind that of export volume. It is therefore clear that Kenya's export performance depends heavily on the performance of coffee and tea.

## 5 Econometric analysis of export performance

In what follows we provide an econometric analysis of Kenya's export performance. We first present a theoretical framework of the model(s) used and, subsequently, the results. Single equations are estimated for coffee, tea, foods, basic raw materials (BARAMA), manufactures (MANUFS), and total non-oil exports (NOX). These equations are estimated using conventional functional forms.

### *Theoretical framework*

The modelling and estimation of export supply and demand functions has a long history. Goldstein and Khan (1985) provide the most recent survey in this area. However, most of this work is based on developed economies. Estimates of trade functions for developing countries are a recent phenomenon; examples are studies by Houthakker and Magee (1969), Khan (1974), Ali (1974), Bond

(1983, 1985), Bahamani-Oskooee (1984, 1986), Arize (1987), and Riedel (1988).

The export supply function is specified in the following log-linear form:

$$\ln x^s_{it} = \gamma_0 + \gamma_1 \ln Cap_t + \gamma_2 \ln REXR_t + \varepsilon_t, \qquad (14.1)$$

where:

$x^s_{it}$ = index of export quantities of commodity $i$ in year $t$.
$Cap_t$ = installed capacity in year $t$, proximated by GDP.
$REXR_t$ = real exchange rate
$\varepsilon_t$ = random error term.

Equation (14.1) is a log-linear function, where $\gamma_1$ and $\gamma_2$ can be interpreted as 'capacity' and 'price' elasticities, respectively. The coefficient $\gamma_1$ is expected to be positive because higher production should lead to increased export supply; and $\gamma_2$ is also expected to be positive because devaluation of the domestic currency increases export earnings and therefore increases production for export.

The above model is an equilibrium model in the sense that it assumes that actual exports adjust to meet desired levels in one year. This may not be so, especially in our study, which includes commodities like tea and coffee with long gestation periods. This could render supply unresponsive in the very shortrun. Even for non-agricultural goods it is possible that high adjustment costs may inhibit market clearing within one year. If that were the case then the estimated coefficients would have a downward bias. To test the importance of adjustment lags, a disequilibrium model is also estimated. This model assumes that exports adjust only partially to the difference between export supply in period $t$ and the actual flow of exports in period $t - 1$. Following Khan (1974) and Goldstein and Khan (1978), the adjustment mechanism is specified as:

$$\ln x_{it} - \ln x_{t-1} = \phi(\ln x^*_{it} - \ln x_{it-1}), \qquad (14.2)$$

where:

$x_{it}$ = actual level of exports
$x^*_{it}$ = desired level of exports
$\phi$ = coefficient of adjustment and $0 \leq \phi \leq 1$.

Substituting equation (14.1) into equation (14.2), we get the disequilibrium model:

$$\ln x_{it} = \gamma_0^* + \gamma_1^* \ln Cap_t + \gamma_2^* \ln REXR_t + \gamma_3^* \ln x_{it-1} + \phi\varepsilon_t, \tag{14.3}$$

where: $\gamma_0^* = \phi\gamma_0$, $\gamma_1^* = \phi\gamma_1$, $\gamma_2^* = \phi\gamma_2$, and $\gamma_3^* = 1 - \phi$. Since $\phi$ is positive and given that $\gamma_1$ and $\gamma_2$ are positive, $\gamma_1^*$, $\gamma_2^*$ and $\gamma_3^*$ are positive. Where $\gamma^*$ is significant, the null hypothesis of adjustment with a lag cannot be rejected.

Equations (14.1) and (14.3) were estimated by OLS method using annual data for the years 1960-85. Export values of coffee, tea, food, manufactures and basic raw materials were obtained from various *Statistical Abstracts* and converted into quantity indices, with 1980 as a base year.

In the absence of a reliable measure of capacity utilization, GDP at 1980 constant prices was used as a scale variable. Production for sale was used as a scale variable in coffee and tea equations. A real effective exchange rate index was used as a relative price.

*Empirical results*

Table 14.11 gives the estimates of the export supply equations (equilibrium model). The short-run *supply* elasticities for all commodities, except BARAMA, are significantly different from zero. For these commodities (including total non-oil exports) an increase in domestic output increases export *supply*. Growth-promoting policies would therefore improve export performance.

All the short-run price elasticities are insignificant. The price elasticity of tea is comparable to those obtained by Akiyama and Trivedi (1987b) of 0.17–0.4 for smallholder output and 0.26–0.86 for estates. It would therefore appear that getting prices 'right' may not be effective in promoting exports. However, these results could reflect the fact that Kenya is a price-taker in world markets. In the case of coffee and tea, the use of prices for export promotion is constrained by the quota system.

Estimates of the disequilibrium model are shown in Table 14.12. As in the case of the equilibrium model, the short-run *supply* elasticities (except for BARAMA) are significantly different from zero and have the correct sign. The size of these coefficients has dropped relative to those of the equilibrium model. However, it is still clear that output is a major determinant of export performance.

The table also shows that the short-run price elasticities have the

Table 14.11 *OLS estimates of the export supply equations for Kenya (equilibrium model)*

| *Commodity* | *Constant* | *GDP*[a] | *REER* | $\bar{R}^2$ | *DW* | δ[b] |
|---|---|---|---|---|---|---|
| Tea | –0.400 | 0.963* | 0.133 | 0.99 | 2.0 | — |
| | (–0.36) | (44.14) | (0.53) | | | |
| Coffee | –2.681 | 0.872* | 0.728 | 0.90 | 2.06 | — |
| | (–1.34) | (11.34) | (1.53) | | | |
| BARAMA | –3.06 | 0.489 | 1.102 | 0.22 | 2.45 | 0.647 |
| | (–0.79) | (1.50) | (1.19) | | | (4.24) |
| MANUF | –0.384 | 0.690* | 0.405 | 0.91 | 1.61 | 0.019 |
| | (–0.28) | (11.71) | (1.24) | | | (0.10) |
| NOX | 0.982 | 0.721* | 0.087 | 0.87 | 1.81 | 0.09 |
| | (–0.61) | (10.10) | (0.22) | | | (0.45) |

*Notes:*
[a] Production for sale as a scale variable for tea and coffee.
[b] Cochrane-Orcut autocorrelation coefficient.
* Significant at 5% level (t-values in brackets).

Table 14.12 *Export supply equations for Kenya (disequilibrium model)*

| *Commodity* | *Constant* | *GDP*[a] | *REER* | *XS(-1)*[b] | $\bar{R}^2$ | *LM*[c] |
|---|---|---|---|---|---|---|
| Tea | –0.593 | 0.988* | 0.186 | –0.037 | 0.99 | 0.76 |
| | (–0.53) | (10.77) | (0.72) | (–0.39) | | |
| Coffee | –2.096 | 0.543* | 0.537 | 0.391* | 0.91 | 10.56 |
| | (1.21) | (3.87) | (1.29) | (3.12) | | |
| BARAMA | –6.466 | 0.061 | 0.718* | 0.598* | 0.73 | 8.13 |
| | (12.36) | (0.50) | (2.54) | (4.63) | | |
| MANUF | –0.564 | 0.518* | 0.402 | 0.212 | 0.92 | 3.86 |
| | (–0.42) | (3.21) | (1.25) | (1.16) | | |
| NOX | –0.666 | 0.436* | 0.397 | 0.313 | 0.88 | 1.17 |
| | (–0.38) | (2.44) | (0.93) | (1.48) | | |

*Notes:*
[a] Production for sale used as a scale variable for tea and coffee.
[b] Lagged dependent variable.
[c] Autocorrelation was tested using Lagrange Multiplier tests.
* Significant at 5% level (t-values in brackets).

Table 14.13 *Long-run elasticities and average time lags for Kenya*

| *Commodity* | *Capacity elasticity* | *Price elasticity* | *Time lag (months)* |
|---|---|---|---|
| Tea | 0.95 | 0.18 | 12 |
| Coffee | 0.89 | 0.88 | 20 |
| BARAMA | 0.15 | 4.27 | 30 |
| MANUF | 1.13 | 1.11 | 15 |
| NOX | 0.63 | 0.58 | 18 |

correct sign, but only that of BARAMA is significantly different from zero. This again casts doubt on the role of price policies in export promotion.

The long-run price elasticities and the average time lags by commodity are given in Table 14.3. The table shows that, except for the price elasticity of BARAMA, all *supply* and price elasticities are less than but close to unity. This conforms to the traditional conclusion (subject to Orcut's critique) that *supply* elasticities are low in LDCs. The long-run price elasticity of 0.58 for NOX is much smaller than Arize's (1987) estimate of 2.3.

The table also shows that the adjustment of export supply to changes in income and prices is on average above one year. The average time lag of eighteen months for total exports concurs with Balassa (1978), who shows that on average LDC exports take about eighteen months to respond to devaluation.

## 6 Conclusion

The aim of this study has been to examine the determinants of Kenya's export performance. An attempt was made to distinguish the effects of internal and external factors. Internal factors were taken to be those over which authorities have some degree of control. Examples are the nominal exchange rate and domestic pricing policies. External factors are exogenous, such as changes in the world economy, in world prices, or in domestic conditions such as the weather. The roles of these factors are inferred from the estimates of export supply.

Estimates of capacity and price elasticities were found to be generally low. In many cases only *supply* elasticities are significantly different from zero, while price elasticities are not. This suggests that policies aimed at increasing the supply of exports may not lead to immediate tangible results. This may in fact explain why, despite the trade changes initiated in 1980, there has been little change in the performance of Kenya's exports. It also points to the conclusion that the determinants of export supply may involve more than price policies. This would mean that successful export promotion would require more than the traditional instruments of export promotion.

## Appendix: Import licensing schedules

| *Schedule* | *1981–82* | | *1982–83* | | *1983–84* | | *1984–85* | |
|---|---|---|---|---|---|---|---|---|
| | *No.* | *%* | *No.* | *%* | *No.* | *%* | *No.* | *%* |
| I | 1,131 | 42 | 1,444 | 53 | n.a.[1] | | n.a. | |
| IA | n.a. | | n.a. | | 784 | 29 | 803 | 30 |
| IB | n.a. | | n.a. | | 673 | 25 | 961 | 35 |
| IIA | 687 | 26 | 398 | 15 | n.a. | | n.a. | |
| IIB | 867 | 32 | 868 | 32 | 869 | 32 | 903 | 33 |
| IIAS | n.a. | | n.a. | | 84 | 3 | 92 | 3 |
| IIAO | n.a. | | n.a. | | 314 | 12 | n.a. | |
| Total | 2,689 | 100 | 2,710 | 100 | 2,724 | 100 | 2,759 | 100 |

*Notes:*
NA: Not applicable.

Schedule I : Essential goods imported freely through automatic licensing and foreign exchange allocation.
IIA : Priority imports for use in industry and agriculture. Receive regular foreign exchange allocation but less than of I.
IIB : Luxury imports and goods produced domestically. Schedule used to protect domestic industry and for BOP purposes, therefore receive residual foreign exchange.
IA : Same as I.
IB : Same as IIA.
IIAS: Goods imported only by authorized agents or requiring ministry approval before licence is issued.
IIAO: Non-luxury imports subject to quota. Receive only residual foreign exchange.

*Source:* Kenya, *Import Licensing Schedules* (various issues), Nairobi.

## Notes

1 The challengers can be grouped into: (1) the terms of trade school of Singer (1950), Prebisch (1950, 1959), Myrdal (1957), (2) the dependencia school of Frank (1978), and (3) the unequal exchange school of Emmanuel (1972).

2 The seriousness of the economic problems facing sub-Saharan African countries is reflected by the high profile it has received from the World Bank and other multilateral and bilateral donors. See, for example, World Bank (1983, 1984, 1986).

3 Several studies have examined the relationship between exports and economic growth, but their results have not been unanimous. Michaely (1977), Balassa (1978), Tyler (1981) and Feder (1983) have found a significant correlation between exports and economic growth; while Love (1984), and Taylor, McCarthy, and Alikhani (1984) found that other factors besides exports are major determinants of growth in LDCs.

4 The 1987 *World Development Report* (World Bank 1987) provides the most up-to-date critique of ISI and advances arguments in favour of EPP.

5 See Lele and Meyers (1987) for comparable analysis.

6 This document is also published as Kenya (1962).

7 Kenya's first structural adjustment loan was approved in March 1980 and the second was approved in July 1982. Kenya has also benefited from the sectoral adjustment credits provided under the Special Facility for sub-Saharan Africa. A loan worth US$40 million to finance the agricultural sector was approved in June 1986.

8 The IMF approved standby credits in 1979, 1980, 1982, 1983 and 1985. The first three standbys were cancelled before they expired because Kenya exceeded IMF ceilings. In February 1988 Kenya reached an agreement with the IMF for a loan worth SDR 175.2 million to be drawn in two stages. SDR 85 million was to be drawn during the first eighteen months under a standby agreement and the rest, SDR 90.2 million, was to be drawn over three years (with SDR 28.4 million available immediately) under the Structural Adjustment Facility.

9 As a means of protecting domestic industry, importers were in certain cases required to obtain a 'non-objection certificate' from the local producer before a licence was granted.

10 See Kenya, *Sessional Paper No. 4*, 1982.

11 A typical example of an import licensing system is represented by Kenya's 1975 system, which had four schedules:

*Schedule I*: listed imports which could be imported subject to specific licences, but for which foreign exchange was readily available.

*Schedule II*: listed imports which could be imported under specific licence, but for which foreign exchange was allocated on a quota basis. This schedule was mainly used for protection.

*Schedule III*: listed goods which were banned. Some of the items falling under this schedule could be imported only after obtaining a 'non-objection certificate' from the domestic producer.

*Schedule IV*: listed goods which were restricted on a quota basis mainly for BOP purposes, so that, depending on the foreign exchange position, their import quota could be increased or decreased.

12 See Kenya, *Sessional Paper No. 4*, 1982.

13 See Budget Speech of 1982/83.

14 The nominal effective exchange rate (NEER) is calculated following Rhomberg (1976). Formally:

$$NEER_t = \sum_{j=1}^{7} (x_{kj}/\Sigma\, x_{kj})\, XR_{kj},$$

where:

$X_{kj}$ = Kenya's exports to country *j*
$XR_{kj} = XR_j/XR_k$

and

$XR_j$ = value of one unit of trading-partner *j* currency in terms of the numeraire currency (the dollar)
$XR_k$ = unit value of the dollar in terms of the Kenya shilling

$XR_{kj}$ is expressed as an index number relative to the base period 1980.

To obtain the real effective exchange rate index (REER), NEER is deflated by a trade-weighted relative price.

$$REER_t = \frac{NEER_t}{TWP_t}$$

where:

$$TWP_t = \sum_{j=1}^{7} (x_{kj}/\Sigma\, x_{kj}) \frac{CPI_{kt}}{WPI_{jt}}$$

$CPI_{kt}$ = Kenya's consumer price index at period *t*.
$WPI_{jt}$ = country *j*'s wholesale price index at period *t*.

15 The aggregated commodities - food, BARAMA, MANUFS and non-oil exports – are made up as follows:

| | |
|---|---|
| *Food*: | meat and meat preparations, milk and cream, butter and ghee, maize, pineapples, beans and peas, and cashewnuts. |
| *BARAMA*: | hides and skins, oil seeds, wool, cotton, sisal, fluorspar, wattle bark, pyrethrum extract, pyrethrum flowers, and animal and vegetable oils. |
| *MANUFS*: | sodium carbonate, cement, wattle extract, steel doors and windows, aluminium ware, and metal containers. |
| *Non-oil exports*: | tea, coffee, foods, BARAMA, MANUFS. |

## References

Akiyama, J. and Trivedi, P. K. (1987), 'Analysis of perennial crop supply', *Journal of Econometrics*, 36, pp. 133–61.

Ali, I. (1974), 'Estimating the determinants of export supply in India', *Indian Economic Journal*, 31, pp. 1–12.

Arize, A. (1987), 'The supply and demand for imports and exports in a simultaneous model', *Applied Economics*, 19, pp. 1233–47.

Bahamani-Oskooee, M. (1984), 'On the effects of effective exchange rates on trade flows', *Indian Journal of Economics*, 65, pp. 57–67.

Bahamani-Oskooee, M. (1986), 'The determinants of international trade flows: The case of developing countries', *Journal of Development Economics*, 20, pp. 107–23.

Balassa, B. (1978), Effects of exchange rate changes in developing countries', World Bank Development Research Department, Discussion Paper DRD 250.

Balassa, B. (1985), *Change and Challenge in the World Economy*, Macmillan, London.

Bhagwati, J. (1978), *Foreign Trade Regimes and Economic Development: Anatomy and Consequences of Exchange Control Regimes*, Ballinger, Cambridge, Mass.

Bond, M. E. (1983), 'An econometric study of primary commodity exports from developing country regions to the world', *IMF Staff Papers*, 30, pp. 703–26.

Bond, M. E. (1985), 'Export demand and supply for non-oil developing countries', *IMF Staff Papers*, 32, pp. 56–77.

Emmanuel, A. (1972), *Unequal Exchange*, New Left Books, London.

Feder, G. (1983), 'On exports and economic growth', *Journal of Development Economics*, 12, pp. 59–73.

Frank, A. G. (1978), *Dependent Accumulation and Under-Development*, Macmillan, London.

Goldstein, M. and Khan, M. (1978), 'The supply and demand for exports: A simultaneous approach', *Review of Economics and Statistics*, 60, pp. 275–86.

Goldstein, M. and Khan, M. (1985), 'Income and price effects in foreign trade', in R. W. Jones, and P. B. Kenen (eds), *Handbook of International Economics*, Vol. II, North Holland, Amsterdam.

Houthakker, H. S. and Magee, S. (1969), 'Income and price elasticities in world trade', *Review of Economics and Statistics*, 51, pp. 111–25.

Kenya (1962), *The Economic Development of Kenya*, World Bank, Report of an Economic Survey Mission.

Kenya, Development Plan, 1966–70, 1970–74, 1974–78, 1979–83 and 1984–88, Nairobi, Government Printer.

Kenya (1974), *Local Manufactures (Export Compensation) Act of 1974*, Nairobi, Government Printer.

Kenya, Sessional Paper No. 4, 1974, 1975, 1980 and 1982, 'On Economic Prospects and Policies', Nairobi, Government Printer.

Kenya, Budget Speeches 1982/83 and 1985/86, Nairobi, Government Printer.

Kenya (1986), 'On Economic Management and Renewed Growth', *Sessional Paper No. 1 of 1986*, Nairobi, Government Printer.

Kenya (1988), *Economic Survey*, Nairobi, Government Printer.

Khan, M. (1974), 'Import and export demand in developing countries', *IMF Staff Papers*, 21, pp. 678–93.

Krueger, A. (1978), *Foreign Trade Regimes and Economic Development: Liberalization Attempts and Consequences*, Columbia University Press, New York.

Lele, U. and Meyers, L. R. (1987), 'Growth and structural change in East Africa: Domestic policies, agricultural performance and World Bank Assistance, 1963–1986', parts I and II, World Bank, Development Research Department Discussion Paper, DRD 274.

Little, I., Scitovsky, T. and Scott, M. (1970), *Trade and Industry*, Oxford University Press, Oxford.

Love, J. (1984), 'External market conditions, competitiveness, diversification and LDCs' exports', *Journal of Development Economics*, 16, pp. 279–91.

Michaely, M. (1977), 'Exports and growth: An empirical investigation', *Journal of Development Economics*, 4, pp. 49–53.

Myrdal, G. (1957), *Economic Theory and Underdeveloped Regions*, University Press, New York; Geraid Duckworth, London, 1956.

Ngeno, N. (1985), 'Kenya's trade relations with PTA: Toward an African common market', paper presented at the Kenyan Economic Association Meeting, 27 September.

Phelps, M. G. and Wasow, B. (1972), 'Measuring protection and its effects in Kenya', Institute for Development Studies, University of Nairobi, DP No. 37.

Prebisch, R. (1950), 'The economic development of Latin America and its principal problems', *Economic Bulletin for Latin America*, 7, pp. 1–22.

Prebisch, R. (1959), 'Commercial policies in the underdeveloped countries', *American Economic Review*, 49, pp. 251–73.

Reimer, R. (1971), 'Effective rates of protection in East Africa', *East African Economic Review*, 3

Rhomberg, R. (1976), 'Indices of effective exchange rates', *IMF Staff Papers*, 23, pp. 88–112.

Riedel, J. (1988), 'The demand for LDC exports of manufactures: Estimates from Hong Kong', *Economic Journal*, 98, pp. 138–48.

Sharpley, J. and Lewis, S. R. Jnr (1988), 'Kenya's industrialisation, 1964–84', Institute of Development Studies, Sussex, DP 242.

Singer, H. (1950), 'The distribution of gains between investing and borrowing countries', *American Economic Review*, 40, pp. 473–85.

Taylor, L., McCarthy, L. and Alikhani, I. (1984), 'Trade patterns in developing countries 1970–81', World Bank, Staff Working Papers No. 642.

Tyler, W. (1981), 'Growth and export expansion in developing countries: Some empirical evidence', *Journal of Development Economics*, 9, pp. 121–30.

Van der Hoeven, R. and Vandemoortele, J. (1987), 'Kenya: Stabilization and adjustment experiences (1979–84) and prospects for future development', WEP WP No. 11. International Labour Organization.

Vandemoortele, J. (1985), 'Kenya data compendium, 1962–1982', University of Nairobi, Institute for Development Studies, Occasional Paper No. 44.

World Bank (1962), *The Economic Development of Kenya*, Johns Hopkins University Press, Baltimore, MD.

World Bank (1975), *Kenya: Into the Second Decade*, Johns Hopkins University Press, Baltimore, MD.

World Bank (1983), *Accelerated Development of Sub-Saharan Africa*, Washington, DC.

World Bank (1984), *Toward Sustained Development in Sub-Saharan Africa : A Joint Program of Action*, Washington DC.

World Bank (1986), *Financing Adjustment with Growth in Sub-Saharan Africa*, Washington, DC.

World Bank (1987), *World Development Report*, Oxford University Press, New York.

# Index